TO RICHARD
MERRY CHRISTMAS
& HAPPY READING
ON YOUR THRONE!
LUV CATHY XMAS97

Uncle John's

GIANT

10th ANNIVERSARY

BATHROOM

READER

The Bathroom Readers' Institute

Bathroom Readers' Press
Ashland, Oregon

D0981334

UNCLE JOHN'S
GIANT 10th ANNIVERSARY
BATHROOM READER

Cover design by Michael Brunsfeld
BRI Technician on back cover: Larry Kelp

Uncle John's Giant 10th Anniversary Bathroom Reader
by The Bathroom Readers' Institute

ISBN: 1-879682-68-0

Printed in the United States of America
First Printing 1997

★　　★　　★

Cleaning House In the Year 2000

When Jane Dobson cleans house she simply turns the hose on everything. Why not? Furniture (upholstery included), rugs, draperies, unscratchable floors— all are made of synthetic fabric or waterproof plastic. After the water has run down a drain in the middle of the floor (later concealed by a rug of synthetic fiber) Jane turns on a blast of hot air and dries everything. ...Jane Dobson throws soiled 'linen' into the incinerator. Bed sheets are more substantial stuff, but Jane Dobson has only to hang them up and wash them down with a hose when she puts the bedroom in order....

—*Popular Mechanics, 1950*

THANK YOU!

The Bathroom Readers' Institute sincerely thanks the people whose advice and assistance made this book possible.

John Javna
John Dollison
Gordon Javna
Jack Mingo
Lenna Lebovich
Tim Harrower
Erik Linden
Sage
Jennifer Massey
Erin Keenan
Casey Bourgeois
Melissa Schwarz
Sharilyn Hovind
Andy Sohn
Michael Brunsfeld
Sherry Powell
Chris Rose-Merkle
Béla Keenan
David Wallechinsky
Scott Dalgarno
Stephanie Keenan
Janis Hunt Johnson

Julie Roeming
Lonnie Kirk
Paul Stanley
Bennie Slomski
Jeff Altemus
Valerie Hendel
Jeff Painter
David Sugar
Shelly Brigham
Mary Kaufman
Erin Reese
Andrea Freewater
Abby Granach
Richard Moeschl
Jenny McCracken
Bill Eriksen
Peter McCracken
Thomas Crapper
Jesse & Sophie, *B.R.I.T.*
Steve Brummett
Sam and Sarah
Hi to Emily and Molly!

★   ★   ★

"The trouble with facts is that there are so many of them."
—Samuel McChord Crothers, *The Gentle Reader*

Hiya Gideon! Hiya Sam!

CONTENTS

NOTE

Because the B.R.I. understands your reading needs, we've
divided the contents by length as well as subject.
Short—a quick read
Medium—1 to 3 pages
Long—for those extended visits, when something
a little more involved is required.
*Extended—for a leg-numbing experience.

★   ★   ★

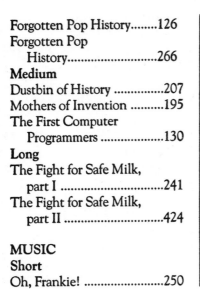

INTRODUCTION

T oday, on the way to work, Uncle John stopped at a coffee stand to brace for the final push to get this book to the printer. He noticed some "French Vanilla" Coffee Mate on a table, and mused that it might make a good article. "Oh, you write?" said the kid making the coffee. "Whaddya write?"

"Books. Something called *the Bathroom Reader.*"

"You're kidding! I grew up with them! My grandma has the whole collection!"

That's when Uncle John realized how long he's been doing this. We at the BRI are actually writing for a *second generation* of bathroom readers! "I can't believe that this series is older than my kids," Uncle John says.

Suddenly it's been 10 years and 1.5 million books since the first *Bathroom Reader*. People know who we are. We've even spawned imitators—there's a burgeoning Bathroom Books segment of the publishing industry. We know we're extremely lucky to have such loyal readers.

We've also been lucky, over the years, to have worked with some wonderful people: John D., Lenna L., Michael B., Sharilyn H., Paul Stanley and Julie Roeming at Banta, Andy S., Eric L., and a whole bunch more. By the way—that's Larry Kelp of the BRI on the back cover, not Uncle John.

This edition of the *Bathroom Reader* is a little different from the others (but not by too much). The biggest difference is the special "Extended Sitting Section" at the end. Over the years, the most persistent request from readers has been for us to add some longer pieces, for times when it's necessary to sit in one place for a while But we've never wanted to limit the rest of the material to do it. This year, we've made the book longer than usual—and now there's room for everything.

This was also the first book we've done in the sleepy little town of Ashland, Oregon, the Institute's new home. We have a whole new staff at the BRI helping to put it together, and you can see for yourself how well they've done. We're proud of them...and amazed that they've come up with even more material to fit the needs of bathroom readers everywhere. We're already hard at work on the next volume!

Until then, thanks for your support, and remember:

Go with the flow.

—Uncle John and the
Bathroom Readers' Institute.

COURT TRANSQUIPS

Do court transcripts make good bathroom reading? Check out these quotes, from a little book called Disorder in the Court. *They're things people actually said in court, recorded word for word.*

Q: "What is your date of birth?"
A: "July fifteenth."
Q: "What year?"
A: "Every year."

Q: "What gear were you in at the moment of impact?"
A: "Gucci sweats and Reeboks."

Q: "Are you sexually active?"
A: "No, I just lie there."

Q: "This myasthenia gravis—does it affect your memory at all?
A: "Yes."
Q: "And in what ways does it affect your memory?"
A: "I forget."
Q: "You forget. Can you give us an example of something that you've forgotten?"

Q: "How old is your son—the one living with you."
A: "Thirty-eight or thirty-five, I can't remember which."
Q: "How long has he lived with you?"
A: "Forty-five years."

Q: "What was the first thing your husband said to you when he woke up that morning?"
A: "He said, 'Where am I Cathy?' "
Q: "And why did that upset you?"
A: "My name is Susan."

Q: "And where was the location of the accident?"
A: "Approximately milepost 499."
Q: "And where is milepost 499?"
A: "Probably between milepost 498 and 500."

Q: "Sir, what is your IQ."
A: "Well, I can see pretty well, I think."

Q: "Did you blow your horn or anything?"
A: "After the accident?"
Q: "Before the accident."
A: "Sure, I played for ten years. I even went to school for it."

Q: "Do you know if your daughter has ever been involved in the voodoo or occult?"
A: "We both do."
Q: "Voodoo?"
A: "We do."
Q: "You do?"
A: "Yes, voodoo."

Q: "Trooper, when you stopped the defendant, were your red and blue lights flashing?"
A: "Yes."
Q: "Did the defendant say anything when she got out of her car?"
A: "Yes, sir."
Q: "What did she say?"
A: "'What disco am I at?'"

First person to refer to a coward as a "chicken": William Shakespeare.

YOUR GOVERNMENT AT WORK

BRI member Tim Harrower found most of these in a book called Goofy Government Grants & Wacky Waste. *Now you can breathe a sigh of relief that your tax dollars are well-spent on things like…*

SCIENTIFIC RESEARCH

• Using bikini-clad women as bait, the National Science Foundation spent $64,000 to study whether distractions such as sex would decrease the honking of drivers stuck in traffic jams.

• Researchers from the National Institute on Alcohol Abuse and Alcoholism spent $102,000 to learn whether sunfish that drink tequila are more aggressive than sunfish that drink gin.

• University of Washington scientists used a government grant to monitor worm defecation. They discovered that all their worms were constipated.

• The National Institutes of Health spent more than $1 million to study cervical cancer using two test groups: nuns who were virgins and "nuns who are sexually active."

BUILDING A STRONG MILITARY

• Martin Marietta, a Department of Defense contractor, was caught charging the government $263,000 for tickets to a Smokey Robinson concert in Denver and $20,194 for professional-quality golf balls.

• In 1981, the U.S. Air Force said it could build 132 B-2 bombers for $22 billion. After eight years it had spent the money and had only *one* plane. A year of tests showed that the B-2 could perform its missions only 26% of the time…and it deteriorated in rain, heat, and humidity. The Air Force said it didn't want any more B-2s; Congress authorized contractors to build 21 of them anyway, at a cost of $44.7 billion.

But its not just us: The government of Japan recently financed a 7-year study to determine whether earthquakes are caused by catfish wiggling their tails.

The saguaro cactus does not grow its first arm until it's at least 75 years old.

SUPERSTITIONS

Here's where some common superstitions come from.

F INDING A FOUR-LEAF CLOVER
The belief that four-leaf clovers are good luck comes from the Druids, ancient residents of the British Isles. Several times a year, they gathered in oak groves to settle legal disputes and offer sacrifices...then they ended their rituals by hunting for four-leaf clovers. Why? They believed a four-leaf enabled its owner to see evil spirits and witches—and therefore avoid them.

THROWING PENNIES INTO A WELL
Ancient people believed spirits living in springs and fountains demanded tribute—usually flesh. Young Mayan girls, for example, were sometimes tossed into the Well of Sacrifice (where they would "marry" the spirits). Today we just toss the spirits a penny or two for luck.

KNOCKING ON WOOD
In the Middle Ages, churchmen insisted that knocking on wood was part of their tradition of prayer, since Christ was crucified on a wooden cross. They were right...but the tradition started several thousands of years earlier, with a different deity. Both Native Americans and ancient Greeks developed the belief (independently) that oak trees were the domain of an important god. By knocking on an oak, they were communicating with him and asking for his forgiveness. The Greeks passed their tradition on to the Romans, and it became part of European lore. The oak's "power" was eventually transferred to all wood.

NAILING A HORSESHOE OVER A DOOR
This "good luck charm" is a combination of two superstitions:

1. In early times, horses were considered magical. Because they can find their way in the dark, for example, people believed they could foresee danger or could guide souls through the underworld so anything connected with a horse was lucky.

2. Horseshoes are made of iron, which was considered protective.

J. Edgar Hoover liked to fire FBI agents who "looked like truck drivers" or had "pointy heads."

The Norse god of battle wore iron gloves and carried an iron hammer. Romans nailed pieces of iron over their doors, believing it could ward off evil spirits.

In the 10th century, Christians added their own twist to the superstition—the tale of a blacksmith named Dunstan, who later became Archbishop of Canterbury. Dunstan had an unusual customer one day, a man with cloven feet who requested iron shoes. Dunstan pretended not to recognize him and agreed to make the shoes. But he knew who the fellow was—he shackled the Devil to the wall, treating him so brutally that Satan cried for mercy. Dunstan released him only after extracting a promise to never enter a dwelling with a horseshoe on the door.

OPENING AN UMBRELLA INDOORS

One of the few superstitions that isn't ancient or irrelevant. In the 18th century, spring-loaded, metal-spoked umbrellas were new and unpredictable. Opening one indoors was courting disaster—it could fly out of control and damage property...or people. It was a practical impulse to regard it as bad luck.

PULLING ON A WISHBONE

Over 2,000 years ago, the Etruscans (an early Italian civilization) believed that chickens—which squawk before they lay their eggs—could tell the future. The powers extended to part of the chicken's skeleton, too, so when a sacred hen died, the Etruscans put its collarbone in the sun until it dried out. Then people would pick it up, rub it, and make a wish. It became known as the "wishbone." Why this particular bone? Apparently because the V-shape looks a little like a human crotch.

Later, as more people wanted to get in on the wishing, the rubbing turned into a symbolic tug-of-war. Not everyone was going to get their wish; it became a contest to see whom the gods favored.

THE STORK BRINGING BABIES

In Scandinavia, storks—gentle birds with strong family ties—habitually nested on top of people's chimneys. So when Scandinavian parents needed to explain to youngsters how babies arrived, the stork was a handy answer. This traditional tale was spread in the 1800s by Hans Christian Andersen, in his fairy tales.

Teddy Roosevelt had 24 pets in the White House, including 4 guinea pigs, 2 cats and 1 bear.

OOPS!

Everyone's amused by tales of outrageous blunders—probably because it's comforting to know that someone's screwing up even worse than we are. So go ahead and feel superior for a few minutes.

HOT CLUE

PHILADELPHIA—"A former Philadelphia fireman, in Federal Court here trying to overturn his dismissal for long hair, set his head on fire.

"William Michini apparently tried to dramatize that his locks were not a safety threat to his job. 'Hair is self-extinguishing. It doesn't burn,' he boasted. With that he struck a match and held it to his head, which caught fire. 'It must have been the hairspray I used,' said the sheepish firefighter."

—*Remarkabilia,* by John Train

...AND HOW'S YOUR WIFE, CARLY?

"Kathie Lee Gifford inadvertently stumbled into talk-show hell on a recent 'Live with Regis and Kathie Lee.'

"Singer-songwriter James Taylor was one of the guests, and the perky one, just making conversation, asked how his older brother, Alex, was doing. Sweet Baby James replied: 'I wish I could say he was doing well....Alex died about four years ago.'

"The *Washington Post* noted: 'Mortification hung in the air for a few long moments.' Blues singer Alex Taylor died of a heart attack in 1993, at age 46."

—*The Portland Oregonian,* May 1, 1997

WHAT ARE YOU DOING HERE?

"The Aldo Oliveri Stadium was meant to be the perfect memorial for one of Italy's greatest sports heroes: a stadium in Verona, dedicated to the memory of the goalie who led Italy to victory in the 1938 World Cup. Everything went smoothly right up to the weekend before it was due to open, when a small problem was discovered. Aldo Oliveri wasn't dead; he was alive, 86, and by all accounts, in the best of health. Plans are now afoot to open the stadium late, under a different name."

—*The Fortean Times,* 1997

The Apaches referred to horses as "God dogs."

...AND WHAT ARE YOU DOING HERE?

"In 1964 Gary Grannai escorted Tricia Nixon to the International Debutante Ball in New York City. Seven years later President Nixon was justifying his prosecution of the Vietnam War, despite the family's loss of a friend: 'Gary was a second lieutenant. He was on patrol duty when it happened. You feel the personal tragedy when it comes into your own home. Yet there is no alternative to the war's going on.' Publication of these remarks was followed by the [embarrassing] reappearance of Gary Grannai, who was very much alive and happily married."

—*Oops*, **by Richard Smith and Edward Recter**

WELL, IN FRANCE KIDS LIKE IT

"French broadcasting system Canal France International blamed a 'technical glitch' that sent an X-rated film instead of children's programming to Arab countries last Saturday. 'We deeply regret this unacceptable incident, and we share in the high feelings prompted in Saudi Arabia and more widely in the Arab world,' a foreign ministry spokesman said. An investigation is under way."

—*USA Today*, **July 23, 1997**

SURE IT WAS A MISTAKE

TORONTO—"Proofreaders at Canada's postal service let a royal error slip through in the production of a souvenir stamp book—a reference to 'the Prince of Whales.'

"Much to Canada Post's chagrin, the book was printed with a passage describing a visit by the 'Prince of Whales' to the snowy shores in 1860. He eventually became King Edward VII.

"It was human error and there was no intended slight to the Royal Family or to Prince Charles, said a spokesman. He also said Canada Post will not pull the book from shelves."

—*Reuters News Service*, **1997**

ALPHABET SOUP

In the 1980s, the Pfeiffer Brewing Company decided to use its successful print ad campaign on the radio. They realized it was a mistake when they heard the announcer say their written slogan aloud: "Pfeiffer's...the beer with the silent P."

On the day that *The Wizard of Oz*'s Judy Garland died, a tornado touched down in Kansas.

HOW THE SPIDER WAS CREATED

Here's the ancient Greek story of the creation of the
spider—and the reason we call spiders "arachnids."
From Myths and Legends of the Ages.

There was a maiden named Arachne who was so skillful at weaving and embroidery that people would come from far and near to marvel at her work. Not only was the work itself beautiful, but Arachne's movements as she wove were so graceful and lovely that people would say, "Minerva herself must have taught you!"

But Arachne had become so vain about her skill that she couldn't bear to hear even the goddess Minerva praised.

"Is that so," scoffed Arachne. "Let Minerva try her skill with me. If I don't surpass her, I will pay the penalty!"

Minerva, hearing this, was angry. But she was also merciful. She disguised herself as an old woman and came to Arachne. "I am an old woman," she said, "and I have learned much in my long lifetime. Challenge your fellow mortals, if you want, but don't challenge a goddess. If I were you, I would beg Minerva's forgiveness and hope she'll pardon you."

But Arachne laughed scornfully. "I am not afraid," she said. "I meant what I said. Let Minerva come down and compete with me...if she dares!"

"She comes!" answered Minerva. And dropping her disguise, she stepped forward.

Arachne paled, but only for a moment. "Let us begin," she said. So the contest began. Minerva wove scenes showing the immense power of the gods. The beauty of her work was so great that the watchers were breathless with admiration.

Then Arachne began to weave. She purposely chose to weave pictures showing the weakness and errors of the gods. Her pictures were so lifelike they almost seemed to move. She wove so marvelously that even Minerva admired her art. But furious at Arachne's insults, Minerva struck her shuttle and it fell apart. Then she touched Arachne's forehead and made her feel guilt and shame.

Arachne, in remorse, rushed away and hung herself. Then Minerva took some pity on her and said, "Live, guilty woman. But from now on, you and your children shall continue to hang."

As she spoke, Arachne's form shriveled up, while her arms and legs grew thinner, until finally she was changed into a spider. Her descendants can be seen to this day, hanging from the thread which they weave into webs.

*   *   *   *

TARANTULA ATTACK!

The poor tarantula is misunderstood—some people still believe its bite is fatal. (In *Dr. No*—the first James Bond film—for example, villains try to kill 007 by putting a tarantula on his pillow.)

• Actually, some species are not poisonous at all. And those that are have a bite generally no more harmful than a bee sting. Unlike bees, however, tarantulas give warnings before they attack—they rear up and bare their fangs. If that doesn't work, they sting.

• John Browning writes in *Tarantulas*, a pet guide for tarantula owners, "Tarantulas have never been known to kill a human being with their venom." However, he suggests caution: just as some people are allergic to bee stings, some can have severe allergic reactions to tarantula bites.

• Of more concern than a bite: Some species have poisonous hairs that can temporarily blind their enemies—including humans. If a tarantula feels threatened, it will rub its abdomen with its hind legs until some strands of hair fall off, then throw the strands at its enemy. (A tarantula with a large bald spot on its abdomen is either old, or under a lot of stress!)

WHY ASK WHY?

*Sometimes, answers are irrelevant—it's the question that
counts. These cosmic queries are from the Internet.*

Why is *abbreviation* such a long word?

Why are there interstate highways in Hawaii?

Why is there an expiration date on sour cream?

Why is it that when you transport something by car, it's called a shipment, but when you transport something by ship, it's called cargo?

Why do we drive on parkways, and park on driveways?

If you're driving in a vehicle at the speed of light, what happens when you turn on the headlights?

Why don't you ever hear about *gruntled* employees?

What is a "free" gift? Aren't all gifts free?

Why do they call it *necking*?

Why isn't *phonetic* spelled the way it sounds?

If you tied buttered toast to the back of a cat and dropped it from a height, what would happen?

Have you ever imagined a world with no hypothetical situations?

If he's arrested, does a mime need to be told he has a right to remain silent?

Why do they call it a TV "set" when you only get one?

What was the best thing *before* sliced bread?

If you throw a cat out a car window, does it become kitty litter?

If one synchronized swimmer drowns, do the rest have to drown, too?

If a cow laughed, would milk come out her nose?

What's another word for *synonym?*

What is the speed of dark?

FAMILIAR PHRASES

Where do these familiar terms and phrases come from? Etymologists have researched them and come up with these explanations.

A CID TEST

Meaning: A test of whether something is true or valuable.

Origin: In the past, gold was traded as currency. To find out if it was genuine, a gold coin could be tested with nitric acid. If the piece was counterfeit, the acid decomposed it. If it was genuine, the gold remained intact.

BUILD A FIRE UNDER SOMEONE

Meaning: Get someone to take action.

Origin: Mules can be stubborn. They sometimes splay all four legs out and refuse to move...and no amount of coaxing or beating will budge them. "When farmers wanted them to move and everything else failed," explains Nigel Rees in *Why You Say It*, "a small fire was built under the mule's belly in hopes that once in action the animal could be guided and kept moving."

BEFORE YOU CAN SAY "JACK ROBINSON"

Meaning: At once; instantly.

Origin: According to lore, the original Jack Robinson was a gentleman who kept his unannounced visits on his neighbors so short that they hardly had a chance to speak before he was gone. The term appears in Dickens's *A Christmas Carol* and Twain's *Huckleberry Finn*.

A FALSEHOOD

Meaning: A lie.

Origin: Before hats came into vogue, men wore hoods of cloth or fur attached to their cloaks. Many professionals—e.g., doctors, and priests—wore distinctive hood styles. If a con man wanted to set himself up as a professional in a town where he wasn't known, all he to do was put on the right hood. This deception came to be labeled as *a falsehood*.

MODERN MYTHOLOGY

These mythological characters may be as famous in our culture as Hercules or Pegasus were in ancient Greece. Here's where they came from.

SNAP!, CRACKLE!, & POP! In 1933, commercial artist Vernon Grant was working at his drawing board when he heard this Rice Krispies ad on the radio:

> Listen to the fairy song of health, the merry chorus sung by Kellogg's Rice Krispies as they merrily snap, crackle and pop in a bowl of milk. If you've never heard food talking, now is your chance.

Inspired, he immediately drew three little elves—which he named after the noises the cereal supposedly made. Then he took the sketches to N. W. Ayer, the Philadelphia ad agency that handled Kellogg's advertising; they bought the cartoons on the spot. They also hired Grant to keep illustrating the little trio for cereal boxes, posters, and ads. He made a good living working for Kellogg's over the next decade, but wasn't happy with the arrangement. So he decided to sue Kellogg's for sole ownership of the characters. Bad move: he lost, Kellogg's fired him, and Grant never made another cent off the characters he created.

THE SUN MAID RAISIN GIRL. "The sun-bonneted woman...who smiles on every box of Sun-Maid raisins was a real person," writes Victoria Woeste in *Audacity* magazine. "Her name was Lorraine Collett and in 1915, she was sitting in her front yard letting her hair dry before participating in Fresno's first Raisin Day parade. A Sun-Maid executive was passing by and was struck by the sight. He had a photographer come take her picture, then had artist Fanny Scafford paint the picture from it." All Collett made from it was a $15 modeling fee and a bit part in a 1936 film called *Trail of the Lonesome Pine*. The original bonnet is now in the Smithsonian.

MR. PEANUT. Amadeo Obici founded the Planters Nut & Chocolate Company in 1906, in Wilkes-Barre, Pennsylvania. Roasted and salted peanuts were still new to most Americans, and the company was an immediate success. As it got bigger, Obici decided he needed a logo. In 1916, he sponsored a contest to find one. The winner: 13-year-old Antonio Gentile, from Suffolk, Virginia, who submitted a drawing of "a little peanut person" and got $5 for it. A commercial artist took Gentile's sketch, added a hat, cane, and monocle (to lend a touch of class to the lowly legume), and Mr. Peanut was born. The elegant gentle-nut made his debut in 1918, in *The Saturday Evening Post.*

MCGRUFF THE CRIME DOG. In the late 1970s, the Ad Council made a deal with the U.S. Justice Department to create an anti-crime ad campaign. Their first task: invent a spokes-character (like Smokey the Bear) to deliver the message in commercials. Adman Jack Keil began riding with the New York police to get ideas. He remembers:

> We weren't getting anywhere. Then came a day I was flying home from the West Coast. I was trying to think of a slogan—*crunch crime, stomp on crime.* And I was thinking of animal symbols—*growling at crime, roaring at crime.* But which animal? The designated critter had to be trustworthy, honorable, and brave. Then I thought, you can't crunch crime or defeat it altogether, but you can snap at it, nibble at it—*take a bite out of crime.* And the animal that takes a bite is a dog.

A bloodhound was the natural choice for a crimefighter, but they still needed a name...so they sponsored a nationwide name-the-dog contest. The most frequent entry was Shure-lock Bones. Others included: Sarg-dog, J. Edgar Dog, and Keystone Kop Dog. The winner was submitted by a New Orleans police officer. In the ads, Keil supplies McGruff's voice.

TONY THE TIGER. In 1952, Kellogg's planned to feature a menagerie of animals—one for each letter of the alphabet—on packages of its Sugar Frosted Flakes. They started with K and T: Katy the Kangaroo and Tony the Tiger. But they never got any further. Tony—who walked on all fours and had a much flatter face than today—was so popular that he became the cereal's official spokes-character. In the first Frosted Flakes commercials, only kids who ate Tony's cereal could see him. His personality has changed a number of times since then, but his voice hasn't. It's Thurl Ravenscroft, an ex-radio star who jokingly claims to have made a career out of just one word: "Grr-reat!"

An adult horse eats 15 pounds of hay and 9 pounds of grain every day.

FAMOUS FOR 15 MINUTES

Here it is again—our feature based on Andy Warhol's prophetic comment that "in the future, everyone will be famous for 15 minutes." Here's how a few people have been using up their allotted quarter-hour.

THE STAR: Pete Condon, 1989 graduate of the University of Georgia

THE HEADLINE: *Case Clothes'd: Job Seeker Wears Resumé, Gets Calls*

WHAT HAPPENED: Condon had graduated from college with a 3.5 grade average, but couldn't get the marketing/advertising job he wanted. Finally, in February 1992, the 25-year-old blew up his resumé, put it on a sandwich board, and stood on an Atlanta street corner during rush hour with a sign saying: "I will work for $25,000 a year." An *Atlanta Constitution* reporter spotted him. The next day his photo and story were in newspapers all over the country.

AFTERMATH: In the next two months, Condon got more than 500 job offers from as far away as Japan and Panama. He was the subject of college lectures and term papers, and women sent photos asking to meet him. Condon finally took a job at Dean Witter…at a salary of considerably more than $25,000.

THE STAR: John (or Tom) Helms

THE HEADLINE: *Lucky Leaper Lands Lightly on Ledge, Likes Life*

WHAT HAPPENED: Just before Christmas in 1977, Helms—a 26-year-old down-and-out artist—decided to commit suicide by jumping off the Empire State Building. He took the elevator to the 86th floor observation deck (more than 1,000 feet up), climbed over the safety rail, and let go. He woke up half an hour later, sitting on a ledge on the 85th floor. Miraculously, a 30-mph wind had blown him back against the building. He knocked on a window, and an astonished engineer in the NBC-TV transmitter room helped him in. "I couldn't believe it," the engineer said. "You don't see a lot of guys coming in through the window of the 85th floor. I poured myself a stiff drink." The story made national news.

The longest-surviving Civil War widow was still alive in 1997.

AFTERMATH: Helms decided life was okay after all, and got hundreds of offers from families who wanted to take him in for the holidays. Two years later a similar incident occurred. On December 2, 1979, Elvita Adams climbed over the 86th floor's safety rail and jumped. She fell about 20 feet before she was blown back onto a 2 1/2-foot ledge, breaking her hip. A guard heard her yelling in pain and rescued her.

THE STAR: Graham Washington Jackson, a Navy musician

THE HEADLINE: *Sobbing Soldier Shows Symbolic Sorrow*

WHAT HAPPENED: President Franklin D. Roosevelt died on April 12, 1945, at the "Little White House" in Warm Springs, Georgia. Jackson was there to see FDR's body taken away. "It seemed like every nail and every pin in the world just stuck in me," he said later. As tears streamed down his face, he spontaneously began playing a tune called "Goin' Home" on his accordion. Edward Clark, a photographer, noticed Jackson and snapped a shot that was published in *Life* magazine. The picture captured the nation's shock and grief so well that both the photo and Jackson became world-famous.

AFTERMATH: Over the next four decades, Jackson was invited to the White House to play for every president. In fact, Jimmy Carter—who regarded the *Life* photo as one of the best ever taken—had Jackson named Georgia's "Official State Musician" when Carter was governor. Jackson died in 1983, at age 79.

THE STAR: Leon Henry Ritzenthaler, possible half-brother of President Bill Clinton

THE HEADLINE: *Surprise Sibling Surfaces in Paradise*

WHAT HAPPENED: In June 1993, a few months after Clinton took office, The *Washington Post* announced that Ritzenthaler—a retired janitor in Paradise, California—was the president's long-lost half-brother.

Clinton's mother had married William Blythe in 1943. Ritzenthaler's mother had married Blythe eight years earlier, in 1935. She and Blythe had divorced in 1936, but continued to "visit" after the divorce; Leon was born in 1938, the result—his mother claimed—of one of those visits. The *Post* spent four months checking, and sure enough, Leon's birth certificate listed Blythe as his father. But

Blythe's sister insisted that it was *another* member of the family who was really the father—that Blythe had merely covered for him.

Meanwhile, the press camped on Ritzenthaler's doorstep. Leon said he wanted nothing from the president except their father's health records, so he could pass them on to his kids. (Although he admitted he wouldn't mind meeting his brother.) Clinton said he'd comment after talking to Ritzenthaler.

The president did call Leon a few days later; they chatted for 15 minutes. And in August, Clinton sent a note that said, "I look forward to meeting you before too long."

AFTERMATH: The story simply died. Clinton seems never to have mentioned Ritzenthaler again, and the press apparently lost interest.

Sidelight: In August 1993, a woman named Wanetta Alexander surfaced, swearing to reporters that the William Blythe she'd married in 1941 was the same man who'd fathered Clinton. That would have made her daughter the president's half-sister…but more interesting, it would have made Clinton "illegitimate." Alexander hadn't divorced Blythe until 1944, and Clinton's mother had married him in 1943. It was apparently never proved.

THE STAR: Ruth Bullis, a waitress at Stanford's Restaurant in Lake Oswego, Oregon

THE HEADLINE: *Tip Tops Charts*

WHAT HAPPENED: In November 1995, a customer ordered a gin-and-tonic and a sandwich from Bullis, paid for it with a credit card, and wrote in a $40 dollar tip. Then he ordered another gin-and-tonic and left $100. Four hours later, after a third gin-and-tonic, he left a whopping $1,000 tip. Bullis said he insisted: "I can leave you whatever I want…I'm a big spender." But she put the tips aside, waiting to see if he'd have second thoughts. A few weeks later, he showed up again…and left $100. She decided it was okay to spend the money. But she was wrong. In February, American Express notified Stanford's that the customer wanted his money back.

AFTERMATH: When the story was picked up by national news media, the company that owned Stanford's decided on its own to avoid publicity and refund the tip to the customer. Bullis kept $1,000 *and* her job.

In the Middle Ages, you were supposed to throw eggs at the bride and groom.

REEL QUOTES

Here are some of our favorite lines from the silver screen.

ON DATING
Allen: "What are you doing Saturday night?"
Diana: "Committing suicide."
Allen: "What are you doing Friday night?"
—*Play It Again, Sam*

ON LOVE
Darrow: "You ever been in love, Hornbeck?"
Hornbeck: "Only with the sound of my own voice, thank God."
—*Inherit the Wind*

"Jane, since I've met you, I've noticed things I never knew were there before: birds singing...dew glistening on a newly formed leaf...stoplights..."
—*Lt. Frank Drebin,*
Naked Gun

ON ANATOMY
Nick Charles: "I'm a hero. I was shot twice in the *Tribune*."
Nora Charles: "I read where you were shot five times in the tabloids."
Nick: "It's not true. They didn't come anywhere near my tabloids."
—*The Thin Man*

ON GOLF
"A golf course is nothing but a poolroom moved outdoors."
—*Barry Fitzgerald,*
Going My Way

ON RELIGION
Sonja: "Of course there's a God. We're made in his image."
Boris: "You think I was made in God's image? Take a look at me. Do you think he wears glasses?"
Sonja: "Not with those frames... Boris, we must believe in God."
Boris: "If I could just see a miracle. Just one miracle. If I could see a burning bush, or the seas part, or my Uncle Sasha pick up a check."
—*Woody Allen's*
Love and Death

ON BEING CLEAR
Ted Striker: "Surely, you can't be serious."
Dr. Rumack: "I *am* serious. And don't call me Shirley."
—*Airplane!*

Ollie: "You never met my wife, did you?"
Stan: "Yes, I never did."
—*Helpmates*

Snakes can get malaria.

READ ALL ABOUT IT!

We've all heard the expression "Don't believe everything you read." Here are a few examples of why that's true.

P LAINFIELD TEACHER'S COLLEGE WINS AGAIN!
(*New York Herald Tribune* and other papers, 1941)
The Story: In 1941 the *Tribune*, the *New York Post*, and a number of other New York papers began reporting the scores of a New Jersey football team called the Plainfield Teachers College Flying Figments as it battled teams like Harmony Teachers College and Appalachia Tech for a coveted invitation to the first-ever "Blackboard Bowl."

The Reaction: As the season progressed and the Figments remained undefeated, interest in the small college powerhouse grew, and so did the press coverage. Several papers ran feature articles about Johnny Chung, the team's "stellar Chinese halfback who has accounted for 69 of Plainfield's 117 points" and who "renewed his amazing strength at halftime by wolfing down wild rice."

The Truth: Plainfield, the Flying Figments, and its opponents were all invented by a handful of bored New York stockbrokers who were amazed that real teams from places like Slippery Rock got their scores into big city newspapers. Each Saturday, the brokers phoned in fake scores, then waited for them to appear in the Sunday papers. The hoax lasted nearly the entire season, until *Time* magazine got wind of it and decided to run a story. In the few days that remained before *Time* hit the newsstands, the brokers sent in one last story announcing that "because of a rash of flunkings in mid-term examinations, Plainfield was calling off its last two scheduled games of the season."

PETRIFIED MAN FOUND IN NEVADA CAVE!
(Virginia City *Territorial Enterprise*, 1862)
The Story: According to the article, a petrified man with a wooden leg was found in a cave in a remote part of the Nevada. The man was found in a seated position, with

the right thumb resting against the side of his nose, the left thumb partially supported the chin, the forefinger pressing the inner corner of the left eye and drawing it partially open; the right eye was closed, and the fingers of the right hand spread apart.

The article claimed the man had been dead for at least 300 years.

The Reaction: The story spread to other newspapers in Nevada, from there to the rest of the country, and from there around the world. The archaeological "find" was even reported in the London scientific journal *Lancet*.

The Truth: The story was the work of the *Territorial Enterprise*'s local editor, Samuel Clemens (later known by his pen name, Mark Twain). Clemens figured people would know it was a hoax by the description of the stone man's hand positions. [Uncle John's note: Try doing it yourself.] But he was wrong. "I really had no desire to deceive anybody," he explained later. "I depended on the way the petrified man was sitting to explain to the public that he was a swindle....[It was] a delicate, a very delicate satire. But maybe it was altogether too delicate, for nobody ever perceived the satire part of it at all."

NOISY GHOST HAUNTS SAN DIEGO BANK BUILDING!
(The San Diego Metropolitan, 1987)

The Story: The article claimed that the Great American Bank Building, one of San Diego's best-known landmarks, was plagued by mysterious footsteps heard late at night, creepy voices, ghost-like images materializing out of thin air; just about all of the classic ghost clichés. The article even claimed the ghost or ghosts had reduced janitorial costs 25% by helping the building's custodians do the vacuuming. The article included a photo of the ghost, and quoted a "parapsychologist" calling it "one of the finest examples of spiritual photography I've ever seen."

The Reaction: The public took the story seriously, and when the tenants of the Great American Bank Building learned of the incidents, they began reporting their own sightings—including power failures, carpeting that had been "mysteriously vacuumed," and cleaning equipment that moved from one floor to another; one electrician even reported seeing his tools float in midair and ghosts walking in the hallway.

The Truth: The article was the brainchild of *Metropolitan* publisher Sean Patrick Reily, who later admitted it had been inspired by Mark Twain's "petrified man" work.

WEIRD CELEBRATIONS

One of Uncle John's bathroom stalwarts is Stabbed with a Wedge of Cheese, *by Charles Downey. There's a lot of offbeat stuff in it, including info on these festivals.*

THE ANNUAL FIRE ANT FESTIVAL

Location: Marshall, Texas

Background: Fire ants are red ants that swarm and bite—a real problem in South Texas. People in Marshall decided that since they couldn't get rid of the ants, they might as well have some fun with them.

Special Events: Fire Ant Call, Fire Ant Roundup, and a Fire Ant Chili Cookoff in which entrants must certify in writing that their fixin's contain at least one fire ant. The ending to the festivities is the Fire Ant Stomp—not an attempt to squash the ants, but an old-fashioned street dance.

THE INTERNATIONAL STRANGE MUSIC FESTIVAL

Location: Olive Hill, Kentucky

Background: Founded to honor people who make music from non-musical items.

Special Events: Every act is a special event. Performers have included:
- A Japanese trio playing "My Old Kentucky Home" on a table (upside down, strung like a cello), tea pot (a wind instrument), and assorted pots and pans (bongo drums)
- A 15-piece orchestra of automobile horns
- A seven-foot slide whistle requiring three people to operate it
- A "Graduated Clanger"—a system of ever-smaller fire alarm bells, played like a xylophone

THE ANNUAL CHICKEN SHOW

Location: Wayne, Nebraska

Background: Held the second Saturday in July, featuring a crowing contest for roosters, a free omelet feed for humans, and a chicken-flying meet, fully sanctioned by the International Chicken Flying Association.

It's impossible to snore in the weightlessness of space.

Special Events: A "Most Beautiful Beak" contest, chicken bingo, and an egg drop (participants risk egg-on-the-face by trying to catch a raw egg dropped from a fully extended cherry picker). The National Cluck-Off selects the person with the most lifelike cluck and most believable crow. Another contest offers prizes to the man and woman who sport the most chicken-like legs.

THE WORLD GRITS FESTIVAL

Location: St. George, South Carolina

Background: World's only celebration honoring the South's staple food. Special grits dishes are offered for all meals of the day. Also featured are a grits mill, a grits-eating contest, and a grits cooking contest. The event was born when someone discovered that the 2,300 citizens of St. George went through about 1,800 pounds of grits a week.

Special Events: "The Roll-in-Grits Contest." A kids' wading pool is filled with hot water and several hundred pounds of grits, then stirred with a canoe paddle till done. Each contestant: 1) weighs in, 2) gets in the pool and wallows in it for seven seconds, 3) gets out and weighs in again. The object: To see how many pounds of grits can stick to your body. All-time winner had 26 pounds stuck to him.

THE UGLY PICKUP PARADE AND CONTEST

Location: Chadron, Nebraska

Background: In 1987, newspaper columnist Les Mann wrote an homage to his junker 1974 pickup, "Black Beauty," claiming it was the ugliest truck on the planet. Irate ugly-truck owners wrote in, saying they could top him. So the first Ugly Truck Contest was born.

Special Events: Experts pick the Ugly Pickup of the Year. An Ugly Pickup Queen leads the three-block parade through town. Official rules: Trucks have to be street-legal, and over a decade old. They have to be able to move under their own power; a majority of the surface area has to be rust and dents; and, most important, they've got to have a good Ugly Truck name. Contestants get extra points for something *especially* ugly on their truck.

IN DREAMS....

We've always been fascinated by our dreams. Where do they come from? What do they mean? D. H. Lawrence put it perfectly when he said, "I can never decide whether my dreams are the result of my thoughts or my thoughts are the result of my dreams." But even if we don't understand dreams, we can use them—sometimes to solve specific problems. On occasion, art, music, and even scientific discoveries / inventions have resulted directly from information received in a dream. Here are some examples.

T HE SEWING MACHINE

Elias Howe had been trying to invent a practical lock-stitch sewing machine for years, but had been unsuccessful. One night in the 1840s, he had a nightmare in which he was captured by a primitive tribe who were threatening to kill him with their spears. Curiously, all that the natives' spears had holes in them at the pointed ends. When Howe woke up, he realized that a needle with a hole at its tip—rather than at the base or middle (which is what he'd been working with)—was the solution to his problem.

DR. JEKYLL AND MR. HYDE

Since childhood, novelist Robert Louis Stevenson had always remembered his dreams and believed that they gave him inspiration for his writing. In 1884, he was in dire need of money and was trying to come up with a book. He had already spent two days racking his brains for a new plot when he had a nightmare about a man with a dual personality. In the dream, "Mr. Hyde" was being pursued for a crime he'd committed; he took a strange powder and changed into someone else as his pursuers watched. Stevenson screamed in his sleep, and his wife woke him. The next morning he began writing down *The Strange Case of Dr. Jekyll and Mr. Hyde.*

INSULIN

Frederick Banting, a Canadian doctor, had been doing research into the cause of diabetes, but had not come close to a cure. One night he had a strange dream. When he awoke, he quickly, wrote down a few words that he remembered: "Tie up the duct of the pancreas of a dog...wait for the glands to shrivel up. Then cut it out, wash it, isolation of the hormone now known as insulin, which has saved

---

Smallest town in the U.S.: Hove Mobile Park City, North Dakota, with a population of two.

millions of diabetics' lives. Banting was knighted for his discovery.

LEAD SHOT

James Watt is remembered for inventing the steam engine, but he also came up with the process for making lead shot used in shotguns. This process was revealed to him in a dream. At the time, making the lead shot was costly and unpredictable—the lead was rolled into sheets by hand, then chopped into bits. Watt began having the same dream each night for a week: He was walking along in a heavy rainstorm—but instead of rain, he was being showered with tiny pellets of lead, which he could see rolling around his feet. The dream haunted him; did it mean that molten lead falling through the air would harden into round pellets? He decided to experiment. He melted a few pounds of lead and tossed it out of the tower of a church that had a water-filled moat at its base. When he removed the lead from the water, he found that it *had* hardened into tiny globules. To this day, lead shot is made using this process.

THE BENZENE MOLECULE

Friedrich A. Kekule, a Belgian chemistry professor, had been working for some time to solve the structural riddle of the benzene molecule. One night while working late, he fell asleep on a chair and dreamed of atoms dancing before him, forming various patterns and structures. He saw long rows of atoms begin to twist like snakes until one of the snakes seized its own tail and began to whirl in a circle. Kekule woke up "as if by a flash of lightning" and began to work out the meaning of his dream image. His discovery of a closed ring with an atom of carbon and hydrogen at each point of a hexagon revolutionized organic chemistry.

JESUS (*as many people think of Him*)

Warner E. Sallman was an illustrator for religious magazines. In 1924 he needed a picture for a deadline the next day, but was coming up blank. Finally, he went to bed—then suddenly awoke with "a picture of the Christ in my mind's eye just as if it were on my drawing board." He quickly sketched a portrait of Jesus with long brown hair, blue eyes, a neatly trimmed beard, and a beatific look—which has now become the common image of Christ around the world. Since 1940, more than 500 million copies of Sallman's "Head of Christ" have been sold. It has been reproduced billions of times on calendars, lamps, posters, etc.

Chief, the U.S. Cavalry's last horse, died in 1968. He was 36.

UNCLE ALBERT SAYS...

Cosmic question: What would Albert Einstein think if he knew we consider his comments great bathroom reading?

"Only two things are infinite, the universe and stupidity—and I'm not sure about the former."

"God is subtle, but He is not malicious."

"'Common sense' is the set of prejudices acquired by age eighteen."

"Nationalism is an infantile disease. It is the measles of mankind."

"I never think of the future. It comes soon enough."

"Try not to become a man of success, but rather, a man of value."

"I experience the greatest degree of pleasure in having contact with works of art. They furnish me with happy feelings of an intensity such as I cannot drive from other realms."

"To punish me for my contempt for authority, Fate made me an authority myself."

"Why is it that nobody understands me, and everybody likes me?"

"A life directed chiefly toward fulfillment of personal desires sooner or later *always* leads to bitter disappointment."

"My political ideal is that of democracy. Let every man be respected as an individual, and no man idolized."

"Whatever there is of God and goodness in the Universe, it must work itself out and express itself through us. We cannot stand aside and let God do it."

"Science without religion is lame, religion without science is blind."

"I am a deeply religious nonbeliever...This is a somewhat new kind of religion."

"With fame I become more and more stupid, which of course is a very common phenomenon."

Chickens are the only birds that have combs.

FLUBBED HEADLINES

These are 100% honest-to-goodness headlines.
Can you figure out what they were trying to say?

Kids Make Nutritious Snacks

ENRAGED COW INJURES FARMER WITH AXE

Red Tape Holds Up New Bridge

BILKE-A-THON NETS $1,000 FOR ILL BOY

PANDA MATING FAILS; VETERINARIAN TAKES OVER

School taxpayers revolting

Eye Drops Off Shelf

HELICOPTER POWERED BY HUMAN FLIES

Circumcisions Cut Back

POPE TO BE ARRAIGNED FOR ALLEGEDLY BURGLARIZING CLINIC

City wants Dead to pay for cleanup

MOORPARK RESIDENTS ENJOY A COMMUNAL DUMP

Montana Traded to Kansas City

Area man wins award for nuclear accident

International Scientific Group Elects Bimbo As Its Chairman

Storm delayed by bad weather

LEGISLATORS TAX BRAINS TO CUT DEFICIT

DEAD GUITARIST NOW SLIMMER AND TRIMMER

Study Finds Sex, Pregnancy Link

Include Your Children When Baking Cookies

Trees can break wind

RANGERS TO TEST PEETERS FOR RUST

Cockroach Slain, Husband Badly Hurt

Living Together Linked to Divorce

ECUADOR'S PRESIDENT DECLARES HE'S NOT DEAD

LACK OF BRAINS HINDERS RESEARCH

Two Sisters Reunited After 18 Years At Checkout Counter

Man, Shot Twice in Head, Gets Mad

MISSOURI WOMAN BIG WINNER AT HOG SHOW

Teacher Dies; Board Accepts His Resignation

PANTS MAN TO EXPAND AT THE REAR

Siberia means "sleeping land."

ANONYMOUS STARS

You've watched them work, you've heard them speak—but you've probably never heard their names. They're the actors inside the gorilla suits, the voices of talking animals, etc. We think they deserve at least a little credit.

THE VOICE OF E.T.

- E.T.'s voice was created by combining the voices of three people, a sea otter and a dog. But the person who spoke the most famous lines—"E.T. phone home" and "Be good"—was Patricia A.Welsh, a former radio soap opera star who'd only been involved in one other movie (*Waterloo*, with Robert Taylor, in 1940).

- By contract, she was forbidden to say her lines (which are copyrighted) even casually in conversation; Steven Spielberg said he "didn't want kids to get confused about E.T.'s image." Her name isn't even listed in the credits.

DARTH VADER

- David Prowse is a 6' 6", 266 pound former heavyweight wrestling champion. George Lucas saw him in *A Clockwork Orange* and offered him his choice between two parts—Chewbacca or Vader. Prowse chose Vader because he didn't like the idea of going around in a "gorilla suit" for six months.

THE LOST IN SPACE ROBOT

- Bob May, a stuntman, had a few small parts in a TV series called "Voyage to the Bottom of the Sea." The Producer, Irwin Allen, told May he was the right size for a part in a new TV series, and asked if he'd be interested. May said yes; Allen said: "Fine, you have the part, go try on the robot costume."

- Cast members goofed on May a lot. One time they locked him in the robot suit and left him there during lunch break. He tried yelling, but no one was around...so he had a cigarette. Irwin Allen wandered in, saw smoke coming from the robot and thought it was burning up. He went to get a fire extinguisher while May yelled from inside the suit. Later, Allen decided he liked the effect and had May smoke a cigar in the suit for a story about the robot burning out.

James Earl Jones (Darth Vader's voice), and David Prowse (who played him onscreen) never met.

MR. ED'S VOICE

• When "Mr. Ed," debuted in 1960, the horses voice was credited to "An actor who prefers to remain nameless."

• *TV Guide* sent a reporter to the studio to figure out who it was. The reporter found a parking space on the "Mr. Ed" set assigned to an old 1930s movie cowboy named Alan "Rocky" Lane

• Lane admitted it was his voice (he'd been embarrassed to let people know). He dubbed Ed's voice off-camera, while the horse was "mouthing the words." A nylon bit concealed in Ed's mouth made him move his lips.

R2-D2

• Kenny Baker, 3'8" tall, was hired simply because he fit into the robot suit. "They made R2-D2 small because Carrie and Mark were small....My agent sent me down. They looked at me and said, "He'll do!' "

• "I thought it was a load of rubbish at first. Then I thought, 'Well, Alec Guinness is in it; he must know what's going on.'"

THE VOICE OF THE DEMON
IN *THE EXORCIST*

• Mercedes McCambridge, an Academy Award-winning actress, was a Catholic. So when she was offered the role, she was uncertain about whether to take it. She consulted Father Walter Hartke at Catholic University, and he approved.

• In the film, the demon's voice is heard as Linda Blair vomits green gunk. According to one report: "A tube was glued to each side of Blair's face and covered with make-up. Two men knelt on either side of Blair holding a syringe filled with the green stuff, ready to shoot on cue."

• "McCambridge had to coordinate her sound effects with the action. A prop man lined up a row of Dixie cups in front of her containing apple pieces soaking in water, and some containing whole boiled eggs. McCambridge held the soft apple chunks in her jaws as she swallowed a boiled egg. On cue, in precise coordination with the screen action, she flexed her diaphragm and spewed everything on the microphone...'It was hard,' she said. ' I sometimes had to lie down after those scenes.' "

THE HISTORY OF ROCK: A QUIZ

How much do you know about the early days of rock 'n' roll?
Here's a test to find out. Answers are on page 492.

1. The song that made Elvis a mega-star was the 1956 smash "(You Ain't Nothin' but a) Hound Dog." How did he come up with it?

a) He used to sing it to his real hound dog, "Buster."

b) He copied it from a Las Vegas lounge act.

c) He overheard a woman singing it in a Memphis bus station.

2. The flip side of "Hound Dog," "Don't Be Cruel," was also a big hit. Elvis not only sang it, but co-wrote it with Otis Blackwell. How did Elvis and Otis wind up working together?

a) They were sitting next to each other on an airplane in 1955. To kill time, they started playing a rhyming game that turned into a hit song.

b) Otis was a nephew of Colonel Tom Parker (Elvis's manager) and needed money to get married. Elvis co-wrote the song with him as a "wedding present."

c) They didn't. Elvis just insisted on getting a writing credit (and half the royalties) as his "reward" for singing the song.

3. In the 1950s, Pat Boone was known as a "cover artist"—which meant he copied black artists' new songs and usually outsold them (because white artists' records got more airplay). In 1956, he covered Fats Domino's classic "Ain't That a Shame." How did he try to change it?

a) He tried to take the word "ain't" out and replace it with "isn't" because he thought it would reflect badly on his education.

b) He tried to slow it down. "It sounds too much like jungle music," he explained.

c) He tried to turn the sax solo into a tuba solo because his parents were polka fans.

If you feed a wild moose often enough, it will begin to attack people who don't feed it.

4. The Platters were one of the biggest vocal groups in the early days of rock. Their hits were often new versions of old standards. Their biggest hit was the 1955 version of Jerome Kern's "Smoke Gets in Your Eyes." Kern was dead when the song was released, but his wife...

a) Threatened a lawsuit to stop the record.

b) Helped the group become the first rock artists with their own TV show.

c) Tried to get them to record three songs *she'd* written.

5. Chuck Berry is one of the fathers of rock 'n' roll. He had more than a dozen hits...but only one of them hit #1 on *Billboard*'s charts. It was...

a) "Johnny B. Goode"

b) "Roll Over Beethoven"

c) "My Ding-a-Ling"

6. Jerry Lee Lewis was one of the wildmen of early rock 'n' roll. His first hit, "Whole Lotta Shakin' Goin' On" (1957), was banned from the radio because...

a) His line, "All you gotta do is stand in one place and wiggle your hips," was considered obscene.

b) It was creating riots. Whenever it played on the radio—even in school—teenagers would jump up and start doing a new dance they called "The Shake."

c) A fundamentalist minister claimed he'd played it backward and heard satanic messages—the first time anyone ever said that.

7. Another crazy man of 1950s rock 'n' roll was Little Richard, who recorded classics like "Tutti Frutti" and "Rip It Up." When he recorded "Long Tall Sally," he had one particular thing in mind. What was it?

a) He sang it as fast as he could, so censors wouldn't be able to distinguish the "dirty" lyrics.

b) He sang it as fast as he could, so Pat Boone wouldn't be able to do a cover version of it.

c) He sang it as fast as he could, because he had to go to the bathroom.

Moscow is closer to Washington, D.C. than Honolulu is.

FORGOTTEN HISTORY

A few tidbits of obscure history from Keep Up
with the World, *a 1941 book by Freling Foster.*

X-RAY-PROOF UNDERWEAR

"A short time after X-rays were discovered in 1895 and news of their penetrating power had spread throughout the world, the women of England believed—and were horrified by—the rumor that a British firm was about to make X-ray spectacles that would enable the wearer to look right through clothing. Within a few months, a manufacturer and a London department store made a small fortune with their new 'x-ray-proof underwear.' "

APE HANGED AS A FRENCH SPY

"In 1705, during Queen Anne's War, between France and England, a small vessel was wrecked in the North Sea off the English coast village of West Hartlepool and the sole survivor, a pet ape belonging to the crew, was washed ashore on a plank and captured by fishermen. The villagers had never before seen such a peculiar character, but they were not to be fooled by his hairy disguise and outlandish chatter. The following day, the monkey was tried by court martial, found guilty and hanged as a French spy."

THE FIRST MOVIE STAR

"The first film star was John Bunny of New York City, who made approximately 100 one-reel comedies for the Vitagraph Company between 1911 and his death in 1915. As his pictures were shown in numerous countries, Bunny's short fat figure soon became more widely known than that of any other living individual. When he went on a world tour in 1913, he became the first movie star ever to be recognized and surrounded by huge crowds in every city he visited."

THE AMPERSAND

"The oldest symbol representing a word is "&," known as the *ampersand*. Originally, it was one of the 5,000 signs in the world's first shorthand system, invented by Marcus Tiro in Rome in 63 B.C."

THE TRUTH ABOUT LOVE

If you want to know something important, ask a kid. These quotes about love were submitted by BRI member Alan Reder, who got them from the Internet and e-mailed them to us.

HOW DO TWO PEOPLE WIND UP FALLING IN LOVE?

Andrew, age 6: "One of the people has freckles and so he finds somebody else who has freckles too."

Mae, age 9: "No one is sure why it happens, but I heard it has something to do with how you smell....That's why perfume and deodorant are so popular."

Manuel, age 8: "I think you're supposed to get shot with an arrow or something, but the rest of it isn't supposed to be so painful."

WHAT IS FALLING IN LOVE LIKE?

John, age 9: "Like an avalanche where you have to run for your life."

Glenn, age 7: "If falling in love is anything like learning how to spell, I don't want to do it. It takes too long."

HOW IMPORTANT IS BEAUTY IN LOVE?

Anita, age 8: "If you want to be loved by somebody who isn't already in your family, it doesn't hurt to be beautiful."

Brian, age 7: "It isn't always just how you look. Look at me. I'm handsome like anything and I haven't got anybody to marry me yet."

Christine, age 9: "Beauty is skin deep. But how rich you are can last a long time."

Pontius Pilate was born in Scotland.

WHY DO LOVERS HOLD HANDS?

Gavin, age 8: "They want to make sure their rings don't fall off because they paid good money for them."

John, age 9: "They are just practicing for when they might have to walk down the aisle someday and do the matchimony thing."

WHAT'S YOUR PERSONAL OPINION ABOUT LOVE?

Jill, age 6: "I'm in favor of love as long as it doesn't happen when *Dinosaurs* is on television."

Floyd, age 9: "Love is foolish…but I still might try it sometime."

Dave, age 8: "Love will find you, even if you are trying to hide from it. I been trying to hide from it since I was five, but the girls keep finding me."

Regina, age 10: "I'm not rushing into being in love. I'm finding the fourth grade hard enough."

WHAT'S A SUREFIRE WAY TO MAKE A PERSON FALL IN LOVE WITH YOU?

Del, age 6: "Tell them that you own a whole bunch of candy stores."

Camille, age 9: "Shake your hips and hope for the best."

Carey, age 7: "Yesterday I kissed a girl in a private place….We were behind a tree."

REFLECTIONS ON THE NATURE OF LOVE

Greg, age 8: "Love is the most important thing in the world, but baseball is pretty good, too."

*　　*　　*

"To love a thing means wanting it to live." —*Confucius*

McREVENGE!

*Don't let all that happy Ronald McDonald stuff fool you—from the begin-
ning, McDonald's has played hardball in the burger business. Not even
the company's namesakes, the McDonald brothers, were exempt.
Here's a classic revenge story on a sesame seed bun*

SETTING THE STAGE

In 1949, Dick and Mac McDonald opened a drive-in restaurant in San Bernardino, California. By 1954, it was so popular
that a salesman named Ray Kroc made a deal to turn it into a national chain and pay the brothers a part of every dollar earned.

That's how McDonald's got started.

Six years later, Kroc offered to buy the brothers' out for $1 mil-
lion apiece. They said yes, but there was a misunderstanding: Kroc
thought he was getting the original San Bernardino restaurant as
part of the agreement; the McDonalds insisted it wasn't part of the
deal.

THE EMPIRE STRIKES BACK

Kroc was furious. He had counted on the cash flow the restaurant
would bring. "I closed the door to my office and paced up and down
the floor calling the [McDonald brothers] every kind of son of a
bitch there was," Kroc recalled. "I hated their guts." Privately, he
told co-workers: "I'm not a vindictive man, but this time I'm going
to get those sons of bitches." According to John Love in *McDonald's Behind the Arches*, that's exactly what he did.

> The moment the deal was completed, Kroc...hopped on a plane to
> Los Angeles, bought a piece of property [in San Bernardino] one
> block away from the brothers' original fast-food drive-in—and or-
> dered the construction of a brand-new McDonald's store. It had
> only one purpose: to put the McDonald brothers' drive-in out of
> business.

THE BIG M SINKS

The brothers had already been forced to take down their "McDonald's" sign, because Kroc's company now owned their trade name.
They renamed it "The Big M," but in every other way it was the

same as it always had been. The problem was, Kroc's restaurant also looked like the Big M...But *his* had the McDonald's name. Customers were a little confused, but figured that the original restaurant had been moved; they took their business to the new McDonald's. Sales at the Big M plummeted, and in 1968, the McDonald brothers finally gave up. They sold their drive-in to a local restauranteur...but he couldn't make it work either. In 1970, Kroc had his final revenge: the birthplace of the fast food industry closed for good.

✂   ✂   ✂

ANIMAL REVENGE

"An ice fisherman in Edwardsburg, Michigan hauled a 4-pound beauty out of the lake, cleanly removed the hook from the mackerel mouth and placed the fish on the ice to re-bait his line. The thrashing mackerel flung itself in the air, locked its teeth on the fisherman's leg and had to be pried loose by two men. The bite required a doctor's attention."

—*Oops,*
by Richard Smith

"In Missouri, Larry Lands was showing off a turkey he had shot and put in his trunk when the not-yet-dead bird started thrashing around and pulled the trigger of lands's gun, also in the trunk. Lands was shot in the leg. 'The turkeys are fighting back,' said county sheriff Ron Skiles."

—*News from the Fringe,*
by John Kohut & Roland Sweet

✂   ✂   ✂

Continental Drift: "In revenge for England's closing of the Libyan embassy in London, Col. Muammar el-Qaddafi ordered that England be deleted from all Libyan maps in the mid-1980s. In its place was put a new arm of the North Sea, bordered by Scotland and Wales."

—*More News of the Weird*

The longest-surviving Civil War veteran died in 1959.

THE BIRTH OF "THE TONIGHT SHOW," PART I

"The Tonight Show" is a television institution that's been around longer than a lot of you Bathroom readers. It's also the forerunner of most of today's TV talk shows—and it's got a fascinating history. So we've decided to include parts of it throughout the book. Tune it in one day at a time, the way you might watch the show.

G OODNIGHT, AMERICA
If you flip through the TV channels between 11:30 p.m. and 1:00 a.m., you'll see a lot of talk shows.

But it wasn't always that way. Before 1950, there weren't many TV shows of *any* kind on that late. Networks ended their programming at 11:00 p.m., and many affiliate stations went off the air, too. If they didn't, chances are they played old movies—*bad* ones. Hollywood, threatened by the inroads TV was making into their business, refused to give them anything good.

Bad movies and test patterns—no wonder hardly anyone was watching.

LEAVE IT TO WEAVER

In 1950, an NBC executive named Sylvester "Pat" Weaver, who'd successfully launched the "The Today Show" and "Your Show of Shows" (a 90-minute variety show starring comic Sid Caesar) turned his attention to late-evening programming.

Weaver (whose daughter, by the way, is actress Sigourney Weaver) figured that a program like "Your Show of Shows," with vaudeville or Broadway review acts, would be successful between 11:30 p.m. and 12:30 a.m.—especially since there was so little competition. He passed around a memo outlining his idea to other NBC executives. It would be called "Broadway Open House," he wrote, and would be "zany, light-hearted...for people in the mood for staying up....It would have the glitter and excitement of Broadway, but the backstage ambience of a party." Through the medium of television, viewers could hobnob with the rich and famous.

At Old English weddings, guests threw shoes at the groom.

Some NBC executives thought it was the dumbest idea they'd ever heard.

"Late night?" one of them supposedly asked at a meeting. "Eleven thirty? At that hour, people are either sleeping or f——."

"Most people aren't that lucky," another NBC exec said, to which Weaver replied: "Let's do something for 'most people.' "

HOST OF PROBLEMS

Finding the right host has always been a problem for talk shows—even from the beginning. "Your Show of Shows" had done well with a comedian for a host, and Weaver thought it would work again with "Broadway Open House." His first choice was a nightclub comic named Jan Murray...but Murray decided to emcee a TV game show instead.

Second choice was Don "Creesh" Hornsby, a cross between Robin Williams and PeeWee Herman. On his own L.A. show, he performed magic tricks, played the piano, ran around the stage shouting "Creesh! Creesh!," and pulled brassieres out of women's blouses. "His stuff was really wild," Weaver remembered years later. "We reasoned, 'What the hell, it'll be late at night and who cares?'"

Creesh took the job, moved his family to New York...and then died suddenly the weekend before "Broadway Open House" was to premiere. NBC executives were shocked by his death, but weren't completely unprepared: his act was so weird that they'd already thought about replacements in case he bombed.

"Broadway Open House" went on the air May 22, 1950, hosted by Tex and Jinx, a husband-and-wife team with their own radio interview show. They were terrible. So Weaver quickly replaced them with comic actor Wally Cox (*Mr. Peepers*)...who lasted only a few days. Then he tried Dean Martin and Jerry Lewis. They were better, but were so overbooked that they couldn't work as regular hosts.

Weaver's next choice was a comedian named Jerry Lester. He took the job...but would only agree to work three nights a week—Monday, Wednesday, and Fridays. So NBC hired Morey Amsterdam (who later became famous on "The Dick Van Dyke Show") to fill in on Tuesdays and Thursdays. A young Neil Simon was hired as a writer.

Educational toy: The Mongols taught their children to ride horses by starting them out on goats.

KEEPING ABREAST

Today, the "sidekick" is a standard part of late-night talk shows. But in 1950, it was a new idea. Few people recall that the first side-kick was Dagmar, a beautiful blonde woman with huge breasts.

Dagmar had an even smaller job on the show than Ed McMahon had on "The Tonight Show"—all she had to do was look stupid on camera. She didn't even talk. "For the first two or three months," Robert Metz writes in *The Tonight Show*, "Dagmar sat on a stool right in front of the band with an off-the-shoulder dress and an enormous overhang that may have influenced the wit who dubbed television the boob tube. Dagmar seemed to fit that phrase on both counts. She was a stereotypical dumb blonde. A large sign under the stool read, 'Girl Singer,' but she never opened her mouth and never sang."

BOOM...AND BUST

"Broadway Open House" quickly built a following. Within two months, Jerry and Dagmar were national celebrities. When the show made a trip to Cleveland, 45,000 people turned out to watch the taping, paying $2.50 apiece for the privilege.

But NBC still had problems with the show: Morey Amsterdam's performance didn't measure up to Lester's, and in November 1950, he quit. Lester still refused to work more than three days a week, so NBC had to find someone to fill in on the other days. They tried a number of young comics, but none of them caught on.

Then Lester and Dagmar—who turned out to have true comic talent—began feuding. The fight got so bad that Lester added a second, less threatening blonde named Agathon to the show to help with the magic tricks.

"Open House" became increasingly stale. Critics who'd lauded it a few months before started attacking it. Finally, in May 1951, Lester quit. The show limped along for three more months as NBC searched frantically for another host...but they never found one. It went off the air on August 23, 1951. Three more years would pass before NBC would attempt another late-night show.

That's just the beginning. See page 133 for Part II.

Clams can live as long as 150 years.

CURSES!

Even if you're not superstitious, it's hard to resist tales of "cursed" ships, tombs, and so on. Who knows—maybe there's something to them. Here are some of our favorites.

THE CURSE OF JAMES DEAN'S PORSCHE

Curse: Disaster may be ahead for anyone connected with James Dean's "death car." It seems to attack people at random.

Origin: In 1955, Dean smashed his red Porsche into a another car and was killed. The wreckage was bought by George Barris, a friend of Dean's (and the man who customized cars like the Munsters' coffin-mobile for Hollywood). But as one writer put it, "the car proved deadly even after it was dismantled." Barris noticed weird things happening immediately.

Among Its Victims:

• The car slipped while being unloaded from the truck that delivered it to Barris, and broke a mechanic's legs.

• Barris put its engine into a race car. It crashed in the race, killing the driver. A second car in the same race was equipped with the Porsche's drive shaft—it overturned and injured its driver.

• The shell of the Porsche was being used in a Highway Safety display in San Francisco. It fell off its pedestal and broke a teenager's hip. Later, a truck carrying the display to another demonstration was involved in an accident. "The truck driver," says one account, "was thrown out of the cab of the truck and killed when the Porsche shell rolled off the back of the truck and crushed him"

Status: The Porsche finally vanished in 1960, while on a train en route to Los Angeles.

THE PRESIDENTIAL DEATH CYCLE

Curse: Between 1840 and 1960, every U.S. president elected in a year ending in a zero either died in office of natural causes or was assassinated. By contrast: Since 1840, of the 29 presidents who were *not* elected in the 20-year cycle, only one has died in office and not one has been assassinated.

Origin: The first president to die in office was William Henry Harrison, elected in 1840. In 1960, when John Kennedy was shot, people began to realize the eerie "coincidence" involved.

Victims:
- William Henry Harrison, dead in 1841 after one month in office
- Abraham Lincoln (elected in 1860), fatally shot in 1865
- James Garfield (1880), assassinated in 1881
- William McKinley (re-elected in 1900), fatally shot in 1901
- Warren G. Harding (1920), died in 1923
- Franklin D. Roosevelt (elected for the third time in 1940), died in 1945
- JFK (1960), assassinated in 1963
- Ronald Reagan (1980) was nearly the eighth victim. He was shot and badly wounded by John Hinckley in 1983

Status: Astrologers insist that 1980 was an aberration because "Jupiter and Saturn met in an air sign, Libra." That gave Reagan some kind of exemption. They say we still have to wait to find out if the curse is over.

THE CURSE OF THE INCAN MUMMY

Curse: By disturbing a frozen mummy's remains, authorities brought bad luck to the region where it had been buried.

Origin: Three Andean mummies were discovered by an archaeologist/mountaineer in October 1995. They had been undisturbed in snow at the top of 20,000-foot Mount Ampato, in Southern Peru, for at least 500 years. Then an earthquake exposed them. One of the mummies was the remains of a young woman, referred to by local shamans as "Juanita." She had apparently been sacrificed to Incan gods.

Among Its Victims:
- Within a year of the discovery, a Peruvian commercial jet crashed and killed 123 people near the discovery site.
- Thirty-five people were electrocuted when a high-tension cable fell on a crowd celebrating the founding of the city of Arequipa (which is near the discovery site).

Status: Local shamans said these were the acts of the angered "Ice Princess." To break the curse, they gathered in the city of Arequipa in August 1996 and chanted: "Juanita, calm your ire. Do not continue to damn innocent people who have done nothing to you." Apparently it worked—we've heard nothing of it since 1996.

THE BIRTH OF THE MICROWAVE

To a lot of us, microwave ovens are "magical mystery boxes." We're not sure how they work…but after a while we can't live without them. Uncle John swore he'd never use one—until he had children. Now he blesses it every time he hauls out an emergency frozen pizza and manages to feed the kids before they kill each other. If you use a microwave, you might be interested to know more about it.

C hances are, you'll use a microwave oven at least once this week—probably (according to research) for heating up leftovers or defrosting something.

Microwave ovens are so common today that it's easy to forget how rare they once were. As late as 1977, only 10% of U.S. homes had one. By 1995, 85% of households had *at least* one. Today, more people own microwaves than own dishwashers.

MICROWAVE HISTORY

Magnetrons, the tubes that produce microwaves, were invented by British scientists in 1940. They were used in radar systems during World War II…and were instrumental in detecting German planes during the Battle of Britain.

These tubes—which are sort of like TV picture tubes—might still be strictly military hardware if Percy Spencer, an engineer at Raytheon (a U.S. defense contractor), hadn't stepped in front of one in 1946. He had a chocolate bar in his pocket; when he went to eat it a few minutes later, he found that the chocolate had almost completely melted.

That didn't make sense. Spencer himself wasn't hot—how could the chocolate bar be? He suspected the magnetron was responsible. So he tried an experiment: He held a bag of popcorn kernels up to the tube. Seconds later they popped.

The next day Spencer brought eggs and an old tea kettle to work. He cut a hole in the side of the kettle, stuck an egg in it, and placed it next to the magnetron. Just as a colleague looked into the kettle to see what was happening, the egg exploded.

BRINGING MICROWAVES TO MARKET

Spencer shared his discovery with his employers at Raytheon and suggested manufacturing magnetron-powered ovens to sell to the public. Raytheon was interested. They had the capacity to produce 10,000 magnetron tubes a week...but with World War II over, military purchases had been cut back to almost nothing. "What better way to recover lost sales," Ira Flatow writes in *They All Laughed*, "than to put a radar set disguised as a microwave oven in every American home?"

Raytheon agreed to back the project. (According to legend, Spencer had to repeat the egg experiment in front of the board of directors, splattering them with egg, before they okayed it.) The company patented the first "high-frequency dielectric heating apparatus" in 1953. Then they held a contest to find a name for their product. Someone came up with "Radar Range," which was later combined into the single word—*Radarange.*

DEVELOPING THE PRODUCT

Raytheon had a great product idea and a great name, but they didn't have an oven anyone could afford. The 1953 model was 5 1/2 feet tall, weighed more than 750 pounds, and cost $3,000. Over the next 20 years, railroads, ocean liners, and high-end restaurants were virtually the only Radarange customers.

• In 1955, a company called Tappan introduced the first microwave oven targeted to average consumers; it was smaller than the Radarange, but still cost $1,295—more than some small homes.

• Then in 1964, a Japanese company perfected a miniaturized magnetron. For the first time, Raytheon could build a microwave oven that fit on a kitchen countertop. In 1967, they introduced a Radarange that used the new magnetron. It sold for $495. But that was still too expensive for the average American family.

• Finally, in the 1980s, technical improvements made it possible to lower the price and improve the quality enough to make microwave ovens both affordable and practical. By 1988, 10% of all new food products in the United States were microwaveable. Surveys showed that the microwave oven was America's favorite new appliance—and it still is today.

How does a microwave oven work? *See p. 235 to find out.*

Q&A: ASK THE EXPERTS

*Everyone's got a question or two they'd like answered.
Here are a few of those questions, with answers from
some of the nation's top trivia experts.*

HOLY COW!

Q: *Why are there holes in Swiss cheese?*

A: Because of air bubbles. "During one of the stages of preparation, while it is still 'plastic,' the cheese is kneaded and stirred. Inevitably, air bubbles are formed in the cheese as it is twisted and moved about, but the viscous nature of the cheese prevents the air bubbles from rising to the surface and getting out. As the cheese hardens, these air pockets remain, and we see them as the familiar 'holes' when we slice the wheel of cheese." (From *A Book of Curiosities*, compiled by Roberta Kramer)

PHOTO FINISH

Q: *Why do eyes come out red in photographs?*

A: "The flash from the camera is being reflected on the rear of the eyeball, which is red from all the blood vessels." The solution: "Use a flash at a distance from the camera, or get your subjects to look somewhere else. Another trick is to turn up the lights in the room, making them as bright as possible, which causes the subject's pupil to contract and admit less of the light from the subsequent flash." (From *Why Things Are*, by Joel Aschenbach)

READ OIL ABOUT IT

Q: *What do the numbers (like 10W-30) mean for motor oil?*

A: "Oil is measured in terms of *viscosity*, which is a measure of a liquid's ability to flow. There are 10 grades, from 0W to 25W for oils... meant for winter weather use (the W stands for winter), and from 20 to 60 for oils rated to work at 212°F. The lower the number, the thinner the oil. Multigrade oils, like 10W-30, were developed to stay thin at low temperatures and still work well at high temperatures. Most experts recommend 5W-30 for very cold weather, 10W-30 for warmer weather." (From *Numbers*, by Andrea Sutcliffe)

Good idea: Turn-of-the-century department stores had "silence rooms" for "nerve-tired shoppers."

HOT STUFF

Q: *How can you cool off your mouth after eating hot peppers?*

A: "Drink milk, says Dr. Robert Henkin, director of the Taste and Smell Clinic in Washington, D.C. Casein, the main protein in milk, acts like a detergent, washing away capsaicin, the substance in hot peppers responsible for their 'fire.'" (From *Parade* magazine, November 14, 1993)

SOMETHING FISHY

Q: *Do fish sleep?*

A: Hard to tell if they sleep in the same sense we do. They never *look* like they're sleeping, because they don't have eyelids. "But they do seem to have regular rest periods....Some fish just stay more or less motionless in the water, while others rest directly on the bottom, even turning over on their side. Some species...dig or burrow into bottom sediment to make a sort of 'bed.' Some fish even...prefer privacy when they rest; their schools disperse at night to rest and then reassemble in the morning." (From *Science Trivia*, by Charles Cazeau)

PICK A BALL OF COTTON

Q: *Should you toss out the cotton after opening a bottle of pills?*

A: Yep. "The cotton keeps the pills from breaking in transit, but once you open the bottle, it can attract moisture and thus damage the pills or become contaminated." (From *Davies Gazette*, a newsletter from Davies Medical Center in San Francisco)

SLIPPERY QUESTION

Q: *A few years ago, we started seeing foods containing "canola oil." What is it?*

A: A variety of rapeseed—which, until recently, was only grown for industrial oils. "Scientists in Canada were able to breed new varieties of rapeseed that were suitable for cooking. They named their creation *canola* to honor Canada. Canola seed contains 40% to 45% oil, of which 6% is saturated fatty acids. Canola oil contains less fat than any other oil: 50% less than corn oil and olive oil, 60% less than soybean oil." (From *Why Does Popcorn Pop*, by Don Voorhees)

TOP-RATED TV SHOWS, 1949–1954

These were the most popular programs of TV's early years. Most weren't filmed, so unless you remember them, they're gone forever.

1949–1950
(1) Texaco Star Theater
(2) Toast of the Town (Ed Sullivan)
(3) Arthur Godfrey's Talent Scouts
(4) Fireball Fun for All
(5) Philco Television Playhouse
(6) Fireside Theatre
(7) The Goldbergs
(8) Suspense
(9) Ford Theater
(10) Cavalcade of Stars

1950–1951
(1) Texaco Star Theatre
(2) Fireside Theatre
(3) Your Show of Shows
(4) Philco Television Playhouse
(5) The Colgate Comedy Hour
(6) Gillette Cavalcade of Sports
(7) Arthur Godfrey's Talent Scouts
(8) Mama
(9) Robert Montgomery Presents
(l0) Martin Kane, Private Eye

1951–1952
(l) Arthur Godfrey's Talent Scouts
(2) Texaco Star Theater
(3) I Love Lucy
(4) The Red Skelton Show
(5) The Colgate Comedy Hour
(6) Fireside Theatre
(7) The Jack Benny Program
(8) Your Show of Shows
(10) Arthur Godfrey and His Friends

1952–1953
(1) I Love Lucy
(2) Arthur Godfrey's Talent Scouts
(3) Arthur Godfrey and His Friends
(4) Dragnet
(5) Texaco Star Theater
(6) The Buick Circus Hour
(7) The Colgate Comedy Hour
(8) Gangbusters
(9) You Bet Your Life
(10) Fireside Theatre

1953–1954
(1) I Love Lucy
(2) Dragnet
(3) Arthur Godfrey's Talent Scouts
(4) You Bet Your Life
(5) The Bob Hope Show
(6) The Buick-Berle Show
(7) Arthur Godfrey and His Friends
(8) Ford Theatte
(9) The Jackie Gleason Show
(10) Fireside Theatre

1954–1955
(l) I Love Lucy
(2) The Jackie Gleason Show
(3) Dragnet
(4) You Bet Your Life
(5) Toast of the Town (Ed Sullivan)
(6) Disneyland
(7) The Bob Hope Show
(8) The Jack Benny Program
(9) The Martha Raye Show
(10) The George Gobel Show

What's the difference between jam and preserves? Jam has minced fruit; preserves have whole.

FREEZE-DRIED CATS AND COTTAGE CHEESE

Uncle John was drinking some freeze-dried coffee when he suddenly got up and started asking everyone in the office what "freeze-drying" is. No one could tell him. So we did some research and wrote this article. We figured if we didn't know, you might not either.

FREEZER BURN

If you've ever had a freezer, you've probably seen "freezer burn"—the discolored, dried-out crust that forms on food when it's been in the freezer too long or isn't wrapped correctly.

What causes it?

Evaporation. Even when something is frozen solid, the water molecules are still moving. And some of them move fast enough to fly right off the surface of the food. Then one of three things happens:

1. They get pulled back by the food's gravitational field.
2. They slam into air molecules and bounce back onto the food.
3. They fly off into space.

Over time, so many water molecules will fly off into space that the surface of the food actually becomes dehydrated. That's freezer burn. It's also known as *sublimation*, the process by which ice evaporates without first turning into water.

That's what freeze-drying is—drying something out while it's still frozen.

FREEZER SCIENCE

In the 19th century, scientists studying sublimation discovered that the process happened faster in a jar when the air was pumped out. (The jars are called *vacuum chambers*.) This is because when you remove air, you're removing the air *molecules*. The fewer air molecules there are to bump into, the greater the chance that the water molecules will escape into space—which speeds the drying.

But the freeze-drying process still took too long. So over the next half-century, scientists tried to find ways to speed it up. They succeeded…and then began freeze-drying anything and everything to see what would happen. The first practical applications they found were in the medical field: many microscopic organisms—including bacteria, viruses, vaccines, yeasts, and algae—could actually survive the process; so could blood plasma.

By World War II, freeze-dried blood plasma and penicillin (which could be reconstituted with sterile water) accompanied soldiers onto the battlefield. And by the end of the war, freeze-dried instant coffee tablets were included in U.S. troops' K rations.

FREEZE-DRIED FOODS

After the war, food companies poured money into making freeze-dried food palatable. It took 10 years, but they finally figured out that when food is "flash frozen" (i.e., frozen as quickly as possible), followed by freeze-drying, much of the flavor is preserved.

The prospects for freeze-dried food seemed limitless: In 1962 *The Reader's Digest* hailed it as "the greatest breakthrough in food preservation since the tin can," and food technologists predicted that sales of freeze-dried food products would rival sales of frozen foods by 1970. Hundreds of food companies rushed new products to the markets. A few, like freeze-dried coffee, were successes. But most wound up in the "fabulous flop" category. For example:

• **Corn flakes with freeze-dried fruit.** As we told you in the first *Bathroom Reader*, in 1964 Post introduced Cornflakes with Strawberries and Kellogg's introduced Cornflakes with Instant Bananas. Both predicted that sales would hit $600 million in a few years. Both were wrong. It turned out that freeze-dried fruit gets soft on the outside when soaked in milk, but stays crunchy on the inside. And by the time the fruit is soft enough to eat, the cereal is soggy. Millions of families bought the cereals once, but never came back for a second helping.

• **Kellogg's Kream Krunch.** Cereal with chunks of freeze-dried ice cream. Different product, same problem: the cereal turned soggy before the ice cream reconstituted.

• **Freeze-dried steak.** "It looks like a brownish sponge," *Business Week* wrote in 1963, "but plop it into hot water and in a few minutes the 'sponge' blossoms into a sirloin steak that tastes almost as good as one from the butcher's." Wishful thinking. It cost as much as a good T-bone, but tasted like a beef sponge.

• **Freeze-dried scrambled eggs.** "Can be prepared by simply cooking with water," *Consumer Reports* wrote in 1962. But that was the only good news. Their tasting panel "came up with a luke warm 'neither like nor dislike'...and at current egg prices, two dozen fresh eggs cost the same as two freeze-dried servings."

Other Freeze-Dried Flops
• Freeze-dried mushrooms in a box, from Armour foods
• Freeze-dried cottage cheese ("with cultured sour cream dressing"), from Holland Dairies
• Freeze-dried milkshake mix, from Borden

PET PROJECTS
• The process of freeze-drying is now widely used in taxidermy (stuffing and mounting dead animals). In the late 1950s, scientists at the Smithsonian Institution discovered that by freeze-drying animals instead of skinning and stuffing them, they could produce more lifelike specimens while reducing labor costs by as much as 80%. Today more than a third of all museums in the United States have freeze-dryers, and some companies will even freeze-dry pets.

• The process is the same as with freeze-drying food, with one exception: the animals are bent into lifelike poses, such as "dining on prey," "fetching a stick," or "resting by fire," before they are frozen.

• Since the internal organs remain in place, animals retain virtually the same shape and dimensions when they're freeze-dried. The only difference is their weight—a freeze-dried animal has roughly the same consistency as styrofoam.

• The process is effective, but is impractical with large animals. Animals weighing as little as 65 pounds can take as long as a year to lose all of their moisture, so most large animals are still skinned and stuffed the old-fashioned way.

NEWS FLASH
"Mrs. Oramae Lewis of Bedford, Ohio, had her cat Felix freeze-dried by a local veterinarian after it was run down by an 18-wheel tractor trailer. The veterinarian used a freeze-drying machine once used by a coffee company. 'Now I can have Felix just like I did when he was alive,' she said. 'He's just like he was in real life, only flatter.' "

—The *Washington Post*, June 27, 1983

MARK TWAIN SAYS...

No one else in the history of American literature has combined sardonic wit, warmth, and intelligence as successfully Mark Twain.

"All you need in this life is ignorance and confidence and then success is sure."

"What a talker he is—he could persuade a fish to come out and take a walk with him."

"The lack of money is the root of all evil."

"Why shouldn't truth be stranger than fiction? Fiction, after all, has to stick to possibilities."

"Be careful about reading health books. You may die of a misprint."

"But who prays for Satan? Who in eighteen centuries, has had the common humanity to pray for the one sinner who needed it most?"

"There are two times in a man's life when he should not speculate: when he can afford to and when he can't."

"Thousands of geniuses live and die undiscovered— either by themselves, or by others."

"We do not deal much in facts when we are contemplating ourselves."

"Envy....the only thing which men will sell both body and soul to get."

"If we had less statesmanship, we would get along with fewer battleships."

"If I cannot swear in heaven I shall not go there."

"It takes me a long time to lose my temper but once lost, I could not find it with a dog."

" Virtue has never been as respectable as money."

" I wonder how much it would take to buy a soap-bubble if there was only one in the world."

THE BEST THINGS EVER SAID?

From The 637 Best Things Anybody Ever Said, *edited by Robert Byrne.*

"If God lived on Earth, people would break his windows."
—*Jewish proverb*

"I have an intense desire to return to the womb. Anybody's."
—*Woody Allen*

"When you don't have any money, the problem is food. When you have money, it's sex. When you have both, it's health. If everything is simply jake, then you're frightened of death."
— *J. P. Donleavy*

"Is sloppiness in speech caused by ignorance or apathy? I don't know and I don't care."
—*William Safire*

"When you have got an elephant by the hind legs and he is trying to run away, it is best to let him run."
—*Abraham Lincoln*

"In the end, everything is a gag."
—*Charlie Chaplin*

"One of the symptoms of an approaching nervous breakdown is the belief that one's work is terribly important."
—*Betrand Russell*

"When ideas fail, words come in very handy."
—*Goethe*

"Victory goes to the player who makes the next to last mistake."
—*Savielly Grigorievitch*

"After all is said and done, more is said than done."
—*Unknown*

"Three o'clock is always too late or too early for anything you want to do."
—*Jean-Paul Sartre*

"A little inaccuracy sometimes saves tons of explanation."
—*H. H. Munro*

"The best way to get praise is to die."
—*Italian proverb*

It takes about 21 pounds of milk to make 1 pound of butter.

STRANGE LAWSUITS

These days, it seems that people will sue each other over practically anything. Here are a few real-life examples of unusual legal battles.

THE PLAINTIFF: Wendy Potasnik, a nine-year-old from Carmel, Indiana

THE DEFENDANT: The Cracker Jack Division of Borden, Inc.

THE LAWSUIT: In 1982, Wendy and her sister Robin each bought a box of Cracker Jacks. Robin got a prize in her box, but Wendy didn't...which made her "really mad."

"They advertise a free toy in each box," she told a reporter. "I feel that since I bought their product because of their claim, they broke a contract with me." So she sued, asking the court to make Borden "pay court costs and furnish a toy."

THE VERDICT: Wendy dropped the suit after Borden apologized and sent her a coupon for a free box of Cracker Jacks...even though the company refused to pay the $19 that Potasnik had spent on court costs.

THE PLAINTIFF: Alan Wald

THE DEFENDANT: The Moonraker Restaurant in Pacifica, California

THE LAWSUIT: In 1993, Wald went to the Moonraker for an all-you-can-eat buffet. He'd already eaten between 40 (Wald's count) and 75 (the restaurant's count) oysters—and was still at it—when the restaurant cut him off. Apparently, other customers were complaining that there were no oysters left. The restaurant offered to refund Wald's $40 to get him to go, but Wald insisted he was within his rights—he hadn't had all he could eat yet. He demanded $400 for "humiliation and embarrassment."

THE VERDICT: Wald was awarded $100 by the judge—but the restaurant was the real winner. "It was great publicity," said the owner. "We're going to get a shovelful of oysters and present them to [Wald] at his table. He can come back anytime."

THE PLAINTIFF: The Swedish government

THE DEFENDANT: Elisabeth Hallin, mother of a five-year-old boy named Brfxxccxxmnpcccclllmmnprxvclmnckssqlbb11116 (which she pronounces "Albin")

THE LAWSUIT: For five years, the Hallins, who say they believe in the surrealist doctrine of "pataphysics," refused to give their son a name. Then Swedish tax officials informed them it was a legal requirement. They chose Brfxxccxxmnpcccclllmmnprxvclmnckssqlbb11116—which was immediately rejected by the authorities. The couple insisted that the "typographically expressionistic" name was merely "an artistic creation," consistent with their pataphysical beliefs.

THE VERDICT: The government disagreed. The Hallins were fined 5000 kronor (about $735) and ordered to come up with a different name.

THE PLAINTIFF: Lorene Bynum

THE DEFENDANTS: St. Mary's Hospital in Little Rock, Arkansas

THE LAWSUIT: In 1992, Bynum visited her husband, a patient at the hospital. She wanted to use the bathroom, but the toilet seat was dirty—and there wasn't enough toilet paper to spread out on it. So she took off her shoes and tried to go to the bathroom *standing* on the toilet seat. Unfortunately the seat was loose. Bynum fell, spraining her lower back. She sued the hospital for negligence.

THE VERDICT: A jury awarded Bynum $13,000. But the Arkansas Supreme Court overturned the verdict. "The injuries resulted from her act of standing on the commode seat, which was neither designed nor intended to be used in that way," they explained.

THE PLAINTIFF: Victoria Baldwin

THE DEFENDANT: Synergy, a hair salon in Sydney, Australia

THE LAWSUIT: In July 1996, Baldwin had her hair cut at the salon. The result was so bad, she complained, that it made her "look like Hillary Clinton." She sued for damages, plus reimbursement for money spent on hats to cover her head until the hair grew back.

THE VERDICT: Baldwin won $750, plus $234 for the hats.

The German language has about 185,000 words. French has less than 100,000.

THE FOOLISH HUNTER

Here's a chance to soak up a little wisdom while you're just sitting around. This is an old Hebrew tale, from a longtime favorite book of Uncle John's, called Myths and Legends of the Ages.

A hunter once caught a bird in a trap. "Let me go," the bird pleaded. "It won't do you any good to kill me—I'm not very big. If you roast me, all you'll get is a mouthful or two at the most. And if you lock me in a cage, I can promise you right now that I'll never sing a note for you. But if you let me go, I'll give you three pieces of wisdom which will bring you great happiness and success."

The hunter pondered over the bird's speech. "All right," he said. "Tell me your three pieces of wisdom, and I'll let you go."

"First," said the bird, "never believe a story that goes against your common sense. Secondly, don't regret what is done and cannot be undone." Then, cocking his head to one side, the bird concluded, "And the third piece of wisdom is, don't try the impossible."

"There's nothing so wise about that," scoffed the hunter. "I practice those teachings all the time. But since you're not much use to me anyway, I'll let you go."

No sooner was the bird released, than he flew to a high branch of a nearby tree. "Foolish man!" he said. "Did you think I was just an ordinary bird? Oh no! Now I can tell you that I am much different from other birds. My heart is made of a precious ruby. If you had cut me open and taken out my heart, you might have been the richest man in the world."

When the man heard this, he cursed his folly in letting the bird go. He shook his fist at the bird in the tree. "I'll catch you, you rogue!" he cried in a rage of disappointment.

The hunter quickly started to climb the tree. But the bird flew to the tip of a high branch, well out of the man's reach. The hunter leaned far out, trying to lay his hands on the bird. But he lost his balance, fell out of the tree, and was badly hurt.

"So!" cried the bird. "You said there was nothing wise about my words—that what I told you is only what you always practice! But the first thing I told you was never to believe anything that was contrary to common sense. Did anyone ever hear of a bird whose heart was made of a ruby? No. Yet you instantly believed my story.

"The next thing I said was don't regret what has been done and cannot be undone. You let me go—but then you instantly regretted it!

"The last piece of wisdom was, don't waste your energies pursuing the impossible. How could you ever hope to catch me, a bird who can fly—just by climbing a tree? Yet, you persisted in your folly and tried to snare a winged bird with your bare hands."

The shaken hunter got to his feet...a bruised but wiser man.

*   *   *   *

AND SPEAKING OF FOOLISHNESS...

The Etruscan Warrior

Background: In 1918 New York's Metropolitan Museum of Art paid $40,000 for the fragments of a 2,500-year-old, 7-foot-tall statue of an Etruscan warrior that predated the Roman Empire. (The Etruscans were conquered by the Romans in 396 B.C.) The museum reassembled the fragments into a nearly intact statue— only the left thumb was missing. The museum made the statue a centerpiece of its Etruscan warrior display, which opened in 1933.

The Truth: In 1936 rumors began circulating that an Italian stonemason had made the statue at the turn of the century...but the exhibit was so popular that the museum refused to investigate. Finally, in 1960, the museum had the statue's glaze tested chemically and proved conclusively that it was a fake.

A few months later, Alfredo Fioravanti (an Italian stonemason, of course) confessed to making the statue...and produced the warrior's missing left thumb as proof.

The water we drink is 3 billion years old.

WHAT'S FOR BREAKFAST?

We take it for granted that bacon, eggs, orange juice, and coffee are breakfast foods. But it's really just a matter of tradition.

COFFEE AND TEA. People started drinking coffee and tea in the morning not because they were pleasant, but because they were hot, dark, and mysterious. Until the 17th century, it was common for Europeans to start their day with alcohol. Queen Elizabeth, for example, had a pot of beer and a pound of beefsteak for breakfast every day. Scottish breakfasts routinely included a dram of whiskey. Coffee, tea, and sugar had the same illicit appeal as alcohol when they reached Europe in the 1600s—so they became suitable substitutes for booze.

EGGS & BACON, SAUSAGE, OR HAM. Colonists brought chickens and pigs with them to America because they were easy to transport by ship, and could provide food on the long voyage. Besides that, it was traditional to eat meat in the morning—and pork was the colonists' first choice. (It was so popular that one writer suggested they rename the U.S. "the Republic of Porkdom.") Eggs probably became a staple at breakfast because "they're freshest when just gathered from the previous night's roosting."

CITRUS FRUIT / ORANGE JUICE. Believe it or not, people started eating oranges in the morning because they thought it would warm them. The ancient Greeks taught that some foods heat your body, and other foods cool it—regardless of the temperature at which they're served. Peas were cold, for example, onions were hot...and oranges were very hot. People still believed this in the Middle Ages, which is why the Spanish began eating candied orange peels the first thing in the morning. The habit was picked up by the British, who brought it to the Colonies. (In Scotland, the orange peel became orange marmalade, which they put on toast with butter—starting another breakfast tradition.)

Orange juice became a staple of the American breakfast table in the 1920s. In 1946, concentrated orange juice was introduced.

THE BIG DIPPER

What's the one constellation everyone knows? The Big Dipper.
After you read this article you'll be able to sound like a know-it-all
the next time you're star-gazing with someone.

THE NIGHT SKY

The Big and Little Dippers are probably the best-known star groups in the northern hemisphere. They're both parts of larger star groups, or constellations, named after bears. The Big Dipper belongs to the constellation Ursa Major, "The Greater Bear," and the Little Dipper is part of Ursa Minor, "The Lesser Bear."

• Ursa Major is the most ancient of all the constellations. For some reason, early civilizations all over the world seem to have thought of it as a bear. This is remarkable, since Ursa Major doesn't look anything like a bear. It's even more remarkable when you consider that most of the ancient world had never seen a bear.

THE NATIVE AMERICAN SKY

In the New World, the Iroquois, who had seen plenty of bears, called it *Okouari*, which means...bear. The Algonquin and Black-foot tribes called it "The Bear and the Hunters." For them, the three stars in the handle of the Big Dipper were three hunters going after the bear.

• In a typical Native American story, a party of hunters set out on a bear hunt. The first hunter carried a bow and arrow. The second hunter brought along a pot or kettle to cook the bear in. The faint star Alcor, which you can just see above the middle star of the Dipper's handle, was the pot. The third hunter carried a bundle of sticks with which to build a fire to cook the bear.

• The bear hunt lasted from spring until autumn. In the autumn, the first hunter shot the bear. Blood from the wounded animal stained the autumn leaves in the forest. The bear died, was cooked, and was eaten. The skeleton lay on its back in the den through the winter months. The bear's life, meanwhile, had entered into another bear, which also lay on its back, deep asleep for the winter.

• When spring returned, the bear came out of the den and the hunters started to chase her again, and so it went from year to year.

THE GREEK SKY

Greek mythology offers another version of how the Bears got into the sky. Calisto, the beautiful daughter of the King of Arcadia, caught the eye of Zeus, the king of the gods. Zeus took her by surprise, leaving her to become the mother of his child. In time, Calisto gave birth to a son, whom she named Arcas. Hera, queen of the gods, changed Calisto into a bear in a jealous rage.

After a number of years had passed, Arcas was out hunting when he saw a bear. Not knowing the bear was his mother, Arcas raised his spear, ready to kill the animal. Before Arcas could throw his spear, Zeus quickly rescued Calisto by placing her in the skies—where she remains today. Arcas also became a constellation, Ursa Minor, next to his mother.

• Some say Zeus swung both bears around by their tails and flung them into the sky, which explains why their tails are so long.

• The Greeks called Ursa Major *Arktos,* which means "Bear." This is where we get our word *Arctic.* The Greek poet, Homer, described the Bear as keeping watch from its Arctic den looking out for the hunter Orion. Homer also remarked that in his day, the Bear never sank into the ocean, which meant that it never set. Hera was responsible for this, having persuaded the ocean gods not to allow the two Bears to bathe in their waters.

HIPPOS AND PLOWS

But not everyone has thought of these constellations as bears. The Egyptians saw the seven stars of the Big Dipper as a bull's thigh or a hippopotamus. Because its stars circled around the north pole of the sky without setting, or "dying," below the horizon, this constellation was a symbol of immortality and figured in rebirth rituals at funerals. Ursa Minor was the Jackal of the god Set that participated in rites for the dead taking place in the Egyptian underworld.

In Mesopotamia, Scandinavia, Italy, and Germany, people referred to the Big Dipper as a wagon, chariot, or cart. In England it was "Charles' Wain" (the word *wain* meant "wagon" and Charles stood for Charles the Great). The Little Dipper was the "Smaller Chariot," or "Little Wain." The four stars that make up the bowl of the dipper are the carriage part of the wain, and the dipper's handle is the part of the wain attached to the horses that pull it.

In some parts of England (and elsewhere), people saw the Big Dipper as "The Plough." The four stars of the dipper's bowl form the blade of the plough, behind which stretches its three-starred handle.

DIPPER DIRECTIONS

At the tip of the handle of the Little Dipper is the most celebrated star in the sky, Polaris, the North Star. While not the brightest star in the heavens, Polaris is certainly the most valuable. It has provided directions to countless travelers. The two stars at the end of the bowl of the Big Dipper, called "The Pointers," point to the North Star.

The Greeks used the Greater Bear and the Phoenicians used the Lesser Bear to find north. American slaves called the Big Dipper "The Drinking Gourd" and followed it northward to freedom.

Seen from the spinning Earth, the sky appears to move during the night, carrying all the stars along with it. Only the North Star stands in the same spot at the hub of the dome of the sky. The Greeks called this star *Cynosure*, a word that has found its way into our language meaning the center of attraction or interest. Others called the North Star the "Lodestar," most likely referring to the magnetic rock lodestone, used in mariners' compass needles to find north.

*   *   *   *

"It is easier to accept the message of the stars than the message of the salt desert. The stars speak of man's insignificance in the long eternity of time. The desert speaks of his insignificance right now."

—*Edwin Way Teale*

A light-year (the distance light travels in a year) is about 6 trillion miles.

GROUCHO MARX, ATTORNEY AT LAW

Here's a script from a recently rediscovered radio show featuring Groucho and Chico Marx. It's from Five Star Theater, *which aired in 1933.*

(*Phone rings*)

MISS DIMPLE: Law offices of Beagle, Shyster, and Beagle . . . No, Mr. Beagle isn't in yet, he's in court...I expect him any minute . .

(*Door opens*)

MISS DIMPLE: Good morning, Mr. Beagle.

GROUCHO: Good morning. Have I any appointments today?

MISS DIMPLE: No, Mr. Beagle,

GROUCHO: Well, make some. Do you expect me to sit here alone all day? Don't you think I ever get lonesome? What do you take me for? (Pause.) Well, go on—make me an offer.

(phone rings)

MISS DIMPLE: Beagle, Shyster, and Beagle ...Just a second. Mr. Flywheel, a man says he found the book you lost.

GROCHO: (*takes phone*) Hello...Yes, this is Flywheel...You found my book?...Oh, don't bother bringing it over—you can read it to me over the phone. Start at page 150. That's where I left off. ...Hello! Hello! (*Sneers*) He hung up on me. After I go to the trouble of putting aside legal business to talk to him!

MISS DIMPLE: *Legal* business? Why Mr. Flywheel, you were doing a crossword puzzle.

GROUCHO: Well, is doing a crossword puzzle *illegal*? Now how about mailing this letter?

MISS DIMPLE: But it has no stamp on it.

GROUCHO: Well, drop it in the box when nobody's looking.

MISS DIMPLE: Anyway, this letter is too heavy for one stamp. I think we'd better put two stamps on it.

GROUCHO: Nonsense. That'll only make it heavier. On second thought, never mind the letter. It's just a note to my friend, Steve Granach, asking for a loan...but he's probably got his own troubles. I hardly think he can spare it. And even if he *had* it, I think he'd be a little reluctant to lend me the dough. He's kind of tight that way. Why, I don't think he'd let me have it if I was going hungry. In fact, that guy wouldn't give me nickel if I were *starving. And he calls himself a friend.* ...the cheap, fourflushing swine. I'll show *him* where to get off. Take a letter to that snake and tell him I wouldn't touch his money. And if he ever comes near this

---

The biggest pumpkin ever recorded weighed 884 pounds.

office again, I'll break every bone in his body.

(*knock on door*)

MAN: Excuse me. Are you Mr. Flywheel or Mr. Shyster?

GROUCHO: I'm both Flywheels. And Shyster doesn't belong to the firm.

MAN: Then why is his name up there on the door?

GROUCHO: Well, Shyster ran away with my wife. And I put his name on the door as a token of my gratitude.

MAN: Oh. Well, Mr. Flywheel, permit me to introduce myself. I'm Bertram T. Bardwell. I suppose you've been hearing about my charity work and my fight against crime?

GROUCHO: Oh yes, I've been hearing about it for a number of years, and I'm getting *pretty sick* of it, too.

MAN: Why...er...I happened to be in court this morning when your thrilling address to the jury sent that man to prison for five years, where he belongs.

GROUCHO: My speech sent him to prison? (Laughs) That's a good

one on the jury. I was defending that guy. As I was...

MAN: Just a moment, Mr. Flywheel. Let me ask you a question.

GROUCHO: No, *I'll* ask *you* one. What has eight legs and sings?

MAN : Why...er...I don't know.

GROUCHO: A centipede.

MAN: But a centipede has a hundred legs.

GROUCHO: Yes, but it can't sing.

MAN (annoyed): Mr. Flywheel, my organization is waging an intensive fight against crime in this city, and I feel you're a man who can help us drive the crooks out of town.

GROUCHO: Drive them? Why not let them walk? ...(*Dramatically*) Bardwell, you've come to the right man. There isn't room enough in this town for gangsters and me.... However, we're putting up a *big hotel* this spring. Now if you'll excuse me, I have a director's meeting at the poolroom across the street.

MAN: Mr. Flywheel! How can you go out to a poolroom?

GROUCHO: I *have* to go out. I can't play pool in *here*—there's no table! Miss Dimple, I'll be back in an hour." (*Door closes*)

*Groucho will be back on page 341,
after a few words from our sponsor.*

*　　*　　*

"Time flies like an arrow. Fruit flies like a banana."

—*Groucho Marx*

Just like Mom? Only 55% of dinners served in the United States include even *one* homemade dish.

WRIGHT ON

Existential wisdom from Steven Wright.

"We had a quicksand box in our backyard. I was an only child, eventually."

"My theory of evolution is that Darwin was adopted."

"I was walking down the street wearing glasses when my prescription ran out."

"I put instant coffee in my microwave oven and almost went back in time."

"My grandfather invented Cliff's Notes. It all started back in 1912...Well, to make a long story short..."

"I'm writing an unauthorized autobiography."

"I wrote a few children's books. Not on purpose."

"Curiosity killed the cat, but for awhile, I was the suspect."

"If all the nations in the world are in debt, where did the money go? "

"If the pen is mightier than the sword, in a duel I'll let you have the pen."

"I own the erasers for all the miniature golf pencils."

"Anywhere is walking distance if you've got the time."

"Ever notice that irons have a setting for 'Permanent Press'? I don't get it..."

"You can't have everything. Where would you put it?"

"I went fishing with a dotted line and caught every other fish."

"I stayed up all night playing poker with Tarot cards. I got a full house and four people died."

"First time I read the dictionary I thought it was a poem about everything."

FOR YOUR READING PLEASURE

*Recently, we stumbled on Bizarre Books, a collection of weird-but-true
book titles, compiled by Russell Ash and Brian Lake. Hard to believe,
but these titles were chosen and published in all seriousness.
How would you like to spend your time reading...*

How to Avoid Intercourse with Your Unfriendly Car Mechanic, by Harold Landy (1977)

Sex After Death, by B.J. Ferrll and Douglas Edward Frey (1983)

The Unconscious Significance of Hair, by George Berg (1951)

Wall-Paintings by Snake Charmers in Tanganyika, by Hans Cory (1953)

The Inheritance of Hairy Ear Rims, by Reginald Ruggles and P. N. Badhuri (no date given)

A Toddler's Guide to the Rubber Industry, by D. Lowe (1947)

The Baron Kinvervankotsdorsprakingatchdern. A New Musical Comedy, by Miles Pewter Andrew (1781)

Manhole Covers of Los Angeles, by Robert and Mimi Melnick (1974)

The History and Romance of Elastic Webbing Since the Dawn of Time, by Clifford A. Richmond (no date given)

Frog Raising for Pleasure and Profit, by Dr. Albert Broel (1950)

Eat Your House: Art Eco Guide to Self-Sufficiency, by Frederic Hobbs (1981)

The Urine Dance of the Zuni Indians of New Mexico, by Captain John G. Bourke (1885)

Constipation and Our Civilization, by James Charles Thomson (1943)

Harnessing the Earthworm, by Thomas J. Barrett (1949)

The Gentle Art of Cooking Wives, Anon. (1900)

Swine Judging for Beginners, Joel Simmonds Coffey (1915)

Fish Who Answer the Telephone, by Yuri Petrovich Frolov (1937)

Proceedings of the Second International Workshop on Nude Mice, University of Tokyo (1978)

The Art of Faking Exhibition Poultry, by George Riley Scott (1934)

Teach Yourself Alcoholism, by Meier Glatt (1975)

Grow Your Own Hair, by Ron MacLaren (1947)

THEY WENT THATAWAY

Malcolm Forbes wrote a fascinating book about the deaths of famous people. Here are a few of the stories he found.

BENJAMIN FRANKLIN
Claim to Fame: American statesman
How He Died: Complications from sitting in front of an open window

Postmortem: Franklin was a big believer in fresh air, even in the middle of winter. He slept with the windows open year-round and, as he wrote, "I rise almost every morning and sit in my chamber without any clothes whatever, half an hour or an hour, according to the season." In April 1790, Franklin, 84, developed an abscess in his lungs, which his doctor blamed on too many hours spent sitting at the open window. The abscess burst on the 17th, sending him into a coma. He died a few hours later.

JOSEPH STALIN
Claim to Fame: Soviet dictator, 1929-1953
How He Died: Stroke

Postmortem: Stalin, who had murdered tens of millions of his own country people, may have been the last victim of his own reign of terror. On the evening of March 1, 1953, Stalin, 74, stayed up drinking with his cronies until 4:00 a.m. His normal habit was to rise again around noon, but that day he didn't.

As the hours passed and Stalin did not emerge from his private quarters, his aides began to panic. They didn't want to risk his wrath, but they were worried. At 10:30 p.m., they finally worked up the nerve to enter his apartments, where they found him sprawled on his living room floor, paralyzed by a stroke and unable to speak. The terrorized aides still did not know what to do...so they didn't call for the Kremlin doctors until 8:30 a.m. the following morning. By then it was too late: according to Stalin's daughter Svetlana, the dictator "died a difficult and terrible death" four days later.

KING GEORGE V

Claim to Fame: King of England, grandfather of Queen Elizabeth

How He Died: Euthanized with morphine and cocaine…to meet a newspaper deadline

Postmortem: The king, a heavy smoker, was in the final stages of lung disease on January 20, 1936. His death was imminent: the date of the State Funeral had been set, and the *London Times* had been instructed to hold the presses—a death announcement would be coming soon. "That night, however, the old king lingered on," Sarah Bradford writes in *The Reluctant King,* and the king's doctor, Lord Dawson,

> seeing that his condition of "stupor and coma" might last for many hours and could easily disrupt all arrangements, therefore "decided to determine the end"… Dawson later admitted that the moment of the King's death was timed for its announcement to be made in the respectable morning papers, and the *Times* in particular, rather than "the less appropriate evening journals."

The king's "last words" as reported to the media: "How is the Empire?" His actual last words: "Goddamn you!"

DIAMOND JIM BRADY

Claim to Fame: Turn-of-the-century millionaire, collector of fine gems (hence the nickname), one of the world's all-time great eaters

How He Died: He ate himself to death. A typical day started with a breakfast of steak, eggs, cornbread, muffins, pancakes, pork chops, fried potatoes, and hominy, washed down with a gallon or more of orange juice. Breakfast was followed with snacks at 11:30, lunch at 12:30, and afternoon tea; all of which involved enormous quantities of food (but no alcohol—Diamond Jim didn't drink). Dinner often consisted of 2 or 3 dozen oysters, 6 crabs, 2 bowls of turtle soup, 7 lobsters, 2 ducks, 2 servings of turtle meat, plus steak, vegetables, a full platter of pastries, and a 2-pound box of chocolate.

Postmortem: When Brady suffered an attack of gallstones in 1912, his surgeons opened him up and found that his stomach was six times normal size and covered in so many layers of fat they couldn't complete the surgery. Diamond Jim ignored their advice to cut back, yet hung on another five years—albeit in considerable pain from diabetes, bad kidneys, stomach ulcers, and heart problems. He died of a heart attack in 1917, at the age of 61.

DEMOCRACY IN ACTION

A democracy is only as weird as the people who participate in it—and you know what that means: anything can happen in an election. Here's proof.

ABSENTEE BALLOT

WESTMORELAND, KAN.—"What if they held an election and nobody came? It happened in Pottawatomie County. Nobody, not even the candidate, showed up to vote in the Rock Creek School Board election Tuesday. 'I don't understand it,' County Clerk Susan Figge said Wednesday. 'I really don't.' Three hundred, twenty-seven people were eligible to vote, but none showed up—not even the candidate, Mike Sotelo, who was running unopposed." The school board wound up appointing a new member themselves.

—Associated Press, April 1997

ELECTING A CORPSE

"A dead man was elected mayor of a small town in Colorado in 1983. The voters of Ward, population 125, elected as the mayor of this old mining town, a resident who died a week before the election. Some of the voters were undoubtedly paying tribute to the man and the community, for as one resident quipped, 'Ward's a ghost town, and we decided to elect a dead man to represent the silent majority.' But not everyone shared this sentiment; another voter was heard to say, 'When he won, I just about died.' "

—The Daily Planet Almanac, 1985

ELECTION FRAUD?

YPSILANTI, MICH.—"When City Councilman Geoffrey Rose turned over a voter list to a college freshman to help get out the vote, it didn't occur to him to ask the kid whom he was getting out the vote for. It turns out, the 18-year-old Eastern Michigan University student was looking out for No. 1." Instead of encouraging voters to cast their ballots for Rose, Frank Houston went door to door urging people to write in *his* name. And he won.

"Rose, who thought he was running unopposed in Monday's

The autographs of what two presidents are most valuable? Washington and Lincoln.

primary, said: 'Frank is 18 years old, and he's already acting like what most people in the country can't stand in elected officials.' Houston, who's thinking about majoring in political science, said he didn't lie to Rose. 'All I ever said was that I was going to get people to vote,' he told reporters.

—*Christian Science Monitor*, **April 1994**

TIE VOTE

NOV. 14, 1994—"In Rice, Minnesota, Virgil Nelson and Mitch Fiedler, who tied 90 to 90 in the November 1996 election for a city council seat, settled the race by drawing cards. On the first try, both drew eights, and on the second, both drew aces. Then Nelson drew a seven, and Fiedler drew an eight for the victory."

—*News of the Weird*

AND ELSEWHERE...

• COPENHAGEN, DENMARK—"Danish comedian Jacob Haugaard, promising better weather, shorter lines, and the right of men to be impotent, got the shock of his life by being elected to parliament in a general election. A stunned Haugaard, the first independent member of parliament elected in Denmark, told crowds of reporters: 'It was all a practical joke, honestly.' He won with 23,211 votes after spending his official campaign money on free hot dogs and beer for voters and providing kettles for old age pensioners."

—*Reuters*, **September 1996**

• "In Britain's April elections, the usual fringe parties were in evidence—such as the Blackhaired, Medium-Build Caucasian Party—but the longest-standing alternative, the Monster Raving Loony Party, ran the most candidates. Its main platform this year was to tow Britain 500 miles into the Mediterranean Sea to improve the country's climate. (Other years, platforms have included setting accountants in concrete and using them as traffic barriers, and putting all joggers on a giant treadmill to generate electricity.)

"Fifty other MRLP candidates made proposals such as requiring dogs to eat phosphorescent food, so pedestrians could more easily avoid stepping in their poops."

—*"The Edge"* in *The Oregonian*, **May 1997**

The portrait of George Washington on the $1 bill was painted by Gilbert Stuart.

A YEN FOR EGG ROLLS

Do the recipes they serve at your local Chinese restaurant really come from China? Don't bet on it. Here are a few food facts to munch on.

Today, Chinese Americans make up less than 1% of the U.S. population, but roughly a third of all ethnic restaurants in the U.S. are "Chinese," and every supermarket carries a line of "Chinese" food.

NEW-FANGLED FOOD

It started with the Gold Rush of 1849. As thousands of "Forty-Niners" streamed into California in search of gold, whole boom-towns—including a tent city named San Francisco—sprang up to supply their needs.

• One merchant who set up shop in San Francisco was a Chinese American named Norman Asing (described by one historian as a "cadaverous but keen old fellow" with a long ponytail and stove-pipe hat). He opened a restaurant called, "The Macao and Woosung" and charged $1 for an all-you-can-eat Chinese buffet.

• It was the first Chinese restaurant on U.S. territory, and it was a hit with miners and other San Franciscans. Asing's success inspired dozens of other Chinese immigrants to open restaurants, called "chow chows."

MADE IN CANTON

Over the next three decades, hundreds of thousands of Chinese migrated to the United States. By 1882—when Congress curtailed Chinese immigration—there were more than 300,000 Chinese nationals living on the West Coast.

• Most came from Kwangtung Province, whose capital city was Canton. So most Chinese restaurants served Cantonese-style food.

• In Cantonese cuisine, very little goes to waste: nearly every part of an animal that can be eaten is used in one dish or another.

• So, says John Mariani in *America Eats Out*, "'Going for Chinese' was considered adventurous eating for most white Americans at the turn of the century." Typically, one food critic who ate in San Francisco's Chinatown in the late 1800s wrote that he was served

---

Yecch: About 15% of U.S. kids say they keep their Halloween candy for at least a year.

Pale cakes with a waxen look, full of [strange] meats...Then giblets of you-never-know-what, maybe gizzards...perhaps toes.

• "Before long, however," Mariani writes, "Chinese cooks learned how to modify their dishes to make them more palatable to a wider American audience." The result: Chinese-American cuisine, food that looked and tasted "Chinese," but was actually invented in the U.S. and was unknown in China. Some examples:

• **Chop Suey.** No one knows for sure when it was invented, or how it got its name. The likely start: In 1850 a bunch of hungry miners busted their way into a chow-chow late at night and demanded to be fed. The chef just stirred all the table scraps and leftovers he could find into a big mess and served it. The miners loved it. When they asked what it was, the chef replied, "*chop sui*," which means "garbage bits" in Cantonese. The dish remained virtually unheard of in China until after World War II; today, it's advertised there as *American* cuisine.

• **Chow Mein.** A mixture of noodles and Chinese vegetables, probably served to railroad crews in the 1850s. From a Mandarin dialect word that means "fried noodles."

• **Egg Foo Yung.** From a Guangdong word that means "egg white." Translated literally, Egg FooYung means "egg egg white."

• **Fortune Cookies.** Invented in 1916 by David Jung, founder of the Hong Kong noodle factory in Los Angeles.

"By the 1920s," says Mariani, "Chinese restaurants dotted the American landscape, and a person

was as likely to find a chop suey parlor in Kansas City as New York, even though the typical menu in such places bore small resemblance to the food the Chinese themselves ate....Won ton soup, egg rolls, barbecued spareribs, sweet-and-sour pork, and beef with lobster sauce were all concocted to whet Americans' appetites....To this day it is standard procedure for an American in a Chinese restaurant to be handed a 2-column menu written in English, while a completely different menu printed in Chinese will be given to a Chinese patron.

Note: Until the 1970s, Chinese-American cuisine was almost exclusively Cantonese. If you're a fan of Szechuan or Hunan cooking, thank Richard Nixon. He opened the People's Republic of China to the West in the '70s...which brought us new Chinese cuisines.

GO ASK ALICE

When Charles Lutwidge Dodgson met a four-year-old girl named Alice Liddell in 1856, he wrote in his diary, "I mark this day with a white stone"—which meant it was a particularly wonderful day for him. It turned out to be a pretty good day for children all over the world: Charles Dodgson became famous as Lewis Carroll...and Alice Liddell was the child who inspired him to write Alice in Wonderland.

B**ACKGROUND**
• Charles Lutwidge Dodgson was a deacon and professor of mathematics at Christ Church College in Oxford.

• He was also a poet and photographer who drew his inspiration from children—especially little girls. In fact, he chose teaching as a career because it left him time to pursue photography and poetry.

• In 1856, the same year Dodgson began teaching at Christ Church, a new dean arrived—Henry George Liddell. He had four children, and Dodgson quickly became friendly with them. He especially enjoyed taking them on outings and photographing the girls.

• The youngest, 4-year-old Alice, had a special relationship with Reverend Dodgson—perhaps because her favorite expression was "let's pretend."

DOWN THE RABBIT HOLE

On what he recalled as a "golden July afternoon" in 1862, Dodgson took the three Liddell girls boating on the river for a picnic.

• As they rowed lazily downstream, Alice begged Dodgson to tell them a story...so he made one up.

• He called his heroine Alice to please her. Then he "sent her straight down a rabbit-hole to begin," he later explained, "without the least idea what was to happen afterwards."

• Amazingly, he made up most of *Alice in Wonderland* on the spot.

SAVING A TREASURE

Alice liked the story so much that she asked Dodgson to write it down. He agreed. In fact, that night—as a gift for his favorite little girl—he sat up and wrote the whole thing out in longhand, adding his own illustrations. He called it *Alice's Adventures Underground.*

In 1997, about one-third of American homes had computers.

• Dodgson had already decided he needed a pseudonym for the humorous poems and stories he'd been contributing to magazines. (He also wrote academic articles on mathematics, and was afraid people wouldn't take him seriously if they knew he was writing nonsense rhymes.)

• He came up with the name Lewis Carroll by scrambling letters in his first two names, and used it for the first time when he signed *Alice's Adventures Underground* for Alice.

A BOOK IS BORN

Fortunately for us, before Dodgson brought the handwritten manuscript to Alice, he happened to show it to a friend named George MacDonald, who read it to his children. If he hadn't, Alice's adventures might have been nothing more than a personal gift to one little girl. But the entire MacDonald family loved the story so much that they urged Carroll to publish it.

• After giving the original to Alice Liddell as promised, Dodgson decided to take their advice. He revised the story, added to it, then hired John Tenniel, a well-known cartoonist, to illustrate it.

• The book was published in 1865 as *Alice's Adventures in Wonderland*. It became so popular that in 1871 Carroll published the further adventures of Alice, entitled *Through the Looking Glass*.

THE ALICE MYSTERY

Shortly after Dodgson presented Alice with the handwritten story, something happened that ended his relationship with the Liddell family. No one knows what it was. But the abruptness of the split has led to speculation about Carroll's sexuality. Why was he so interested in little girls in the first place?

• In fact, however, there's no evidence that his relationships with children were in any way improper. His biographers interviewed many of the women Carroll entertained as children and they always spoke of him with great respect and fondness. It's more likely, say some biographers, that Carroll broached the subject of marriage to one of the Liddell girls and was rejected.

• At any rate, the lazy days of games, and stories were over for Alice and Dodgson. By the time Alice received her copy of the published edition of, *Alice's Adventures in Wonderland*, the author was no longer a part of her life.

In 1926, Alice Liddell sold the original manuscript of *Alice's Adventures Underground* to an American book dealer for $25,000. He resold it to a group of Americans. They took it to England and presented it as a gift to the British people in gratitude for their bravery in World War II. It remains there today, in the British Museum.

*   *   *   *

FAMILIAR FACES

Many of the now-classic characters in Carroll's stories were easily recognizable to the Liddell children. For example:

The White Rabbit: Was modeled after Carroll himself. Like the rabbit, he was very proper, usually dressed in an old-fashioned formal black suit and top hat. He always wore gloves—no matter what the weather—which he frequently misplaced.

The Dodo: Carroll had taken the girls to a museum, where they were fascinated by a stuffed Dodo bird. He incorporated the bird into the story as himself because he stammered and his name came out as "Do-Do-Dodgson."

The Duck, Lory, and Eaglet: The Duck was Carroll's friend, Robinson Duckworth, who'd accompanied him on many of the outings with the children. The Lory was Lorina Liddell, the Eaglet, Edith Liddell. The three sisters show up again in the Dormous's story as Elsie (from L.C., Lorina's initials), Lacie (an anagram for Alice), and Tillie (a family nickname for Edith).

The Mock Turtle's Song: "Beautiful Soup" was a parody of one of the children's favorite songs, "Star of Evening," and the way they sang in their childish voices.

The Mad Hatter: Supposedly modeled after an eccentric man named Theophilus Carter, who'd been at Christ Church but became a furniture dealer.

In the 1600s in Europe, "fashion" wigs were often made of plaster of Paris.

THE WORLD ACCORDING TO ALICE

The Alice books are among the most quotable children's stories ever written. There's a gem on practically every page—and some passages are packed with them. In the 1st and 6th Bathroom Readers we included a few sections of Lewis Carroll's work. Here are some more.

In that direction," the Cheshire Cat said, waving its right paw round, "lives a Hatter: and in that direction," waving the other paw, "lives a March Hare. Visit either you like: they're both mad." "But I don't want to go among mad people," Alice remarked.

"Oh, you can't help that," said the Cat: "we're all mad here. I'm mad. You're mad."

"How do you know I'm mad?" said Alice.

"You must be," said the Cat, "or you wouldn't have come here."

*   *   *   *   *

"It was much pleasanter at home," thought poor Alice, "when one wasn't always growing larger and smaller, and being ordered about by mice and rabbits. I almost wish I hadn't gone down that rabbit hole and yet it's rather curious, you know, this sort of life! I do wonder what can have happened to me! When I used to read fairy tales, I fancied that kind of thing never happened, and now here I am in the middle of one! There ought to be a book written about me, that there ought! And when I grow up, I'll write one but I'm grown up now," she added in a sorrowful tone, "at least there's no room to grow up any more here."

*   *   *   *   *

"Alice took up the fan and gloves, and, as the hall was very hot, she kept fanning herself all the time she went on talking: "Dear, dear! How queer everything is today! And yesterday things went on just as usual. I wonder if I've been changed in the night? Let me think: was I the same when I got up this morning? I almost think I can remember feeling a little different. But if I'm not the same, the next question is, Who in the world am I? Ah, that's the great puzzle!" And she began thinking over all the children she knew, that were of the same age as herself to see if she could have been changed for any of them."

*　　*　　*　　*　　*

"Who are you?" said the Caterpillar.

This was not an encouraging opening for a conversation. Alice replied, rather shyly," I, I hardly know, sir, just at present at least I know who I was when I got up this morning, but I think I must have been changed several times since then."

"What do you mean by that?" said the Caterpillar sternly. "Explain yourself!"

"I can't explain myself, I'm afraid, sir," said Alice, "because I'm not myself, you see."

"I don't see," said the Caterpillar.

"I'm afraid I can't put it more clearly," Alice replied very politely," for I can't understand it myself to begin with; and being so many different sizes in a day is very confusing."

"It isn't," said the Caterpillar.

"Well, perhaps you haven't found it so yet," said Alice; "but when you have to turn into a chrysalis—you will some day, you know—and then after that into a butterfly, I should think you'll feel a little queer, won't you?"

"Not a bit," said the Caterpillar.

"Well, perhaps your feelings may be different," said Alice; "all I know is, it would feel very queer to me."

"You!" said the Caterpillar contemptuously. "Who are you?"

*　　*　　*

"The two *Alices* are not books for children; they are the only books in which we *become* children."

—Virginia Woolf

PRIMETIME PROVERBS

TV comments about everyday life, from Primetime
Proverbs, *by Jack Mingo and John Javna.*

ON ROMANCE

"Gomez, I've been yours since
that first day you carved my
initials in your leg."
—Morticia Addams,
The Addams Family

Emily Hartley: "Bob, do you
love me?"
Bob Hartley: "Sure."
Emily: "Why?"
Bob: "Why not?"
—*The Bob Newhart Show*

"We've come to realize that
you can be in love without
making others want to puke."
—Michael Harris,
Newhart

ON BIGOTRY

"Look, Archie Bunker ain't no
bigot. I'm the first to say—
look, it ain't your fault you're
colored."
—Archie Bunker,
All in the Family

ON WOMEN'S ISSUES

Game Show Host: "Complete
this famous phrase: Better late
than..."
Blanche: "Pregnant!"
—*The Golden Girls*

ON BEING WEALTHY

"If God had not meant for there
to be poor people, He wouldn't
have given you all their money."
—Minister addressing a
wealthy congregation, SCTV

"As my old Pappy used to say, if
the Lord had more respect for
money, he'd have given it to a
better class of people.
—Bret Maverick,
Maverick

ON WORKING
FOR A LIVING

Napoleon Solo: "Are you free?"
Illya Kuryakin: "No man is free
who has to work for a living. But
I am available."
—*The Man from U.N.C.L.E.*

"I don't have anything against
work. I just figure, why deprive
somebody who really loves it?"
—Dobie, *The Many
Loves of Dobie Gillis*

"My old Pappy used to say, hard
work never hurt anyone—who
didn't do it."
—Bret Maverick,
Maverick

When a waitress draws a happy face on a check, tips go up 18%; when a *waiter* does, tips rise 3%.

IT'S A MIRACLE!

They say the Lord works in mysterious ways. Do you believe it?
These people obviously do…In fact, they may be the proof.

T HE GLASS MENAGERIE
   The Sighting: A 35-foot-high image of the Virgin Mary on
   the side of a building in Clearwater, Florida

Revelation: In 1996, workers chopped down a palm tree in front of
the Seminole Finance Company building. Not long afterward, a
customer noticed a discoloration in the building's tinted windows
that resembled the Madonna. The discovery was reported on the
afternoon news. By the end of the week, an estimated 100,000 people visited the site…including a Baptist minister who was ejected
after he "condemned the crowd for worshipping an image on glass."

Impact: The city set up a "Miracle Management Task Force" to install portable toilets at the site, arrange police patrols, and erect a
pedestrian walkway over the adjacent road (Route 19) to stop the
faithful from dodging in and out of traffic. "That's the busiest highway in Florida," one policeman told reporters. "You want to know
the real miracle? Half a million people have crossed that intersec-
tion and nobody's been injured or killed."

STRANGE FRUIT

The Sighting: The words of Allah in a sliced tomato in Hudders-
field, England

Revelation: In June 1997, 14-year-old Shasta Aslam sliced a tomato in half for her grandparents' salad and saw what appeared to be
the Koranic message "There is no God but Allah" spelled out in
Arabic in the veins of one half of the tomato, and the words "Mo-
hammed is the messenger" written in the other half. "There were
some letters missing and it was hard to decipher," her grandmother
told reporters, "but the message was clear."

Impact: Hundreds of Muslims from all over the United Kingdom
went to view the tomato. "They knock on the door and I take
them through to the kitchen and open the fridge door for them to
have a look," the grandmother explained. The tomato has since
been moved to the freezer.

In 1900, the average American slept 9 hours, 20 minutes. Now it's 7 hours, 20 minutes.

NICE BUN

The Sighting: The face of Mother Teresa in a cinnamon bun in Nashville, Tennessee

Revelation: In the fall of 1996, bakers at the Bongo Java coffeehouse were baking cinnamon buns when they noticed one that bore a striking resemblance to Mother Teresa.

Impact: Bongo Java owner Bob Bernstein shellacked the bun and put it in a display case beneath the coffeehouse's cash register. The story was reported in newspapers and on national television. The coffeehouse, now a tourist attraction, set up a Web site and began selling "Immaculate Confection" T-shirts, mugs, cards, and "Mother Teresa's Special Roast" coffee beans. More than 2 million people from 80 different countries have visited the Web site, and many have left messages. "I hate to burst your bubble," one visitor wrote, "but to me, it looks more like Abe Vigoda in a hooded sweatshirt."

When Mother Teresa—who didn't even allow her own order to use her image in fundraising—learned of the bun, her lawyers asked the coffeehouse to remove it from display. "If it were sacrilege, we'd stop," a Bongo spokesman said. "But it's not."

THIRSTY FOR ENLIGHTENMENT

The Sighting: A statue of Lord Ganesh, the elephant-headed Hindu god of wealth and power, drinking milk through its trunk.

Revelation: On September 21, 1995, a Hindu in India had a dream that Ganesh, the god of wealth and power, "wanted some milk." So he held an offering of a teaspoonful of milk up to the trunk of his Ganesh statue…and it drank it. As word spread over the next few days, the same phenomenon was observed in Hindu communities in England, Hong Kong, Malaysia, Nepal, the Netherlands and the United States. (Skeptics point to capillary action—the ability of porous stone and metals to absorb liquids—as a likely culprit.)

Impact: According to Indian news reports, "So many Hindus were caught up in the mass hysteria that milk supplies were depleted and shopkeepers raised the price of milk 20 times. The military used bamboo canes to control the worshippers flooding Hindu temples." The phenomenon spread to other religions. "After reading news reports," one man in Kuala Lumpur wrote, "I tried the same thing on Mother Mary and baby Jesus. They drank a whole spoonful."

OLYMPIC MYTHS

Every four years, we're treated to another round of Olympics. Whether you watch them or not, it's impossible to avoid all the hype—which, it turns out, isn't all true. Next time someone refers to "Olympic tradition," read them this.

THE MYTH: Athletes who competed in the ancient Greek Olympics were amateurs.

THE TRUTH: Technically, maybe. But in fact, they were handsomely rewarded for their victories. "Contrary to popular belief," says David Wallechinsky in his *Complete Book of the Olympics*, "the Ancient Greek athletes were not amateurs. Not only were they fully supported throughout their training, but even though the winner received only an olive wreath at the Games, at home he was amply rewarded and could become quite rich." Eventually, top athletes demanded cash and appearance fees—even back then.

THE MYTH: In ancient Greece, the Olympics were so important that everything stopped for them—even wars.

THE TRUTH: No war *ever* stopped because of the Olympics. But wars didn't interfere with the games because: 1) participants were given nighttime safe-conduct passes that allowed them to cross battlefields after a day's fighting was done and 2) the Olympics were part of a religious ceremony, so the four olympic sites—including Delphi and Olympia—were off-limits to fighting.

THE MYTH: To honor ancient tradition and discourage commercialism, organizers of the modern Olympics decided that only amateur athletes could compete.

THE TRUTH: Not even close. It was "amateurs only" strictly to keep the riff-raff out. Baron Coubertin, the man responsible for bringing back the Olympics in 1896, was a French aristocrat who wanted to limit competitors to others of his social class. "He saw the Olympics as a way to reinforce class distinctions rather than overcome them," writes one historian. Since only the rich could afford to spend their time training for the games without outside support, the best way to keep lower classes out was to restrict them to amateurs.

THE MYTH: The torch-lighting ceremony that opens the games originated with the ancient Greeks.

THE TRUTH: It has no ancient precedent—it was invented by the Nazis. The 1936 Olympics took place in Berlin, under Hitler's watchful eye. Carl Diem, who organized the event for the Führer, created the first lighting of the Olympic flame to give the proceedings "an ancient aura" Since then, the ceremony has become part of Olympic tradition...and people just assume it's much older than it really is.

THE MYTH: The 5-ring Olympic symbol is from ancient Greece.

THE TRUTH: The Nazis are responsible for that myth, too. According to David Young's book, *The Modern Olympics*, it was spread in a Nazi propaganda film about the Berlin Games.

THE MYTH: Adolf Hitler snubbed U.S. runner Jesse Owens at the 1936 Olympics in Berlin.

THE TRUTH: This is one of the enduring American Olympic myths. Hitler, the story goes, was frustrated in his attempt to prove Aryan superiority when Owens—an African American—took the gold. The furious Führer supposedly refused to acknowledge Owens's victories. But according to Owens himself, it never happened. Hitler didn't congratulate anyone that day because the International Olympic Committee had warned him he had to congratulate "all winners or no winners." He chose to stay mum.

THE MYTH: The Olympic marathon distance was established in ancient times to honor a messenger who ran from Marathon to Athens—about 26 miles—to deliver vital news...then died.

THE TRUTH: The marathon distance—26 miles, 385 yards—was established at the 1908 games in London. It's the distance from Shepherd's Bush Stadium to the queen's bedroom window.

THE MYTH: Drugs have always been taboo in the Olympics.

THE TRUTH: Drugs weren't outlawed until 1967. In fact, according to the *Complete Book of the Olympics*, drugs were already in use by the third modern Olympic Games: "The winner of the 1904 marathon, Thomas Hicks, was administered multiple doses of strychnine and brandy *during* the race."

FAMILIAR PHRASES

More unusual origins of everyday phrases

CARRY A TORCH FOR SOMEONE

Meaning: Be devoted to (in love with) someone

Origin: During the 19th century, a dedicated follower showed support for a political candidate by carrying a torch in an evening campaign parade. Only enthusiastic followers took part in such rallies. A fellow who carried a torch didn't care who knew that he was wholeheartedly behind his candidate. Later, the term was applied to someone publicly (and obsessively) in love.

SELL LIKE HOTCAKES

Meaning: Go over big; have a big commercial success

Origin: In the early 1800s, hotcakes were *the* popular fast food at carnivals and country fairs. Anyone who set up a hotcake stand was sure to make a killing.

PUT THE SCREWS TO SOMEONE

Meaning: Pressure someone mercilessly

Origin: According to Robert Claiborne in *Loose Cannons and Red Herrings*, "The screws aren't those used to fasten a piece of woodwork together, but the much larger screws used to compress such things as cotton bales. If someone's putting the screws on you, they're squeezing you for all you're worth."

BAWL SOMEONE OUT

Meaning: Berate (or yell at) someone for doing something wrong.

Origin: "The word *bawl* for a loud, rough cry goes back to the fifteenth century and probably derives from the Latin for *baulare*, to bark like a dog, the word first meant to bark or howl the way a dog does, but it was also applied to the sounds of other animals, especially cows and bulls. This supports the theory that *to bawl out* originated as ranch slang, suggested by the bawling or bellowing of angry bulls." (*Animal Crackers*, by Robert Hendrickson)

PULL YOUR OWN WEIGHT

Meaning: Do your share

Origin: Surprisingly, a rowing term. "Each member of a crew must pull an oar at least hard enough to propel his or her own weight." (*Have a Nice Day No Problem*, by Christine Ammer)

DEAD SET AGAINST SOMETHING

Meaning: Unalterably opposed to something

Origin: An industrial term. When a machine is bolted down or fastened so it can't move, it's said to be "dead set."

DRUM UP BUSINESS

Meaning: Find a way to sell things

Origin: "Before the practice of advertising in printed media became so common, traveling hawkers of various wares would enter a village in their wagons and attract an audience by beating a drum." (*The Whole Ball of Wax*, by Lawrence Urdang)

A BOOBY TRAP

Meaning: A hidden hazard, designed to surprise the victim

Origin: Literally a trap for a *booby* (or *boob*)—a term that probably came from the Spanish word *bobo*, meaning stupid.

FIT AS A FIDDLE

Meaning: In tip-top shape

Origin: "The phrase was originally 'fit as a fiddler,' and referred to the stamina of fiddlers, who could play for a dance all night long without even getting tired." (*Why Do We Say It*, by Castle Books)

MONKEY SUIT

Meaning: Formal wear; a tuxedo

Origin: "The organ grinder's monkey, dressed in a little jacket and given a hat in which to collect coins, was a familiar sight in the 18th and 19th centuries. About 1820 a close-fitting, short jacket was called a *monkey jacket* for its resemblance to the street musician's monkey; toward the end of the 19th century this name was also used for tuxedo jacket." Eventually the tux itself was nicknamed *monkey suit*. (*Raining Cats and Dogs*, Christine Ammer)

COURT TRANSQUIPS

Here are some more great moments in American jurisprudence.
(These quotes are taken from actual court transcripts.)

Q: "How many trucks do you own?"
A: "Seventeen."
Q: "Seventy?"
A: "Seventeen."
Q: "Seventeen?"
A: "No, about twelve."

Q: "The respiratory arrest means no breathing, doesn't it?"
A: "That's right."
Q: "And in every case where there is death, isn't there no breathing?"

Q: "Tell us your full name, please.
A: Mine?"
Q: "Yes, sir."
A: "555-2723."
Q: "Mr. Daniels, do you have any problems hearing me?"
A: "Not really."
Q: "Where do you live?"
A: "Pardon?"

Q: "To the charge of driving while intoxicated, how do you plead?"
A: "Drunk."

Q: "Are you qualified to give a urine sample?"
A: "Yes, I have been since childhood."

Q: "Where do you live?"
A: "LaPosta Tailer Court."
Q: "How do you spell that trailer court?"
A: "T-r-a-i-l-e-r C-o-u-r-t."

Q: "Do you wear a 2-piece bathing suit now that you have a scar?"
A: "I don't wear a bathing suit at all now."
Q: "That can be taken two ways."

Q: "Are you restricted in some way by having your third finger shot off?"
A: "Yeah, a little."
Q: "What could you do before the accident that you can't do now?"
A: "Wear a ring on it."

Q: "What device do you have in your laboratory to test alcohol content?"
A: "A dual column gas chromato-gragh, Hewlett Packard 5710A with flame analyzation detectors."
Q: "Can you get that with mag wheels?"
A: "Only on the floor models."

Q: "Do you recall examining a person by the name of Rodney Edgington at the funeral chapel?"
A: "Yes."
Q: "Do you recall approximately the time that you examined the body of Mr. Edgington?"
A: "It was in the evening. The autopsy started at about 8:30 p.m."
Q: "And Mr. Edgington was dead at that time, is that correct?"
A: "No, you dumb asshole. He was sitting on the table wondering why I was doing an autopsy."

It's estimated that 75% of all U.S. dollars contain traces of cocaine.

BRAND NAMES

*You already know these names—
here's where they come from.*

ACE BANDAGES. When World War I broke out in 1914, the Becton Dickinson Company had to stop importing German elastic bandages and start making them in the U.S.A. They held a contest to give the new product a name. The winners: a group of doctors who called it *ACE*, for All Cotton Elastic.

ALPO. The original canned dog food, introduced in 1937 as *All-Pro*. Shortened in 1944 to *Alpo*.

ARM & HAMMER. In the 1860s, the Church family owned the Vulcan Spice Mills. Their logo was an arm and a hammer, representing the Roman god Vulcan (who was a blacksmith). When the family formed a baking soda company in 1867, they used the same logo…and eventually named the company after it.

DELTA AIRLINES. Huff-Daland Dusters, formed in 1924, was the world's first crop-dusting service. When they moved to Louisiana a year later, they changed the name to Delta Air Service (because they were serving the Mississippi Delta). In 1929 they began their first passenger route, between Dallas and Jackson.

GRAPE-NUTS. The first Post cereal, introduced in 1897. The reference to *grapes* comes from the baking process, in which part of the starch in the dough is converted to dextrose—commonly called "grape sugar." And C. W. Post thought the cereal's small granules looked like nuts.

SARA LEE. Charles Lubin and his brother-in-law owned three bakeries in the Chicago area. But Lubin dreamed of bigger things—he wanted a product that would be distributed nationally. In 1949 he created a cheesecake that he could sell through supermarkets, and named it after his daughter, Sara Lee Lubin. Within five years the company had developed a way to quick-freeze Sara Lee cakes and was selling them all over the U.S.

In June 1989, two original carbon scripts of *Citizen Kane* sold for $231,000.

WORD GEOGRAPHY

Did you know that many words are taken from place names? Here are some examples, from a book called Toposaurus, *by John D. Jacobson.*

BUNGALOW

From: Bengal, India
Explanation: England's 200-year occupation of India led to many borrowed Hindi words. An Indian *bangla* is a one-story house, often with a roofed porch (in Hindi, a *veranda*). *Bangla*—which literally means "from Bengal"—was anglicized to *bungalow*.

BIBLE

From: Byblos (a city now called Jubayl in present-day Lebanon)
Explanation: The ancient city of Byblos was where the Phoenicians converted a plant called papyrus into a type of paper. Greeks called the paper *biblios*, after the city, and soon a *biblion* meant "a little book." In 400 A.D. Greeks started using the word *Bible* to refer to the Christian scripture. Lower-case *bible* today means any authoritative source work.

SLEAZY

From: Silesia, Poland
Explanation: The Eastern European region of Silesia was known for its fine cloth. Eventually, so many low-quality imitations wound up on the market that *Silesian* turned into *sleazy*.

JEANS

From: Genoa, Italy
Explanation: Genoa—called *Gene* by sixteenth-century Europeans—was the first city to make the denim cloth used for jeans. The pants were named after the city.

SPA

From: Spa, Belgium
Explanation: The Belgian resort town of Spa was known for its healthful mineral springs. As a result, the term *spa* became associated with mineral water. Today it means "a place to rejuvenate."

The fingerprints of humans and koalas are virtually identical.

THE EIFFEL TOWER, PART I

It's hard to believe now, but when the Eiffel Tower was proposed in the late 1800s, a lot of Parisians—and French citizens in general— opposed it. Here's a look at the story behind one of the most recognizable architectural structures on earth.

REVOLUTIONARY THINKING

In 1885, French officials began planning the Great Exposition of 1889, a celebration of the 100th anniversary of the French Revolution. They wanted to build some kind of monument that would be as glorious as France itself.

The Washington Monument, a masonry and marble obelisk, had recently been completed. At 557 feet high, it was the tallest building on earth. The French decided to top it by constructing a 1,000-foot-tall tower right in the heart of Paris.

Now all they had to do was find somebody who could design and build it.

OPEN SEASON

On May 2, 1886, the French government announced a design contest: French engineers and architects were invited to "study the possibility of erecting on the Champ de Mars an iron tower with a base 125 meters square and 300 meters high."

Whatever the contestants decided to propose, their designs had to meet two other criteria: 1) the structure had to be self-financing—it had to attract enough ticket-buying visitors to the exposition to pay for its own construction; and 2) it had to be a temporary structure that could be torn down easily at the end of the Exposition.

MERCI...BUT NON, MERCI

More than 100 proposals were submitted by the May 18 deadline. Most were fairly conventional, but some were downright weird. One person proposed building a huge guillotine; another suggested

---

No wonder he's fat: U.S. kids leave an estimated 812 million cookies out for Santa on Christmas Eve.

erecting a 1,000-foot-tall sprinkler to water all of Paris during droughts; a third suggested putting a huge electric light atop the tower that—with the help of strategically placed parabolic mirrors—would provide the entire city "eight times as much light as is necessary to read a newspaper."

NO CONTEST

The truth was, none of them had a chance. By the time the contest was announced, Alexandre-Gustave Eiffel—a 53-year-old structural engineer already considered France's "master builder in metal" had the job sewn up. (He would later become as *le Magicien du Fer*—"the Iron Magician.")

Weeks earlier, he had met with French minister Edouard Lockroy and presented plans for a wrought iron tower he was ready to build. Eiffel had already commissioned 5,329 mechanical drawings representing the 18,038 different components that would be used. Lockroy was so impressed that he rigged the contest so only Eiffel's design would win.

JOINT VENTURE

In January 1887, Eiffel signed a contract with the French government and the City of Paris. Eiffel & Company, his engineering firm, agreed to contribute $1.3 million of the tower's estimated $1.6 million construction cost. In exchange, Eiffel would receive all revenues generated by the tower during the Exposition...and for 20 years afterward. (The government agreed to leave the tower up after the Exposition.) Afterward, full ownership reverted to the City of Paris. They could tear it down if they wanted.

MONEY MACHINE

Unlike other public monuments, the Eiffel Tower was designed to make money from the very beginning. If you wanted to take the elevator or the stairs to the first story, you had to pay 2 francs; going all the way to the top cost 5 francs (Sundays were cheaper). That was just the beginning: restaurants, cafes, and shops were planned for the first story; a post office, telegraph office, bakery, and printing press were planned for the second story. In all, the tower was designed to accommodate up to 10,416 paying customers at a time.

Which goes up, stalactites or stalagmites? Try this: "When the mites go up, the tights come down."

GROUNDBREAKING

Construction began on January 26, with not a moment to spare. With barely two years left to build the tower in time for the opening of the Exposition, Eiffel would have to build the tower more quickly than any similar structure had been built before. The Washington Monument, just over half the Eiffel Tower's size, had taken 36 years to complete.

PARISIAN PARTY POOPERS

A 1,000-foot tower would dwarf the Parisian skyline and overpower the city's other landmarks, including Notre Dame, the Louvre, and the Arc de Triomphe. When digging started on the foundation, more than 300 prominent Parisians signed a petition protesting the tower. They claimed that Eiffel's "hollow candlestick" would "disfigure and dishonor" the city. But Eiffel and the city ignored the petition, and work continued uninterrupted.

OTHER FEARS

The tower still had its critics. A French mathematics professor predicted that when the structure passed the 748-foot mark, it would inevitably collapse; another "expert" predicted that the tower's lightning rods would kill all the fish in the Seine.

The Paris edition of the New York *Herald* claimed the tower was changing the weather; and the daily newspaper *Le Matin* ran a headline story claiming "The Tower Is Sinking." "If it has really begun to sink," *Le Matin* pontificated, "any further building should stop and sections already built should be demolished as quickly as possible." As the tower's progress continued unabated, however, a sense of awe began to replace the fear.

Part II of the story begins on page 349.

*   *   *

Interesting Sidelight

August Eiffel also designed and built the iron skeleton that holds up the Statue of Liberty.

In her films, Shirley Temple always had 56 curls in her hair.

SPACED-OUT SPORTS

Our friend Tim Harrower, an awesome talent in sniffing out Bathroom Reader material, came up with these quotes from sports announcers and interviews and graciously sent them our way.

"We have only one person to blame, and that's each other."
—**Barry Beck,
N.Y. Ranger, explaining
how a brawl stared**

"He fakes a bluff!"
—**Ron Fairly,
S.F. Giants announcer**

"Winfield goes back to the wall. He hits his head on the wall—and it rolls off! It's rolling all the way to second base! This is a terrible thing for the Padres."
—**Jerry Coleman,
S.D. Padres radio announcer,
describing a fly ball hit by a
member of the opposing team**

"We are experiencing audio technicalities."
—**Ralph Kiner,
N.Y. Mets announcer**

"If I wasn't talking, I wouldn't know what to say."
—**Chico Resch,
N.Y. Islanders goalie**

"Arnie, usually a great putter, seems to be having trouble with his long putt. However, he has no trouble dropping his shorts."
—**Golf broadcaster,
during a tournament**

"Kansas City is at Chicago tonight—or is that Chicago at Kansas City? Well, no matter…Kansas City leads in the eighth, 4 to 4."
—**Jerry Coleman,
Padres announcer, going
through the scoreboard on air**

"His reputation preceded him before he got here."
—**Don Mattingly,
N.Y. Yankees' star, on
new pitcher Dwight Gooden**

"Lintz steals second standing up! He slid, but he didn't have to."
—**Jerry Coleman,
Padres announcer**

"I don't want to tell you any half-truths unless they're completely accurate."
—**Dennis Rappaport, boxing
manager, explaining his silence
regarding boxer Thomas Hearns**

"It's about 90 percent strength and 40 percent technique."
—**Johnny Walker,
wrist-wrestling champion, on
what it takes to be a winner**

"Today is Father's Day, so everyone out there: Happy Birthday!"
—**Ralph Kiner,
Mets announcer**

The average meteor is no larger than a grain of sand.

ELVIS SINGS OPERA

In 1956 it would have been impossible to imagine swivel-hips Elvis Presley singing "O Sole Mio." But when he did, it sold 20 million copies. This piece is from Behind the Hits, *by Bob Shannon and John Javna.*

In March 1960, Elvis returned to the United States after serving a two-year hitch in the Army. He was greeted not only by loyal fans, but by a friendly press. Reporters who'd derided him in the 1950s as a "no-talent" or worse were impressed by his role as a model soldier.

Elvis rewarded these new allies in a number of ways. He appeared on TV with Frank Sinatra, the man who'd scathingly denounced rock 'n' roll as "a rancid-smelling aphrodisiac." He launched a series of innocuous film musicals that were more Pat Boone than raunchy rocker. And in his records, he moved away from rock 'n' roll. The new "improved" Elvis was suddenly acceptable to radio stations that wouldn't go near his material even a year earlier. By the mid-1960s, he was winning Grammys for *religious* music; eventually he became a mainstream demigod.

And it all started with "It's Now or Never."

THE KING...OF OPERA?

"It's Now or Never" is based on an Italian operatic theme called "O Sole Mio," composed in 1901 by Eduardo di Capua. It was popularized in America by Mario Lanza, who sang it in Italian; then it was popularized again in 1949 by Tony Martin, who sang an English "translation" called "There's No Tomorrow."

But what was Elvis the Pelvis doing, singing like Mario Lanza? Actually, the King had always admired crooners like Dean Martin and operatic voices like Lanza's. As he told a reporter later:

"O Sole Mio" has always been one of my favorite songs. I liked the Tony Martin version...and I often played the record by Jan Pierce, the opera singer. I used to sing it myself. I don't read music, but I know what I like.

Assuming Rudolph's in front, there are 40,320 ways to arrange Santa's eight other reindeer.

CREATING THE SONG

Elvis decided to record the song while he was still stationed in Germany. He told music publisher Freddie Bienstock, who was there to visit him, that he wanted new lyrics to it. Bienstock returned to New York and went straight to his office with the news. As it happens, only two writers were working there that day—Wally Gold and Aaron Schroeder. By being in the right place at the right time, they picked up the most coveted assignment in pop music.

Wally Gold: "Elvis was a plum....All the writers, we all wrote our behinds off when a project like that was presented to us. This time we were lucky because we were the only ones sitting in the office. We jumped in a cab to go to Aaron's studio. We got the title in the cab, the melody was already written, and in half an hour we knocked off the lyric. We brought it back to Freddie the same day and he said, "Great! Terrific! Go do a demo." [A demonstration recording, so the artist can hear what the song sounds like with instruments, etc.] And we did."

THE ELVIS METHOD

This was a typical Elvis procedure. If a song was accepted by Bienstock, the writers would make a demo—and if Elvis liked it, he'd record it exactly as it was on the demo. For "It's Now or Never," Gold and Schroeder made an up-tempo, cha-cha-flavored arrangement. Elvis loved it (it became his favorite of all his records), and recorded it in the same sessions as the *Elvis Is Back* LP, right after he got out of the Army.

Wally Gold: "It was enormous. Number one in every market of the world, which made it, I believe, the #1 single of his entire recording career. Worldwide it sold more than twenty million. For a few issues we were in the *Guinness Book* as the largest-selling single in the history of music....Aaron wrote other hits, I wrote other hits, but a song we finished in a half hour was the biggest of our career!"

*   *   *   *

"I don't know anything about music. In my line, you don't have to."

—*Elvis Presley*

World record: A tornado blew a canceled check 137 miles, from Wisconsin to Michigan, in 1996.

CANINE QUOTES

A few thoughts about man's best friend.

"You can say any fool thing to a dog, and the dog will give you this look that says, 'My God, you're right! I *never* would have thought of that!'"

—*Dave Barry*

"They say the dog is man's best friend. I don't believe that. How many friends have you had neutered?"

—*Larry Reeb*

"My dog is half pit bull, half poodle. Not much of a guard dog, but a vicious gossip."

—*Craig Shoemaker*

"Outside a dog, a book is man's best friend. Inside a dog it's too dark to read."

—*Groucho Marx*

"If a dog will not come to you after he has looked you in the face, you should go home and examine your conscience."

—*Woodrow Wilson*

"Dogs laugh, but they laugh with their tails."

—*Max Eastman*

"Acquiring a dog may be the only opportunity a human ever has to choose a relative."

—*Morecai Siegal*

"Every dog should have a man of his own. There is nothing like a well-behaved person around the house to spread the dog's blanket for him, or bring him his supper when he comes home mantired at night."

—*Corey Ford*

"To his dog, every man is Napoleon; hence the constant popularity of dogs."

—*Aldous Huxley*

"To err is human, to forgive canine."

—*Anonymous*

"Dogs have more love than integrity. They've been true to us, yes, but they haven't been true to them selves."

—*Clarence Day*

"Every dog is entitled to one bite."

—*English proverb*

The average American buys 17 yards of dental floss each year.

AFTER THE FUNERAL

Your grave is supposed to be your final resting place. But that isn't always the case, especially if you're famous. Take a look at what happened to these unfortunate folks.

ABE LINCOLN

Claim to Fame: 16th president of the United States

How He Died: Assassinated by John Wilkes Booth on April 14, 1865

After the Funeral: On April 21, his body was laid to rest in a temporary vault in Springfield, Illinois, while a permanent mausoleum was under construction. The body was moved three more times, then entombed in the National Lincoln Monument on October 15, 1874. But in 1876 a ring of counterfeiters made two attempts to kidnap the body and hold it hostage until an accomplice was freed from prison; the second attempt was nearly successful—it was foiled just as the conspirators were prying open the sarcophagus.

Between 1876 and 1901, Lincoln's body was moved *14 more times*—sometimes for security reasons, other times to repair the dilapidated crypt. In 1901 Old Abe was laid to rest a final (so far) time. As his son Robert supervised, the coffin was encased in steel bars and buried under tons of cement. As far as anyone can tell, Abe hasn't been moved since.

FRANCISCO PIZARRO

Claim to Fame: 16th-century Spanish explorer and conquistador of the Incas

How He Died: Stabbed to death by his countrymen in 1541 in a feud over Incan riches

After the Funeral: Pizarro's body was buried behind the cathedral in Lima on the night he died, where it remained for 2 1/2 years. In 1542, his bones were exhumed, placed in a velvet-lined box, and deposited under the main altar of the cathedral.

Pizarro's remains were moved repeatedly over the next 350 years because of earthquakes, repair work on the cathedral, and other reasons. On the 350th anniversary of his death, in 1891, a mummified body authenticated as his was placed in a glass and marble sarcophagus, which was set out for public display.

Then in 1977, some workers repairing a crypt beneath the main altar found two boxes—one lined with velvet and filled with human bones. The other box bore the Spanish inscription, "Here is the skull of the Marquis Don Francisco Pizarro who discovered and won Peru and placed it under the crown of Castile."

Which body was Pizarro's? In 1984, forensics experts from the United States flew to Peru to compare the two sets of remains and determined that the bones in the boxes were those of Pizarro. (The box itself fit the historical description, and of the two sets of bones, the ones in the boxes were the only ones with stab wounds.)

Aftermath: When Pizarro's bones were positively identified, they were placed in a box in the glass sarcophagus, and the "impostor" mummy (who was never identified) was returned to the crypt underneath the altar.

JOHN PAUL JONES

Claim to Fame: Revolutionary War hero, founding father of the U.S. Navy, and the man who said, "I have not yet begun to fight"

How He Died: Kidney disease and bronchial pneumonia. Jones was one of the greatest heroes of the American Revolution, but that counted for little when he died in Paris on July 18, 1792. Rather than pay to ship the body back to the United States for burial, the American ambassador to France instructed Jones's landlord to bury him "in the most private manner, and at the least possible expense."

After the Funeral: In 1899, 107 years later, another U.S. ambassador to France, Horace Porter, became obsessed with locating Jones's grave and returning it to the United States for a proper hero's burial. Nobody knew where in Paris Jones was buried, but after six years of searching, Porter was pretty sure he was buried in a cemetery for Protestants. The cemetery, abandoned decades earlier, had since had an entire neighborhood built on top of it.

Acting on information that Jones had been buried in a lead casket, Porter hired a digging party to tunnel under the neighborhood and search for a lead casket among the hundreds of rotting and exposed wooden caskets. They found three lead coffins—and Jones was in the third. His body was so well preserved that it was identified by comparing the face to military medals inscribed with Jones's likeness. An American Naval Squadron returned him to the U.S. Naval Academy in July 1905...where the body was stored under a staircase in a dormitory for seven more years until Congress finally appropriated enough money to build a permanent crypt.

JESSE JAMES

Claim to Fame: Wild West bank and train robber

How He Died: Shot by one of his gang members on April 3, 1882

After the Funeral: In the years after his death, several men came forward claiming to be the "real" Jesse James, arguing that the person in the grave was someone else. In September 1995, the remains were exhumed and their DNA was compared with James's living descendants. Result: It was him.

ZACHARY TAYLOR

Claim to Fame: 12th president of the United States

How He Died: On July 4, 1850, Taylor ate a bowl of fresh cherries and iced milk. Hours later, he complained of stomach pains and diarrhea; on July 9 he died.

Historians have always assumed Taylor died of natural causes; but rumors that he was poisoned with arsenic have persisted since his death. Taylor opposed the extension of slavery into newly admitted states; conspiracy theorists speculated he was murdered by pro-slavery forces.

After the Funeral: In 1995, Taylor's heirs consented to an exhumation to settle the controversy once and for all. Result: The tests were negative. "President Taylor had in his remains only minuscule levels of arsenic—consistent with any person who lived in the 19th century," forensic anthropologist Dr. William Maples writes in *Dead Men Do Tell Tales*. "The possibility that another poison was used to kill Taylor is extremely remote....On the face of this evidence, the verdict of history must be that Zachary Taylor died of natural causes."

How long will a person wait for an elevator without fidgeting? Researchers say about 40 seconds.

WILDE ABOUT OSCAR

Wit and wisdom from Oscar Wilde, one of the most popular—and controversial—writers of the 19th century.

"When people agree with me I always feel that I must be wrong."

" I never put off till tomorrow what I can possibly do the day after."

"I sometimes think that God, in creating man, somewhat overestimated His ability."

"As long as woman can look ten years younger than her own daughter, she is perfectly happy. "

"Women are meant to be loved, not to be understood."

"After a good dinner one can forgive anybody, even one's own relations."

" I like men who have a future, and women with a past. "

"Women give to men the very gold of their lives, but they invariably want it back in small change."

"Nowadays people know the price of everything and the value of nothing."

"The Americans are certainly great hero-worshipers, and always take their heroes from the criminal classes."

"No great artist sees things as they really are. If he did he would cease to be an artist."

"In this world there are only two tragedies. One is not getting what one wants and the other is getting it."

"Experience is the name everyone gives to their mistakes."

"A gentleman is one who never hurts anyone's feelings unintentionally."

"The one duty we owe to history is to rewrite it."

"The basis of action is lack of imagination. It is the last resource of those who know not how to dream."

FART FACTS

You won't find trivia like this in any ordinary book.

THE NAME

The word *fart* comes from the Old English term *foertan*, to explode. *Foertan* is also the origin of the word *petard*, an early type of bomb. *Petard*, in turn, is the origin of a more obscure term for fart—*ped*, or *pet*, which was once used by military men. (In Shakespeare's *Henry IV*, there's a character whose name means fart—Peto.)

WHY DO YOU FART?

Flatulence has many causes—for example, swallowing air as you eat and lactose intolerance. (Lactose is a sugar molecule in milk, and many people lack the enzyme needed to digest it.) But the most common cause is food that ferments in the gastrointestinal tract.

• A simple explanation: The fats, proteins, and carbohydrates you eat become a "gastric soup" in your stomach. This soup then passes into the small intestine, where much of it is absorbed through the intestinal walls into the bloodstream to feed the body.

• But the small intestine can't absorb everything, especially complex carbohydrates. Some complex carbohydrates—the ones made up of several sugar molecules (beans, some milk products, fiber, etc.) can't be broken down. So they're simply passed along to the colon, where bacteria living in your intestine feed off the fermenting brew. If that sounds gross, try this: the bacteria then excrete gases into your colon. Farting is how your colon rids itself of the pressure the gas creates.

FRUIT OF THE VINE

So why not just quit eating complex carbohydrates?

• First, complex carbohydrates—which include fruit, vegetables, and whole grains—are crucial for a healthy diet. "Put it this way," explains Jeff Rank, an associate professor of gastroenterology at the University of Minnesota. "Cabbage and beans are bad for gas, but they are good for you."

Record for most costume changes by an actor in one film: 65, by Elizabeth Taylor in *Cleopatra* (1963).

• Second, they're not the culprits when it comes to the least desirable aspect of farting: smell.

• Farts are about 99% odorless gases—hydrogen, nitrogen, carbon dioxide, oxygen, and methane (it's the methane that makes farts flammable). So why the odor? Blame it on those millions of bacteria living in your colon. Their waste gases usually contain sulfur molecules—which smell like rotten eggs. This is the remaining 1% that clears rooms in a hurry.

AM I NORMAL?

• Johnson & Johnson, which produces drugs for gas and indigestion, once conducted a survey and found that almost one-third of Americans believe they have a flatulence problem.

• However, according to Terry Bolin and Rosemary Stanton, authors of *Wind Breaks: Coming to Terms with Flatulence*, doctors say most flatulence is healthy. What's unhealthy is worrying about it so much.

NOTABLE FARTERS

• Le Petomane, a 19th-century music hall performer, had the singular ability to control his farts. He could play tunes, as well as imitate animal and machinery sounds rectally. Le Petomane's popularity briefly rivalled that of Sarah Bernhardt.

• A computer factory in England, built on the site of a 19th-century chapel, is reportedly inhabited by a farting ghost. Workers think it might be the embarrassed spirit of a girl who farted while singing in church. "On several occasions," said an employee, "there has been a faint girlish voice singing faint hymns, followed by a loud raspberry sound and then a deathly hush."

• Joseph Stalin was afraid of farting in public. He kept glasses and a water pitcher on his desk so that if he felt a wind coming on, he could mask the sound by clinking the glasses while pouring water.

• Martin Luther believed, "on the basis of personal experience, that farts could scare off Satan himself."

BATHROOM BEGINNINGS

*A few interesting odds and ends from under
the sink and in the medicine cabinet.*

AUTOMATIC TOILET BOWL CLEANER. A guy named Eisen cleaned the toilets in his house because his wife wouldn't—but he hated it. One day in 1977, while hanging out at a swimming pool, he started thinking that if chlorine keeps pools sanitary, it could do the same for his toilets—and then he wouldn't have to scrub them. But how to keep the bowl water chlorinated? Later at dinner, Eisen was inspired by the sour cream on his baked potato: he figured that if he put chlorine in a sour cream container, punched holes in it, and put it in his toilet tank, it would get a dose of chlorine every time it was flushed. It worked. He turned it into a product called 2000 Flushes, now the best selling toilet cleaner in America.

BRECK SHAMPOO. In 1898, at age 21, John Breck became America's youngest fire chief. It didn't make him happy, though— he was obsessed with the fact that he was going bald. He decided to take chemistry classes at a nearby college to see if he could save his hair. There, he hit on a solution: liquid shampoo. (At the time, Americans used bar soap on their hair—shampoos were used only in Europe). The shampoo he developed didn't save his hair, but in 1908 it did become the inspiration for America's first shampoo company.

DRAMAMINE. In 1949, a woman with a bad case of hives went to the Johns Hopkins Allergy Clinic in Baltimore. Her doctor gave her a prescription for a new drug he thought was an antihistimine. On her next visit, the woman's hives were just as bad...but she was in good spirits. For once, she said, the motion of the streetcar she took to get there hadn't made her sick. The doctor suspected the drug had something to do with it. So he gave her a placebo to see if she'd get motion sickness again. She did. He gave her the drug again—the motion sickness vanished. The clinic got the army to try it on soldiers "making a rough trans-Atlantic crossing via ship." Worked fine. The drug—Dramamine—became the standard treatment for motion sickness.

It's estimated you'll eat some 35,000 cookies in your lifetime.

OTHER PRESIDENTIAL FIRSTS

We all know the first president (Washington), the first president to serve more than two terms (FDR), and so on. But who was the first to be cloned? For that info, you need to turn to the Bathroom Reader.

T he president: Gerald Ford
Notable first: First president to be a fashion model.
In the late 1930s, he was a student at Yale Law School. His girlfriend, a model, convinced him to put $1,000 into a modeling agency. His reward: He got to pose in skiwear ads with her.

The president: Richard Nixon
Notable first: First president to host a rock concert at the White House. Unlikely as it seems, Nixon invited the Guess Who and the Turtles to Washington to play for his daughters.

The president: Abraham Lincoln
Notable first: First president to be cloned.
Someday this may be big news. Now it's just a curiosity. In 1990 a group of research scientists got permission to duplicate the DNA from Lincoln's hair, blood, and skull (which they got from the National Museum of Health and Medicine in Washington, D.C.), to find out whether he had a disease called Marfan's syndrome.

The president: John Quincy Adams
Notable first: First president with a pet reptile.
Adams kept a pet alligator in the East Room of the White House. Historians say he enjoyed "the spectacle of guests fleeing from the room in terror."

The president: George Washington
Notable first: First president to use "help wanted" ads to hire staff.
Washington moved to New York—the U.S. capital—in 1789 and put a classified ad in the *New York Daily Gazette* requesting a coachman and a cook "for the Family of a President." Apparently it was no great honor to work for a First Family—the ads ran for six weeks before the jobs were filled.

NOW HEAR THIS!

If you weren't reading right now, you might be listening to a "personal tape player"—like a Walkman. But then when people started banging on the door, asking what you were doing in there, you wouldn't hear them. Maybe they'd panic and think you were dead, like Elvis. They'd run outside and get a bunch of people to help break down the door. Wham! And there you'd be, completely oblivious. They'd get so mad that they'd attack you with the toilet plunger, which would get stuck to the top of your head. You'd have to go to the emergency room...and...well, aren't you glad you're reading Uncle John's Bathroom Reader *instead? Since it's not safe to* listen *to a Walkman, we'll* print *a story about it instead. It's by Jack Mingo.*

THE PRESSMAN

In the mid-1970s, a team of Sony engineers headed by Mitsuro Ida created the Pressman—a portable tape recorder that could fit into a shirt pocket. As Sony expected, it quickly became standard equipment for journalists. But there was one small problem: the Pressman recorded in mono, and radio journalists preferred working in stereo. They requested a stereo version.

Sony's engineers put their best into it, shrinking stereo components, trying to get them into a small, pocket-sized case. They almost made it—but could only fit in the playback parts and two tiny speakers. Since the whole point was to come up with a tape recorder, the attempt was an embarrassing and expensive failure. Still, the quality of the sound was surprisingly good. So Ida kept the prototype around the shop instead of dismantling it. Some of the engineers started playing cassettes on it while they worked.

THE MISSING LINK

One day Masaru Ibuka wandered by. Although he'd co-founded the company with Akio Morita, he was considered too quirky and creative to fit into day-to-day operations. So he was made "honorary chairman"—a title that gave him much respect, little authority, and lots of time to wander the halls of Sony.

Ibuka stopped to watch the Pressman engineers working on their design problem. He heard music coming from the unsuccessful prototype and asked, "Where did you get this great little tape player?" Ida explained that it was a failure because it couldn't record.

Ibuka spent a lot of his time roaming around, so he knew what was going on all over the company. He suddenly remembered another project he'd seen that was being developed on the other side of the building—a set of lightweight portable headphones.

"What if you got rid of the speakers and added the headphones?" he asked Ida. "They'd use less power and increase the quality of the sound. Who knows, maybe we can sell this thing even if you can't record on it." The engineers listened politely and respectfully— while privately thinking the old man had finally lost it. Why make a tape recorder that can't record?

LISTENING WELL

Ibuka took the gadget, with headphones attached, to Morita. He too was skeptical...until he heard the quality of the stereo music. To the shock of the engineering team, Morita gave it a green light. It was dubbed the Walkman, to go along with the Pressman.

The marketing department thought it was a terrible idea. They projected that the company would lose money on every unit sold. Even the name seemed wrong. According to American distributors, "Walkman" sounded "funny" to English ears. So Sony rolled the product out as the "Soundabout" in the U.S. and the "Stowaway" in England. Their 1979 publicity campaign—a low-budget, lukewarm affair aimed at teens—got virtually no results. It seemed as though the Walkman's critics were right.

As it turned out, though, Sony had just targeted the wrong market. Teens had boom boxes...it was *adults* who wanted the Walkman. The little unit was perfect for listening to Mozart while jogging or the Stones while commuting, and was small enough to fit into a briefcase or the pocket of a business suit. To Sony's surprise, white collar workers discovered the Walkman on their own. It became a sudden, raging success. Sony had prepared an initial run of 60,000 units; when the first wave hit, they sold out instantly.

The world still loves the Walkman and its offspring. By 1997, four million personal cassette players were sold a year.

FOUNDING FATHERS

You already know the names. Here's who they belonged to.

Godfry Keebler. Opened a bakery in Philadelphia in 1853. His family expanded it. Today, Keebler is second-largest producer of cookies and crackers in the U.S.

Linus Yale, Jr. Invented the first combination locks and the first flat-key cylinder locks, in the 1860s. In 1868, the Yale Lock Company was formed to mass-produce his creations.

Joseph Campbell. A fruit merchant, he opened a canning factory in 1869. His specialties included jellies, salad dressing, and mincemeat—but not soup. The company added condensed soup in 1897. (First variety: tomato.)

Pleasant and John Hanes. Brothers who built a tobacco business in the late 1800s, then sold it in 1900. Each invested his profits in a textile company. John's made socks and stockings; Pleasant's made new-fangled two-piece men's underwear. They were separate companies until 1962, when the families joined forces.

Carl Jantzen. Part owner of the Portland Knitting Mill. In 1910, at the request of a member of the Portland Rowing Club, he developed the first elasticized swimsuits. They became popular around the country as "Jantzens." In 1920, the company changed its name to Jantzen.

John M. Van Heusen. Started the Van Heusen Shirt Company. In 1919 it became the first to sell dress shirts with collars attached. Developed a way to weave cloth on a curve in 1920, which made one-piece collars possible...and revolutionized the shirt industry.

Arthur Pitney and Walter Bowes. In 1901 Pitney created a machine that could stick postage stamps on letters. In 1920 he joined forces with Bowes. Because of WWI, there was a letter-writing boom, and the post office needed a machine to keep up. In 1920 Congress passed a bill allowing the Pitney-Bowes machine to handle the mail.

HERE COMES THE SUN

Some facts about that big lightbulb in the sky, from astronomer (and BRI member) Richard Moeschl.

It takes 8.3 minutes for the sun's light—traveling at 186,282 miles a second—to reach Earth. (At that speed, light can travel around the Earth seven times in one second.)

The sun looks yellow-gold because we're viewing it through the Earth's atmosphere. Judging from its surface temperature, the sun's color is probably closer to white.

The temperature of the sun at its core is around 73 million degrees F. It takes 50 years for this energy to reach the sun's surface, where we can see it as light.

The English astronomer James Jeans once figured that if you placed a piece of the sun's core the size of the head of a pin on Earth, its heat would kill a person 94 miles away.

The temperature of the sun's photosphere, the part that sends us light, is about 10,000 degrees F.

The sun contains 99.9% of the matter in the solar system.

The sun produces more energy in one second than human beings have produced in all of our history. In less than a week, the sun sends out more energy than we could make by burning all the natural gas, oil, coal, and wood on Earth.

The total energy output of the sun is 1.92 calories per minute per square centimeter, or 3.83 x 1,000,000,000,000,000,000,000,000,000 watts.

The Earth receives 2 one-billionths of the sun's power.

The amount of power that falls on each square foot of the Earth's surface per minute is about 126 watts, enough to light two standard 60-watt lightbulbs.

The surface gravity on the sun is 28 times that of Earth. If you weigh 120 pounds on Earth, on the sun you would weigh 3,360 pounds.

The sun rotates once every 26.8 days.

With every passing day, the sun is losing energy—but it still has about 5 billion years of life left in it.

The most widely used surname in the world is Li. About 87 million people have it.

CELEBRITY GOSSIP

*Here's the BRI's cheesy tabloid section—a
bunch of gossip about famous people.*

ALBERT EINSTEIN

- He applied to the Federal Polytechnic Academy in Zurich, but flunked the entrance exam. When his father asked his headmaster what profession Albert should adopt, he got the answer, "It doesn't matter, he'll never amount to anything."

- For many years, Einstein thought of his work in physics as something of a hobby. He regarded himself as a failure because what he really wanted to do was play concert violin. Einstein was uncharacteristically intense when he played his violin, cussing a blue streak whenever he made a mistake. One evening, while playing violin duets with Queen Elizabeth, Einstein suddenly stopped in the middle of the piece and unceremoniously told her she was playing too loudly.

MUHAMMAD ALI

- For some reason, as a child, he always walked on his tiptoes. When he got older, he played touch football, but wouldn't play tackle because he thought it was too rough.

- Because he was afraid to fly, Ali (then going by his original name, Cassius Clay) almost didn't make it to the 1960 Rome Olympics, where he won the gold medal that launched his career.

JANIS JOPLIN

- In 1965, when she was on the verge of becoming a blues star, strung out on heavy drugs, hanging out with Hells Angels, Joplin wrote to her parents and asked them to send her one present for Christmas: "a *Betty Crocker* or *Better Homes and Gardens* cookbook."

- She once went on a blind date with William Bennett. He was apparently so traumatized that he eventually became drug czar under Ronald Reagan, and a conservative "family values" advocate.

Most-performed rock song in history: "You've Lost That Lovin' Feeling."

GENERAL GEORGE PATTON

• On the way through Europe during World War II with his troops, Patton was continuously in danger from shelling, strafing, and bombing. In the middle of one scorched, scarred, and burning landscape, with the sound of explosions around him, he threw out his arms and looked to the skies as if bathing in a warm spring rain. "Could anything be more magnificent?" he shouted to the soldiers all around him. "Compared to war, all other forms of human endeavor shrink to insignificance. God, how I love it!"

MICHAEL JACKSON

• Jackson's favorite song? He told a group of reporters that it was "My Favorite Things," performed by Julie Andrews.

• His opinion of other singers: Paul McCartney? Okay writer, not much of an entertainer. "I do better box office than he does." Frank Sinatra? "I don't know what people see in the guy. He's a legend, but he isn't much of a singer. He doesn't even have hits anymore." Mick Jagger? "He sings flat. How did *he* ever get to be a star? I just don't get it. He doesn't sell as many records as I do." Madonna? "She just isn't that good....She can't sing. She's just an OK dancer....She knows how to market herself. That's about it."

FIDEL CASTRO

• For Castro's first revolutionary attack on a military post, he forgot his glasses. As a result, he could barely drive to the post, much less aim his gun accurately.

• Castro fancies himself quite a lady's man. In fact, there are dozens of children in Cuba who claim him as father. His technique? One purported lover, a dancer at the Tropicana Hotel, said he read while making love. A French actress complained that he "smoked his damned cigar." An American woman said he never took his boots off. Other women said he took them to romantic spots and then talked for hours on end about things like agricultural reform.

ALFRED HITCHCOCK

• When he sat on a public toilet and another man entered the room, he'd quickly raise his legs in the stall "so that no one could tell anyone was there."

LUCKY FINDS

In our last Bathroom Reader, we included a section about valuable things people have found. Since then we've found many more stories. Hey —maybe it's not such a rare occurrence. It could happen to you!

GARAGE SALE TREASURE

The Find: Two Shaker "gift" paintings

Where They Were Found: Inside a picture frame

The Story: In 1994, a retired couple from New England bought an old picture frame for a few dollars at a garage sale. When they took the frame apart to restore it, two watercolor drawings—dated 1845 and 1854—fell out.

A few months later, the couple was traveling in Massachusetts and noticed a watercolor on a poster advertising the Hancock Shaker Village Museum. It was similar to the two they'd found. Curious, they did some research and found out the works were called "gift paintings."

It turns out that the Shakers, a New England religious sect of the 1800s, did not allow decorations on their walls; Shaker sisters, however, were permitted to paint "trees, flowers, fruits and birds...to depict the glory of heaven." The paintings were then "gifted" to other sisters and put away as holy relics. And one of the couple's paintings was signed by the most famous of all "gift" artists, Hannah Cohoon.

They called a curator of the Hancock Museum with the news, but he didn't believe them. Only 200 Shaker "gift" paintings still exist...and very few are of the quality they described. Moreover, all known paintings were in museums—none in private hands. Nonetheless, in January 1996, the couple brought the paintings to the museum, where they were examined and declared authentic. A year later, in January 1997, Sotheby's sold them for $473,000. ·

BIZARRE BITE

The Find: A diamond

Where It Was Found: In a plate of pasta

The Story: In October 1996, Liliana Parodi of Genoa, Italy, went

---

The market value of the raw materials in a 170-lb. man's body, at 1997 prices: About $25.

to her favorite restaurant for some pasta. The meal was uneventful...until she bit down on something hard and it wedged painfully between her teeth. She complained to the management, then left. The next morning, she went to a dentist, who extracted the object —a one-carat, uncut diamond worth about $3,000. Parodi took it to a jeweller and had it set in a ring. How it got into the pasta is still a mystery.

A BEATLE'S LEGACY

The Find: Dozens of sketches by John Lennon

Where They Were Found: In a notebook

The Story: In 1996, a man named John Dunbar—who'd been married to British singer Marianne Faithfull in the 1960s—was going through some old belongings and came across a notebook he hadn't seen in over 25 years. He'd had it with him at a London party in 1967, on a night when he and his friend John Lennon were taking LSD together. But he'd stashed it away and forgotten about it.

During that week in 1967, Lennon had seen an ad in the newspaper offering "an island off Ireland," for about $2,000. At the party, the drugged-out Beatle suddenly decided to buy it. He and Dunbar immediately flew to Dublin, traveled across Ireland in a limousine, and hired a boat to get there. "The island was more like a couple of small hills joined by a gravelly bar with a cottage on it," Dunbar recalled. "When we got there, John sat down and started drawing." The pair stayed on the island for a few days. Lennon did buy it, but never lived there. (In fact, he gave it away a few years later, to a stranger who showed up at Apple Records.)

Dunbar kept the notebook as a memento of the trip, and today, experts estimate the drawings at about $165,000. The incredulous Dunbar can always look at it as a belated "thank you"—he was the fellow, it turns out, who introduced Lennon to Yoko Ono.

LOTTERY TICKET

The Find: A wallet with $224.

Where It Was Found: On a street in Adelaide, Australia

The Story: In the 1970s, Joan Campbell found a wallet and tracked down the owner, hoping for a nice reward. She was disappointed—all the man gave her was a 55¢ lottery ticket. Later, she cheered up: the ticket paid $45,000.

Gadsby, a 50,000-word, novel by Ernest Wright, contains no words with the letter "e."

PARLEZ-VOUS PENTAGONESE?

The phrases in the left column are actual terms used by the Pentagon (as reported in Williams Lutz's book, The New DoubleSpeak). The words in the right column are plain English. Can you understand Pentagonese well enough to match the military term to its meaning?

Pentagonese

1. "Civilian irregular defense soldiers"

2. "Ambient noncombat personnel"

3. "Interdictional nonsuccumbers"

4. "Force packages"

5. "Visit the site"

6. "Revisit the site"

7. "Accidental delivery of ordnance equipment"

8. "Suppression of assets"

9. "Airborne sanitation"

10. "Disruption"

11. "Area denial weapons"

12. "Sanitizing the area"

13. "Servicing the target"

Real English

A. Bombs

B. Cluster bombs

C. Mercenaries

D. Jamming enemy radar and radio, blowing up anti-aircraft weapons, and shooting down enemy planes

E. Refugees

F. Bombing attack

G. Enemy troops who survive bombing attacks

H. Bombs that miss the target (hitting instead children, hospitals, schools, and so on)

I. Bombing

J. Bombing everything from enemy soldiers to sewage plants

K. Killing the enemy

L. Bomb it

M. Bomb it again

Answers

1. C, 2. E, 3. G, 4. A, 5. L, 6. M, 7. H, 8. D, 9. F, 10. I, 11. B, 12. J, 13. K

Highest price ever paid for a movie prop: $275,000, for 007's Aston Martin from *Goldfinger*.

A CLEAN FIGHT: BATH VS. SHOWER

Which is a better way to stay clean—a bath or a shower? Everyone's got an opinion. This article by Jay Stuller originally appeared in InHealth magazine.

PRE-FIGHT INFORMATION

First, you should know that whatever their chosen method, Americans bathe zealously. A study conducted for the Colgate-Palmolive Company found that women who preferred the tub took an average of 4.5 baths per week, while those who preferred the spray showered 7.5 times each week. Male bathers averaged 3.2 a week; shower-lovers averaged nearly 8.

It's no wonder, then, that in the ranks of nonedible items purchased by grocery store customers, bar soap ranks second, right after toilet paper. We spend more than $700 million annually on the stuff.

CHOOSE YOUR WEAPON

There are, of course, many kinds of soaps. Some contain abrasives, others deodorants, and some, ostensibly, a whiff of springtime in Ireland. But all work the same way to remove the dirt, oil, and bacteria that collect upon the human skin. (The latter is why the unwashed masses are so massively unpleasant—the bacteria feed off the fat in sweat. It's their waste products—bacteria poop, if you will—that make us stink.) Soap is composed of molecules that at one end attract water and at the other end attract oil and dirt, while repelling water. With a kind of pushing and pulling action, the soap loosens the bonds holding dirt to the skin, and lifts it from the body.

"Unless you're using a germicidal soap, it usually doesn't kill the bacteria," says Shyam Gupta, the Dial Corporation's manager for new technology. "For the most part, soap simply removes bacteria along with dirt and oil."

ROUND 1

Rank and fetid armpits notwithstanding, neither baths nor showers are all that necessary for one's physical health.

Or so says University of Pennsylvania dermatologist Albert Kligman. "The skin doesn't give the slightest damn whether or not it's clean," he says. "Unless you're in a Third World country where infectious diseases are common, or you have open sores on your skin, the dirt and bacteria aren't going to hurt. In fact, soap can irritate and sometimes do more damage than good, especially with elderly people who have dry skin. The only reason for showering or bathing is to feel clean and refreshed."

ROUND 2

Baths, on the other hand, have enormous psychological benefits, Kligman insists. "Everyone is in such a hurry with showers. If a person just took an hour every day to listen to nice music, read a book, or do whatever while floating in a tub of water, he or she would be lot better off."

Dedicated bathers know well that shower-takers are missing out on a relaxing ritual, akin to a vodka martini without the liver damage....There is a physiological basis for this relaxed feeling. For one thing, your limbs become slightly bouyant in bathwater, which takes a load off muscles and triggers a drop in muscular tension. Moreover, if the water is hotter than normal body temperature, the body attempts to shed heat by expanding the blood vessels near the surface of the skin. This lessens the circulatory system's resistance to blood flow, and blood pressure gently drops.

(However, when all that blood goes to the skin, it limits the oxygen going to vital organs such as the heart. For this reason, people with heart trouble should take cool or warm baths.)

ROUND 3

In a shower, only part of your body is exposed to hot water, and the rest to cooler air. This temperature disparity, and the fact that you're still on your feet instead of reclining, is likely what makes a shower more invigorating. Indeed, in the Colgate-Palmolive survey, only 58% of the tubbers felt that bathing was "an invigorating experience." But about 75% of the shower-takers felt exhilarated after standing under the nozzle.

ROUND 4

A bath is also the most effective way to hydrate the skin, says Gupta.

"The longer you soak, the more water gets into the skin,"

he says. "And because soap lowers the surface tension of the water, it helps you hydrate more rapidly." The slippery water, in other words, more easily seeps into the skin.

"The big advantage with a bath over a shower is that you can add oils to the water," says Peter Elias, a dermatologist with the University of California at San Francisco. The oil traps all that water you've soaked up.

"But the real key after either a bath or a shower is to partially dry yourself and then seal in the moisture with a cream or ointment that contains a lot of oil, which doesn't have to be expensive to be good." He adds that one should avoid lotions that contain mostly water, which tend to dry the skin.

AND THE WINNER IS...

But back to the core question in the debate: Which method—a bath or a shower—gets you the cleanest? "When you're washing," says Gupta, "you're not only trying to remove dirt and oil, but also flakes of dead skin.

And the best way to remove them is to get your skin extremely hydrated in a tub of water so that the flakes float away." Of course, one can [scrub] the hell out of one's skin in a shower, but Gupta explains that the mechanical process is simply not as effective as a deep soak.

[So] the bath wins.

"But just a minute," Gupta adds. "In a bath, all the dirt and grime and the soap in which it's suspended float on the surface. So when you stand up, it covers your body like a film."

"The real solution," he concludes, "is to take a bath and then rinse off with a shower."

THE REAL CHAMPION

So there you have it—except for one more thing. After leaving a tub or shower, that freshly exposed skin becomes a playground for microbes. In two hours, says Gupta, you probably have as many bacteria on certain parts of the body, such as the armpits, as before the bath or shower—a bunch of little stinkers.

* * *

A POEM TO TOMATO KETCHUP
If you shake the bottle,
None'll come...and then a lot'll.

Chef's tip: Is your soup too salty? Slice up two potatoes and boil them in it for a short time.

BOND...JAMES BOND

Here's a shaken—not stirred—history of the most popular (and profitable)
British secret agent in Hollywood history...and of the former World
War II intelligence officer who brought the character to life.

SPY STORY

Even before World War II started, Great Britain knew it would never be able to patrol the entire northern Atlantic and defend all its ships against the German Navy. But the British also knew that if they could learn the locations of Nazi ships and submarines by deciphering coded German radio communications, they'd be able to reroute convoys of food and weapons around German patrols. In 1939 they launched a massive effort, codenamed Ultra, to do just that.

The Enigma. The Germans sent coded messages using an encryption machine called the "Enigma." By September 1940 the British had managed to put together a working model of the Enigma using parts captured in several raids on German ships. But the Enigma was so sophisticated that even when the British had one in their possession, they couldn't crack the German codes. They needed a copy of the Nazis' special codebook.

FLEMING...IAN FLEMING

How were they going to get one? The wildest suggestion came from the assistant to the Director of Naval Intelligence, a man named Ian Fleming. On September 12, 1940, Fleming wrote the following memo to his boss:

Director of Naval Intelligence:

I suggest we obtain the loot [codebook] by the following means:

1. Obtain from Air Ministry an air-worthy German bomber.

2. Pick a tough crew of five, including a pilot, wireless telegraph operator and a word-perfect [fluent] German speaker. Dress them in German Air Force uniform, add blood and bandages to suit.

3. Crash plane in the Channel after making S.O.S. to rescue service in plain language.

As a boy, young Ian Fleming also gave his mother the nickname "M."

4. Once aboard the rescue boat, shoot German crew, dump over-board, bring rescue boat back to English port.

In order to increase the chances of capturing a small or large minesweeper, with their richer booty, a crash might be staged in mid-[English] Channel. The Germans would presumably employ one of this type for the longer and more hazardous journey.

OPERATION RUTHLESS

The Director of Naval Intelligence passed the plan along to Prime Minister Winston Churchill, who gave it his personal approval. A German twin-engine Heinkell 111, shot down during a raid over Scotland, was restored to flying condition and a crew was recruited to fly it. "Operation Ruthless " was ready to go....But as David Kahn writes in *Seizing the Enigma,*

> In October, Fleming went to Dover to await his chance. None came. Air reconnaissance found no suitable German ships operating at night, and radio reconnaissance likewise found nothing.... The navy awaited favorable circumstances. But they never materialized, and the plan faded away.

Even though Great Britain never did attempt a raid as daring as Fleming proposed, it did manage to capture codebooks from Ger-man ships. By 1943 they were cracking Enigma codes regularly; and by May of that year the Battle of the Atlantic was effectively over.

A NOVEL IDEA

After the war Fleming got out of the intelligence business and be-came an executive with the company that owned the London *Sunday Times.* He never forgot his wartime experiences.

First Person. By 1952 Fleming was in his forties and about to be married for the first time. He was apparently tense at the thought of giving up his batchelorhood, and his future wife suggested he try writing a novel to ease the strain. Fleming had wanted to write a novel for years, so he decided to give it a try. Drawing on his intel-ligence background, he wrote a spy thriller called *Casino Royale* during his two-month winter vacation in Jamaica.

Picking a Name. The book was filled with murders, torture, and lots of action. It was an autobiographical fantasy, the adventures of a British secret agent named James Bond that Fleming—who spent

---

In Italy, James Bond is known as "Mr. Kiss-Kiss-Bang-Bang."

World War II stuck behind a desk in London—wanted to be, but couldn't.

Fleming thought that giving the agent an unexciting name would play off well against the plot. But what name? As Fleming later recounted, he found it "in one of my Jamaican bibles, *Birds of the West Indies* by James Bond, an ornithological classic. I wanted the simplest, dullest, plainest-sounding name that I could find. James Bond seemed perfect."

ON HIS WAY

Casino Royale was published in England in April 1953, and in the U.S. a year later. The book was a critical success, but sales were disappointing. Luckily for Fleming, he took a two-month vacation in Jamaica *every* year, and in each of the next several years he wrote a new Bond novel during his vacation, including *Live and Let Die* (1954), *Moonraker* (1955), and *Diamonds are Forever* (1956).

Live and Let Die became a bestseller in England, and Fleming began building a considerable following in the U.K. But in America, sales remained sluggish for the rest of the 1950s.

Thanks, JFK. The Bond bandwagon got rolling in the U.S. beginning in 1961, when *Life* magazine published a list of President John F. Kennedy's favorite books. Among the scholarly tomes was one work of popular fiction—*From Russia, With Love*. "This literally made Bond in America overnight," Raymond Benson writes in *The James Bond Bedside Companion*. "From then on, sales improved almost immediately....It was good public relations for Kennedy as well—it showed that even a President can enjoy a little 'sex, sadism, and snobbery.' "

How did a little-known Scottish actor named Sean Connery land the role of the most famous secret agent in Hollywood history? The story continues on page 211.

*   *   *

Happy Anniversary! The first push-button phones were installed Nov. 18, 1963. They were put into service between Carnegie and Greensburg, Pennsylvania.

Most types of lipstick contain fish scales as an ingredient.

ALLENISMS

Thoughts from one of America's leading wits, Woody Allen.

"My success has allowed me to strike out with a higher class of women."

"My parents put a live teddy bear in my crib."

"When I was kidnapped, my parents sprang into action. They rented out my room."

"The world is divided into good and bad people. The good ones sleep better... while the bad ones seem to enjoy the working hours much more."

"Life is full of loneliness, misery, and suffering, and it's all over much too soon."

"I do not believe in an afterlife, although I am bringing a change of underwear."

"How is it possible to find meaning in a finite world, given my waist and shoe size?"

"The difference between sex and love is that sex relieves tension and love causes it."

"My parents stayed together for forty years, but that was out of spite."

"Basically my wife was immature. I'd be at home in the bath and she'd come in and sink my boats."

"Don't pay attention to what your schoolteachers tell you. Just see what they look like and that's how you know what life is really going to be like."

"If God would only give me some clear sign. Like making a large deposit in my name in a Swiss bank account."

"Eternal nothingness is fine, if you happen to be dressed for it."

"I think crime pays. The hours are good, you travel a lot."

"It is a gorgeous gold pocket watch. I'm proud of it. My grandfather, on his deathbed, sold me this watch."

TOP-RATED TV SHOWS, 1955–1960

The late 1950s and early 1960s were the heyday of the "adult Western." And take a look at #3 in 1956–1957. That was Ronald Reagan's TV show.

1955-1956

(1) The $64,000 Question
(2) I Love Lucy
(3) The Ed Sullivan Show
(4) Disneyland
(5) The Jack Benny Program
(6) December Bride
(7) You Bet Your Life
(8) Dragnet
(9) I've Got a Secret
(10) General Electric Theater

1956-1957

(1) I Love Lucy
(2) The Ed Sullivan Show
(3) General Electric Theater
(4) The $64,000 Question
(5) December Bride
(6) Alfred Hitchcock Presents
(7) I've Got a Secret
(8) Gunsmoke
(9) The Perry Como Show
(10) The Jack Benny Program

1957-1958

(1) Gunsmoke
(2) The Danny Thomas Show
(3) Tales of Wells Fargo
(4) Have Gun, Will Travel
(5) I've Got a Secret
(6) Wyatt Earp
(7) General Electric Theater
(8) The Restless Gun
(9) December Bride
(10) You Bet Your Life

1958-1959

(1) Gunsmoke
(2) Wagon Train
(3) Have Gun, Will Travel
(4) The Rifleman
(5) The Danny Thomas Show
(6) Maverick
(7) Tales of Wells Fargo
(8) The Real McCoys
(9) I've Got a Secret
(10) Wyatt Earp

1959-1960

(1) Gunsmoke
(2) Wagon Train
(3) Have Gun, Will Travel
(4) The Danny Thomas Show
(5) The Red Skelton Show
(6) Father Knows Best
(7) 77 Sunset Strip
(8) The Price Is Right
(9) Wanted: Dead or Alive
(10) Perry Mason

1960-1961

(1) Gunsmoke
(2) Wagon Train
(3) Have Gun, Will Travel
(4) The Andy Griffith Show
(5) The Real McCoys
(6) Rawhide
(7) Candid Camera
(8) The Untouchables
(9) The Price Is Right
(10) The Jack Benny Program

One big difference between canned and fresh vegetables is salt—there's up to 40 times more in cans.

FORGOTTEN POP HISTORY

Here are a few tidbits of obscure Americana, from the 1941 book Keep Up with the World, *by Freling Foster.*

INSTANT HEIRLOOMS

In 18th-century America, before cameras, portrait painters traveled from town to town with an assortment of pictures of men and women, complete except for the face and hair. People who wanted an oil portrait of themselves merely had to select the body they liked best. The head and features would then be painted in by the artist.

THE CORPSE WOULDN'T TALK

As late as the 17th century, America held "trials by touch," in which the defendant in a murder case was made to touch the corpse. If the accused was guilty, the dead man was supposed to move or to indicate the fact in some other way.

BANANAS IN TINFOIL

Bananas were virtually unknown in this country until 1876, when they were featured at the Philadelphia Centennial Exposition. Wrapped individually in tinfoil, they were sold as novelties at 10¢ apiece.

I GET A WHOLE BED TO MYSELF?

The greatest event in hotel history was the opening of Boston's Tremont House in October 1829. It surpassed every other inn and tavern in size (it had 180 rooms), furnishings, and accommodations. Instead of making four or five people—usually strangers to one another—sleep together in one bed in an unlocked room, the Tremont gave each guest a whole room with a lock on the door and clean linen on the bed. Instead of having to use an outside pump to wash, the guest was supplied with a bowl and a pitcher of water. Moreover, the Tremont was the first to install a device in its rooms to signal the office for service; and it was the first hotel to employ bellboys who, at that time, were known as "rotunda men."

Poll results: 44% of Americans think God is a man; only 1% think God is a woman.

WHY A RABBIT'S FOOT?

Good question. When we were kids, they sold rabbits' feet at the local variety store "for luck." We always wondered how a rabbit's foot could be lucky for us, since it obviously didn't do the rabbit any good. Anyway, one day someone wondered aloud where the idea came from, and we went to our BRI library to look it up. To our surprise, no two books gave the same answer. After a while, we were just looking to see how many "reasons" we could find. Here are some favorites.

ORIGINS AND FIRSTS, by Jacob M. Braude
"The rabbit's foot originated as a good luck symbol in show business, where it was used as a powder puff in makeup, and when lost or misplaced, it might delay a performance...bad luck. Hence the reverse when it wasn't."

SUPERSTITIOUS!, by Willard Heap

"The rabbit is a prolific animal, producing large numbers of off-spring. For that reason, it was thought to possess a creative power superior to other animals, and thus became associated with prosperity and success. If a person carries a rabbit's foot, preferably the left hind foot, good luck is sure to follow. True believers stroke their hands or faces with it, so they will have success in a new venture."

SUPERSTITIOUS? HERE'S WHY, by Julie Forsyth Batchelor and Claudia De Lys

"The first fears and superstitions developed about the European hare....Since most of the habits of these two are alike, superstitions about the hare also apply to the bunny.

"The ancients noticed many things about these timid creatures that they couldn't explain, so they considered them both good and evil. They saw how rabbits came out at night to feed, and how they gathered in bands on clear moonlit nights to play as if influenced by the moon. Another astonishing fact was that northern hares were brown in summer and white in winter.

"But one thing especially impressed primitive man, and that was how the rabbit used his hind legs. There are only two other animals, the greyhound and cheetah, whose rear feet hit the ground in front of the forefeet when running swiftly. Also, rabbits thump the ground with their hind legs as if 'speaking' with them. So their hind feet came to be looked upon as a powerful charm against evil forces."

SUPERSTITIONS, by Peter Lorie

"The idea of a hare's foot as a lucky charm...arose out of the primitive medical belief that the bone of a hare's foot cured gout and cramp, though the bone had to be one with a joint in it intact, to be effective. Carrying a hare's foot bone, with joint, would keep away all forms of rheumatism."

ENCYCLOPEDIA OF SUPERSTITIONS, by Edwin and Mona Radford

"The origin of the superstitions concerning the luck of the rabbit's foot lies in the belief that young rabbits are born with their eyes open, and thus have the power of the Evil Eye, and can shoo away the Evil One."

EXTRAORDINARY ORIGINS OF EVERYDAY THINGS, by Charles Panati

"The rabbit's habit of burrowing lent it an aura of mystery. The Celts, for instance, believed that the animal spent so much time underground because it was in secret communication with the netherworld of numinia. Thus, a rabbit was privy to information humans were denied. And the fact that most animals, including humans, are born with their eyes closed, while rabbits enter the world with eyes open, imbued them with an image of wisdom for the Celts; rabbits witnessed the mysteries of prenatal life. (Actually, the hare is born with open eyes; the rabbit is born blind. And it is the rabbit that burrows; hares live aboveground. Confusion abounded.)"

BUILDING A BETTER SQUIRT GUN

When Uncle John was a kid, he had squirt guns that shot 5 to 10 feet at most, and that was only if you pulled the trigger so hard it hurt. Today, there are water toys that shoot 50 feet or more. Here's the story.

BOY WONDER

Lonnie Johnson loved to tinker. As a kid, he used to take his brothers' and sisters' toys apart to see how they worked. By high school, he'd graduated to mixing rocket fuel in the family kitchen. One year he used scrap motors, jukebox parts, and an old butane tank to create a remote-controlled, programmable robot ...which won first prize in the University of Alabama science fair. Not bad for a kid from the poor side of Mobile, Alabama.

UNDER PRESSURE

Johnson got an engineering degree from Tuskeegee Institute and wound up working at the Jet Propulsion Lab in Pasadena, California. But he still spent his spare time tinkering. He recalls that one evening in 1982, "I was experimenting with inventions that used water instead of freon as a refrigeration fluid. As I was shooting water through a high-pressure nozzle in the bathtub, I thought 'Wow, this would make a neat water pistol.'"

He built a prototype squirt gun out of PVC pipe, plexiglass, and a plastic soda bottle. Then he approached several toy companies...but none of them thought a squirt gun with a 50-foot range would sell. Johnson even looked into manufacturing the toys himself, but couldn't afford the $200,000 molding cost.

BREAKTHROUGH

In March 1989, he went to the International Toy Fair in New York and tried to sell his invention again. This time, the Larami Corporation was interested. They arranged a meeting with Johnson at their headquarters in Philadelphia. When everyone was seated, Johnson opened his suitcase, whipped out his prototype, and shot a burst of water across the entire room. Larami bought the gun on the spot. Within a year, the "Super Soaker" was the bestselling squirt gun in history.

The firefly is the official insect of the state of Pennsylvania.

THE FIRST COMPUTER PROGRAMMERS

Uncle John was sitting in the bathroom, thumbing through the
Wall Street Journal *(surprisingly good bathroom reading, on*
occasion), when he came across this historical tidbit.

This, in brief, is the story of the first computer programmers—
how much they gave to history, [and] how little history gave
back to them....

FOR WOMEN ONLY

The year was 1945. The clacking of adding machines and clouds of
cigarette smoke filled a university-owned row house along Walnut
Street [in Philadelphia]. Inside, dozens of women calculated trajec-
tories to help wartime artillery gunners take aim. Men, the Army
reasoned, lacked the patience for such tedium—a single problem
might require months of work.

The army called the women "computers." One of them, Jean
Bartik, was a 20-year-old math prodigy recruited from the farms of
Missouri. Another, Betty Holberton, was the granddaughter of an
astronomer who spent her childhood steeped in classical literature
and language. The women formed a tight fellowship, drawn together by youth, brains, and the war effort...

THE COMPUTER AGE

One day word spread that the brightest "computers" were needed
to work on a new machine called the Electronic Numerical Inte-
grator and Computer, or *ENIAC*—a steel behemoth, 100 feet long
and 10 feet high, built of 17,480 vacuum tubes in an engineering
building at the University of Pennsylvania. It was the first electronic computer, intended to automate the trajectory calculations the
female computers performed by hand.

Running the ENIAC required setting dozens of dials and plugging a ganglia of heavy black cables into the face of the machine, a
different configuration for every problem. It was this job—
"programming," they came to call it—to which just six of the

young women were assigned: Marlyn Meltzer, Ruth Teitelbaum, Kay Antonelli, and Frances Spence, as well as Ms. Bartik and Ms. Holberton. They had no user's guide. There were no operating systems or computer languages, just hardware and human logic. "The ENIAC," says Bartik, "was a son of a bitch to program."

HOW THEY DID IT

The first task was breaking down complex differential equations into the smallest possible steps. Each of these had to be routed to the proper bank of electronics and performed in sequence.... Every datum and instruction had to reach the correct location in time for the operation that depended on it, to within 1/5,000th of a second.

Yet despite this complexity, the Army brass considered the programming to be clerical work; that it was women stringing the cables only reinforced this notion. Their government-job rating was SP, as in "subprofessional." Initially they were prohibited as security risks even from *entering* the ENIAC room, forcing them to learn the machine from wiring diagrams. When finally admitted, they sometimes had to straighten the clutter of gear the engineers left overnight.

Finally, in February 1946, the scientists were ready for the ENIAC official unveiling. A test problem involving the trajectory of a 155-millimeter shell was handed to Jean Bartik and Betty Holberton for programming. The machine performed flawlessly, calculating the trajectory in less time than it would take the bullet to land. After the demonstration, the men went out for a celebratory dinner. The programmers went home.

LIFE ISN'T FAIR

In the 50 years since, their legacy is confined mainly to Movietone footage and sepia photos—women standing alongside the machine, as if modeling a Frigidaire. Why was history so ungenerous? Partly because in the awe surrounding the machine itself, the hardware was seen as the whole story. In addition, three of the programmers married engineers with top jobs on the ENIAC, making them wives first in the eyes of the history makers and history writers.

A copious, definitive history of the ENIAC, written by the Army ordnance officer who commanded the project, merely lists

Food for thought: In a 1997 survey, 87% of people said they were "likely" to go to heaven.

the programmers' names (misspelling one of them) and identifies which of the engineers they married.

The greater injustice is not history's treatment of the women but its resistance to revision.…[For example,] until [an enthusiastic historian] made an issue of it, most of the programmers had not even been invited to the gala dinner…celebrating the 50th anniversary, of the ENIAC.

*   *   *   *

MOTHERS OF INVENTION

Here are two women you may never have heard of, but who may have affected your life.

Mother of Invention: Kate Gleason, a New York architect in the 1920s.

The Invention: Tract housing

Background: After watching engines being put together on a Cadillac assembly line, Gleason decided to try using mass production techniques to build affordable housing for soldiers who'd returned from World War I. Her first development was "Concrest," a 100-unit concrete housing project. Its six-room homes sold for $4,000 each.

Mother of Invention: Ruth Wakefield, owner of the Toll House Inn and restaurant in Whitman, Massachusetts, in the 1930s.

The Invention: Chocolate chip cookies

Background: One afternoon Wakefield was baking a batch of "chocolate butter drop" cookies for her restaurant. She decided to smash a semisweet chocolate bar into tiny chunks and dump the pieces into the batter, rather than take the time to melt the bar first. She figured the chunks would melt into the batter in the oven, and the cookies would be indistinguishable from her regular ones. She was wrong—and her customers loved the difference. Today Americans consume more than 150 million pounds of chocolate chip cookies every year.

More than half of Americans say they regularly watch TV while eating dinner.

THE BIRTH OF "THE TONIGHT SHOW," PART II

On page 46 we told you the story of "Broadway Open House," the first late-night TV talk show. The show had its problems and was cancelled after 13 months, but it led to "The Tonight Show," the most successful talk show in history. Here's the next installment in the story.

SILENT NIGHT

"Broadway Open House" went off the air on August 24, 1951, and NBC's late-night airwaves remained dark for three years. But Pat Weaver was still convinced that a late-night talk show could be successful. In 1954 he gave it another shot.

This time, rather than create a show himself, he hired comedian Steve Allen, a panelist on the CBS quiz show "What's My Line," to do it for him.

MR. TONIGHT

Allen had been working on his own talk-show format off and on for several years. In the 1940s, he was the midnight disc jockey on L.A.'s CBS radio affiliate. He spent so much time telling jokes between songs—and building a huge following in the process—that the station changed the show's format to live comedy, complete with a studio audience.

Before Allen went on the air, hardly anyone in Los Angeles had listened to radio late at night. But the show quickly became an institution. Big celebrities began dropping by to plug upcoming movies and do interviews.

CBS recognized Allen's promise and brought him to New York, where he briefly hosted a daytime TV show. But CBS didn't have a whole lot more for him to do. He was cooling his heels on "What's My Line" when he got the call from NBC.

"THE TONIGHT SHOW" IS BORN

On September 27, 1954, "The Tonight Show" premiered. Gene Rayburn (who later hosted "Match Game") was the announcer, Steve Lawrence and Eydie Gorme made regular appearances, and

---

The average American spends 1,600 hours a year watching TV, and 323 hours reading.

Skitch Henderson conducted the orchestra—which even then included Doc Severinsen on the trumpet. Don Knotts, Tom Poston, and other comedians performed skits, and Bill Dana, one of Allen's writers, invented his character Jose Jimenez on the show.

JUST PLAIN FOLKS
Allen also had several ordinary—albeit odd—folks who made regular appearances, including Mr. Shafer, a fast-talking farmer from upstate New York; Mrs. Sterling, an elderly woman who pestered Allen for presents; and Professor Voss, a quack who advocated bare-chested walks in the snow and drinking a gallon of water before breakfast each morning.

But the highlight of the show was Steve Allen and his improvisational comedic style. Today ad-lib gags are a staple of late-night talk shows, but in the early 1950s *everything* was scripted in advance—and Allen's make-it-up-as-you-go-along format was revolutionary. He conducted man-on-the-street interviews with pedestrians walking past his studio; he dressed up as a border patrol officer and flagged down motorists to inspect their cars for illegal fruit. A few minutes later he flagged a taxi, threw a salami into the back, and told the driver to take it to Grand Central Station. (He did.)

THANKS, STEVE
Allen's freewheeling style was more like David Letterman's than Johnny Carson's. And the similarity is no accident. Letterman, only seven years old when the first segment of "The Tonight Show" aired, grew up watching the program. Years later, he sent his writers to the Museum of Television and Radio in New York to screen old Steve Allen shows and look for ideas. Steve Allen covered himself in tea bags and was dunked in a huge teacup; David Letterman covered himself in Alka-Seltzer tablets and got dunked in a huge glass of water. Steve Allen jumped in huge vats of Jell-O, so did Dave. Steve Allen sent a camera out the back door and into the street, and then ad-libbed with the people who walked by; Dave did the same, making neighborhood merchants some of the biggest stars of his show.

END OF THE ROAD
As "The Tonight Show" grew in popularity, Allen began to feel

constrained in his late-night hours. He wanted to prove himself in prime time. So NBC created "The Steve Allen Show" in October 1956 and ran it directly against the popular Ed Sullivan's "Toast of the Town" on Sunday night at 8:00 p.m. on CBS.

Allen kept working at "The Tonight Show" three nights a week, with comedian Ernie Kovacs and announcer Bill Wendell (who also announced "Late Night with David Letterman") replacing him on Monday and Tuesday. NBC also cut "The Tonight Show" from 90 to 60 minutes.

By the end of the year, Allen recalls, "I realized I'd bitten off more than I could chew. One show had to go." The choice was simple: "The Tonight Show" had an audience of about 3 million; "The Steve Allen Show" had an audience of 35 million, and paid five times as much. Besides, Allen admits, "in those days none of us connected with 'The Tonight Show' thought it was a big deal at all. It's amazing. It seems a big deal now. It's now part of the national psychological furniture."

"The Tonight Show" went off the air on January 25, 1957. No one knew if it would return.

* * * *

INTERLUDE

In 1956, Pat Weaver had been forced out of NBC. The reason: General David Sarnoff, head of RCA (NBC's parent company), wanted to make his son, Robert, chairman of the network.

When Steve Allen quit "The Tonight Show," the new chairman replaced it with his own idea—"America After Dark," a combination news and entertainment show. It was disaster. Sleepy viewers just couldn't get used to the jarring shifts between light entertainment and hard news reports. "A typical night might have coverage of a new jazz club, followed by a live report from the site of an airplane crash," Ronald Smith writes in *The Fight for Tonight*. "It was as if someone was flicking the dial back and forth between David Letterman and Ted Koppel....At that hour of the night, bewildered viewers simply turned the set off and went to sleep."

Chastened, Robert Sarnoff decided to resurrect "The Tonight Show" with a new host. But who was the right person for the job?

To find out, turn to page 199 for Part III of the story.

DUMB CROOKS

Many Americans are worried about the growing threat of crime, but the good news is that there are plenty of crooks who are their own worst enemies. Want proof? Check out these news reports.

CAREFUL, THIS FINGER'S LOADED

MERCED, Calif.—"A man tried to rob a bank by pointing his finger at a teller, police said.

"Steven Richard King just held up his finger and thumb in plain sight and demanded money. The Bank of America teller told Mr. King to wait, then just walked away. Mr. King then went across the street to another bank...jumped over the counter, and tried to get the key to the cash drawer. But an employee grabbed the key and told him to 'get out of here.'

"Police officers found Mr. King sitting in the shrubs outside the bank and arrested him."

—*New York Times*, April 1997

STRANGE RESEMBLANCE

OROVILLE, Calif.—"Thomas Martin, former manager of a Jack In the Box restaurant, reported that he'd been robbed of $307 as the store was closing. He provided police sketch artist Jack Lee with a detailed description of the suspect. When Lee put his pad down, he observed that the drawing looked just like Martin. When questioned, Martin confessed."

—*Parade* magazine, December 1996

KEYSTONE KROOK

OAKLAND, Calif.—"According to the Alameda County District Attorney's office, in 1995 a man walked into an Oakland bank and handed the teller a note reading: *This is a stikkup. Hand over all yer mony fast.*

"Guessing from this that the guy was no rocket scientist, the teller replied, 'I'll hand over the cash as long as you sign for it. It's a bank policy: All robbers have to sign for their money.'

The Elvis Presley hit "Hound Dog" was written in about ten minutes.

"The would-be robber thought this over, then said, 'I guess that's OK.' And he signed his full name and address.

"That's where the cops found him a few hours later."

—*Jay Leno's Police Blotter*

SHAKE YOUR BOOTIES

WICHITA, Kan.—"Charles Taylor was on trial for robbing a shoe store at knifepoint, accused of taking a pair of tan hiking boots and $69. As he listened to testimony in court, he propped his feet on the defense table. He was wearing a pair of tan boots.

"'I leaned over and stared,' the judge told a reporter later. 'I thought, Surely nobody would be so stupid as to wear the boots he stole to his own trial.' But when an FBI agent called the shoe store, he found out that the stolen boots were size 10, from lot no. 1046 —the same size and lot number as the boots Taylor was wearing. The jury found Taylor guilty, and officers confiscated the boots. 'We sent him back to jail in his stocking feet,' the judge said."

—From wire service reports, March 1997

NEXT WEEK HE'S COMING BACK FOR BRAINS

"In March 1995, a twenty-six-year-old inmate walked away from his community release facility in South Carolina. He was recaptured a week later when he went back to pick up his paycheck."

—*Knuckleheads in the News*, by John Machay

OH, JUST BAG IT

"Not wishing to attract attention to himself, a bank robber in 1969 in Portland, Oregon, wrote all his instructions on a piece of paper rather than shouting.

"'This is a hold-up and I've got a gun,' he wrote and then held the paper up for the cashier to read.

"The bemused bank official waited while he wrote out, 'Put all the money in a paper bag.'

"This message was pushed through the grille. The cashier read it and then wrote on the bottom, 'I don't have a paper bag,' and passed it back. The robber fled."

—*The Book of Heroic Failures*, by Stephen Pile

In his youth, President William Howard Taft was recruited by a professional basketball team.

PRESIDENTIAL INFLUENCE

*Public service is only a part of our presidents' importance to us—
they're also pop icons. Their clothes, their hobbies, and so on,
have an impact on our lives, too. Here are some examples.*

THE ROCKING CHAIR

President: JFK

Influence: Until the 1960s, Americans only thought of rocking chairs as furniture for old folks or porches. Then Kennedy's physician recommended he use a rocking chair whenever possible, for back therapy. In 1961 he was photographed at the White House sitting in an "old-fashioned cane-backed porch rocker." Overnight, the company that made the chair was inundated with orders. Sensing a hot fad, furniture makers started cranking out rockers. B. Altman, a New York department store, even devoted an entire floor to them. The result: rocking chairs became furniture for living rooms.

BROCCOLI

President: George Bush

Influence: In 1992, Bush commented that he didn't like broccoli when he was a kid, and he didn't like it now. "I'm president of the United States," he said, "and I'm not going to eat any more broccoli." The story was reported worldwide. Feigning outrage, a major broccoli producer shipped the White House 10 tons of the veggie. The arrival of the truck was carried *live* by CNN.

Campbell's Soups and *Women's Day* magazine co-sponsored a recipe contest called "How to Get the President to Eat Broccoli." With all the publicity, broccoli sales shot up 40%. "I can't begin to tell you how wonderful this has been for us," a broccoli industry spokesperson said. "The asparagus people were saying they wished Bush had picked on them instead."

PAINT-BY-NUMBERS

President: Dwight D. Eisenhower

Influence: Paint-by-number were already becoming popular when Eisenhower was elected in 1952. He helped turn it into a national

---

President Dwight Eisenhower helped popularize Izod alligator shirts.

craze. As the media reported, Ike loved to paint, but didn't care about originality (his paintings were copied from postcards, photos, etc.) or results ("They're no fun when they're finished," he said). Plus, he couldn't draw—so he often had other artists outline pictures on his canvas. Naturally, he thought paint-by numbers kits were great, and gave them his "official" endorsement in 1953 by handing out sets to his staff as Christmas presents. The craze peaked around 1954, but thanks in part to Ike, they're still with us.

GOING HATLESS
President: JFK

Influence: Believe it or not, kids, in 1960 "respectable" men were still expected to wear hats in public. (Not baseball caps but fedoras—the kind you see in old movies). JFK ignored tradition and usually went hatless. When other men began copying him, there were storms of protest from the fashion industry. The *New York Times*, for example, reported on July 6, 1963:

> A British fashion magazine today stepped up its campaign to persuade President Kennedy to wear a hat and pointedly asked him how a hatless man could properly greet a lady. "How does the president acknowledge such an encounter?" asked *Tailor & Cutter* in an editorial....."The deft touch of a raised hat, politely pinched between thumb and forefinger ...would bring a bright spark of gallantry to modern diplomatic moves."

JFK ignored their entreaties, and the hat industry ultimately bowed to the inevitable.

THE SAXOPHONE
President: Bill Clinton

Influence: When he was running for office, Clinton played his sax on TV—and received a ton of favorable publicity. At his inauguration he did it again, playing "Your Mama Don't Dance." In 1993, the *Wall Street Journal* noted that "thanks in part to President Clinton's willingness to toot his horn on national television, sales of saxophones are way up." Music teachers also reported a big increase in sax students...and CD sales of sax music—from Kenny G to John Coltrane—have been booming.

FASHIONABLE MATERNITY CLOTHES

First Lady: Jacqueline Kennedy

Influence: Before 1960, most pregnant women resigned themselves to staying out of public, and to looking embarrassingly dowdy when they ventured out. In the early 1960s, Jackie Kennedy brought maternity clothes out of the closet. Although she was pregnant, she remained visible in public life, wearing stylish clothes adapted for her. As *Newsweek* commented:

> *Vogue* and *Harper's Bazaar* view [pregnancy] as mere plump frumpery, too impossibly unchic and rarely, if ever, mentionable. But with Jacqueline Kennedy being [as important as she is], the issue can hardly be obscured much longer. Pregnancy is fashionable; at the very least, it is no longer an excuse for looking *un*fashionable.

Clothesmaker Lane Bryant cashed in on the publicity with their new First Lady Maternity Fashion Ensemble. It was a hit, and maternity clothes have never been the same.

MISCELLANEOUS INFLUENCE

• George Bush loved playing horseshoes. During his presidency, sales of the game went up 20%.

• In 1962, *Newsweek* wrote: "When Jackie Kennedy sported Capri pants, women raced to buy them. When Jackie appeared in a roll-brimmed hat, millenary shops were rocked with orders or copies. So it was inevitable that when the president's wife took to wraparound sunglasses, a fad would follow. Indeed, despite a recent White House request that merchants not use the presidential family to push products, many of the fast-selling wraparounds still managed to focus their promotion on the First Lady. A big seller, for example, is the $15 *Jaqui*."

• President Eisenhower helped popularize TV trays. Every night, reporters told the nation, Ike and his wife "eat supper off matching tray-tables in front of a bank of special TV consoles built into one wall of the White House family quarters." Ordinary families followed suit.

• President Kennedy publicized the fact that he had taken the Evelyn Woods speed-reading course. For a time, enrollment at Evelyn Wood—and other courses—boomed.

VIDEO TREASURES

How many times have you found yourself at a video store staring at the thousands of films you've never heard of, wondering which ones are worth watching? It happens to us all the time—so we decided to offer a few recommendations for relatively obscure, quirky videos you might like.

DREAMCHILD (1985) *Drama*
Review: "A poignant story of the autumn years of Alice Hargreaves, the model for Lewis Carroll's *Alice in Wonderland*. Film follows her on a visit to New York in the 1930s, with fantasy sequences by Jim Henson's Creature Shop." *(Video Hound's Golden Movie Retriever) Stars:* Coral Brown, Ian Holm, Peter Gallagher. *Director:* Gavin Millar.

THE STUNT MAN (1980) *Mystery / Suspense*
Review: "Nothing is ever quite what it seems in this fast-paced, superbly crafted film. It's a Chinese puzzle of a movie and, therefore, may not please all viewers. Nevertheless, this directorial tour de force by Richard Rush has ample thrills, chills, suspense, and surprises for those with a taste for something different." *(Video Movie Guide) Stars:* Peter O'Toole, Steve Railsback, Barbara Hershey.

SUGAR CANE ALLEY (1984. French, with subtitles) *Drama*
Review: "Beautifully made drama about an 11-year-old boy and his all-sacrificing grandmother, surviving in a Martinique shantytown in the 1930s. Rich, memorable characterizations; a humanist drama of the highest order." *(Leonard Maltin's Movie & Video Guide) Stars:* Gary Cadenat, Darling Legitimus. *Director:* Edwin L. Marian.

SMILE (1975) *Satire*
Review: "Hilarious, perceptive satire centering around the behind-the-scenes activity at a California 'Young American Miss' beauty pageant, presented as a symbol for the emptiness of American middle-class existence." *(Leonard Maltin's Movie & Video Guide) Stars:* Bruce Dern, Barbara Feldon. *Director:* Michael Ritchie.

It figures: Brain cells are the only human cells that don't reproduce.

WRONG IS RIGHT (1982) *Comedy*

Review: "Sean Connery, as a globe-trotting television reporter, gives what may be the best performance of his career, in this outrageous, thoroughly entertaining end-of-the-world black comedy, written, produced, and directed by Richard Brooks. An updated version of *Network* and *Dr. Strangelove.*" (*Video Movie Guide*) *Stars:* Sean Connery, Robert Conrad. *Director:* Richard Brooks.

MIRACLE MILE (1989) *Thriller*

Review: "A riveting, apocalyptic thriller about a mild-mannered misfit who,...standing on a street corner at 2 a.m., answers a ringing pay phone. The caller...announces that bombs have been launched for an all-out nuclear war....A surreal, wicked farce sadly over looked in theatrical release." (*Video Hound's Golden Movie Retriever*) *Stars:* Anthony Edward, Mare Winningham. *Director:* Steve DeJamatt.

TIME BANDITS (1981) *Fantasy*

Review: "This subversive kid's adventure teams a youngster with a criminally minded pack of dwarves on the run from the Supreme Being through holes in time. A highly imaginative, quirky mix of Monty Python humor, historical swashbuckler, and kid's gee-whiz adventure." (*Seen That, Now What?*) *Stars:* Sean Connery, David Warner. *Director:* Terry Gilliam.

DEFENSE OF THE REALM (1985) *Thriller*

Review: "A British politician is accused of selling secrets to the KGB through his mistress and only a pair of dedicated newspapermen believe he is innocent....They discover a national cover-up conspiracy. An acclaimed, taut thriller." (*Video Hound's Golden Movie Retriever*) *Stars:* Gabriel, Byrne, Greta Scacci. *Director:* David Drury.

NIGHT MOVES (1975) *Mystery*

Review: "While trying to deal with his own sour private life, a P.I. is hired by a fading Hollywood star to track down her reckless daughter, involving him in art smuggling, murder, and sex on Florida's Gulf Coast. This incisive psychological drama manages to be both intelligent and entertaining." (*Seen That, Now What?*) *Stars:* Gene Hackman, Jennifer Warren. *Director:* Arthur Penn.

LITTLE SHOP OF HORRORS

In this chapter, we feeeed you the story of one of the most unlikely—but most popular—cult films of all time.

ALL SET TO GO

A few days after he finished work on a film called A *Bucket of Blood* in 1959, director Roger Corman had lunch with the manager of Producers Studio, the company that rented him office space. The manager mentioned that another company had just finished work on a film, and the sets were still standing.

"I said, just as a joke, 'If you leave the sets up, I'll come in for a couple of days and see if I can just invent a picture, because I have a little bit of money now and some free time," Corman recalled years later. "And he said, 'Fine.' The whole thing was kind of a whim. I booked the studio for a week."

TO B OR NOT TO B

Corman, 32, had only been directing films for five years (*The Monster from the Ocean Floor* and *Attack of the Crab Monsters* were two early titles). But he was already developing a reputation for making profitable movies very quickly on minuscule budgets—a skill that would later earn him the title "King of the B films."

He had filmed A *Bucket of Blood*, a "beatnik-styled horror comedy" in only five days, a personal record. He bet his friend at Producers Studio that he could make this next film in 48 hours.

COMING UP WITH A SCRIPT

Corman called scriptwriter Chuck Griffith, who'd written A *Bucket of Blood*, and told him to write a new variation of the same story. The only limitations: it had to be written for the existing sets, and Corman had to be able to rehearse all of the scenes in three days...and then film them in two.

Griffith took the assignment. He and Corman went bar-hopping to brainstorm an outline for the film. It was a long night: Griffith got drunk, then got into a barroom brawl. Somehow, he and Corman still managed to come up with a story about a nerdy flower shop employee and his man-eating plant.

Rule of thumb: The right rear tire on your car will wear out before the others do.

DEJA VU

Griffith turned in the final script a week later. It was essentially a warmed-over version of *A Bucket of Blood*.

• In *A Bucket of Blood*, a well-meaning sculptor accidentally kills his landlord's cat, then hides the evidence by turning it into a sculpture, which he titles *Dead Cat*. When the sculpture brings him the notoriety he's always sought, he starts killing people and making them into sculptures, too.

  • In *Little Shop of Horrors*, a well-meaning flower shop employee becomes a local hero after he accidentally creates a man-eating plant (which he names *Audrey Jr.*, after his girlfriend) by crossbreeding a Venus flytrap with a buttercup. He then begins killing people to keep the plant—and his fame—alive.

LOW BUDGET

• The filming took place between Christmas and New Year's Eve 1959. Corman spent a total of $23,000 on the film, including $800 for the finished script and $750 for three different models of Audrey Jr.: a 12-inch version, a 6-foot version, and a full-grown 8-foot version.

• Corman pinched pennies wherever he could. Jack Nicholson, 23 years old when Corman hired him to play a masochistic dental patient named Wilbur Force, remembers that Corman wouldn't even spend money making copies of the script: "Roger took the script apart and gave me only the pages for my scenes. That way he could give the rest of the script to another actor or actors."

• Corman also paid a musician named Fred Katz $317.34 for the musical score...but as John McCarty and Mark McGee write in *The Little Shop of Horrors* book,

> Katz simply used the same score he'd written for *A Bucket of Blood*, which has also been used in another Corman film, *The Wasp Woman* and would be used yet again in Corman's *Creature from the Haunted Sea*. Whether or not Corman was aware he was buying the same score three times is unknown.

• Even if a shot wasn't perfect, Corman would use it if he could. In the first day of shooting, Jackie Haze and Jack Nicholson accidentally knocked over the dentist's chair, spoiling the shot and breaking the chair. When the property master said it would take an hour to fix the chair so they could reshoot the scene, Corman changed the script to read, "The scene ends with the dentist's chair falling over."

• Corman was legendary for getting as much work out of his actors and writers as he could. One example: Chuck Griffith, who wrote the script, also played a shadow on a wall, the man who runs out of the dentist's office with his ear bitten, and the thief who robs the flower shop. He also directed the Skid Row exterior shots and provided the voice for Audrey Jr. (Griffith's voice wasn't supposed to make it into the final film—he was just the guy who stood off camera and read the plant's lines so the actors would have something to react to. Corman had planned to dub in another actor's voice later. "But it got laughs," Griffith says, "so Corman decided to leave it the way it was.")

• Corman also saved money by filming all of the Skid Row exteriors actually in Skid Row, and using "real bums to play the bums." Griffith, who directed the scenes, paid them 10¢ per scene, using the change he had in his pocket.

THAT'S A WRAP
• Corman finished all of the interior shots in the required two days, then spent a couple more evenings filming the exterior shots. To this day, *Little Shop of Horrors* is listed in the *Guinness Book of World Records* for "the shortest shooting schedule for a full-length, commercial feature film made without the use of stock footage."

• In its original release, *Little Shop of Horrors* was only a modest success. It didn't develop its cult following until the late 1960s, when it became a Creature Feature classic on late-night TV. It was adapted into an off-Broadway musical in 1982, which was itself adapted into a new $20 million film in 1987.

• "*Little Shop of Horrors* is the film that established me as an underground legend in film circles," Corman says. "People come up to me on the street who have memorized parts of the dialogue. I suppose you could say it was *The Rocky Horror Picture Show* of its time."

PUBLIC PROPOSALS

*Asking someone to marry you used to be a solemn, private matter. No
longer. Now it's a public event, complete with trumpeters, billboards, and
an audience—ranging from a few passersby to hundreds of thousands of
TV viewers. (Incidentally, the answers to these proposals were all "yes"!)*

DAN CAPLIS

Proposed: On television

Story: Caplis and Aimee Sporer worked for Channel 4
news in Denver—he was the legal expert, she was the anchorwom-
an. One night they were sitting next to each other during a broadcast. After explaining how judges decide on criminal sentences,
Caplis looked at the camera and told the audience that since they
were like family, he wanted to share an important moment with
them. He took a ring out of his pocket and put it in front of Sporer.
Choked up, she said, "I would love to marry you," then turned away
from the camera. The quick-thinking cameraman cut for a commercial break.

LOU DROESCH

Proposed: At a city council meeting

Story: Pam Ferris, the city clerk of Louisville, Colorado, was taking
notes at the council meeting when Droesch, a local mortgage banker, went up to the microphone to voice his opinion about an issue.
It wasn't the issue anyone expected. He said: "I'm crazy about your
city clerk. And I ask that the city fathers approve my asking for
her hand in marriage." Then he got down on one knee and popped
the question.

NEIL NATHANSON

Proposed: In a crossword puzzle

Story: Neil and his girlfriend, Leslie Hamilton, liked doing the San
Francisco *Examiner* crossword puzzles together. "One Sunday,"
writes Michael Kernan in *Smithsonian* magazine, "Leslie noticed
that many of the puzzle answers struck close to home.

"State or quarterback" turned out to be MONTANA, which is

Job-search rule of thumb: For every 1,470 resumes an employer receives, 1 person is hired.

where she came from. "Instrument" was CELLO, which she plays. "I was about halfway through the puzzle," she remembers, "when I figured out that a string of letters running across the middle of the puzzle said 'DEAR___ WILL YOU MARRY ME NEIL.'...Sure enough, it was Leslie."

Neil, it turns out, had been working with Merl Reagle, the *Examiner*'s puzzlemaker, for four months. They invited him to the wedding. "I never did finish the puzzle," Leslie added.

JIM BEDERKA
Proposed: During a college graduation ceremony
Story: Paige Griffin was sitting with her class, ready to graduate from Ramapo College in Mahwah, New Jersey, when her boyfriend Jim showed up and asked her to leave the group for a minute. She said no—she didn't want to cause a disturbance. He kept insisting, getting more and more aggravated. Finally she gave in. As she stepped into the aisle, she saw two trumpeters decked in medieval garb standing at the stage. Between them: a sign reading "Paige, will you marry me?" When she accepted, the trumpeters held up a "She said yes" sign; 1,500 people applauded.

MARK STEINES
Proposed: At an AIDS benefit
Story: Leanza Cornett, 1993's Miss America, paused during her performance at the 1994 AIDS mastery Benefit in Los Angeles to select a raffle winner. She stuck her hand in a bag, pulled out a piece of paper, and read: "Let's get married. Wanna? Check the appropriate response: Yes or Yes." She thought it was a joke...until she realized there was a ring attached.

BOB BORNACK
Proposed: On a billboard
Story: In the Chicago suburb of Wood Dale, Bornack put up a billboard that read: "Teri, Please Marry Me! Love, Bob." The sign company immediately got 10 calls from women named Teri who wanted to know if it was "their" Bob. "One Teri called in a total panic because she's dating two Bobs," said an employee. "She didn't know which one to answer." (It wasn't either of them.)

Female spiders spin better webs than males do.

BRAND NAMES

Here are more origins of commercial names.

ADIDAS. Adolph and Rudi Dassler formed Dassler Brothers Shoes in Germany in 1925. After World War II, the partnership broke up, but each brother kept a piece of the shoe business: Rudi called his new company Puma; Adolph, whose nickname was "Adi," renamed the old company after himself—*Adi Dassler.*

PENNZOIL. In the early 1900s, two motor oil companies—Merit Oil and Panama Oil—joined forces and created a brand name they could both use: Pennsoil (short for William Penn's Oil). It didn't work—consumers kept calling it Penn-soil. So in 1914 they changed the *s* to a *z.*

DIAL SOAP. The name refers to a clock or watch dial. The reason: It was the first deodorant soap, and Lever Bros. wanted to suggest that it would prevent B.O. "all around the clock."

WD-40. In the 1950s, the Rocket Chemical Company was working on a product for the aerospace industry that would reduce rust and corrosion by removing moisture from metals. It took them 40 tries to come up with a workable *Water Displacement* formula.

LYSOL. Short for *lye solvent.*

MAZDA. The Zoroastrian god of light.

NISSAN. Derived from the phrase *Nissan snagyo,* which means "Japanese industry."

ISUZU. Japanese for "50 bells."

MAGNAVOX. In 1915 the Commercial Wireless and Development Co. created a speaker that offered the clearest sound of any on the market. They called it the *Magna Vox*—which means *great voice* in Latin.

PRIMETIME PROVERBS

TV comments about everyday life, from Primetime Proverbs, *by Jack Mingo and John Javna.*

ON FIGHTING

Farrah: "A swordsman does not fear death if he dies with honor."
Doctor Who: "Then he's an idiot."
—*Doctor Who*

Student: "What is the best way to deal with force?"
Teacher: "As we prize peace and quiet above victory, there is a simple and preferred method—we run away."
—*Kung Fu*

"If all the men who lived by the gun were laid end to end, I wouldn't be surprised."
—Pappy Maverick, *Maverick*

ON BIG IDEAS

Ralph Kramden (working on a new scheme): "This is the biggest thing I ever got into!"
Alice Kramden: "The biggest thing you ever got into was your pants."
—*The Honeymooners*

"If we ever needed a brain, now is the time!"
—Squiggy Squiggman, *Laverne and Shirley*

ON TV

"Dealing with network executives is like being nibbled to death by ducks."
—Eric Sevareid, *CBS News*

"Imitation is the sincerest form of television."
—Mighty Mouse, *The New Adventures of Mighty Mouse*

ON EDUCATION

School principal: "I'm sure your children will be very happy here."
Gomez: "If we wanted them to be happy, we would've let them stay at home."
—*The Addams Family*

Jane: "Do you like Kipling?"
Jethro: "I don't know—I ain't never kippled."
—*The Beverly Hillbillies*

"You know somethin'? If you couldn't read, you couldn't look up what's on television."
—Beaver, *Leave It to Beaver*

ON SUICIDE

"I don't believe in suicide. It stunts your growth."
—Vila Restal, *Blake's 7*

Among other things, ancient Egyptian embalmers preserved mummies with cinnamon.

THE FIRST LADY

Many Americans don't recall that Eleanor Roosevelt was the first modern first lady (1933-1945) to take an active interest in America's political life, supporting causes and speaking out about issues.

"Courage is more exhilarating than fear, and in the long run it is easier."

"We started from scratch, every American an immigrant who came because he wanted a change. Why are we now afraid to change?"

"For a really healthy development of all the arts, you need an educated audience as well as performers."

"People grow through experience if they meet life honestly and courageously. That is how character is built."

"Every effort must be made in childhood to teach the young to use their own minds. For one thing is sure: If they don't make up their own minds, someone will do it for them."

"It is curious how much more interest can be evoked by a mixture of gossip, romance, and mystery than by facts."

"The important thing is neither your nationality nor the religion you professed, but how your faith translated itself in your life."

"In this world, most of us are motivated by fear— governments more, perhaps, even than individuals."

"Remember always that you have not only the right to be an individual; you have the obligation to be one. You cannot make any useful contribution in life unless you do this."

"The idea of rugged individualism, completely divorced from the public interest, has a heroic sound, a kind of stalwart simplicity. The only trouble is that for many years it has been inapplicable to American life."

"The function of democratic living is not to lower standards, but to raise those that have been too low."

THE INSANE EXPERIMENT

BRI member Ben Brand sent us this article by Ron Perlman, which he found in an old edition of the S.F. Chronicle. It's a little scary—but frankly, isn't this what you always suspected?

LOONEY TUNES

"We cannot distinguish the sane from the insane in psychiatric hospitals," says Dr. David Rosenhan of Stanford University. In fact, he adds, it's the hospitals themselves that might be "insane," rather than the patients confined there.

This is not mere speculation by Rosenhan (a professor both of psychology and law at Stanford). He has just completed one of the most remarkable experiments in the annals of psychological research. He and seven sane colleagues posed as patients worried about their mental health: they were admitted to mental hospitals diagnosed as insane, were treated for periods as long as 52 days, and finally were released—not as cured, but merely as improved, or "in remission," as their doctors said. And during all the time they were being treated—mostly with tranquilizers and only rarely with any psychotherapy—the only people who suspected that they weren't really crazy were some of their fellow patients. Nurses, ward attendants, and psychiatrists never tumbled to the fact that the pseudopatients were at least as sane as they were—and perhaps saner.

A METHOD TO HIS MADNESS

Here is how Rosenhan's experiment worked: He chose his colleagues carefully as being apparently sane in every measurable respect, with no record of past mental problems. Three were professional psychologists, one was a psychiatrist, one a pediatrician, one a well-known, established painter, one a housewife, and one a psychology graduate student.

They obtained appointments at a total of 12 mental hospitals on both the East and West coasts of the United States, using false names and in some cases false professions. All told the same tale of trouble: they had been hearing voices which seemed to be saying "empty" or "hollow" or "thud." This was the only symptom they the pseudopatient's were scrupulously truthful about all other aspects of their lives during interviews and therapy sessions.

As soon as they were admitted to the hospitals, they stopped simulating any symptoms at all, and whenever they were asked they all said they felt fine and that their brief hallucinations were gone. They were cooperative as patients and behaved completely normally. The only symptom they might then have shown was a little nervousness at the possibility of being found out....

Of the eight experimenters, seven were firmly diagnosed as suffering from schizophrenia; one was labeled by doctors as a victim of "manic-depressive psychosis."

OKAY, LET'S TRY IT AGAIN

What may be more remarkable, Rosenhan reported, is what happened at one hospital, which was told about the experiment later but which doubted whether such errors could occur.

To the skeptics Rosenhan proposed another experiment: he told them that more "pseudopatients" would soon be seeking admission to the hospital, and asked the psychiatrists and their staffs to detect the phonies. The hospital staffs took extra pains diagnosing the next 193 patients admitted for psychiatric treatment.

And sure enough, 41 new patients were determined by at least one staff member to be a "pseudopatient"—a sane person posing as insane. Twenty-three patients were judged to be sane by at least one psychiatrist.

But, in fact, Rosenhan reported, none of the 193 patients was actually a pseudopatient at all. It's an open question, he added, whether all the 193 were really insane, and whether the doctors were preening their diagnostic egos by finding some of them sane just because they had been led to expect sane people in the group. "But one thing is certain," he commented. "Any diagnostic process that lends itself so readily to massive errors of this sort cannot be a very reliable one."

WHO'S RUNNING THE ASYLUM?

In the main experiment, Rosenhan related, all eight pseudopatients kept careful daily notes on their treatment and their observations of life in the mental wards. At first they took their notes secretively and hid them, lest staff members become suspicious. But when they found the staff paid no attention to them and never asked them why they were writing, they took their notes openly.

At that point many real patients became suspicious, either because of the note taking or because the pseudopatients behaved so sanely. Many of the real patients challenged them. "You're not crazy," they insisted. "You're a journalist, or a professor. You're checking up on the hospital."

But the staff never tumbled. One nurse, noticing that a pseudopatient was taking regular notes, saw it as a symptom of a crazy compulsion. "Patient engages in writing behavior," she wrote portentously in his chart day after day.

On this point Rosenhan commented dryly, "The fact that the patients often recognized normality when staff did not raises important questions."

*   *   *   *

AND NOW...BEHIND THE TITLE

Here's how a pair of well-known books got their titles.

1984, by George Orwell

Readers assume that Orwell was predicting the year his bleak vision would come true. He wasn't. He was concerned that people would interpret his story as a description of contemporary life. So, to put it into the future, he just transposed the numbers of the year he completed it—1948 became 1984.

GONE WITH THE WIND, by Margaret Mitchell

First the book was called *Pansy*, after the lead character. Then Pansy's name was changed to Scarlett and the title became *Tote the Weary Load*. That didn't last long, either—Mitchell decided on *Tomorrow Is Another Day* (Scarlett's famous line)...then backed away from it when she realized that more than a dozen books in print already started with the word "Tomorrow." Publication was imminent—and she needed a title. Finally, she just picked a line she'd used in the book.

According to the California Medical Association, 87% of pro boxers have brain damage.

TELEVISION HOAXES

A majority of Americans say they get their info and opinions on world events from TV news and documentaries. When you consider how easy it is to fake TV "news," that's a pretty scary thought.

THE TAMARA RAND HOAX

Background: On March 30, 1981 President Ronald Reagan was shot by John Hinkley, Jr. A few days later, KNTV in Las Vegas, ran a segment of the "Dick Maurice and Company" show that had been taped on January 6, 1981—nearly two months earlier.

Incredibly, the tape showed a psychic named Tamara Rand predicting that Reagan would be shot in March or April "by a young, fair-haired man who acted alone" and had the initials "J. H." The prediction-come-true was so amazing that a few days later ABC's "Good Morning America" and NBC's "Today" also broadcast it.

The Truth: An Associated Press reporter noticed that Rand was wearing different rings on her fingers during the assassination segment than on the rest of the show. Her microphone was attached to her shirt a different way, too. The reporter did some investigating…and discovered that the day *after* the assassination, Rand and Maurice had sneaked back to the TV studios wearing the same clothes they'd worn in the first interview, and taped a new one. Then they combined the two videotapes to make it look as if Rand had predicted the assassination.

What Happened: Maurice and Rand admitted the hoax. Maurice was suspended from his show; Rand faded back into obscurity.

BLOOD SPORT

Background: On April 29, 1991, Denver's Channel 4 KCNC News began airing "Bloodsport," a four-part series on Denver's dog-fighting underworld. Exhibit A was an anonymous home video that someone had mailed to KCNC reporter Wendy Bergen. The footage showed dogs working out on treadmills and fighting one another. The story launched a police investigation into illegal dog-fighting in Denver.

The world's oceans have risen an average of six inches in the past 100 years.

The Truth: On May 2, 1991, the broadcasting columnist for the *Rocky Mountain News* reported that the "anonymous home video" was actually footage of a dogfight that had been staged for KCNC. Bergen and her cameraman denied the charge, but a few days later the man who staged the fights agreed to cooperate with the police in exchange for immunity. It turned out that the fights *had* been staged, and that the workout scenes had even been filmed on the cameraman's own treadmill.

As Bob Tamarkin writes in *Rumor Has It,* "After finding out that attending a dogfight was a felony punishable by up to four years in prison, Bergen re-edited the tape to make it look like a home video. She sent it to herself and told executives that it had arrived anonymously."

What Happened: Bergen and her cameraman eventually confessed; both were fired and each was indicted on felony charges. Bergen was found guilty of conspiracy, being an accessory, and one count of dogfighting. She was fined $20,000.

THE PREGNANT MAN OF THE PHILIPPINES

Background: In May 1992 newspapers in the Philippines began running stories about "Carlo," a male nurse who was actually a hermaphrodite—a person born with complete sets of both male and female sexual organs. Carlo claimed he was six months pregnant, and he had a bulging belly to prove it. "I feel proud that I'm going to be the mother of a baby boy," he told reporters. "I'm happy now that I'm really feeling fulfilled like a complete woman." NBC's "Today" picked up the story, and Bryant Gumbel interviewed Carlo on the air.

The Truth: A few days after the "Today" interview, a gynecologist examined Carlo and quickly discovered that 1) he wasn't pregnant; 2) he wasn't a hermaphrodite, and 3) he looked pregnant because he was wearing a fake belly under his shirt. "Carlo" was actually Edwin Bayron, and the pregnancy was part of a scheme to have his gender legally changed to female so that he could marry his male lover, a 21-year-old Army officer, in the Catholic Church.

What Happened: Bayron went underground after the hoax was exposed; Gumbel apologized on the air.

DATELINE NBC

Background: On November 17, 1992, "Dateline NBC" aired a story attacking the safety record of GM trucks that had "sidesaddle" gas tanks. The story included NBC's own crash tests, which showed two of the trucks exploding into flames when hit by another car in a side impact.

The Truth: As a multi-million-dollar lawsuit filed by GM later alleged, NBC had attached tiny model rocket engines to the trucks to make them burst into flames. Furthermore, the lawsuit alleged, "NBC did not disclose that the fire lasted only 15 seconds, that gasoline had leaked from an ill-fitting cap, and that its own correspondent had argued that the tests were unscientific and should not be aired."

What Happened: NBC settled the lawsuit with GM in February 1993 and as part of the settlement, apologized to GM publicly for staging the crash. NBC News president Michael Gartner was fired 21 days later, and the incident became famous as "a video-age symbol of irresponsible journalism."

* * * *

LIFE'S LITTLE IRONIES

• Astronaut Buzz Aldrin's mother's maiden name was *Moon*.

• The only member of the band ZZ Top without a beard has the last name *Beard*.

• On Jan. 4, 1971 George Mellendorf, a soldier in Vietnam, sent Pres. Richard Nixon this letter: "Dear President Nixon: It seems nobody cares if we get our mail. We are lucky to get it twice a week. Sir, someone is not doing their job." It was delivered to Mr. Nixon in Feb. 1978, seven years later.

• On Jan. 2, 1997, famous psychic Jeanne Dixon made this celebrity prediction: "A famous entertainer [will] leave a nation in mourning within weeks." On Jan. 25, three weeks later, she died of a heart attack.

FAMOUS FOR BEING NAKED

We know—this sounds a little off-color. Butt...er...we mean but...it's just another way to look at history.

L ADY GODIVA, wife of Earl Leofric, lord of Coventry, England, in the 1100s

Famous for: Riding horseback through Coventry, covered only by her long blonde hair.

The bare facts: Lady Godiva was upset by the heavy taxes her husband had imposed on poor people in his domain. When she asked him to give the folks a break, he laughingly replied that he'd cut the taxes if *she* would ride through the town naked. To his shock, she agreed. But she requested that townspeople stay indoors and not peek while she rode through the streets. Legend has it that they all complied except for one young man named Tom, who secretly watched through a shutter...which gave us the term "peeping Tom."

ARCHIMEDES (287–212 B.C.), a "classic absent-minded professor" and one of the most brilliant thinkers of the Ancient World

Famous for: Running naked through the streets of ancient Syracuse, screaming "Eureka!"

The bare facts: Archimedes' friend, King Hieron II of Syracuse, Sicily, was suspicious that his new crown wasn't solid gold. Had the goldsmith secretly mixed in silver? He asked Archimedes to find out. As Peter Lafferty recounts in his book, *Archimedes:*

> Archimedes took the crown home and sat looking at it. What was he to do? He weighed the crown. He weighed a piece of pure gold just like the piece the goldsmith had been given. Sure enough, the crown weighed the same as the gold. For many days, he puzzled over the crown. Then one evening,...the answer came to him.
>
> That night, his servants filled his bath to the brim with water. As Archimedes lowered himself into the tub, the water overflowed onto the floor. Suddenly, he gave a shout and jumped out. Forgetting that he was naked, he ran down the street to the palace shouting "Eureka!" ("I have found it!")

A selenologist is someone who studies the moon.

Archimedes, presumably still wearing his birthday suit, explained his discovery to the king: "When an object is placed in water," he said, "it displaces an amount of water equal to its own volume."

To demonstrate, he put the crown in a bowl of water and measured the overflow. Then he put a lump of gold that weighed the same as the crown into the bowl. "The amount of water was measured," writes Lafferty, "and to the King's surprise, the gold had spilled less than the crown." It was proof that the goldsmith really *had* tried to cheat the king. The secret: "Silver is lighter than gold, so to make up the correct weight, extra silver was needed. This meant that the volume of the crown was slightly larger than the gold, so the crown spilled more water."

Archimedes became famous for his discovery. We can only guess what happened to the goldsmith.

RED BUTTONS, popular red-headed actor of the 1940s and 1950s
Famous for: Being the first person ever to appear naked on TV.
The bare facts: In the early 1950s, Red did a guest spot on the "Milton Berle Show," which was broadcast live. One skit featured Berle as a doctor and Buttons as a shy patient who wouldn't disrobe for his exam. Buttons wore a special "breakaway" suit—the coat, shirt, and pants were sewn together so they'd all come off when Berle yanked on the shirt collar. As he explained in *The Hollywood Walk of Shame*:

> When my character refused to get undressed, Milton was supposed to grab my shirt front and rip the entire thing off—and I'd be left standing there in old-fashioned, knee-to-neck one-piece underwear. That was the laugh.
>
> Well, Milton reached for my shirt and accidentally grabbed me *under* the collar. And when he yanked at my breakaway suit, everything came off—including my underwear! We were on live television and there I stood—nude in front of a studio audience and all the people watching at home. When I realized what had happened, I got behind Milton, who was as shocked as I was, but had the presence of mind to announce the next act and have the curtain closed.

Buttons said he turned "as red as my hair."

Poet Henry Wadsworth Longfellow was the first American to have indoor plumbing.

COUNTDOWN TO 2000

You probably still don't know what you're going to be doing when the year 2000 arrives...but some people have had their plans set for decades. Here's a chronological list of what some of the real trailblazers have been busy with over the last 30 or 40 years, compiled by Eric Lefcowitz.

1957: THE FIRST HOTEL RESERVATION.

Inspired by a novel about soldiers who agree to meet at the Waldorf-Astoria hotel in New York if they survive World War II, Jim Hoogerwert and his two best friends decided to meet at the Waldorf on December 31, 1999...and made reservations at the hotel. Hoogerwert, who'll be 56 in 1999, told the *Los Angeles Times* in 1993: "I could never imagine, then, being 56. It seemed so far off."

1963: THE FIRST "YEAR 2000" ORGANIZATION.

The World Association for Celebrating the Year 2000 (WACY) was founded in England. It began when the *Daily Telegraph* published a letter by John Goodman inquiring how people celebrated the year 1000. A clergyman replied that the year 1000 had been filled with apocalyptic fears. Goodman saw a parallel with contemporary life...and decided to form an organization to try to avert nuclear war. He wrote to Khrushchev, Kennedy and other world leaders with a plan to plant trees for the year 2000 rather than make bombs. When his plea was ignored, Goodman began travelling around England, planting "celebration-trees." His motto: "An Un-disaster must be found for the world to think about."

Eventually WACY blossomed into a worldwide foundation with members in 30 countries. Goodman, however, did not live to see the fruits of his labor—he died at age 65 in 1994.

1966: THE FIRST "YEAR 2000" TIME CAPSULE.

The Mutual of New York Insurance Co. buried a time capsule at its Syracuse, New York office building to be opened in 2000.

Justice Department prediction: 1 in 20 babies born today will serve time in prison.

1979: THE FIRST YEAR 2000 PARTY PLANS

Twenty students at Yale University formed the Millennium Society. Their goal: throw the biggest party in history, on December 31, 1999. Through annual Millennium Society Balls, the group planned to finance free public festivals in each of the world's 24 time zones, including celebrations at China's Great Wall, the Taj Mahal, Mount Fuji, the Eiffel Tower, and of course, Times Square.

1982: THE FIRST BIMILLENNIAL ANTHEM

Prince released the song "1999."

1987: THE FIRST COUNTDOWN CLOCK.

In 1987, on the tenth anniversary of the opening of the Pompidou Centre in Paris, President Francois Mitterand inaugurated a countdown clock which displays the number of seconds left till 2000. "A nation must orient its gaze toward the future," Mitterand declared.

1991 FIRST PRIVATE PARTY BOOKED.

Wendy Warren of Portland, Oregon leased the Space Needle, Seattle's landmark after being turned down for six years. For an undisclosed amount, Warren and 14 other families got exclusive use of the Needle beginning at 8 p.m., December 31, 1999. She plans a party of 900 people. "People go *Oh My God! Are you Nuts?*" Warren told the *Seattle Post Intelligencer*, "but I love big parties."

1992: FIRST YEAR 2000 POLL.

The Millennium Poll by Yankelovich Clancy Shulman found that 59% expected to do "the same old thing" on New Year's Eve, 1999.

1993: FIRST EMCEE HIRED.

ABC-TV signed up eternal teenager Dick Clark to host "New Year's Rockin' Eve" in Times Square on December 31, 1999.

1995: FIRST CALENDAR PUBLISHED.

The first-ever calendar of the year 2000 was published as a part of "The Millennium Planner." It invited buyers to "enter in your own millennium resolutions for the beginning of the only change of millennium ever to be experienced by the currently living human race, then sit back and wait for the future to catch up with you."

Back to nature: You can't get athelete's foot if you never wear shoes.

LITTLE THINGS MEAN A LOT

"The devil's in the details," says an old proverb. And in the profits too. The littlest thing can mean big bucks. Here are a few examples.

A MINUS SIGN

The story: In 1962, an Atlas-Agena rocket that was carrying the Mariner 1 satellite into space was launched from Cape Canaveral. Unfortunately, the rocket went off course and ground controllers had to push the self-destruct button. The whole thing exploded. Investigators found that someone had left a minus sign out of the computer program. Cost to U.S. taxpayers: $18.5 million.

A LETTUCE LEAF

The story: In 1993, Delta Airlines was looking for ways to reduce costs to compete in the cutthroat airline industry. They discovered that by just eliminating the decorative piece of lettuce served under the vegetables on in-flight meals, they could save over $1.4 million annually in labor and food costs.

A SHOE

The story: On September 18, 1977, the Tennessee Valley Authority had to close its Knoxville nuclear power plant. The plant stayed shut for 17 days, at a cost of $2.8 million. Cause of the shutdown: "human error." A shoe had fallen into an atomic reactor.

A DECIMAL POINT

The story: In 1870, the government published a table of nutritional values for different foods. According to the charts, spinach had ten times as much iron as other vegetables. Actually, a decimal point had been misplaced; spinach has about the same amount as other veggies. But a popular misconception had already taken hold that spinach promotes strength. Long-term benefit: It ultimately gave us Popeye the Sailor, who's "strong to the finish, 'cause I eats my spinach."

Diamonds have been worth more than pearls for only about a century.

FAMILIAR PHRASES

*Where do these familiar terms and phrases mean? Etymologists
have researched them and come up with these explanations*

WHAT A SUCKER!

Meaning: A pushover, an easy mark for a con.

Origin: Settlers in the New World found a strange fish
that fed along the bottom of rivers and streams. They called it a
sucker. Soon, any fish that resembled it was referred to as a a sucker—and this included so many types of fish that practically any
time someone threw a hook in the water, they caught "a sucker."
Eventually, the term was applied to a person who'd fall for anything.

TO HECKLE SOMEONE

Meaning: To disturb a speaker, jeer at.

Origin: In medieval times, a brush with iron teeth, called a *heckle,*
was used to split and comb the fibers from flax stalks in clothmak-
ing. By the 15th century the word had become a verb meaning "to
scratch with a steel brush" or "to look for weak points."

DIDDLY-SQUAT

Meaning: Very little of something; small change.

Origin: Carnival lingo. Carny barkers referred to nickels and
dimes—the going rate for games of chance—as *"Diddle-e-squat,*
yelling to passers-by: "Step right up…All it costs is diddle-e-squat."

FROM PILLAR TO POST

Meaning: Driven from one difficulty to another.

Origin: The sport of tennis arrived in England in the early 1600s.
It was played in grassy estate courtyards. The gate was at one end of
the court and the mansion was at the other. So a spirited game
would see competitors running back and forth between the pillars
of the mansion to the post of the gate.

Even today, scientists don't completely understand why thrown stones skip across the water.

THE SPIDER DANCE

Here's an interesting little tale about a classic folk dance.

DANCE FEVER
Over the last 2000 years there have been occasional instances of mass hysteria that scientists call "epidemic dancing." Entire towns or provinces will begin a wild, spontaneous dancing, often accompanied by hallucinations.

Perhaps the most serious outbreak took place in July 1374, in the French town of Aix-la-Chapelle. As Frederick Cartwright writes in *Disease and History*,

> The sufferers began to dance uncontrollably in the streets, screaming and foaming at the mouth. Some declared they were immersed in a sea of blood, others claimed to have seen the heavens open to reveal Christ enthroned with the Virgin Mary....Streams of dancers invaded the Low Countries, moved along the Rhine, and appeared throughout Germany....In the later stages, the dancers often appeared to be entirely insensible to pain, a symptom of hysteria.

Today, scientists and historians speculate the dancing was caused by eating rye bread contaminated with "ergot," a fungus that infects bread cereals. One of the chemical compounds created by ergot is lysergic acid diethylamide—LSD. So the dancers were essentially high on LSD. And long after the effects of the drug had worn off, mass hysteria kept them going.

We know about the hallucinogenic effects of LSD today...but until a few decades ago, no one had any idea what caused the mysterious outbreaks. In the 16th century, when a similar incident took place near Taranto, Italy, the townspeople blamed the *tarantula*, a local spider named after the town.

The tarantula was known for its painful bite, which was thought to be deadly. So when the dancers survived, the Tarantans were surprised. "In due course," John Ayto notes in *The Dictionary of Word Origins*, "the dancing came to be rationalized as a method of counteracting the effects of the spider's bite, and so the dance was named the *tarantella*."

Italians don't dance away their spider bites anymore, but they still have a lively folk dance called the *tarantella*.

UNLUCKY STARS

They had successful acting careers...but might have been even more successful if it hadn't been for one single decision. Here are some stories about "the one that got away."

BUDDY EBSEN
Background: Ebsen eventually became famous as Jed Clampett in the 1962–71 sitcom "The Beverly Hillbillies." But in the 1930s, he was an up-and-coming young singer/dancer.

The Story: After appearing in several films as an MGM contract player, Ebsen got his big break in 1938 when he got the part of the Scarecrow in *The Wizard of Oz*. But Ray Bolger, cast as the Tin Man, was determined to play the Scarecrow instead. He launched a relentless campaign for the part...and Ebsen, tired of saying no, finally agreed to swap roles.

It was a costly decision. The make-up department was using aluminum powder to make the Tin Man's face look metallic; Ebsen developed a severe allergy to it. Nine days after the film went into production, Ebsen wound up in an oxygen tent at Good Samaritan Hospital; he'd inhaled so much of the powder that his lungs were coated with aluminum. Unsympathetic studio execs kept calling the hospital, wondering when he was coming back to work. Finally director Mervyn LeRoy simply hired another actor (Jack Haley) to play the Tin Man.

Ebsen recovered from the aluminum allergy in a few weeks. His career didn't bounce back as fast, though. He appeared in a handful of movies in the 1940s, but didn't make a real impression until 1955, when he played Davy Crockett's sidekick in Disney's *Davy Crockett, King of the Wild Frontier*. He became a TV star in the "Hillbillies" in 1962, but never made it big in the movies.

ELVIS PRESLEY
Background: Elvis left a legacy of about 30 movies, most of them inane formula films like *Harum Scarum* and *Tickle Me*. But at the end of his career, the King came close to doing something really special onscreen.

The Story: In Joe Esposito's book *Good Rockin' Tonight*, he reveals that in 1974, Barbra Streisand offered Elvis "the kind of part he'd dreamed of." Elvis was performing at the Las Vegas Hilton. After the show, Streisand and her boyfriend Jon Peters (then a well-known Hollywood hairdresser) visited him backstage.

> "Elvis, can we go someplace where we can talk in private?" she asked. "I have something I would like to tell you about." I suggested the room next to his dressing room, where Elvis rested between shows. Elvis asked me to come in with them. Barbra and Jon sat on the two chairs, Elvis on the bed, and I sat on the floor....
>
> Barbra explained the purpose of her visit.
>
> "Elvis, I bought the rights to the Judy Garland movie, *A Star Is Born*," she said. "I'm going to remake it, and I thought you might be interested in starring in it with me." Elvis hadn't been interested in making movies for a long time, but Barbra explained the entire story. Two hours later, he was hooked.
>
> "I'll have to think about it. [My agent], the Colonel, will get back to you," he told her before she left. But to the guys he was more enthusiastic. "I'm going to do it!" he vowed.

It never happened. First, Presley's pals suggested that since Peters was going to produce the film, he'd make sure it showcased Barbra—not Elvis. Then they pointed out that Elvis and Barbra might have a hard time getting along. Elvis was shaken. He called his manager, Colonel Tom Parker, the next night and said he wanted to do the film—but had a few reservations. "Colonel, you think I'm going to take orders from that hairdresser?" he asked.

> "I've got news for you, the Colonel said. "I guarantee that they'll turn the contract down because I'm going to request that you get top billing."
>
> A few days later, the Colonel reported back to Elvis. He'd asked for top billing. "That took care of that," the Colonel said. Streisand and Peters never even responded to his offer.

Elvis, who never made another film, lost what *he* described as "an opportunity parallel to Frank Sinatra's performance in *Here to Eternity*." That performance won Sinatra an Oscar in 1954 and revived his sagging career. Who knows? If Elvis had made the film, it might have turned his life around.

BURT WARD

Background: In 1966 Ward was playing Robin on ABC's phenomenally popular TV series, "Batman" (produced by 20th Century Fox). He was one of the hottest properties in the country—quoted, copied, and mobbed by fans wherever he went—and he was ready to break into the movies.

The Story: "My agents submitted me to Larry Turman, a talented producer who was getting ready to produce *The Graduate* for Fox," Ward wrote in his autobiography, *Boy Wonder: My Life in Tights.*

> I met with Larry and he told me that he wanted me for the lead role in his upcoming movie. The timing was perfect. The film was set to shoot during my hiatus from "Batman." Wow, was I ever excited.
>
> Unfortunately, not only did Fox not want me to work for any other studio, but they refused to let me star in Larry's film. I was told that "Batman" was such an important series to Fox that they didn't want any dilution of Robin's character by having the same actor portray a movie role whose character wasn't the Boy Wonder.
>
> At the time, I was sad and disappointed. When the movie was released and made a superstar out of the actor who replaced me—[Dustin Hoffman]—I wanted to jump off a building without my Batrope.

"Batman" went off the air about a year after *The Graduate* was filmed. Dustin Hoffman became one of America's best-known actors; Ward quickly faded from sight. "Over the course of the last 20 years," he writes, "I have run into Larry three times. Each time he said the same thing: 'Burt, I wanted you for that role.' I WANTED THAT ROLE! Pardon me while I scream."

TOM SELLECK

Could Have Starred In: *Raiders of the Lost Ark* (1981)

Background: After years of bouncing around Hollywood, Selleck got his break as a guest on "The Rockford Files" in the 1979-80 TV season. He was brought back for several episodes "by popular demand." But as the season ended, "Rockford" star James Garner quit. That left CBS with a hole in its schedule where a successful detective program had been...and a distaste for unmanageable "big stars." The network also had an empty studio in Hawaii, since the long-running "Hawaii Five-O" had just ended. CBS's solution "Magnum, P.I."—a detective show based in Hawaii, starring newcomer Tom Selleck. It was scheduled for the 1980-81 season.

Story: As Cheryl Moch and Vincent Virga describe it in their book *Deals:*

> Then the actor's dream became the actor's nightmare. [He was of-
> fered] two sensational jobs at once. Steven Spielberg and George Lu-
> cas cast him [as Indiana Jones] in *Raiders of the Lost Ark.* They want-
> ed a new face. They asked CBS to postpone "Magnum"...*Ark* would
> most likely make Selleck a superstar, a big plus for any aspiring TV
> series. Selleck held his breath when he wasn't praying.
>
> CBS refused, fearful of losing the already announced "Magnum"
> idea to a competitor and worried about the demands superstars
> make. The two jobs conflicted and Selleck belonged to CBS. He
> packed for Hawaii. As it happened, an actor's strike delayed [the
> "*Magnum*"] production for three months. *Raiders*, shooting abroad,
> was exempt. "I could have gone to Europe and Africa," Selleck said
> with a sigh, "done *Raiders*, then come back to Hawaii to do
> "Magnum."

"Magnum" ran for eight years and made Selleck famous, but he
never really made it as a movie star. *Raiders of the Lost Ark*, starring
Harrison Ford, became one of the top-grossing films of all time and
helped establish Ford as the biggest box office attraction in history.

* * *

RANDOM INFO: FIVE FOOD FLOPS

1. Cold Snap. An imitation ice cream mix introduced by Procter
& Gamble in the 1960s."It had the taste of cold Crisco, took hours
to prepare, and had directions similar to a model airplane."

2. Prest-O-Wine. Like alcoholic Kool-Aid. Just add sugar and water to a purple powder (secret ingredient: yeast), and wait a month.

3. Square Eggs. Introduced in In 1989, a French company called
Ov'Action, Inc. "Fully cooked, reconstituted egg cubes," 2/3"
square. Had a 21-day shelf life and could be microwaved.

4. Spudka. A vodka-like beverage from Idaho potato-growers.

5. Whisp Spray Vermouth. "Good news for martini-drinkers"—
vermouth in an aerosol spray container. Also recommended as a
seasoning "for fresh fruit, meat, and seafood!"

TOP-RATED TV SHOWS, 1961–1966

More of the annual Top 10 TV shows of the past 50 years.

1961-1962
(1) Wagon Train
(2) Bonanza
(3) Gunsmoke
(4) Hazel
(5) Perry Mason
(6) The Red Skelton Show
(7) The Andy Griffith Show
(8) The Danny Thomas Show
(9) Dr. Kildare
(10) Candid Camera

1962-1963
(1) The Beverly Hillbillies
(2) Candid Camera
(3) The Red Skelton Show
(4) Bonanza
(5) The Lucy Show
(6) The Andy Griffith Show
(7) Ben Casey
(8) The Danny Thomas Show
(9) The Dick Van Dyke Show
(10) Gunsmoke

1963-1964
(1) The Beverly Hillbillies
(2) Bonanza
(3) The Dick Van Dyke Show
(4) Petticoat Junction
(5) The Andy Griffith Show
(6) The Lucy Show
(7) Candid Camera
(8) The Ed Sullivan Show
(9) The Danny Thomas Show
(10) My Favorite Martian

1964-1965
(1) Bonanza
(2) Bewitched
(3) Gomer Pyle, U.S.M.C.
(4) The Andy Griffith Show
(5) The Fugitive
(6) The Red Skelton Hour
(7) The Dick Van Dyke Show
(8) The Lucy Show
(9) Peyton Place (II)
(10) Combat

1965-1966
(1) Bonanza
(2) Gomer Pyle, U.S.M.C.
(3) The Lucy Show
(4) The Red Skelton Hour
(5) Batman (II)
(6) The Andy Griffith Show
(7) Bewitched
(8) The Beverly Hillbillies
(9) Hogan's Heroes
(10) Batman (I)

1966-1967
(1) Bonanza
(2) The Red Skelton Hour
(3) The Andy Griffith Show
(4) The Lucy Show
(5) The Jackie Gleason Show
(6) Green Acres
(7) Daktari
(8) Bewitched
(9) The Beverly Hillbillies
(10) Gomer Pyle, U.S.M.C.

Season's greetings: Americans sent about 2.6 *billion* Christmas cards in 1996.

YOU SHOULD NEVER...

A *few pearls of wisdom from 599* Things You
Should Never Do, *edited by Ed Morrow.*

"Never argue with an idiot—folks might not be able to tell the difference. "

—*Anonymous*

"Never believe anything until it's been officially denied."

—*Antony Jay*

"Never sell the sheep's hide when you can sell the wool."

—*German adage*

"Never say 'that was before your time,' because the last full moon was before their time."

—*Bill Cosby*
(on talking to children)

"Never cut what you can untie."

—*Joseph Joubert*

"Never slap a man who chews tobacco."

—*Willard Scott*

"Never be flippantly rude to elderly strangers in foreign hotels. They always turn out to be the King of Sweden."

—*Hector Hugh Munro*

"Never whisper to the deaf or wink at the blind."

—*Slovenian adage*

"Never test the depth of a river with both feet."

—*African adage*

"Never fight an inanimate object."

—*P. J. O'Rourke*

" Never think you've seen the last of anything. "

—*Eudora Welty*

"Never eat anything whose listed ingredients cover more than a third of the package."

—*Joseph Leonard*

"Never play leapfrog with a unicorn."

—*American adage*

"Never try to outsmart a woman, unless you are another woman."

—*William Lyon Phelps*

"Never judge a book by its movie."

— *J. W. Eagan*

Ouch! There are 1,000 barbs in a single porcupine quill.

JAPAN'S SPACE-AGE TOILETS

We've come a long way from the outhouse. This article, by Mary Jordan and Kevin Sullivan, first appeared in the Washington Post.

AN EMBARRASSING MOMENT

TOKYO—An American diplomat was at a dinner party in a Japanese home when he excused himself to go to the bathroom. He did his business, stood up, and realized he didn't have a clue about how to flush the toilet

The diplomat speaks Japanese, but he was still baffled by the colorful array of buttons on the complicated keypad on the toilet. So he just started pushing. He hit the noisemaker button that makes a flushing sound to mask any noise you might be making in the john. He hit the button that starts the blower for your bottom. Then he hit the bidet button and watched helplessly as a little plastic arm, sort of a gun shaped like a toothbrush, appeared from the back of the bowl and began shooting a stream of warm water across the room and onto the mirror.

And that's how one of America's promising young Foreign Service officers ended up frantically wiping down a Japanese bathroom with a wad of toilet paper.

"It was one of my most embarrassing experiences in Japan," said the embassy employee, who diplomatically asked not to be identified.

TOILET TECHNOLOGY

Forget that you need to know three alphabets to read a Japanese newspaper. Forget that the new fashion in Tokyo is women gluing their bras in place. Forget horse sushi. The most puzzling thing for many foreigners here is Japanese toilets.

Just as many foreigners had finally mastered the traditional Japanese "squatter" with no seat, they are being confused anew by the latest generation of Japanese toilets—super-high-tech sit-down models with a control panel that looks like the cockpit of a plane.

Japan is the world leader in high-tech toilets, and its biggest toilet company, Toto, is working on a *itijine* model that will chemically analyze urine. Already selling well are toilets that clean themselves, have coatings that resist germs and spray pulsating water to massage your backside.

A LUXURY...OR A HAZARD?

The toilets basically look like a standard American model, except for the control pad, which sometimes comes with a digital clock to tell you how long you've been in the bathroom. Some of the buttons control the temperature of the water squirted onto your backside. The bottom-washer function, combined with the bottom blower, is designed to do away with the need for toilet tissue. Other buttons automatically open and close the lid; the button for men lifts lid and seat; the button for women lifts the lid only. Some toilets even have a hand-held remote control: a clicker for the loo.

Many foreigners say once you get used to these toilets—which cost $2,000 to $4,000—it's hard to do without them, especially the automatic seat warmer. Harry Sweeney, an Irishman who raises horses on Japan's cold north island of Hokkaido, said he knows a man who drives a mile and a half out of his way each morning to use a public toilet with a heated seat. "It gets very cold up here in the winter; those heated seats aren't a luxury, they're a necessity," Sweeney said. But some people never get the hang of it—they find themselves panicked, trapped in stalls, unable to figure out how to flush. Worse, they find themselves stranded on the toilet, unsure how to shut off the spraying bidet and unable to get up without soaking themselves and the bathroom.

DO YOUR BUSINESS, TOTO

Toto sells about $400 million worth of high-tech Washlet toilets a year, and they estimate they have only half the market here.

They have expanded that market with the Travel Washlet, a portable hand-held bottom washer. Going on a trip where they might not have top-of-the-line toilets? No problem: Just fill your Travel Washlet with warm water at home. Then after nature calls on the road, unfold the little squirt-nozzle and wash your behind just like at home. At $100 each, Toto has sold 180,000 of these gizmos in the last two years.

Horses don't breath through their mouths.

Toto now wants a piece of the U.S. market. So it is starting with a less expensive, less complicated model. The U.S. Toto is a $600 seat, lid, and control panel that attaches to a regular American toilet bowl. It features a heated seat, the bottom washer and a deodorizing fan that "breaks down odorous molecules and returns clean air to the bathroom environment," according to Toto literature.

TOILET SWEET TOILET

Toto has gone to great lengths to make its toilets, bathtubs, and other products user-friendly. Thousands of people have collected data on the best features of a toilet, and at the company's "engineering laboratory," volunteers sit in a Toto bathtub with electrodes strapped to their skull, to measure brain waves and "the effects of bathing on the human body."

A Toto spokesperson said the toilets are also popular because they make the bathroom a place where people want to spend relaxed time. Japanese homes are generally so small that the bathroom is often the only place where someone can be alone, he said. "Particularly middle-aged salarymen have no personal space in their lives. So especially for them, bathrooms can be the only place where privacy is guaranteed."

Tom Quinn, a Californian who does play-by-play analysis of sumo matches on Japanese television, said he has a high-tech toilet at home but wishes he had a plain old American one. "I don't like anything startling in the bathroom," he said. "I don't want rocket controls on my toilet."

*　　*　　*　　*

LIFE'S LITTLE IRONIES

• In 1978 Saudi Arabia had to import five tons of sand from Holland (for use in swimming pool filters).

• Mel Blanc, the voice of Bugs Bunny, was allergic to carrots.

• "Eric II, King of Denmark, died in 1104. He was known as Eric the memorable"…but no one can remember why."

Artichokes are flowers.

CLASSIC RUMORS

Some rumors have been around so long that they deserve a special place in the annals of gossip. Have you heard any of these?

ORIGIN: Mid-1940s.

RUMOR: The Harvard School of Medicine will buy your body for $500. All you have to do is let them tattoo the words "Property of Harvard Medical School" on the bottom of your feet. When you die, your body will be shipped C.O.D. to Harvard.

HOW IT SPREAD: By word of mouth, back when $500 was a lot of money.

THE TRUTH: Harvard says it has never paid people for their bodies, and only accepts donations from people who specify in their wills that they want their bodies to go to the school. Even then, surviving relatives have to agree with the bequest. To this day, the school receives several calls a week asking about the program.

ORIGIN: The 1950s, heyday of big hair.

RUMOR: A teenager got a beehive hairdo, and liked it so much that she didn't wash it out—not even after a couple of weeks. She sprayed it every morning with hair spray...and suddenly one morning got a terrible stabbing pain on the top of her head. She went to the doctor, who found a black widow that had stung the woman on her scalp. She died from the sting a few days later.

THE TRUTH: This story changes with fashion trends. In the 1960s, it was a mouse that tunneled into the brain of a "dirty hippie"; in the 1970s, a man died on the floor of a disco when the cucumber he stuffed down the front of his tight pants cut off circulation to his legs. Most versions have two morals: 1) bathe regularly; and 2) avoid loony fashion fads.

ERA: The 1970s, during the energy crisis

RUMOR: The oil companies have a pill that can make a car go 100 miles on one gallon of gas. But they're sitting on it to keep gasoline sales high. (Similar stories abounded about super-carburetors and experimental cars that went 1,000 miles on a gallon of gas.)

Einstein couldn't read until the age of nine.

HOW IT SPREAD: Word of mouth, perhaps as an explanation for the fuel crisis, and/or a manifestation of public fear and suspicion of huge corporations.

THE TRUTH: Oil companies scoff at the idea, and no one has ever produced a shred of evidence. The story can be traced to an old gas station con, when hucksters would pull into a gas station, fill a fake gasoline tank with water, and then convince the gas station owner that the car ran on water and a magic pill. The con man then sold the owner a jar of the pills for all the cash he had.

ORIGIN: Late 1930s.

RUMOR: If the wrapper of your Tootsie Roll Pop has a picture of the Indian aiming his bow and arrow at a star (called "Shooting Star" by the company) on it, you can send it in for a free bag of candies.

HOW IT SPREAD: From one kid to another since the Tootsie Roll Pop was introduced in 1936.

THE TRUTH: The Tootsie Roll Company has never redeemed an Indian wrapper for bags of candy. Even if it wanted to, it couldn't afford to, since nearly half of all Tootsie Roll Pops have the Indian on the label. The company responds to such requests with a legend of its own: in a special form letter, it explains that Shooting Star is the one who invented the process of putting the Tootsie Pop inside the lollipop. Every once in a while, Shooting Star returns to the factory and inspects the candy to make sure the company is following his instructions. The Indian on the wrapper is Shooting Star's seal of approval: it shows that he has personally inspected that piece of candy himself.

ORIGIN: The 1960s

RUMOR: It's against the law to kill a praying mantis. If you're caught, you can be fined.

THE TRUTH: Praying mantises are good for gardens, but there's no law protecting them—they're not endangered. (In fact, this rumor predated the Endangered Species Act by many years.) The tale was probably invented years ago by a gardener trying to keep kids from destroying the weird-looking, but beneficial, bugs.

If an octopus is hungry enough, it will eat its own arms.

ALIAS "ALAN SMITHEE"

Next time you're thinking about seeing a movie, check to see who the director is. If it's Alan Smithee, you might just want to reconsider. Here's why.

WHO IS THIS GUY?

He has directed westerns, sci-fi epics, thrillers, even a comedy set in Australia (*The Shrimp on the Barbie*). His range seems boundless. His name is Alan (sometimes Allen) Smithee, he makes lousy movies, and he does not exist.

The name is a pseudonym regularly used in Tinseltown by directors who wish to disown their work, usually because the studio has tampered with it in the cutting room and altered it beyond recognition.

BIRTH OF AN ICON

"Alan Smithee" dates from 1969, when Don Siegel was brought in to replace Robert Totten as director of *Death of a Gunfighter*, which had already been in production for 25 days. In the end, neither director was happy with the result so they approached the Directors Guild of America, the filmmakers' trade union, seeking a way to dissociate themselves from it. The guild ruled that the fictitious Alan Smithee should be created to shoulder the blame for this film ...and for similar foul-ups in the future.

The invention of the name is credited to John Rich, an Emmy-winning television director. His first choice was "Smith," but this was rejected on the grounds that sooner or later there would be a real director of that name. Adding an "e" was also considered but rejected as an affectation...until Mr. Rich hit upon the notion of doubling it, and changing the pronunciation. "Alan" was chosen because it is short and comes at the beginning of the alphabet.

A PROLIFIC CAREER

Despite an unpromising start, Alan Smithee proved more gifted than anybody originally dreamed. When *Death of a Gunfighter* opened in America, critics praised the director's sensitivity, adding that this was only to be expected from a man who had served a

---

A *puwo* is an animal that's a cross between a poodle and a wolf.

long apprenticeship with the veteran John Ford.

He has been a prolific filmmaker. In the past 25 years he has taken director's credit for some 30 films and television plays, sometimes in lieu of well-known names. *Catchfire* (1991), with Jodie Foster, Charlie Sheen, and Bob Dylan, was an Alan Smithee production—but for only the100-minute version. The original 180-minute film, which was never released, carried the name of Dennis Hopper.

When David Lynch's sci-fi saga *Dune* was shown in cinemas, it ran for 140 minutes. For still unsated television viewers in America, a special edition was prepared running 50 minutes longer and incorporating substandard material that had been axed from the original. As a way of registering his disapproval, Lynch promptly invoked the Alan Smithee convention.

POPULAR NAME

Other filmmakers who have used the name include John Frankenheimer, the director of *The Manchurian Candidate*, who opted for it on the television movie *Riviera* (1987); Stuart Rosenberg (who made *Cool Hand Luke* but not—officially—*Let's Get Harry*); and even Jud Taylor, a former president of the Directors Guild, who in 1970 sulked as Alan Smithee rather than let the world know he had made the Burt Reynolds film *Fade-in*. One director has used the name twice. Rob Holcomb passed the buck for a made-for-television comedy, "Moonlight" (1982), to the hapless Smithee and did so again in 1985 with "Stitches."

In fact, Smithee is a man of many talents. Besides making films, he is a gifted journalist and linguist. In 1985, he helped Anne Thompson with the research for a dictionary of Hollywood slang and in the same year popped up in the Dutch-language magazine *Skoop* with an article on Freud in Disneyland. And although Smithee will never win an Oscar, he moves in charmed circles. His cousin George Spelvin is in the same line of business—an actor who wants to remain anonymous can hide behind this name. Strenuous efforts, however, are being made to suppress information about his sister, Georgina Spelvin, last seen impersonating future stars in porno pictures.

THE RESURRECTION OF ELVIS

Since his death in 1977, Elvis's popularity has grown. Once he was just a singer. Now he's an icon with his own church (the Church of Elvis), and his own holy site (Graceland). It's an amazing phenomenon—but it hasn't been entirely accidental. Behind the scenes, a handful of people have orchestrated Elvis's return from the dead for their own benefit. Here's part of the inside story. For a more complete story, we recommend Elvis, Inc., by Sean O'Neal. It's entertaining bathroom reading.

BACK FROM THE DEAD

B Ironically, the tale of Elvis's resurrection begins with the story of a vampire.

In 1960 Universal Studios dusted off a number of its classic horror films and released them for TV broadcast. It was the first time baby boom kids had ever seen the original *Frankenstein* (starring Boris Karloff), *The Wolfman* (starring Lon Chaney) or *Dracula* (starring Bela Lugosi)—and the films were phenomenally popular. In fact, a huge "monster" fad swept America...and Universal cashed in by licensing its characters for T-shirts, posters, lunch boxes, etc. One of the most popular images was Bela Lugosi in his Count Dracula costume.

Courting Universal

When Lugosi's widow and son found out about the merchandising deals, they filed suit to block them. Their argument: Lugosi's name and likeness should be passed on to his family, as his worldly assets had been. At the very least, they had a right to share in the profits.

The Lugosis won their lawsuit. But Universal appealed the decision. The second time around, appellate judges reasoned that if the names and likenesses of famous people could be inherited, the relatives of all public figures—past and present—could sue for royalties. Even George Washington's descendants could charge the federal government for the right to use his image on the $1 bill. The judges ruled in favor of Universal.

Boris Yeltsin's favorite Elvis song: "Are You Lonesome Tonight?"

Laurel and Hardy

In 1975, after Laurel and Hardy's old films became popular on TV, the heirs of Stan Laurel and Oliver Hardy filed a similar lawsuit against the Hal Roach Studios. This time, the *heirs* won, throwing the entire issue of posthumous "intellectual property" into chaos.

Based on legal decisions, it was impossible to tell who owned the rights to a dead celebrity's image—the public…or the celebrity's family.

ELVIS PRESLEY

That was the situation when Elvis died from a drug overdose on August 16, 1977. His death was announced at 3:30 that afternoon; within a few hours, newspapers were speculating about his estate's value.

The media figured the King *had* to be worth a bundle: in his more than 20 years as a performer, he'd recorded 144 Top 40 songs, starred in more than 30 films (at one point he was the highest-paid actor in Hollywood), performed in hundreds of sold-out concerts, and sold more than *600 million* records. No other recording artist had ever even come close to his accomplishments.

Estimates of Presley's fortune were as high as $150 million. (When John Lennon was assassinated three years later, he left an estate valued at more than $200 million). But they were way off.

The Awful Truth

What the media failed to take into account was that Elvis was one of the most poorly managed and morbidly self-indulgent superstars in entertainment history. True, he had generated more than $4 billion in revenues during his career. But surprisingly little of the money found its way into his pockets—and even less stayed there.

Bad management and bad financial advice ate up about 60¢ of every dollar Elvis earned; letting the IRS fill out his tax forms (he really did—Elvis hated audits) took an extra 20¢ on the dollar. And the King had no trouble finding ways to blow the rest.

BUT WAIT! THERE'S MORE...

Unfortunately, that turned out to be just the tip of the iceberg. It turned out that his manager, Colonel Tom Parker, had made a deal

that cost Elvis more than $500 million in potential earnings—
including $320 million in lost royalties from records sold *after*
Elvis's death alone. In March 1973, he'd sold RCA the royalty
rights to *all* of Elvis's songs up to that point for $5.4 million. After
Parker extracted his usual 50% commission, Elvis was left with $2.7
million—$1.35 million after taxes—for virtually his entire life's
work. (Nearly all of that went to pay off ex-wife Priscilla Presley,
who divorced him in October 1973.)

As Sean O'Neal writes in *Elvis, Inc.*, "The final agreement
signed by Colonel Parker…may have been the single most finan-
cially damaging contract in the history of the music industry….Elvis sold the rights to the greatest master catalog in music
history and was left with virtually nothing to show for it. Thereafter, his estate received no royalties at all for any songs Elvis recorded prior to March 1973."

ALL THE KING'S WEALTH
When the probate court tallied up the King's assets, all they found
was Graceland, two airplanes, eight cars, two trucks, seven motor-
cycles, guns, jewelry, and miscellaneous other personal property.
Total value: about $7 million. Elvis left everything to his 9-year-
old daughter, Lisa Marie, who would inherit when she turned 25.
Elvis's father, Vernon Presley, a man with a seventh-grade education, was charged with keeping the estate solvent until then.

Going, Going...
What little was left of the King's estate dwindled fast: In February
1978 the National Bank of Commerce sued the estate to collect
$1.4 million in unpaid loans to the King. A short time later, the
IRS upgraded its estimate of the estate's value and slapped it with
millions in new inheritance taxes—payable immediately. Security
and upkeep on Graceland ate up $500,000 a year.

Vernon Presley sold off the airplanes, jewelry, and Cadillacs,
and even the house that Elvis had bought him, in a desperate
scramble to keep the estate off the auction block. But the Presley
estate was edging closer and closer to bankruptcy.

How was Graceland saved? *To find out, turn to page 376.*

It takes an estimated 2,893 licks to get to the center of a Tootsie Roll pop.

BARRYISMS

Dave Barry is one of the funniest columnists in America. Here are some of his "observations."

"If you surveyed a hundred typical middle-aged Americans, I bet you'd find that only two of them could tell you their blood types, but every last one of them would know the theme song from the 'Beverly Hillbillies.'"

"A child can go only so far in life without potty training. It is not mere coincidence that six of the last seven presidents were potty trained, not to mention nearly half of the nation's state legislators."

"If a woman has to choose between catching a fly ball and saving an infant's life, she will choose to save the infant's life without even considering if there are men on base."

"I reached puberty at age thirty. At age twelve, I looked like a fetus."

"Although golf was originally restricted to wealthy, overweight Protestants, today it's open to anybody who owns hideous clothing."

"Skiing combines outdoor fun with knocking down trees with your face."

"I have come up with a sure-fire concept for a hit television show, which would be called 'A Live Celebrity Gets Eaten by a Shark.'"

"Basically, a tool is an object that enables you to take advantage of the laws of physics and mechanics in such a way that you can seriously injure yourself."

"I've noticed that the one thing about parents is that no matter what stage your child is in, the parents who have older children always tell you the next stage is worse."

"One popular new plastic-surgery technique is called lipgrafting, or 'fat recycling, wherein fat cells are removed from one part of your body that is too large, such as your buttocks, and injected into your lips; people will then be literally kissing your ass."

Central Park, in New York City, is almost twice as big as Monaco.

THE FORTUNE COOKIE

Confucius says: "Good book in bathroom is worth ten on library shelf."

HISTORY

- "Legend has it," a TV reporter told CNN viewers recently, " that the first secret message was sent hundreds of years ago during the Teng Dynasty. A pastry chef was in love with the daughter of the Lotus Queen, and slipped her rice paper love notes in baked wontons."

- It's a romantic idea—but fortune cookies are actually American, not Chinese. They were invented by George Jung, a Los Angeles noodlemaker, in 1916, who gave them to customers at his Hong Kong Noodle Company to distract them while they waited for their orders.

HOW THEY'RE MADE

- A mixture of rice flour and other ingredients is squirted onto small griddles and forms a little pancake. While it's still pliable, it's taken off the grill and folded around a paper fortune

- Traditionally, it was folded by hand. But in 1967 Edward Louie, owner of the Lotus Fortune Cookie Co., invented a machine that automatically inserts the fortunes as the cookies are folded. The strips of paper are sucked in by a vacuum.

THE FORTUNES

- The first fortunes were sayings from Confucius, Ben Franklin, etc. But today they're upbeat messages. "Basically," says Edward Louie's son Gregory, "we're in the entertainment business. "We give people what they want."

- Edward Louie was once asked the secret of his success. He answered: "'Nobody can resist reading their fortune, no matter how corny it is."

- Louie's favorite fortunes were, "If you see someone without a smile, give them one of yours" and, "'Don't wait any longer, book that flight."

- Overall the ten most popular fortunes are : 1. You will have great

---

Big surprise: 41% of Americans call Geraldo Rivera "the most annoying news personality on TV."

success; 2. You will soon be promoted; 3. You will step on the soil of many countries; 4. Your destiny is to be famous; 5. Your love life will be happy and harmonious; 6. Your present plans are going to succeed; 7. Good news will come to you from far away; 8. Now is the time to try something new; 9. Be confident and you will succeed; 10. You will be rich and respected.

A REAL FORTUNE COOKIE
Some fortunes have lottery numbers on the other side. Believe it or not, some people have played those numbers and won.

According to one account: "In March 1995, Barbara and Scott Turnbull got a fortune cookie at a China Coast restaurant in the Texas town of McAllen. They both bought tickets with the same numbers—and won $814,000 each. Meanwhile, Nealy LaHair got a fortune cookie with the same numbers from a China Coast restaurant in Dallas. She played the numbers and won $814,000 for herself. "

BACK IN ASIA...
• In 1989 an entrepreneur on Hong Kong began importing fortune cookie and selling them as luxury items. They were offered as "Genuine American Fortune Cookies"
• On Dec. 27, 1992, the Brooklyn-based Wonton Foods, signed a joint venture agreement with a company in mainland China to build a fortune cookie plant there. The cookies had *never been sold there before!* Chinese fortunes are less direct than American ones. So instead of predictions, they offer comments like "True gold fears no fire," "The only way to catch a tiger cub is to go into the tiger's den," and "Constant grinding can turn an iron rod into a needle."

THE UNFORTUNATE COOKIE
• In the 1970s, a company in New England called the Unfortunate Fortune Cookie Company offered "dismal forebodings... for misanthropes, masochists or what some might regard simply as realists."

What happened to them? They went out of business,.

There are an estimated 28 million Jennifers in the United States.

MR. MOONLIGHT

Some facts about our night-light in the sky, from astronomer (and BRI member) Richard Moeschl.

It takes 29 days, 12 hours, 44 minutes, and 3 seconds for the moon to go through all of its phases (from one full moon to the next). This is close to the length of a month—which is why the word *month* means "moon."

The light that comes from the moon is sunlight reflected off the moon's surface. It takes 1 1/4 seconds for the light to travel to Earth.

The moon only reflects 7% of the light it receives from the sun.

The moon is smaller than any planet in the solar system, but relative to the size of the planets they orbit, our moon is the largest of the moons.

The moon is 2,160 miles in diameter—about a quarter of the Earth's diameter.

If the Earth was as big as a fist, the moon would be the size of a stamp…placed 10 feet away.

The average temperature on the Moon is -283° to 266°F.

Since the moon spins once on its axis every 27 1/3 days—the same amount of time it takes to go around the Earth once—we end up seeing only one side of the moon (about 59% of its surface).

The side of the moon we always see is called "the near side." The side we never see from Earth is "the far side." That's probably where Gary Larsen got the name of his comic strip.

There is no sound on the moon. Nor is there weather, wind, clouds, or colors at sunrise and sunset.

If you weigh 120 pounds on Earth, you would weigh 20 pounds on the Moon—1/6 of your Earth weight.

A 3-foot jump on Earth would carry you 18 feet, 9 inches, on the moon.

Astronauts have brought over 843 pounds of moon samples back to Earth.

The moon is moving away from the Earth at the rate of about 1/8 inch a year.

President Clinton's favorite movie: *High Noon.*

TOP-RATED TV SHOWS, 1967–72

More of the annual Top 10 TV shows of the past 50 years.

1967-1968
(1) The Andy Griffith Show
(2) The Lucy Show
(3) Gomer Pyle, U.S.M.C.
(4) Gunsmoke
(5) Family Affair
(6) Bonanza
(7) The Red Skelton Hour
(8) The Dean Martin Show
(9) The Jackie Gleason Show
(10) Saturday Night at the Movies

1968-1969
(1) Rowan and Martin's Laugh-In
(2) Gomer Pyle, U.S.M.C.
(3) Bonanza
(4) Mayberry R.F.D.
(5) Family Affair
(6) Gunsmoke
(7) Julia
(8) The Dean Martin Show
(9) Here's Lucy
(10) The Beverly Hillbillies

1969-1970
(1) Rowan and Martin's Laugh-In
(2) Gunsmoke
(3) Bonanza
(4) Mayberry R.F.D.
(5) Family Affair
(6) Here's Lucy
(7) The Red Skelton Hour
(8) Marcus Welby, M.D.
(9) The Wonderful World of Disney
(10) The Doris Day Show

1970-1971
(1) Marcus Welby, M.D.
(2) The Flip Wilson Show
(3) Here's Lucy
(4) Ironside
(5) Gunsmoke
(6) ABC Movie of the Week
(7) Hawaii Five-O
(8) Medical Center
(9) Bonanza
(10) The F.B.I.

1971-1972
(1) All in the Family
(2) The Flip Wilson Show
(3) Marcus Welby, M.D.
(4) Gunsmoke
(5) ABC Movie of the Week
(6) Sanford and Son
(7) Mannix
(8) Funny Face
(9) Adam-12
(10) The Mary Tyler Moore Show

1972-1973
(1) All in the Family
(2) Sanford and Son
(3) Hawaii Five-O
(4) Maude
(5) Bridget Loves Bernie
(6) NBC Sunday Mystery Movie
(7) The Mary Tyler Moore Show
(8) Gunsmoke
(9) The Wonderful World of Disney
(10) Ironside

Start counting: On average, an adult laughs about 15 times a day; a child laughs 400 times.

LEMONS

*At one time or another just about everyone has owned a car
that they thought was a lemon. But chances are, your car
was nothing compared to these losers.*

THE WOODS SPIDER (1900)

In 1900, the Woods Motor Vehicle Company of Chicago came out with a carriage powered by a tiny electric motor. Like in horse-drawn taxicabs of the day, the driver sat in an elevated back seat, behind the passengers (who sat in the front seats). But instead of using reins, the driver steered with a "tiller," or steering stick, that was connected to the front wheels via two long rods running underneath the passenger seats.

Fatal Flaw: The steering. Horses *pulled* a carriage, so they easily turned the wheels when they changed direction. But in the Woods Spider, the driver had to wrestle the wheels himself to get them to turn—which was nearly impossible, since he was sitting in the rear of the car, behind the center of gravity. Bad weather was another problem. The passenger seat had its own convertible top. When it was closed, it blocked the driver's view—he had to crouch and peek through a tiny window, over the passengers' shoulders, to see the road ahead. If passengers were too tall or fat, he couldn't see at all. In 1901, Woods succumbed to logic and moved the driver up front.

THE MACDUFF AEROPINION/ PNEUMOSLITO (1904)

Impressed by early aeroplanes, the folks at MacDuff designed a propeller-driven *car*. (The prop was placed in back, like a giant fan.) In heavy snow, you could slap small wooden skis onto each tire and—viola! The Aeropinion became the Pneumoslito, a propeller-driven sled that flew over frozen turf.

Fatal Flaw: First and foremost, it was tough to handle. But it was a menace, too. In summer, the propeller kicked up enough dust on dirt roads to blind everyone behind it for about a block and a half—a big problem when nearly all roads were unpaved. And the whirling blades were also potential disasters: they could make sausage out of any pedestrian who walked into them, or easily fly off in a car accident. The car was produced for just one year.

Watches get their name because they were originally worn by night watchmen.

THE ARTHUR SELDEN CAR (1908)

The Arthur Selden Car was a front-wheel-drive car with an unusual feature: the front wheels didn't turn...and neither did the rear wheels. Instead, the car itself was hinged in the middle, with the steering connected to the hinge instead of the wheels.

Fatal Flaw: The car jackknifed easily, and the hinges wore out quickly. Besides, the car was so goofy-looking that nobody would have bought it even if it was easy to steer. Selden made a couple of prototypes, then quickly went out of business.

THE LE ZEBRE (1916–1920)

The Le Zebre was a cheap, stylish two-seat convertible that appealed to drivers who wanted expensive sports cars but couldn't afford them. It had a four-cylinder engine, slender lines, a fancy horn, and a spare wheel that sat on the running board. Ooh-la-la!

Fatal Flaw: Quality control at the factory was so bad that the car was like a prop in a slapstick comedy—it fell apart, piece by piece. For example, the axles shattered like clockwork every 200 miles, and the wheel nuts—frequently followed by the wheels themselves—popped off even at low speeds. People bought them anyway, because they were low-priced. The model lasted for four years.

THE DAVIS (1947–1949)

Produced by the Davis Motor Car Company of Van Nuys, California, the Davis was a three-wheeled car, shaped like a gumdrop, that looked like something out of "The Jetsons." Power was provided via the two rear wheels; the driver steered the single front wheel. The company also made a special military version. (No word on whether the Pentagon actually bought any.)

Fatal Flaw: Bizarre looks and unconventional design would surely have killed the Davis, but they didn't have the chance. Misleading claims made by the company's founder, G. G. "Gary" Davis, beat them to it. Davis swore the car got 116 mph on the highway, and that it could make sudden, sharp turns at speeds as high as 55 mph. Actual fuel economy turned out to be 65 mph (not bad, but not as advertised). And in high-speed turns, one of the rear wheels lifted off the ground and spun freely, causing the speedometer to register artificially high speeds. The company was shut down following a financial scandal in 1949.

About three-quarters of American adults wear some kind of fragrance.

THE WRITING ON THE WALL

At some time, all bathroom readers have found themselves in a public stall with nothing to read. Your eye starts to wander…and then you spot —graffiti! Here's a tribute to that emergency reading material.

You might be surprised to learn that graffiti aren't new…or even recent. The term comes from the Italian word for "scribbling"…and it was coined by archeologists to describe wall-writing found in ancient ruins. It has been discovered in the catacombs of Rome, the Tower of London, medieval English alehouses, and even Mayan pyramids.

Some of the earliest examples of graffiti were preserved on the walls of Pompeii when Mt. Vesuvius erupted in 79 A.D. As you can see from the following examples, it hasn't changed much in nearly 2,000 years:

Appolinaris, doctor to the Emperor Titus, had a crap here

NO ONE'S A HANDSOME FELLOW UNLESS HE HAS LOVED

Whoever loves, goes to hell. I want to break Venus' ribs with blows and deform her hips. If she can break my tender heart, why can't I hit her over the head?

HULLO, WE'RE WINESKINS

Artimetus got me pregnant

In Nuceria, near Porta Romana, is the district of Venus. Ask for Novellia Primigenia

He who sits here, read this before anything else: If you want to make love ask for Attice. The price is 16 asses.

LOVERS, LIKE BEES, ENJOY A LIFE OF HONEY
Wishful thinking

O Chius, I hope your ulcerous pustules reopen and burn even more than they did before

IN NUCERIA VOTE FOR LUCIUS MUNATIUS CAESARNINUS: HE IS AN HONEST MAN

Romula tarried here with Staphylus

The most common word spoken by a dying person is "Mother" or "Mommy."

A RECORD OF HISTORY

People have been studying and collecting graffiti for centuries. Hurlo Thrumbo, an English publisher, put out the first printed collection in the 1700s. In the early 1900s, German sociologists collected scrawls from public toilets and turned them into the first academic study of graffiti. In America, the Kinsey researchers collected bathroom messages as part of their study of men's and women's sex habits. But it wasn't until the 1960s, when graffiti became an outlet for the counterculture and anti-Vietnam protest movement, that academics really started to pay attention.

Now these "scribblings" are regarded as important adjuncts to the "official" history of a culture. They provide a look at what the average person was thinking and give evidence of the social unrest, political trends, and inner psychology of a society.

COLLECTING INFO

After decades of study, experts have decided that graffiti fit into four major categories.

• *Identity graffitists:* Want to immortalize themselves or a part of their lives (a romance, an accomplishment)

• *Opinion* or *message graffitists:* Want to let the world know what they think: "UFOs are real—the Air Force doesn't exist."

• *Dialogue graffitists:* Talk back to other graffitists. "I've got what every woman wants"...(*underneath:*) "You must be in the fur coat business."

• *"Art" graffitists:* The most recent trend, with spray cans of paint used to create intricate designs signed with pseudonyms. Either vandalism or modern design, depending on your point of view.

THE GRAFFITI HERO

The most famous graffitist in history was Kilroy. Beginning in World War II, the line "Kilroy was here" started showing up in outrageous places. Kilroy left his signature on the top of the torch of the Statue of Liberty, on the Marco Polo Bridge in China, and even on a Bikini atoll where an atomic bomb was to be tested. The original Kilroy was an infantry soldier who was sick of hearing the Air Force brag about always being first on the spot. But the phrase has appeared for so many years in so many places that "Kilroy was here" has become synonymous with graffiti.

MORE WRITING ON THE WALL

A sampling of contemporary graffiti, collected since the 1960s.

Q: How do you tell the sex of a chromosome? A: Pull down its genes.

If Love is blind, and God is love, and Ray Charles is blind, then God plays the piano.

Mafia: Organized Crime
Government: Disorganized Crime

Flush twice, it's a long way to Washington.

Death is just nature's way of telling you to slow down.

How come nobody ever writes on the toilet seats?

Things are more like they are now than they have ever been before.

I can't stand labels, after all, I'm a liberal.

Although the moon is smaller than the earth, it's farther away.

Free Chile!
...Free tacos!
...Free burritos!

Only Jackie knows what her Onasis worth.

Did you ever feel like the whole world was a white wedding gown, and you were a pair of muddy hiking boots?

Standing room only.
[written on top of a men's urinal]

The chicken is an egg's way of producing another egg.

If you think you have someone eating out of your hands, it's a good idea to count your fingers.

The typical Stanford undergrad is like a milkshake: thick and rich.

Blessed is he who sits on a bee, for he shall rise again.

Please remain seated during the entire program.—The Management

There are those who shun elitism.
Why?
...Because it is there.
...It's the elitist thing to do.

Please do not throw cigarette butts in the toilet, as they become hard to light.

You can lead a horticulture, but you can't make her think.

Abraham Lincoln hated being called "Abe."

FAMOUS PUBLISHING HOAXES

They say you shouldn't judge a book by its cover—and sometimes, as these hoaxes reveal, you can't even judge them what's inside.

NAKED CAME THE STRANGER

The Book: In 1966 Mike McGrady, editor of the Long Island newspaper *Newsday*, interviewed "sex-novelist" Harold Robbins and was shocked to learn that Robbins had received a $2 million advance for a book he hadn't even written yet. McGrady decided to see if he could repeat Robbins's success: he deliberately set out to write a bad book, just to see how it would be received by publishers and the public. He came up with a title: *Naked Came the Stranger*, and a pen name: Penelope Asche.

Next, McGrady wrote up a story outline about a suburban housewife who gets even against her philandering husband by seducing married men. He recruited twenty-four *Newsday* reporters to write one chapter apiece, complete with two sexual encounters per chapter, one of which had to be bizarre. "There will be an unremitting emphasis on sex," he explained. "Also, true excellence in writing will be blue-pencilled into oblivion."

When the book was finished, McGrady gave it to his sister-in-law, who, posing as Penelope Asche, shopped it around to several New York publishing houses. Dell Publishing paid $37,500 for it, and published it in 1970.

What Happened: *Naked Came the Stranger* became a bestseller—it sold 20,000 copies in the first month alone, thanks in part to McGrady's sister-in-law, who made TV and radio appearances promoting the book. McGrady eventually revealed the hoax, but sales remained strong, eventually topping well over 100,000 copies. McGrady, et al. were offered $500,000 to write a sequel; instead, he wrote a book called *Stranger Than Naked, or How to Write Dirty Books for Fun and Profit.*

THE MAN WHO WOULDN'T TALK

The Book: At the end of World War II, George DuPre, a Canadian, returned from Europe and began telling neighbors of his exploits in the secret service. DuPre said he was part of the anti-Nazi French underground until he was captured by the Germans, who tortured him to get him to talk. At one point, DuPre said, they even gave him a sulphuric acid enema—but somehow he managed to keep silent, and later escaped.

As word of DuPre's exploits spread, he became a Canadian national hero. *Reader's Digest* printed an interview with him, which inspired Random House to publish *The Man Who Wouldn't Talk*, the story of his experiences, in 1953.

What Happened: Not long after his book was published, DuPre broke down during an interview with the Calgary Herald and admitted he'd made up the entire story. He'd actually spent the entire war in Canada and England. Random House realized it had been fooled and pulled *The Man Who Wouldn't Talk* from its nonfiction list. But rather than destroy the books, the publisher changed the title to *The Man Who Talked Too Much* and began selling it as fiction. Sales went up 500%.

THE MEMOIRS OF LEE HUNG CHANG

The Book: In 1913 Houghton Mifflin posthumously published *The Memoirs of Li Hung Chang*, the autobiography of one of the most famous Chinese statesmen of the era. The book was praised by many China experts—including John W. Foster, Secretary of State under Benjamin Harrison, who had worked with Li Hung Chang during an 1897 peace conference. Chapters of the work were serialized in the *London Observer* and *The New York Sun*.

What Happened: American Chinese experts praised the book. But *Chinese* experts immediately denounced it as a fake. They pointed out so many inaccuracies and discrepancies that Houghton Mifflin finally had to admit a problem and "look into the matter." They discovered that the book's "editor," a man named William Mannix, was actually its author. Using books on China sent to him by friends, and a typewriter sent to him by the Governor of Hawaii, Mannix had written the book in 1912—while serving time for forgery in a Honolulu prison.

Strangely enough, the book can still be found in many university and public libraries today.

LAUNCHING
AIR JORDAN

*If you had to name just one person associated with an athletic shoe,
it would be Michael Jordan, right? Here's how he became Air
Jordan, from the BRI's long-time pop historian, Jack Mingo.*

WALKING ON AIR

The air-filled shoe wasn't Nike's idea. The first air sole
was patented in 1882, and over 70 more were registered
with the U.S. Patent Office before 1969. They all failed because of
technical problems.

In 1969, a designer named Frank Rudy gave it a shot. He left a
job at Rockwell International during a downturn in the aerospace
industry, and invested his time and money in an effort to develop a
running shoe with air soles. After many attempts, he finally succeeded by using a thin polyurethane bag for an air cushion. Then
he convinced the Bata shoe company to try it out.

The first prototypes worked great. Unfortunately, it was the middle of the oil embargo of 1974, and Bata's supplier quietly changed
its polyurethane formula to use less oil. The new formula wasn't as
strong as the old one; when the soles warmed up and air pressure
increased, they would explode like a rifle shot. Bata suddenly lost
interest.

LAST ATTEMPT

Nearly broke and desperate, Rudy flew to France to show Adidas
what he had. He didn't get anywhere with them, but while he was
hanging around the Adidas offices, he heard an employee mention
a little U.S. company named Nike that was selling running shoes
on the West Coast. Rudy made some calls, found out there was a
running shoe trade show that weekend in Anaheim, and caught
the next flight to Southern California.

He stopped by the Nike booth in Anaheim just as it was closing
and got the name of the company's president, Phil Knight. Rudy
immediately found a pay phone and called Knight at Nike's head-

quarters in Beaverton, Oregon. Knight listened to Rudy's story, then invited him for a visit.

NIKE JUMPS IN

Knight, an amateur runner, personally took Rudy's air-filled shoes for a run. They slowly deflated as he ran, but he saw their potential. "It was a great ride while it lasted," he told Rudy. Then he put Rudy on retainer for six months, to see if he could make the idea work.

After much trial and error, Nike finally came up with something they liked—an inflated midsole that went between the regular sole of a shoe and the runner's foot. Nike called their new creation the *Tailwind* and rushed it into production at $50 retail—the highest price anyone had ever charged for a mass-produced running shoe. But runners bought them anyway. Unfortunately, a last-minute fabric switch resulted in a shoe that fell apart after a short time, infuriating customers. About half of the shoes were returned as defective.

Nike eventually got the bugs out. This time they decided not to release the shoe directly into the marketplace. They were going to wait and try something special.

LUCKY CHOICE

Meanwhile, Nike was reevaluating its marketing strategy. The company had been paying professional athletes anywhere from $8,000 to $100,000 apiece to wear and endorse their shoes. One day in 1983, Nike execs did an analysis and found they "owned" about half of the players in the NBA—at a cost of millions of dollars a year. In fact, they had 2,000 athletes on their endorsement roster. It was getting more expensive all the time and it wasn't necessarily winning them any any more business.

So they decided to switch tactics and find one promising rookie… then sign him to a long-term contract before he got too expensive. They considered Charles Barkley and Patrick Ewing, but finally settled on 20-year-old college junior Michael Jordan. Their plan was to design a brand-new shoe for him, push it hard, and tie the product to the man (and vice versa), so when consumers saw the player, they'd think "shoes!"

LAUNCHING AIR JORDAN

They had just the right product—the air-cushioned shoe. Nike offered Jordan $2.5 million for a five-year contract, plus royalties on every Air Jordan shoe sold. But Jordan turned them down. He didn't particularly like Nike shoes. In fact, he loved Adidas and was willing to make concessions to sign with them. He told their representatives, "You don't even have to match Nike's deal—just come close." But Adidas wasn't interested. They offered only $100,000 a year, with no special shoe and no royalties. So, in August 1984, Jordan signed with Nike.

Nike came up with the distinctive black and red design for the Jordan shoe. In fact, it was so distinctive that the NBA commissioner threatened to fine him $1,000 if he wore Air Jordan shoes during games, because they violated the NBA "uniformity of uniform" clause. Jordan wore them anyway, creating an uproar in the stands and in the press...and Nike gladly paid the fine.

FLYING SOLO

It was the beginning of a brilliant advertising campaign. Air Jordans went on to become the most successful athletic endorsement in history, selling over $100 million worth of merchandise in the first year alone. The dark side: Air Jordans became so popular that it became dangerous to wear them in some cities, as teenagers began killing other teenagers for their $110 sneakers. And the company was embarrassed—or should have been—by the revelation that a worker in its Far East sweatshops would have to work for several weeks to make enough money to buy a pair.

Despite occasional bad publicity and considerable competition over the years, however, Air Jordans became so successful that in 1997, Michael Jordan and Nike announced that after his retirement from professional basketball, Jordan would be heading his own division of Nike.

MOTHERS OF INVENTION

There have always been women inventors—even if they've been overlooked in history books. Here are a few you may not have heard of.

MELITTA BENTZ, *a housewife in Dresden, Germany*
Invention: Drip coffeemakers
Background: At the beginning of the 20th century, people made coffee by dumping a cloth bag full of coffee grounds into boiling water. It was an ugly process—the grounds inevitably leaked into the water, leaving it gritty and bitter.

One morning in 1908, Frau Bentz decided to try something different: she tore a piece of blotting paper (used to mop up after runny fountain pens) from her son's schoolbook and put it in the bottom of a brass pot she'd poked with holes. She put coffee on top of the paper and poured boiling water over it. It was the birth of "drip" coffeemakers—and the Melitta company. Today, Melitta sells its coffeemakers in 150 countries around the world.

LADY ADA LOVELACE, *daughter of British poet Lord Byron*
Invention: Computer programming
Background: The forerunner of modern computers—called the "analytical engine"—was the brainchild of a mathematical engineer named George Babbage. In 1834 Babbage met Lady Lovelace, and the two formed a partnership, working together on the engine's prototype. In the process, Lovelace created the first programming method, which used punch cards. Unfortunately, tools available to Babbage and Lovelace in the mid-1800s weren't sophisticated enough to complete the machine (though it worked in theory). Lovelace spent the rest of her life studying cybernetics.

LADY MARY MONTAGU, *a British noblewoman*
Invention: Smallpox vaccine
Background: In 1717, while traveling in Turkey, she observed a curious custom known as *ingrafting*. Families would call for the services of old women, who would bring nutshells full of "virulent"— live smallpox—to a home. Then it would be "ingrafted" into a patient's open vein. The patient would spend a few days in bed with a

slight illness but was rendered immune to smallpox. This technique was unknown in England, where 30% of smallpox victims died. Montagu convinced Caroline, Princess of Wales, to try it on her own daughters. When it worked, she anonymously published *The Plain Account of the Inoculating of the Small-pox by a Turkish Merchant*. Despite vehement opposition from the church and medical establishments, the idea took hold. Lady Montagu lived to see England's smallpox death rate drop to 2%.

MARGARET KNIGHT, *an employee of the Columbia Paper Bag Company in the late 1800s*

Invention: The modern paper bag

Background: Knight grew so tired of making paper bags by hand that she began experimenting with machines that could make them automatically. She came up with one that made square-bottomed, folding paper bags (until then, paper sacks all had V-shaped bottoms). But her idea was stolen by a man who'd seen her building her prototype. A court battle followed in which the main argument used against Knight was her "womanhood." But she proved beyond a doubt that the invention was hers and received her patent in 1870. Knight was awarded 27 patents in her lifetime, but was no businesswoman—she died in 1914 leaving an estate of only $275.05.

BETTE NESMITH GRAHAM, *a secretary at the Texas Bank & Trust in Dallas in the early 1950s*

Invention: Liquid Paper

Background: Graham was a terrible typist...but when she tried to erase her mistakes, the ink on her IBM typewriter just smeared. One afternoon in 1951, while watching sign painters letter the bank's windows, she got a brilliant idea: "With lettering, an artist never corrects by erasing but always paints over the error. So I decided to use what artists use. I put some waterbase paint in a bottle and took my watercolor brush to the office. And I used that to correct my typing mistakes." So many other secretaries asked for bottles of "Mistake Out" that in 1956 she started a small business selling it. A year later, she changed the formula and founded Liquid Paper, Inc. In 1966 her son, Michael Nesmith, made more money as a member of the Monkees than she did with Liquid Paper. But in 1979, she sold her company to Gillette for $47 million.

MISSED IT BY *THAT MUCH*

Often success and disaster are a lot closer than we'd like to think. Here are some classic "near misses."

AN ASSASSINATION

Theodore Roosevelt: On October 14, 1912, the former president was on his way to a speech in Milwaukee when a man named John Schrank drew a revolver, pointed it at Roosevelt, and pulled the trigger. Roosevelt staggered but didn't fall. No blood could be detected, but Roosevelt's handlers begged him to go to the hospital. He refused and delivered a 50-minute speech to a cheering throng. However, when he pulled the 100-page speech out of his vest, he noticed a bullet hole in it. It turned out that the bullet had ripped through the paper and penetrated four inches into Roosevelt's body, right below his right nipple. If the written speech hadn't slowed the bullet down, he would have been killed. After speaking, Roosevelt was treated for shock and loss of blood.

A PLACE IN HISTORY

Elisha Gray: Gray was an electrical genius who independently developed his own telephone. Incredibly, he filed a patent for the invention on February 14, 1876—the *exact same day* that Alexander Graham Bell did—but a few hours *after* Bell. "If Bell had been a few hours late," says one historian, "what we know of as the Bell System would have been the Gray System." Gray was successful with other inventions, but was bitter for the rest of his life about not receiving credit for the telephone.

James Swinburne: Leo Baekeland patented the first modern plastic on June 14, 1907; he called it "Bakelite." A day later, a Scottish electrical engineer named James Swinburne filed a patent for almost exactly the same thing. He'd been experimenting with the same chemicals on his own halfway around the world, and had come up with the substance completely independently. Unlike Gray, though, he made peace with his near-miss and wound up chairman of the Bakelite company.

The word "love" appears in more film titles than any other word. Second place: "Paris."

A CAREER-ENDING "INJURY"

Frank Sinatra: "Gangster Sam Giancana once ordered a hit on Frank Sinatra. He was going to have Sinatra's throat cut to ruin his voice. But on the night the hit was supposed to go down, Giancana was enjoying an intimate moment with [his girlfriend] Phyllis McGuire, who played Sinatra records to heighten the romantic mood. After listening for a while, Giancana decided he couldn't in good conscience silence that voice. He cancelled the hit." (*The Portland Oregonian*, August 29, 1997)

MILITARY DEFEAT

George Washington: "On Christmas night, 1776, Washington was preparing to cross the Delaware with his army to attack the British. The commander of forces at Trenton, Colonel Rall, was German. He was drinking and playing cards when he received a note from a British loyalist warning him of the attack. But the note was in English, which Rall couldn't read, and he was groggy anyway, so he put it in his pocket. At dawn, Washington attacked and because the British were unprepared, he won. As Rall lay dying on the battlefield, the note was translated into German and Rall admitted if he'd read it, 'I would not be here.' " (From *Oh Say Can You See?*)

THE PRESIDENCY

John Janney: "In 1840, Janney was chairman of the Whig Party Convention in Virginia. This convention nominated William Henry Harrison for president. John Janney and John Tyler were the nominees for vice president. When the vote of the convention was a tie, Janney, as chairman, did the "honorable" thing and voted for Tyler. Harrison won the election but died soon after, and John Tyler became president. John Janney lost the presidency by one vote—his own." (From *Dear Abby*, December 17, 1996)

Sen. Ben Wade: When Lincoln was shot in 1865, Andrew Johnson became president. In 1867 the Republican Congress tried to impeach him, but was one vote shy of the two-thirds majority needed to remove him from office. Wade, as president of the Senate, would have become the 18th American president. He became the second man in history to miss the U.S. presidency by one vote.

Only pharoahs were allowed to eat mushrooms in ancient Egypt.

"THE TONIGHT SHOW" PART III: JACK PAAR

In his day, Jack Paar left as big a mark on "The Tonight Show" as Johnny Carson. But he only hosted the show for five years...and it's been more than 35 years since he left the stage...so his contribution is largely forgotten. Here's Part III of our look at "The Tonight Show."

STARTING OVER

With "America After Dark" going down in flames, NBC began looking for someone to host a new version of "The Tonight Show." The search didn't take long: when Steve Allen had cut back to three days a week in 1956, two comedians had been contenders for the Monday and Tuesday slots: Ernie Kovacs (who got the job) and Jack Paar, an out-of-work television personality.

This time, NBC decided give Paar a chance. They weren't confident he could pull it off—with good reason. He seemed to have a knack for turning opportunity into disaster.

Army Brat

• Paar first attracted notice in the Army during World War II. He performed as part of the Special Service Company at USO shows, and was notorious for his satirical putdowns of military brass. Enlisted troops loved him, and he drew bigger applause than even Jack Benny or Bob Hope when he appeared with them. But the act nearly got him court-martialed after he insulted a commodore.

• After he was discharged, he moved to Hollywood. In 1947 Jack Benny took time off from his radio program and arranged for Paar fill in over the summer. It might have been a big break, but Paar let his ego and his temper get in the way. Three of his four writers walked out one afternoon after he insulted them once too often. Then he was quoted in *Time* magazine referring to Jack Benny's style of humor as "old hat" and pledging to bring a fresh approach to radio comedy.

"When the summer ended," Robert Metz writes in *The Tonight Show*, "so did Jack's Hollywood career. He had made lots of enemies there, partly because of unbending attitudes, and, his critics say, his unwillingness to show humility."

• Paar moved on to New York and did a number of TV game, news, and variety shows, but none worked. Then he got a job as Walter Cronkite's replacement on "The Morning Show," which ran on CBS against "The Today Show." The "Morning Show's" ratings went up during Paar's tenure, but he developed a reputation for being "uncooperative." CBS fired him after he refused to attribute his wife's "newfound" beauty to a sponsor's lipstick.

• Paar lost his job, but won an important fan—NBC executive Mort Werner...who hired him for "The Tonight Show."

THE JACK PAAR STYLE
At first, Paar tried to mimic Steve Allen's format. "The first night," he recalled years later, "I grappled with a heavyweight wrestler, threw vegetables at the audience, and fed catnip to a lion." But where Allen had been a gifted and very physical comedian, Paar was uncomfortable and wooden. The critics panned the July 29, 1957 premiere.

Paar struggled with Allenesque skits and physical humor for another six months before he finally told his writers that from now on, he would open with a short monologue, then move to his desk, where he would chat with his guests. Paar was a strong conversationalist, and he wanted to make that the backbone of the show. He also figured that dumping the hijinks would help him attract more serious guests, such as politicians and journalists.

UP, UP, AND AWAY
"The Tonight Show" was building an audience even before the changes in format, and this helped it grow even more. "Before long," Paar remembered years later, "we had 154 stations, an estimated 30 million viewers weekly, and so many sponsors I felt guilty when I interrupted the commercials with the program." By the end of the second year, Paar's ratings were higher than Steve Allen's had been.

For the first time in its difficult history, "The Tonight Show" was selling out its advertising. And because the show was cheap to produce by TV standards—Paar had only three writers and a weekly budget of $50,000—it made big profits for NBC.

TALK SHOW

Guests were booked on the show not because they had a new movie or television show coming out (as most guests are booked today), but because Paar found them interesting to talk to. Some big celebrities never got on, while Betty White, then an unknown comedian, appeared more than 70 times. "Jack was fascinated [by the guests on the show]," says Hal Gurnee, who directed Paar's show and years later would also direct David Letterman's. "He was good at talking to people and convincing them he was interested in what they had to say."

HOT TALENT

It wasn't just Paar's talent for conversation that followed him to "The Tonight Show." His ego, stubbornness, and bad temper also came along. Ironically, these qualities—which had nearly derailed his career several times—became an important a part of "The Tonight Show's" success. If he was mad about something, he'd vent his anger onstage. If he was emotional, he'd cry. If he didn't like a guest, he'd insult them to their faces, right on national TV. Sometimes he even chewed out his staff on the air. Audiences, which were used to the tightly scripted TV shows of the 1950s, were mesmerized. There was nothing else like it on TV.

Unlike today's talk-show hosts, who tend to keep personal disputes off the air and wage their wars through publicists, Paar fought his feuds on camera and in person. He attacked columnists who criticized his show and could become jealous of any guests who got bigger laughs than he did. One night comedian Jack E. Leonard scored big with the studio audience. Paar told him, "Keep going. You're doing great!" throughout his routine, but a few days later, he announced that Leonard was history. "You'll be seeing a lot of him in the future," Paar told viewers, "but not on my show!"

Even regular guests had to watch their step. Dody Goodman was a ditsy comedian Paar discovered on the first week of the show. She was so funny that he made her a regular. But one night when she got too many laughs, he dumped her.

MR. NICE GUY

Paar could also be a sentimental family man—especially during his monologues, which he peppered with stories about his wife and daughter. When his daughter got her first training bra, he told the world. And when the family vacationed in foreign countries, Paar always packed a movie camera to record their trips for the show.

"Paar was in essence hosting a nightly gathering at his 'house,' " Ronald Smith writes, "complete with home movies, guests who should not have been invited and the atmosphere that 'anything might happen.' Some guests were quietly invited to leave, the subject of catty insults. Others were embraced and urged to come back over and over, long overstaying their welcome."

A NATIONAL HABIT

Viewers didn't just *want* to watch "The Tonight Show," they felt they *had* to, out of fear that they'd miss something if they didn't.

"Jack in all his work let his own quirks, neuroses, suspicions and dislikes play freely on the surface," Dick Cavett (a writer on the show) recalled in his autobiography. "There was always the implied possibility in his manner that he would explode one day, and you might miss seeing a live nervous breakdown viewed from the comfort of your own bedroom."

As viewers flocked to "The Tonight Show," so did celebrities from all walks of life. Richard Nixon played piano accompanied by an orchestra of "15 Democratic violinists"; Liberace tickled the ivories while a young Cassius Clay read poetry. "For a change, do that one about you," he goaded the champ. Even Eleanor Roosevelt and Albert Schweitzer made appearances.

A LITTLE POLITICS ON THE SIDE

"The Tonight Show" may even have helped decide the outcome of the 1960 presidential elections. Both Kennedy and Nixon made appearances on the show to explain their positions, and on the eve of the election, Paar invited Bobby Kennedy, JFK's campaign manager, on the show to explain "in three minutes" why his brother should be president. (Nixon, of course, was not pleased.) As James Reston of The *New York Times* put it, there were two litmus tests in the 1960 campaign: "Who can stand up to Nikita Khrushchev. And who can sit down with Jack Paar."

Want to hear a censored joke? Turn to page 271 for Part IV.

According to a 1997 poll, about 2/3 of Americans believe a UFO may have crashed at Roswell.

CELEBRITY ALSO-RANS

It helps to be a celebrity if you want to run for political office. Take a look at Congress today: there's a member of the "Love Boat" cast, a Hall of Fame pitcher, even a former rock star. Here are four famous Americans who aren't known as politicians...because they lost.

HENRY FORD
Ran for: U.S. Senate seat from Michigan

The Story: Ford was one of the richest, most famous men in America when Woodrow Wilson called him into the White House in 1918 and asked him to run for the open senate seat in Michigan. He agreed to do it.

It was a bizarre campaign. Although he had unlimited cash, Ford refused to spend any. He also refused to make any public speeches. And while Ford said nothing, his opponent—Truman H. Newberry—attacked the carmaker mercilessly for his pacifism.

Outcome: Surprisingly, Ford lost by less than 5,000 votes. *Then* he got interested in the election. He demanded a recount and hired private detectives to prove Newberry had cheated. Over the next four years, Ford had more than 40 investigators scouring Michigan, looking for proof that Newberry had spent money on his campaign illegally. This, he claimed (and perhaps believed), would be proof that Wall Street had conspired to beat him.

In the end, he got the revenge he wanted. The Democrats regained control of the Senate in 1922 and announced they were reopening "the Newberry case." Newberry gave in to the inevitable and resigned. Ford never ran for office again.

P. T. BARNUM
Ran for: U.S. House of Representatives

The Story: In 1865, the world-famous showman (known for his alleged comment: "There's a sucker born every minute") ran for—and won—a seat in the Connecticut state legislature. The reason: he wanted to have a hand in abolishing slavery permanently. He

---

USDA recommends 5 servings of fruits & veggies a day. The average adult eats 4.4; kids eat 3.4.

was rewarded in 1867 with the Republican nomination for U.S. Congress. Strangely, his opponent was also named Barnum.

The rest of the country seemed appalled by the idea. In a typical editorial, *The Nation* called him a "depraving and demoralizing influence" and said Connecticut should be ashamed of itself. Barnum himself noted that by the election time, "half the Christian community" believed he wore "horns and hoofs."

Outcome: A Democratic landslide swept Connecticut, and Barnum was soundly defeated. The man responsible for innumerable hoaxes said *he* wanted nothing more to do with "oily politicians." But in 1875, he was elected mayor of Bridgeport; and in 1877 he was again elected to the state legislature.

HUNTER THOMPSON

Ran for: Sheriff of Aspen, Colorado

The Story: In 1970 Thompson, the infamous "Gonzo" journalist, jokingly ran for sheriff of the glitzy ski resort as a "freak power" candidate. His platform: He promised to ban cars, tear up the roads and turf them, rename Aspen "Fat City," and put stocks on the courthouse lawn to punish "dishonest" dope dealers.

Outcome: Amazingly, he lost the race by less than 1,000 votes.

SHIRLEY TEMPLE BLACK

Ran for: U.S. House of Representatives

The Story: In the 1930s, little Shirley Temple was one of the world's most famous movie stars. In 1966 she was Shirley Temple Black, a committed conservative Republican.

In 1967, the U.S. representative from her district died, and she ran for the Republican nomination in a special election. She started out as the odds-on favorite...but lost steam as her positions seemed more and more at odds with her compassionate little-girl movie character. In a magazine interview, for example, she belittled funds spent on rat control in slums, scoffing, "I'd like to know who *counted* the rats." She was also a Vietnam hard-liner, while her opponent—a Vietnam vet with a war injury—was a moderate.

Outcome: She lost the primary, 69,000 to 35,000, and was bitter about it for years. For some reason, she thought that if she'd had two more weeks to campaign, she would have won.

INFORMAL WRITING

Can't find anything to write on when you get a brainstorm? Do what these people did—grab whatever's in front of you and start scribbling.

WRITTEN ON: A cocktail napkin
BY: Rollin King and Herb Kelleher
THE STORY: Kelleher was a lawyer. King was a banker and pilot who ran a small charter airline. In 1966, they had a drink at a San Antonio bar. Conversation led to an idea for an airline that would provide short intrastate flights at a low cost. They mapped out routes and a business strategy on a cocktail napkin. Looking at the notes on the napkin, Kelleher said, "Rollin, you're crazy, let's do it," and Southwest Airlines was born.

WRITTEN ON: Toilet paper
BY: Richard Berry
THE STORY: Berry, an R&B performer, was at a club in 1957 when he heard a song with a Latin beat that he liked. He went into the men's room, pulled off some toilet paper, and wrote down the lyrics to "Louie, Louie."

WRITTEN ON: The back of a grocery bill
BY: W. C. Fields
THE STORY: In 1940 Fields needed money quickly. He scribbled down a plot idea on some paper he found in his pocket, and sold it to Universal Studios for $25,000. Ironically, the plot was about Fields trying to sell an outrageous script to a movie studio. It became his last film, *Never Give a Sucker an Even Break* (1941). Fields received screenplay credit as Otis Criblecoblis.

WRITTEN ON: The back of a letter
BY: Francis Scott Key
THE STORY: In 1814 Key, a lawyer, went out to the British fleet in Chesapeake Bay to plead for the release of a prisoner. The British agreed, but since Key had arrived as they were preparing to attack, they detained him and his party until the battle was over. From this vantage point Key watched the bombardment, and "by

---

Nice doggie: In 1996, U.S. postal workers were bitten by dogs 2,795 times.

the dawn's early light" saw that "our flag was still there." He was so inspired that he wrote the lyrics to "The Star Spangled Banner" on the only paper he had, a letter he'd stuck in his pocket.

WRITTEN ON: A cocktail napkin
BY: Arthur Laffer
THE STORY: In Sept. 1974, Arthur Laffer (professor of business economics at USC) had a drink at a Washington, D.C. restaurant with his friend Donald Rumsfeld (an advisor to President Gerald Ford). The conversation was about the economy, taxes, and what to do about recession. Laffer moved his wine glass, took the cocktail napkin, and drew a simple graph to illustrate his idea that at some point, increased taxes result in decreased revenues. The graph, known as the "Laffer Curve," later became the basis for President Reagan's "trickle-down" economics.

WRITTEN ON: A napkin
BY: Roger Christian and Jan Berry
THE STORY: In the early 1960s Roger Christian, one of the top DJs in Los Angeles, co-wrote many of Jan and Dean's hits with Jan Berry. One night he and Jan were at an all-night diner and Christian began scribbling the lyrics to a new song, "Honolulu Lulu," on a napkin. When they left the restaurant, Jan said, "Give me the napkin...I'll go to the studio and work out the arrangements." "I don't have it," Christian replied. Then they realized they'd left the napkin on the table. They rushed back in...but the waitress had already thrown it away. They tried to reconstruct the song but couldn't. So the two tired collaborators went behind the diner and sorted through garbage in the dumpster until 4 a.m., when they finally found their song. It was worth the search. "Honolulu Lulu" made it to #11 on the national charts.

WRITTEN ON: The back of an envelope
BY: Abraham Lincoln
THE STORY: On his way to Gettysburg to commemorate the battle there, Lincoln jotted down his most famous speech—the Gettysburg Address—on an envelope. Good story, but just a myth. Several drafts of the speech have been discovered—one of which was written in the White House on executive stationery.

Tomato ketchup was once sold in the U.S. as a medicine.

THE DUSTBIN
OF HISTORY

*Think your heroes will go down in history for something they've done?
Don't count on it. These folks were VIPs in their time...but they're
forgotten now. They've been swept into the Dustbin of History.*

FORGOTTEN FIGURE: Fanny Elssler, Viennese ballerina
CLAIM TO FAME: A superstar of the 1840s, Elssler
toured America for two years and inspired what newspapers
referred to as "Elssler Mania." Wherever she went, "The Divine
Fanny" drew hordes of admirers. They rioted outside her hotel in
New York and mobbed her carriage in Baltimore. In Washington,
Congress adjourned so lawmakers wouldn't miss her performance.
Poems and songs were written about her. At the end of her tour,
she went back to Europe and (as far as we know) never returned.

FORGOTTEN FIGURE: Peter Francisco, American soldier
CLAIM TO FAME: Every war has its working-class heroes. During the Revolutionary War, this 19-year-old, known as the "strongest man in the Colonies" and "the American Samson," was the
people's favorite. They told stories of Private Francisco's exploits
—like the time in 1780, during a retreat, when he "lifted a 1,100-
pound cannon and *carried* it to the rear"; the time when he was ordered by a British cavalryman to drop his musket and he used his
bayonet to "lift the hapless horseman from the saddle"; the time in
1781 at Guilford Courthouse when, "with his thigh laid open by a
bayonet, Francisco chopped down 11 British troops before collaps-
ing." By the end of the war, he had become the most famous regular soldier in the Continental Army. After the war, he was rewarded with a job as sergeant at arms for the Virginia legislature.

FORGOTTEN FIGURE: Belva Ann Lockwood (née Bennett),
pioneering crusader for women's rights
CLAIM TO FAME: One historian writes: "Lockwood's entire career was a living example of women's potential, even in the stifling
atmosphere of the 19th century." In 1873, at age 43, she became an
attorney; and in 1879, she was the first woman to plead a case be-

---

Flush away! The average toilet will last about 50 years before it has to be replaced.

fore the United States Supreme Court. She persuaded male law-makers in Washington to pass a bill awarding equal pay to women employed by the federal government. In 1884 and 1888, she ran for president as the candidate of the National Equal Rights Party...and won Indiana's electoral votes—something no woman candidate has done since (at least, not yet).

FORGOTTEN FIGURE: Dr. Mary Edwards Walker, Civil War soldier, the only woman to win the Congressional Medal of Honor

CLAIM TO FAME: Achieved national prominence during the Civil War, serving as a nurse and later as a spy and surgeon (she was the first woman to hold a medical commission). In the field she dressed like male officers, wearing gold-striped trousers, a felt hat encircled with gold braid, and an officer's greatcoat. She always wore her hair in curls, though, so that "everyone would know that I was a woman." For her service to the sick and wounded, President Andrew Johnson awarded Walker the Congressional Medal of Honor; she was the first and only woman in history thus recognized.

"Immediately after the war," writes one historian, "her attire was so notorious that she was arrested on several occasions for 'masquerading as a man.' However, Walker was never prosecuted, since a grateful Congress had passed a special act granting her the right to wear trousers, in recognition of her wartime services."

Walker avidly campaigned for women's political rights...and for their right to wear pants. She also campaigned against cigarettes; she always carried an umbrella "with which she batted offending cigarettes from the mouths of startled men."

She wore her medal proudly, but in 1917, when Walker was 85, a government review board revoked it (along with the medals of 911 other Civil War veterans) on the grounds that "nothing in the records show the specific act or acts for which the decoration was originally awarded." When asked by the Army to return her medal, she replied, "Over my dead body!" "She wore the medal every day, and was wearing it when she took a bad fall on the Capitol steps" on her way to petition Congress for one of her reform causes. A few months later she died...and when she was buried, the medal was still pinned securely to her Prince Albert coat.

Poll results: Only 2% of women think they should keep their last name when they marry.

THERE'S EGG ON YOUR FACE!

Businesses spend plenty of time and plenty of money setting up elaborate promotions. Sometimes they backfire so badly that they're funny (to us—not them). A tip of the BRI hat to Nash and Zullo's Misfortune 500 *for much of the info here.*

Company: United Airlines
Promotion: "Fly Your Wife for Free"
Businessmen were invited to buy a ticket and bring their wives along at no charge. Part of the promotion included a letter from the airline thanking people for taking advantage of the offer. Soon letters poured in to United from angry wives saying *they* hadn't been their husbands' companions, and demanding to know who had.

Company: MCA Records, Canada
Promotion: Press kit for the "Miami Vice" soundtrack
The cops on TV's "Miami Vice" nailed a lot of drug smugglers in the 1980s. When the show's soundtrack was released, MCA Canada sent reviewers copies of the tape...plus a small bag of white powder (it was sugar). Bad idea. Critics howled that MCA was promoting cocaine use. MCA Canada tried to blame the idea on their California parent company. Then they found out it came from their own promotions department. "Well," a spokesman explained, sheepishly, "normally our promotions staff isn't that creative."

Company: Rival Dog Food
Promotion: A media event to publicize Rival's new dog food
In the mid-1960s, the president of Rival invited the press to lunch. He brought along a special guest—a pedigreed collie—which sat at the main table with him and was served Rival's new "all-beef dinner" for its meal. A clever way to get attention, except that the dog wouldn't eat it. Wouldn't even sniff it. "In desperation," write Nash and Zullo, "the Rival president reached into the dog's bowl and ate the stuff himself—to the cheers of reporters. The next day, news-

papers carried stories with headlines such as RIVAL PRESIDENT EATS DOG FOOD, BUT DOG WON'T." "I've never used an animal since," said the chairman of Rival's PR firm, who was fired the next day.

Company: Charleston RiverDogs (a class A minor league baseball team in South Carolina)
Promotion: "Free Vasectomy Day"
The RiverDogs announced they'd be offering a free vasectomy to anyone who showed up at the ballpark on June 13, 1997—Father's Day. The idea didn't go over too well with the general public, particularly the Roman Catholic Diocese of Charleston.

The RiverDogs' marketing VP defended the idea— "Some men find it very useful," she claimed—but less than 24 hours later, the promotion was canceled.

Company: Kellogg Co.
Promotion: They put a photo of Miss Venezuela (19-year-old Alicia Machado), winner of the 1996 Miss Universe contest, on boxes of Special K cereal in her native country.
"In Venezuela," said news reports, "where beauty queen titles launch careers, Special K cereal boxes featured the 19-year-old brunette sitting on an inflatable globe above the slogan, 'Nothing to hide.' Buyers who stocked up on the cereal in the hope of keeping their figures trim now want their money back."

The reason: Four months after winning the crown, Machado had gained 11 pounds and had acquired the nickname "the eating machine." Local newspapers were flooded with angry letters, and after a slew of bad publicity, Kellogg's discontinued the promotion.

Company: Weight Watchers
Promotion: An ad campaign featuring Weight Watchers spokeswoman Sarah Ferguson, the former Duchess of York.
Ferguson appeared on brochures and in ads saying that losing weight is "harder than outrunning the paparazzi." A week later her former sister-in-law, Princess Diana, was killed in a car wreck while trying to outrun the paparazzi. The ad campaign was quickly withdrawn.

BOND ON FILM

*Sean Connery is so closely associated with the role of James Bond
that it's hard to believe he was initially a long shot for the part. Here's
the story of how Ian Fleming's 007 thrillers found their way onto film.*

BOND-AGE FILMS

In the late 1950s Albert R. "Cubby" Broccoli and Harry Salzman, two movie producers, teamed up to turn Ian Fleming's Bond novels into action films. *Thunderball* was their choice for the first Bond film, but it was tied up in a lawsuit between Fleming and some other writers. So they settled on *Dr. No.* They shopped the idea around to every film studio in Hollywood...and were rejected by nearly everyone. Finally, United Artists agreed to back the film—as long as they didn't want to spend a lot of money. *Dr. No*'s budget was set at a paltry $1 million

Casting Call

The first task was to find the right James Bond. Broccoli and Saltzman knew what kind of actor they were looking for: a top-notch British performer who was willing to work for low-budget wages, and who would commit to making several sequels (in the unlikely event that *Dr. No* was successful).

But as Broccoli and Salzman quickly realized, no actor like that existed. Broccoli's friend Cary Grant was one of the first people to say no; many others followed. Stage actor Patrick McGoohan rejected the role on moral grounds (too violent); and up-and-coming British actor Richard Johnson refused to commit to a multipicture deal, fearing it would hurt his career. (Both men later ended up playing James Bond knock-offs on TV and in film.) Ian Fleming suggested either David Niven or Roger Moore; Niven wasn't interested, and Moore was already committed to *The Saint*, a TV detective/spy series.

SERENDIPITY

Not long after it was announced that *Dr. No* was being made into a film, *The Daily Express*, which ran the James Bond comic strip, held a readers' poll to see who should be cast as Bond. The winner was Sean Connery, a little-known Scottish actor and former Mr. Universe contestant. Connery was beginning to build a following in Great Britain, and had recently been interviewed by the paper.

At about the same time, Cubby Broccoli and his wife saw the Disney film *Darby O'Gill and the Little People*, in which Connery played a "farmer and country bumpkin." Neither of the Broccolis was particularly impressed with Connery's acting, but Cubby Broccoli liked his accent, and Mrs. Broccoli thought he had the raw sex appeal that the Bond part needed.

Coincidentally, a short time later film editor Peter Hunt sent Broccoli several reels of a film he was working on called *Operation Snafu*, with the recommendation that one of the stars—Sean Connery again—would make a great Bond.

TOUGH GUY

Connery's career prior to the Bond films was nothing to brag about, but he still played hard to get. When Broccoli asked him to test for the part, he refused, telling Broccoli, "Either take me as I am or not at all."

"He pounded the desk and told us what he wanted," Broccoli recounted years later. "What impressed us was that he had balls." The producers finally tricked him into auditioning on film by telling him they were experimenting with camera setups.

Mr. Right

Connery came from a working-class background and he showed up at the audition wearing grubby clothes, but by the time he finished his screen test Broccoli and Saltzman knew the search for Eton-educated Bond was over. "He walked like he was Superman," Broccoli recalled, "and I believed we had to go along with him. The difference between him and the other young actors was like the difference between a still photo and film. We knew we had our Bond." Connery remembers getting the part somewhat less romantically:

> Originally, they were considering all sorts of stars to play James Bond. Trevor Howard was one. Rex Harrison was another. The character was to be a shining example of British upper-crust elegance, but they couldn't afford a major name. Luckily, I was available at a price they could afford.

Casting an unknown in the lead part did not go down well at the studio—one executive rejected him and told the producers to, "see if you can do better." Connery did not impress Ian Fleming, either. "I'm looking for Commander James Bond," he complained, "not an overgrown stuntman." But Connery stayed.

THE BOND THEME

Composer Monty Norman created the musical score for *Dr. No*, and while Broccoli and Saltzman were happy with his work on the rest of the film, they didn't like his theme song. So they hired a new composer named John Barry. They told him they needed a song exactly 2-1/2 minutes long to fit into the soundtrack where the old song had gone. Without even seeing the film, Barry composed the "James Bond theme," one of the most recognizable themes in Hollywood history. He was paid £200 (less than $500) for his effort.

BOND MANIA

Dr. No premiered in 1962 and was a smash hit. The film earned huge returns for Broccoli, Saltzman, and United Artists; and launched the most successful film series in history. By 1996 a total of 19 Bond films had been made, including 7 with Sean Connery, 1 with George Lazenby, 1 with David Niven, 7 with Roger Moore, 2 with Timothy Dalton, and 1 with Pierce Brosnan, who signed on for three more through the 21st century.

  Dr. No and and the second Bond film, *From Russia with Love*, also launched a "Bond mania" complete with 007 toys, board games, spy kits, decoder rings, cartoons, toiletries, clock radios, and even lingerie. The fad peaked in 1965 and continued well into the 1970s, inspiring numerous TV knock-offs such as *The Man from U.N.C.L.E.*, *I Spy*, and *The Avengers*.

For the Boys

But the success of *Dr. No* went beyond launching a spy fad or a film series, as Suzanna Andrews writes in The *New York Times*,

> *Dr. No* also marked the beginning of the big-budget "boy" movies that today dominate the film industry, movies marked by action, special effects, and men who never fail. In spirit and style, Bond is godfather to such movies as "Lethal Weapon" and "Die Hard," and many films that star Sylvester Stallone or Arnold Schwarzenegger.

UNTIMELY END

James Bond's creator Ian Fleming, did not live to see the full impact of the genre he created: in 1964, after only two Bond films had been completed, he died from a massive heart attack brought on by years of heavy drinking and a 70-cigarette-a-day smoking habit. He was 56.

In his lifetime Fleming earned nearly $3 million in book royalties; but his heirs would lose out on many of the profits his work generated after he died. Less than a month before his death, Fleming, who suspected the end was near, sold 51% of his interest in the James Bond character to reduce the inheritance taxes on his estate. He collected only $280,000, even though it was worth millions.

❊   ❊   ❊

FOOD NOTES

Ian Fleming made James Bond into a connoisseur of fine wine, women, weapons, and food, but Fleming's own tastes left a lot to be desired, especially when it came to food. As his friend and neighbor on Jamaica, Noel Coward, recounted years later,

> Whenever I ate with Ian at Goldeneye (Fleming's Jamaican hideaway) the food was so abominable I used to cross myself before I took a mouthful....I used to say, "Ian, it tastes like armpits." And all the time you were eating there was old Ian smacking his lips for more while his guests remembered all those delicious meals he had put into the books.

BOND'S FIRST MARTINI

> "A dry Martini," [Bond] said. "One. In a deep champagne goblet."
> "Oui, Monsieur."
> "Just a moment. Three measures of Gordon's, one of vodka, half a measure of Kina Lillet. Shake it very well until it's ice cold, then add a large thin slice of lemon peel. Got it?"
> "Certainly, Monsieur." The barman seemed pleased with the idea.
>
> —*Casino Royale,* 1953

ANIMALS FAMOUS FOR 15 MINUTES

When Andy Warhol said, "In the future, everyone will be famous for 15 minutes," he obviously didn't have animals in mind. Yet even they haven't been able to escape the relentless publicity machine that keeps cranking out instant celebrities.

HEADLINE: *Cat Makes Weather Forecasters Look All Wet*
THE STAR: Napoleon, a cat in Baltimore, Maryland
WHAT HAPPENED: A severe drought hit Baltimore in the summer of 1930. Forecasters predicted an even longer dry spell, but Frances Shields called local newspapers and insisted they'd have rain in 24 hours. The reason: Her cat was lying down with his "front paw extended and his head on the floor," and he only did that just before it rained. Reporters laughed...until there *was* a rainstorm the next day.

AFTERMATH: Newspapers all over the country picked up the story, and Napoleon became a feline celebrity. He also became a professional weather-cat and newspaper columnist. His predictions were printed regularly—and he did pretty well. All told, he was about as accurate as human weather forecasters.

HEADLINE: *Nuts to Him! California Dog Wins Nutty Contest*
THE STAR: Rocky, a 100-pound male Rottweiler
WHAT HAPPENED: In 1996 a Fresno radio station ran a contest offering free Neuticles to the dog submitting the best ghost-written essay on why he wanted them. (Neuticles are artificial plastic testicles, implanted after a dog is neutered, that supposedly make the dog feel better about itself.) The appropriately named Rocky won.

AFTERMATH: The contest made national news. *Parade* magazine called it the "Best Canine Self-Improvement Story" of 1996.

HEADLINE: *Dog Makes List of Notable Americans*
THE STAR: Otis P. Albee, family dog of the Albees, in South Burlington, Vermont (breed unknown)

Research reports: An average 4-year-old child asks 437 questions a day.

WHAT HAPPENED: In the 1980s George Albee, a professor at the University of Vermont, was invited to submit biographical information for a book called *Community Leaders and Noteworthy Americans.* Instead, he filled out the forms for his dog—"a retired explorer, hunter and sportsman with a Ph.D. in animal husbandry."

AFTERMATH: Otis made it into the book. When this was reported nationwide, Albee announced that Otis had no comment. Apparently, neither did the book's publishers.

HEADLINE: *A Dog Is Man's...Best Man?*

THE STAR: Samson, a six-year-old Samoyed mix

WHAT HAPPENED: In 1995 Dan Anderson proposed to Lori Chapasko at the Wisconsin animal shelter where they both volunteered. She said yes...and approved when Dan chose their dog Samson to be "best man" at the wedding. "He epitomizes everything a best man should be," Anderson explained to reporters.

AFTERMATH: The dog was news, but apparently the wedding wasn't. Reporters seem to have ignored it.

HEADLINE: *World Gets Charge from Nuclear Kittens*

THE STARS: Four black kittens—Alpha, Beta, Gamma, and Neutron—who were living at the shut-down San Onofre Nuclear Power Plant in San Diego, California

WHAT HAPPENED: How do you make a nuclear power plant seem warm and fuzzy? Find some kittens there. In February 1996, just as the owner of the San Onofre power plant was kicking off a pro-nuclear PR campaign, a worker happened to find four motherless kittens under a building. A pregnant cat, the story went, had slipped through security at the shut-down power plant, given birth to a litter of kittens, and disappeared. When the worker tried to carry them off the grounds, alarms went off. It turned out that the cute little animals were slightly radioactive...though officials explained that they were in no danger. The story was reported worldwide. *The Nuclear News*, a nuclear industry publication, called it "the biggest nuclear story in years."

AFTERMATH: Seven months later, the Atomic Kittens were pronounced "radiation-free"...proving that nuclear power *isn't* so bad after all. Offers to adopt the pets flooded in from all over the world, but workers at the plant decided to keep them.

THE DISCOVERY OF THE PLANETS

As early as kindergarten, we're taught that there are nine planets. but 200 years ago, even scholars were sure there were only six planets. Here's how we got the three new ones.

THE END OF THE SOLAR SYSTEM

People have always known about Mercury, Venus, Mars, Jupiter, and Saturn. Early civilizations named the days of the week after each of these planets, plus the sun and moon. The Greeks watched them move through the night sky, passing in front of the stars that make up the constellations of the zodiac, and called them *planetes*—which means "wanderers."

As recently as the 1700s, people still believed that the planet Saturn was at the farthest extent of the solar system. That there might be other planets wasn't even a respectable idea. But as technology and science became more sophisticated, other members of the solar system were discovered.

URANUS

In 1781 a self-taught astronomer, William Herschel, was "sweeping the skies" with his telescope. By March, he had reached the section included the constellation Gemini, and he spotted an object that appeared as a disk rather than a glowing star. Because it moved slightly from week to week, Herschel thought it was a comet. After a few months, however, he decided the orbit was circular...and came to the shocking conclusion that it wasn't a comet, but an unknown planet. People were astonished.

Finding a Name

No one since ancient times had named a planet. Herschel felt that it should be called "Georgium Sidus" (George's Star) in honor of his patron, George III—the king of England who reigned during the American Revolution. Some people wanted to name it "Herschel" after its discoverer. But one influential astronomer suggested

---

No surprise: People laugh least in the first hour after waking up in the morning.

they call it "Uranus," after the Greek god of the heavens. That made sense, since this new planet was certainly the limit of the skies of the solar system. Or so they thought.

NEPTUNE

The newly found planet had a slight variation in its orbit, almost as if something were tugging at it. Could there be another planet affecting Uranus? A century earlier, Isaac Newton had come up with laws describing the effects that the gravitational forces of planets have on one another. Using Newton's laws, two young scientists set out independently in 1840 to find the unknown planet whose gravitational forces might be pulling on Uranus. One of the scientists was a French mathematician, Jean Leverrier. The other was an English astronomer, John Couch Adams. Both hoped the unknown planet would be where their calculations said they could find it.

The Hidden Planet

Adams finished his calculations first, in September 1845. The following August, Leverrier completed his. Neither had access to a large telescope, so they couldn't verify their projections—and no one would make one available to them. Finally, Leverrier traveled to the Berlin Observatory in Germany, and the young assistant manager, Johann Gottfried Galle, agreed to help search for the planet.

That was September 23, 1846. That night, Galle looked through the telescope, calling out stars and their positions while a young student astronomer, Heinrich Louis d'Arrest, looked at a star chart, searching for the stars Galle described. Finally Galle called out an eighth-Magnitude star that d'Arrest couldn't locate on the charts. They had found the unknown planet! It had taken two years of research—but only a half hour at the telescope. The honor of the discovery belongs to both Adams and Leverrier, who had essentially discovered the new planet with just a pen and a new set of mathematical laws. The greenish planet was named after Neptune, god of the sea.

VULCAN

Leverrier was on a roll. He started looking for other planets...and became convinced that there was one between the Sun and Mercury. He called his planet "Vulcan," the god of fire, because it was so close to the Sun. Leverrier noted that, like Uranus, Mercury experienced disturbances that caused it to travel farther in one point in its orbit. Since Neptune was one of the causes of similar pulls on Uranus, it made sense that another planet was affecting Mercury.

Leverrier never found Vulcan, but people believed it was there until 1916, when Einstein's general theory of relativity was published. Einstein gave a satisfactory explanation for the discrepancies in Mercury's orbit, scientists no longer needed Vulcan. It thereby ceased to exist...until decades later, when Gene Roddenberry, creator of "Star Trek," appropriated the planet and made it the home of Spock.

PLUTO

The discovery of Neptune did not completely account for the peculiar movements of Uranus. Once again, scientists considered the pull of another planet as a cause and set out to find "Planet X." Using the telescope at his observatory in Flagstaff, Arizona, Percival Lowell searched for Planet X for 10 years. After he died in 1916, his brother gave the observatory a donation that enabled it to buy a telescope-camera. The light-sensitive process of photography allowed astronomers to capture images of dim and distant stars that they couldn't see, even with the aid of a telescope.

In 1929 the Lowell Observatory hired Clyde Tombaugh, a young self-taught astronomer from Kansas, to continue the search for Planet X. Lowell had suggested that the unknown planet was in the Gemini region of the sky. Using an instrument called the *blink microscope*, Tombaugh took two photographs of that area of the sky a few days apart and placed them side by side under the microscope. If something moved in the sky, as planets do, it would appear as a speck of light jumping back and forth as Tombaugh's eyes moved from one photograph to the other, looking through the microscope.

That's just what happened. The observatory announced the discovery of the ninth planet on March 13, 1930. An 11-year-old girl, the daughter of an Oxford astronomy professor, chose the name Pluto—the god of the netherworld—for the new planet.

For years before his death, Tombaugh repeatedly declared that there were no more planets in our solar system. If there were, he said, he would have found them.

The Indian hero Geronimo was once kicked out of church for gambling.

OOPS!

More goofs, blunders, and dumb mistakes.

CHURCH MUSIC
"A funeral in 1996 in an English church ended with Rod Stewart singing:

> If you want my body,
> And you think I'm sexy,
> C'mon baby let me know.

The vicar admitted that when he was recording the deceased's last request—a hymn—he'd apparently failed to erase the entire cassette tape."

—*Fortean Times*, 1996

UNPLUGGED
"In 1978 workers were sent to dredge a murky stretch of the Chesterfield-Stockwith Canal. Their task was to remove all the rubbish and leave the canal clear....They were disturbed during their tea-break by a policeman who said he was investigating a giant whirlpool in the canal. When they got back, however, the whirlpool had gone...and so had a 1 1/2-mile stretch of the canal....A flotilla of irate holidaymakers were stranded on their boats in brown sludge.

Among the first pieces of junk the workers had hauled out had been the 200-year-old plug that ensured the canal's continued existence. 'We didn't know there was a plug,' said one bewildered workman...All the records had been lost in a fire during the war."

—*The Book of Heroic Failures*, by Stephen Pile

YIKES!
"Defense lawyer Phillip Robertson, trying to make a dramatic point in front of the jury at his client's recent robbery trial in Dallas, pointed the pistol used in the crime at the jury box, causing two jurors to fling their arms in front of their faces and others to gasp. Though Robertson was arguing that his client should be sentenced only to probation, the horrified jury gave him 13 years."

—"The Edge," in The Portland *Oregonian*, September 10, 1997

Denny's restaurants used to be known as "Danny's" restaurants.

THE WRONG NOTE

A 61-year-old woman and her daughter made a deposit at the drive-up window of an Albuquerque, New Mexico, bank Thursday, and were waiting for a receipt when police cars surrounded them and officers ordered them out of their vehicle at gunpoint. It turned out the New Mexico grandmother had accidentally held up the bank; she'd handed in a deposit slip on which a prankster had scrawled a hold up message. The FBI said investigators believe someone wrote the note on the deposit slip and left it in a pile inside the bank, where the woman picked it up and used it, unaware of what was written on the back."

—*Washington Post*, May 24, 1997

A PAIR OF BIRDBRAINS

"Each evening, birdlover Neil Symmons stood in his backyard in Devon, England, hooting like an owl—and one night, an owl called back to him.

"For a year, the man and his feathered friend hooted back and forth. Symmons even kept a log of their 'conversations.'

"Just as Symmons thought he was on the verge of a breakthrough in interspecies communication, his wife had a chat with next-door neighbor Wendy Cornes.

"'My husband spends his night in the garden calling out to owls,' said Mrs. Symmons.

"'That's odd,' Mrs. Cornes replied. 'So does my Fred.'

"And then it dawned on them."

—"The Edge," in The Portland *Oregonian*, August 29, 1997

GOVERNMENT EFFICIENCY

"In 1977, a government clerk in Australia made a slight error in paperwork. As a result, a $300,000 police headquarters was built in St. Arnaud's (population 3,000) instead of in St. Alban's (population 40,000). Part of the new construction was a 50-car parking lot. It is currently being used by the two cars and two bicycles of the St. Annaud's police department."

—*Encyclopedia Brown's Book of Facts,* by Donald Sobol

Rather than sell the first story he ever wrote, Charles Dickens traded it for a bag of marbles.

GREAT MOMENTS IN TELEPHONE HISTORY

Everyone's got a telephone—but it seems the only thing anyone knows about it is that Alexander Graham Bell invented it. In our Encyclopedia Bathroomica *(page 473), we talk about how the phone works. Here's a little history to go along with it.*

FEB. 14, 1876. Beating out a competing inventor by only a few hours, Alexander Graham Bell arrives at the U.S. patent office and patents the telephone in his name. Three days later, he builds the first telephone that actually works. Hoping to earn a page in the history books, he memorizes lines from Shakespeare to use in the world's first telephone conversation. But when the magic moment arrives, he spills acid on himself and barks out "Mr. Watson, come here. I want you."

Fall 1876. Bell offers to sell the rights to his invention to the Western Union Telegraph Co. for $100,000. He is laughed out of the office.

• Stage fright becomes a significant obstacle in expanding telephone sales. To reassure the public, Bell takes out ads claiming that "Conversations can be easily carried on after slight practice and with occasional repetitions of a word or sentence."

1877. Charles Williams of Somerville, Massachusetts, becomes the first American to install a telephone in his house. (But since no one else had a phone, he couldn't call anyone. So he installed a telephone in his office, where his wife could reach him during the day).

1877. A woman named Emma Nutt becomes the first female telephone operator in the United States. Initially the phone company preferred to hire young boys as operators, but eventually had to phase them out because of their foul language and penchant for practical jokes.

First prize in the 1850 French national lottery: a one way ticket to the San Francisco Gold Rush.

1879. In the middle of a measles epidemic in Lowell, Massachusetts, a physician, worried about what would happen if the town's operators succumbed to the disease, suggests to the local phone company that it begin issuing the nation's first phone numbers to telephone subscribers. At first the public resists the idea, attacking phone numbers as being too impersonal.

1881. Thomas Edison comes up with a new way to answer the telephone. "Originally," writes Margaret Cousins in *The Story of Thomas Edison*, "people wound the phone with a crank, which rang a bell, and then said: 'Are you there?' This took too much time for Edison. During one of the hundreds of tests made in his laboratory, he picked up the phone one day, twisted the crank and shouted: "Hello!" This became the way to answer the telephone all over America, and it still is."

*   *   *   *

GREAT MOMENTS IN EMERGENCY DIALING

In 1995, a woman in Devizes, England, was awakened from a sound sleep by a phone ringing.

Upon answering it, she was greeted by moans, groans, and yelling. The woman dismissed the call as a prank and hung up.

A short while later the phone rang again. This time the woman heard outright screaming, followed by a female shouting ,"Oh my God!" Terrified, the woman hung up. There was no mistaking it: the voice on the other end belonged to her daughter, who lived about a hundred miles away.

The woman phoned the police. They sent squad cars to the daughter's house, broke down the door, and stormed the bedroom.

There they found the daughter making love to her boyfriend on the bed.

Apparently, during two wild moments of passion, the daughter's big toe accidentally hit the speed-dial button on the phone, which was on a nightstand by the bed.

"This is a warning for other people," a police spokesman said. "If you're going to indulge in that sort of thing, move the phone."

—Knuckleheads in the News

The White House was originally called the "Presidential Palace."

THE LEANINGEST TOWER ON EARTH

The Leaning Tower of Pisa is one of the most recognizable buildings in the world, a visual symbol of Italy itself. Here's a look at its unusual history.

CIVIC RIVALRY

In 1155, builders in Venice, Italy, finished work on a bell tower next to the Cathedral of San Marco. Legend has it that citizens in the seaport town of Pisa—determined not to be outdone by the Venetians—decided to build their own bell tower next to the Cathedral of Pisa.

Work began in 1173. The plans called for a seven-story marble tower with more than 200 columns, plus a belfry with seven large bells at the top. The building would be 184 feet tall but only 52 feet in diameter.

The entire building was supposed to stand on a foundation less than 2240 feet deep. But as it turned out, the ground—largely sandy soil and waterlogged clay—was too spongy to support it.

BACK AND FORTH

By the time the second floor was finished, the building had already begun leaning slightly to the north. But rather than start over, the builders just lengthened the northern walls on the third floor and shortened the southern ones, levelling off the top of the building in the process. That way, they figured, the rest of the building would be level, too.

Stop and Go

As luck would have it, political unrest in Pisa forced builders to stop work on the building for 90 years. That meant the clay soil beneath the tower was allowed to compact and strengthen over time. Soil experts now believe that if it hadn't, the tower would have collapsed when the upper floors were added.

But they didn't. Six more stories were successfully added between 1270 and 1278. This time, however, the added weight

---

A brown bear can run faster than a horse at full gallop.

caused the building to lean to the *south,* the direction it still leans today. The builders applied the same solution to the fifth floor that they'd used on the third, only in reverse: they lengthened the southern walls and shortened the northern ones, giving the building a slight banana shape. Once again, the top was level.

Final Addition
Political unrest halted construction again, this time until 1360. By now the building was terribly off-center, but builders added the belfry anyway—again making the southern walls taller than the northern ones, to level out the roof. One hundred eighty-seven years after it was begun, the tower was finally finished.

But the tilt was only beginning. Over the next six centuries, the building moved a fraction of an inch each year. By the early 1990s, it was more than 14 feet off-center.

SAVING THE TOWER
By 1900, the Leaning Tower of Pisa had already become one of the world's great tourist attractions. So the Italian government just appointed a commission to figure out how to keep it from falling over.

The commission wasn't much help—except to the government, which was able to take credit for actively trying to save the tower. After that, whenever scientists speculated that the tower was falling, the government just appointed another commission. The only one that had any lasting impact was the 1933 commission...which made things worse. They drilled 361 holes in the ground surrounding the tower and filled them with 1,800 tons of concrete. Instead of stabilizing the ground, the concrete added weight to the tower's foundation, causing it to tip six times faster.

THE FINAL FIX
In 1989, the Italian government appointed its 15th commission. This time, it actually helped. In 1992, scientists began implementing a three-phase plan to halt the tilting:

1. In April 1992, five steel bands were strapped around the second floor of the building (judged to be weakest part). The belts act like girdles—when a masonry building collapses at the base, the part that gives way bursts *outward,* not inward. The bands hold everything in place.

In the 1880s, waterskiing was known as "plankgliding."

2. In the summer of 1993, scientists began placing 75 eight-ton weights on the north side of the tower, hoping that by compressing the earth to the north, the building would stop leaning so much to the south. By November, the tower had actually straightened up about a quarter of an inch.

3. In 1995, the scientists began removing clay soil from beneath the tower, extracting the water, and replacing it all in a process they called "controlled subsistence." When they're finished, the tower will be resting on a drier, firmer soil base that will be better able to support the building.

The End?
In April 1997, John Burland, the British soil mechanics expert who devised the plan, announced that the Leaning Tower of Pisa had finally stopped its tilt. Has the tower been saved? Only time—a lot of it—will tell.

TOWER FACTS
• Six of the tower's eight floors are without safety rails. More than 250 people have fallen to their deaths since 1174.

• According to Italian officials, there's little danger anyone will be hurt if the tower does come crashing down. They predict that a collapse won't be sudden—that there will be plenty of rumbling and groaning in the building ahead of time to warn people. Besides: The building is open to tourists only eight hours a day. That means there's a two-in-three chance it'll be empty when it falls.

• Restoration officials get an average of two letters a week with suggestions on how to keep the tower upright. Some of the weirdest: building an identical tower to lean against the first one; building a huge statue of a man who looks like he's holding the tower up; tying helium balloons to the roof; anchoring the top of the tower to a hillside several miles away with a large steel cable.

• Of course, officials could tear the tower down, stone by stone, and rebuild it—this time perfectly vertical—on a strengthened foundation. But there's no chance of that—the tower brings in $300 million a year from tourists. "Let's face it, the tower would have no significance if it were straight," caretaker Spartaco Campani admitted in 1983. "Its lean is Pisa's bread-and-butter."

What do Siberian tigers, river otters, and polar bears have in common? They're all blind at birth.

FIRST FILMS

People like Arnold Schwarzenegger would probably just as soon you forgot about the films they had to make before hitting it big. But Jami Bernard didn't forget—she wrote First Films, *a book we used to research this section. We recommend it. The best of its kind.*

M ERYL STREEP

First Film: *Julia* (1976)

The Role: She plays a snooty, shallow friend of the lead characters (played by Jane Fonda and Vanessa Redgrave). If you blink, you might miss her—her two scenes last a total of 61 seconds and her back is to the camera most of the time. She's also wearing a black wig (which she hated).

Memorable line: "Oooh...you're so famous."

PAUL NEWMAN

First Film: *The Silver Chalice* (1954)

The Role: Newman plays Basil, a Roman slave selected to make the chalice for Jesus's last meal because he can whittle better than anyone in Jerusalem. Publicity posters called it *The Mightiest Story of Good and Evil Ever Told, Ever Lived, Ever Made into a Motion Picture!* Newman called it "The worst film made in the entirety of 1950s." At one point, he even took out a magazine ad urging people not to see it.

ARNOLD SCHWARZENEGGER

First film: *Hercules in New York* (1969): rereleased on video as *Hercules Goes Bananas.*

The Role: Arnold plays Hercules, of course. Viewers got their first look at his pumped-up body (including a ludicrous scene in which he "bounces one pectoral muscle at a time"). But they never heard his voice. The 22-year-old Austrian's accent was so thick, no one could understand him. Result: His entire part (but *only* his) had to be dubbed. The film is so bad that Schwarzenegger—who was originally billed as "Arnold Strong"—won't acknowledge it.

Memorable line: (When a cabbie demands payment) "Bucks? Doe? What is all this zoological talk about the male and female species?"

JANE FONDA

First film: *Tall Story* (1960)

The role: Not what you'd expect. The future feminist plays June, a 21-year-old home economics major and cheerleader who's got her sights set on the school's basketball star and top scholar (Anthony Perkins). Once she gets him—about a third of the way through the film—she fades into the background. The story then focuses on Perkins's basketball dramas.

Memorable line: (On why she came to college) "The same reason that every girl, if she's honest, comes to college—to get married."

NICOLAS CAGE

First film: *Fast Times at Ridgemont High* (1982)

The role: "Brad's Bud"—a part so small that the writers didn't even bother giving him a name (or any lines). Most of his part was cut out, but you can still see him looking miserable behind the grill at All-American Burger. He was billed as Nicolas Coppola, but got so much flak from the cast about being director Francis Coppola's nephew that by his next film he'd changed his name to Cage.

MICHELLE PFEIFFER

First film: *Hollywood Knights* (1980)

The role: "Sporting her old nose and too much eye-liner...she [plays] Suzy Q, a carhop at Tubby's Drive-In, where her job requires her to wear tall, white go-go boots." On the side, she's an aspiring actress and girlfriend of Tony Danza—who also makes his screen debut in this "low-rent ripoff of *American Graffiti*."

Memorable line: "I have an audition in the morning."

TOM HANKS

First film: *He Knows You're Alone* (1980)

The role: Hanks is on for 3 1/2 minutes in this low-budget psycho-slasher film. He plays a college student who meets two of the killer's future victims and takes them on a date to a Staten Island amusement park. That's about it.

Memorable line: "Want a goober?"

ROSEANNE SEZ...

A few choice thoughts from Roseanne.

"My husband said he needs more space. So I locked him outside."

"You may think you married the man of your dreams... but 15 years later, you're married to a reclining chair that burps."

"My husband and I found this great new method of birth control that really, really works... Every night before we go to bed, we spend an hour with our kids."

"Men can read maps better than women, because only the male mind could conceive of one inch equaling one hundred miles."

"The other day on "Donahue," they had men who like to dress up as women. When they do, they can no longer parallel park."

"I quit smoking. I feel better. I smell better. And it's safer to drink out of old beer cans laying around the house."

"The day I worry about cleaning my house is the day Sears comes out with a riding vacuum cleaner."

"My son is into that nose-picking thing. The least he can do is act like an adult— buy a car and sit in traffic."

"You get a lot of tension. You get a lot of headaches. I do what it says on the aspirin bottle. Take two and keep away from children."

"The way I look at it, if the kids are still alive when my husband comes home from work, then I've done my job."

"Women are cursed, and men are the proof."

"Women complain about premenstrual syndrome, but I think of it as the only time of the month I can be myself."

"It's okay to be fat. So you're fat. Just be fat and shut up about it."

Paradise, South Dakota, was named by two residents named Adam and Eve.

WHO PAINTED THE ELEVATOR?

We found this list of words and phrases people use instead of saying "fart" in a book called Opus Maledictorum. *We figured, if you can't put a list like this in a* Bathroom Reader, *where can you put it?*

Some people simply cannot bring themselves to use the word "fart." Although the word is commonly used in many classics of English literature...and on every schoolyard in America (by even the most innocent of children), it's still considered vulgar and offensive to some people. The result: over the years all sorts of "more acceptable" terms have been invented to cover the subject. So if you don't like saying "fart"....

YOU CAN ALWAYS SAY...

Bark: A sharp report, as in a "barking" gun...a natural for a noisy passage of gas: "Are you barking for your supper or because of it?"

Barking Spider: A family-type expression to cover the subject in reasonably good humor: "It's about time to call the exterminators; those barking spiders are back again."

Bucksnorter: A farting hunter who, when tromping through the woods with a buddy, stops, lifts his leg, lets one rip, and then says: "Did you hear that buck snort?"

Cushion Creeper: A muffled fart that seems never to end, and lingers—both sound and smell—in, around, and on the soft cushion of an overstuffed chair or sofa.

House Frog: Another family-type term used to explain the situation nicely, as in "What was that?"—"Just a house frog."

Painting the Elevator: After you have just let a real stinker on an elevator (thinking you are all alone) and somebody gets on at the next floor, you wrinkle up your nose and say, "They must have just painted this elevator."

Count for yourself: The average dictionary contains entries for 278,000 words.

Pets: A French-Canadians term. Farting is called "petting"— not because they're fond of it;...[it's] short for the French word *petard*, meaning "to crack, to explode, to break wind."

Poot: An interjection used to express disgust. In the South it's a popular euphemism for fart, especially among the women-folk.

Rattler: A reverberating blast powerful enough to rattle cups and saucers, or, perhaps, even the windows and doors of rickety buildings — like army barracks.

S.B.D.: The abbreviation for the worst kind of fart — "silent-but-deadly"; in medical circles, this is called a "tacit" fart. In Spanish, a "pedo sin zapatos."

Shooting Rabbits: What one says when one hears a fart of unknown origin: "Somebody is shooting rabbits!" or "Are you the one that's been shooting rabbits all night?"

Silent Horror: Very smelly fart inflicted upon another without fair warning; illegal chemical warfare, something akin to mustard gas.

Snappers: Beans, for obvious reasons; served every Saturday night throughout New England, "to put life into the old boy!" Also used to describe what happens after the beans have had a chance to work.

Sputter: Sound imitations are sometimes useful: "I've been sputtering (or spluttering) all day." However, one can go too far with this if the imitation is too close to the real thing, as in "Who just sphtttttt?"

Squeaking Chair: A clever way to bring the passage of gas to public attention, asking: "Are you sitting in a squeaking chair?" or "I think my chair squeaks." A variation on this theme can be: "Is there a mouse in here?"

Stepping on a Frog: If you have ever stepped on a frog, or can imagine the complaints the frog would give you if you did, no further explanation is necessary.

The world's first recorded tonsillectomy was performed in the year 1,000 B.C.

THE
PROVERBIAL TRUTH

Is blood really thicker than water? How much would you have to eat if you "ate like a horse"? We found the answers in The Column of Lists.

At a snail's pace: The fastest-moving land snail is probably the common garden snail. Its top speed is 55 yards per hour, or 0.0313 mph.

Only skin deep: The skin on your eyelid is one one-thousandth of an inch deep (the thinnest); the skin on your back is one-fifth of an inch (the thickest).

Eat like a horse: A 1,200-pound horse eats about 15 pounds of hay and nine pounds of grain every day (seven times its own weight each year).

Quick as a wink: The average wink, or blink, lasts one-tenth of a second.

Knee-high to a grasshopper: The knee-high measurement of an average-sized grasshopper is about 1/2 inch.

High as a kite: The official record is 12,471 feet. Abbott Rotch, director of the U.S. Weather Bureau station in Milton, Massachusetts, set that record on February 28, 1898. Weather bureau people used to be master kite fliers, and their kites carried instruments that measured not only the temperature and humidity but also the altitude.

Faster than a speeding bullet: Los Angeles Police Department ballistics experts say that the fastest bullet is fired from a .223-caliber rifle and travels at 3,500 feet per second, more than three times the speed of sound.

Blood is thicker than water: In chemistry, water is assigned a relative density, or specific gravity, of 1.00—it is used as the standard for all other densities. By comparison, blood has a specific gravity of 1.06—only slightly thicker than water.

THE PERSONALS

We admit it—we like to sneak a peek at the personal ads every once in a while. Even when they're completely serious, they're fascinating. And when they're strange, they're irresistible. Most of these ads were collected by Kathy Hinckley for her book Plain Fat Chick Seeks Guy Who Likes Broccoli.

WOMEN SEEKING MEN

Me: buxom blonde with blue eyes. You: elderly, marriage-minded millionaire with bad heart.

I like driving around with my two cats, especially on the freeway. I make them wear little hats so that I can use the carpool lane. Way too much time on your hands too? Call me.

Lonely Christian woman has not sung Glory Hallelujah in a long time. Write soon!

Cute guy with snowplow sought by head-turnin', zany, brainy, late-30s Babe to share happy time in the big driveway of love. A rake for springtime a big plus!

Coldhearted, insensitive unconscionable, selfish, hedonistic, drunk liar seeks next gullible male without enough sense to stay away from me.

Gorgeous blonde model, tired of being patronized. Looking for sincere, understanding man. Must be willing to listen to stories of alien abduction.

MEN SEEKING WOMEN

Mentally Ill? Are you restrained in a straight-jacket? Do you think you're a chicken? Did you kill and eat your last boyfriend? I don't mind. This tall, educated, professional SWM would like to meet an interesting woman!

I drink a lot of beer, smoke a lot of cigars, and watch football nonstop from September to January. I seek a woman, 18–32, to share this with.

If it takes a three-legged elephant with one tusk 5 days to cross the Sahara Desert, how many times do I have to put an ad in to get one call?

Award-winning poet, 27 yrs., seeks short-term, intense, doomed relationship for inspiration. Must be attractive, sensual, articulate, ruthless, 21–30 yrs., under 5'6". Break my heart, please.

Desperate lonely loser, SWM, 32, tired of watching TV and my roommate's hair fall out. Seeks depressed, unattractive SWF, 25–32, no sense of humor, for long talks about the macabre.

Pound for pound, spiders, flies, and grasshoppers all contain more protein than beef does.

WHY ASK WHY?

*Here are more cosmic queries you don't need to answer,
from the Internet and our friends at "The Edge."*

Who needs rhetorical questions?

Why do they sterilize the needles for lethal injections?

How do they get the deer to cross the road at the yellow sign?

Why do kamikaze pilots wear helmets?

What do you do when you discover an endangered animal that eats only endangered plants?

If women wear a pair of pants and a pair of glasses, why don't they wear a pair of bras?

Twenty-four hours in a day...twenty-four beers in a case...coincidence?

Why do they put braille dots on the keypad of the drive-up ATM?

When you're sending someone styrofoam, what do you pack it in?

If 7-11 is open 24 hours a day, 365 days a year, why are there locks on the doors?

If someone with multiple personalities threatens to kill himself, is it considered a hostage situation?

How can there be self-help *groups*?

What's another word for *thesaurus*?

Do witches run spell-checks?

If it's tourist season, why can't we shoot them?

Is it true that cannibals don't eat clowns because they taste funny?

When you choke a Smurf, what color does it turn?

If dolphins are so smart, why did Flipper work for television?

If you haven't understood me to this point, why do I bother? If you have understood me, why are you listening?

HOW A
MICROWAVE WORKS

*We gave you a brief history of the microwave oven on page 51. Now
here's the rest of the story—the science that makes it work.*

WHAT ARE MICROWAVES?

Here's the first thing you should know about "microwaves": Like visible light, radio waves, and X-rays, they
are waves of electromagnetic energy. What makes the four waves
different from each other? Each has a different length (*wavelength*)
and vibrates at a different speed (*frequency*).

• Microwaves get their name because their wavelength is much
shorter than electromagnetic waves that carry TV and radio signals. (For more info about electromagnetic waves, see page 381.)

• The microwaves in a microwave oven have a wavelength of
about four inches, and they vibrate 2.5 billion times per second—
about the same natural frequency as water molecules. That's what
makes them so effective at heating food.

• A conventional oven heats the air in the oven, which then
cooks the food. But microwaves cause water molecules in the food
to vibrate at high speeds, creating heat. The heated water molecules are what cook the food.

• Glass, ceramic, and plastic plates contain virtually no water
molecules, which is why they don't heat up in the microwave.

MICROWAVE MECHANICS

• When the microwave oven is turned on, electricity passes
through the magnetron, the tube which produces microwaves. The
microwaves are then channeled down a metal tube (*waveguide*) and
through a slow rotating metal fan (*stirrer*), which scatters them into
the part of the oven where the food is placed.

• The walls of the oven are made of metal, which reflects microwaves the same way that a mirror reflects visible light. So when the
microwaves hit the stirrer and are scattered into the food chamber,
they bounce off the metal walls and penetrate the food from every

---

The Netherlands used to be known as the United States.

direction. Some ovens have a rotating turntable that helps food cook more evenly.

• Do microwave ovens cook food from the inside out? Some people think so, but the answer seems to be no. Microwaves cook food from the outside in, like conventional ovens. But the microwave energy only penetrates about an inch into the food. The heat that's created by the water molecules then penetrates deeper into the food, cooking it all the way through. This secondary cooking process is known as "conduction."

• The metal holes in the glass door of the microwave oven are large enough to let out visible light (which has a small wavelength), but too small to allow the microwaves (which have a larger wavelength) to escape. So you can see what's cooking without getting cooked yourself.

YOU CALL THAT COOKING?

According to legend, shortly after Raytheon perfected its first microwave oven in the 1950s, Charles Adams, the chairman of Raytheon, had one installed in his kitchen so he could taste for himself what microwave-cooked food was like. But as Adams's cook quickly discovered, meat didn't brown in the oven, french fries stayed limp and damp, and cakes didn't rise. The cook, condemning the oven as "black magic," quit.

When sales of microwave ovens took off in the late 1980s, millions of cooks discovered the same thing: Microwaves just don't cook some foods as well as regular ovens do. The reason: Because microwaves cook by exciting the water molecules in food, the food inside a microwave oven rarely cooks at temperatures higher than 212°F, the temperature at which water turns to steam.

Conventional ovens, on the other hand, cook at temperatures as high as 550°F. High temperatures are needed to caramelize sugars and break down proteins, carbohydrates, and other substances and combine them into more complex flavors. So microwave ovens can't do any of this, and they can't bake, either.

Some people feel this is the microwave's Achilles heel. "The name 'microwave oven' is a misnomer," says Cindy Ayers, an executive with Campbell's Soup. "It doesn't do what an oven does."

"It's a glorified popcorn popper," says Tom Vierhile, a researcher with *Marketing Intelligence*, a newsletter that tracks microwave sales. "When the microwave first came out, people thought they had stumbled on nirvana. It's not the appliance the food industry thought it would be. It's a major disappointment."

Adds one cooking critic: "Microwave sales are still strong, but time will tell whether they have a future in the American kitchen." In the meantime, Uncle John isn't holding his breath—he's too busy heating up leftovers.

MICROWAVE FACTS

• Have you heard that microwave ovens are dangerous? In 1968 the Walter Reed Hospital tested them to see if the microwaves leaked out. They did—and the government stepped in to set the first federal standards for microwave construction. Today all microwaves sold in the U.S. must be manufactured according to federal safety standards.

• If you microwave your foods in a square container and aren't happy with the results, try cooking them in a round one. "Food cooks better in a round container than in a square one," says Jim Watkins, president of the company that makes Healthy Choice microwave food products. "No one really knows why."

• Irregularly shaped foods, such as a leg of chicken that is thick at one end and thin at the other end, cook unevenly.

• Food that has been cut up will also cook faster than a single, large piece of food, for the same reason: the microwaves penetrate completely through smaller pieces of food, but not through larger pieces.

• Aluminum foil reflects microwave energy the same way mirrors reflect light energy. That's why you can't use foil in a microwave…unless, for example, you're using it to shield some food items on a plate while others are being cooked. But be careful: if too much food is shielded with foil, the microwaves can overload the oven and damage the magnetron.

MYTH-CONCEPTIONS

Common knowledge is frequently wrong. Here are a few examples of things that most people believe…but just aren't true.

Myth: Watching TV in a dark room is bad for your eyesight.

Fact: As Paul Dickson and Joseph C. Goulden write in *Myth-Informed*, "The myth was created in the early 1950s by an innovative Philadelphia public relations man named J. Robert Mendte, on behalf of a client who manufactured lamps."

Myth: For every cockroach you see in your house, there are 10 more you didn't see.

Fact: According to studies conducted by the Insects Affecting Man and Animals Laboratory of the U.S. Department of Agriculture, the number is actually closer to 1,000 to 1.

Myth: Flamingos are naturally pink.

Fact: Flamingos are grey when chicks. They turn pink as adults because the sea creatures they eat turn pink during digestion. The pigment is then absorbed by the bird's body and colors its feathers. If flamingos are fed a different diet, they're white.

Myth: Johnny Weissmuller's famous Tarzan yell was his own voice.

Fact: His voice was combined with a high C sung by a soprano, and a hyena's howl recorded on tape and played backward.

Myth: All your fingernails grow at the same rate.

Fact: If you're right-handed, nails on your right hand grow faster; if you're left-handed, nails on your left will.

Myth: Tonto's nickname for the Lone Ranger, Kemo Sabe, means "faithful friend."

Fact: In Apache *Kemo Sabe* means "white shirt," and in Navaho it means "soggy shrub." But George Trendle, who created the Lone Ranger, didn't know that. He took the name from a summer camp he went to as a boy.

In Nepal, Mt. Everest is known as "Gauriosankar."

Myth: The artist Vincent Van Gogh cut off his entire ear.
Fact: The famous episode followed two months of hard work, hard drinking, and an argument with his best friend, Paul Gauguin. Van Gogh was despondent and cut off only a small part of his earlobe.

Myth: Hens cannot lay eggs without a rooster.
Fact: Almost all eggs we buy in the store are unfertile eggs, laid by hens with no help from a rooster.

Myth: More women in the U.S. have had face lifts than any other type of cosmetic surgery.
Fact: Nope, the cosmetic surgery performed most frequently on women in the U.S. is liposuction. The second most popular process: collagen injections.

Myth: John Kennedy is one of many presidents buried in Washington, D.C.
Fact: Actually, there are only three. William Howard Taft (27th president) and Woodrow Wilson (28th president) are the other ones.

Myth: The largest pyramid in the world is in Egypt.
Fact: The Quetzalcoatl pyramid southeast of Mexico City is 177' tall, with a base covering 45 acres and a volume of 120 million cubic feet. Cheops, the largest in Egypt, though originally 481' tall, has a base covering only 13 acres and a volume of only 90 million cubic feet.

Myth: Giraffes have more vertebrae in their necks than other mammals.
Fact: They're the same as the rest of us. Although giraffes have the longest neck of any animal—10 to 12 feet—they have the same number of vertebrae as all mammals, including humans. The giraffe's neck bones *are* farther apart, though.

Myth: Air fresheners remove offending odors from the air.
Fact: Not even close. Actually, they either cover smells up with a stronger scent, or make your nose numb so you can't smell the bad stuff. The only way you can get *rid* of odors is with expensive absorption agents like charcoal or silica gel.

The word *mattress* originally meant "place to throw things."

SEINFELD-OLOGY

Commentary from one of America's most popular comedians.

"Now they show you how detergents take out bloodstains, a pretty violent image there. I think if you've got a T-shirt with bloodstains all over it, maybe laundry isn't your biggest problem. Maybe you should get rid of the body before you do the wash."

"Nothing in life is 'fun for the whole family.'"

"It's amazing that the amount of news that happens in the world every day just exactly fits the newspaper."

"My parents didn't want to move to Florida, but they turned sixty, and that's the law."

"A date is like a job interview that lasts all night. The only difference between the two is that there are very few job interviews where there's a chance you will wind up naked at the end of it."

"Let me ask you something. If someone's lying, are their pants really on fire?"

"One of the powers of adulthood is the ability to be totally bored and remain standing. That's why they could set up the DMV that way."

"Where lipstick is concerned, the important thing is not what color to choose, but to accept God's decision on where your lips end."

"Seventy-five percent of your body heat is lost through the top of your head. Which sounds like you could go skiing naked if you got a good hat."

"Why does McDonald's have to count every burger that they sell? What is their ultimate goal? Do they want cows to surrender voluntarily?"

"You know why dogs have no money? No pockets. 'Cause they see change on the street all the time and it's driving them crazy when you're walking them. He is always looking up at you: 'There's a quarter...'"

In one 4-year period, inventor Thomas Edison obtained an average of one patent every five days.

THE FIGHT FOR SAFE MILK, PART I

"Milk and kids" are virtually synonymous in our culture with "good health." But that wasn't always the case. Until the early 1900s, milk was often adulterated with foreign substances, taken from sick cows, or mis-handled during milking and storage. As a result, it was often host to tuberculosis, cholera, typhoid fever, and other life-threatening diseases. But few people knew that the milk made them sick. It wasn't until the late 19th century, when scientists began to understand germ theory, that they realized diseases were being transmitted through milk—and that they could do something to eliminate the hazard. Here's a fascinating but little-known story from American history.

THE GOOD OLD DAYS

In the days before refrigeration, farmers who lived near towns delivered milk the old-fashioned way: they brought a cow into town and went door to door looking for customers. Anyone who wanted milk could step out into the street with a pitcher or a bucket, and watch the farmer milk the cow right before their eyes.

Since customers were standing only a few feet away, it paid for the farmer to take good care of his cows. Nobody wanted to buy milk from a beast that looked mistreated, dirty, or sick. So although there was a risk of buying bad milk, it was kept to a minimum.

City Slickers

But in cities, where door-to-door cow service wasn't practical or possible, buying milk was another matter. "Milk sellers" acted as middlemen between farmers and townspeople. Like used car dealers today, they were widely mistrusted and said to possess "neither character, nor decency of manner, nor cleanliness." Whether or not the reputation was deserved, they were notorious for diluting milk with water to increase profits. People said their milk came from "black cows," the black cast-iron pumps that provided towns with drinking water. And if the pump was broken, horse troughs were always a handy source of water.

Although it actually spread serious diseases, watered-down milk was seen as more of an annoyance than a health hazard, and nothing much was done about it. It wasn't until the 1840s that scandals in the *liquor* industry led to the first demands for milk reform.

THE SWILL MILK SCANDALS

In the mid-1800s, it was common for whiskey and other liquor distillers to run dairy and beef businesses on the side. The manufacture of grain alcohol requires huge amounts of corn, rye, and other fresh grains, which are cooked into a mash and then distilled. Once the distillation is complete, the remaining "swill" can be discarded...or, as the distillers discovered, it could be fed to cows.

Profit, not quality, was the priority with "swill herds." As a result, conditions in many distillery-owned dairies were atrocious. The cows spent their entire lives tied up in tiny pens, which were rarely cleaned. They received no food other than the swill—and no fresh water at all since, distillers thought, there was already plenty of water in the swill.

Spoiled Milk

With no exercise, no real food, and no water, even the hardiest cattle sickened and died in about six months. The failing herds were milked daily until the very end; when a cow became too weak to stand on its own, it was hoisted upright with ropes so that it could be milked until it died.

Milk produced by swill herds, as muckraking journalist Robert Hartley wrote in 1842, was "very thin, and of a pale bluish color," the kind nobody in their right mind would buy. So distilleries added flour, starch, chalk, plaster of Paris, or anything else they could get away with to make the milk look healthy. This adulteration only increased the amount of bacteria in milk that was already virtually undrinkable.

TAKING NOTICE

The toll that adulterated milk took on public health was severe: in New York City, where five million gallons of swill milk were produced and sold each year, the mortality rate of children under five tripled between 1843 and 1856.

Crab-eating seals don't eat crabs.

No one knew for sure what was causing the child mortality rate to soar, and there was probably no single cause. But people began to suspect that bad milk was at least partially to blame. In May 1858, *Frank Leslie's Illustrated Newspaper,* one of the most popular journals of the day, published a series of articles describing in graphic detail the conditions in some of New York's swill dairies.

REFORMS
Public exposure had a devastating impact on the industry. Some distilleries got out of the milk business entirely; others cleaned up their act. Those that remained were forced out of business in 1862, when the state of New York outlawed "crowded or unhealthy conditions" in the dairy industry. Two years later, the state outlawed the industry outright, declaring that "any milk that is obtained from animals fed on distillery waste, usually called swill, is hereby declared to be impure and unwholesome."

Several other states followed suit, including Massachusetts, Pennsylvania, Illinois, Kentucky, and Indiana. As they took action, the spiraling infant death rate in the U.S. leveled off—and even began to decline. But there was still plenty of work to be done to ensure that milk was safe.

For the next part of the story, turn to page 424

*   *   *

TWO-LETTER SCRABBLE WORDS

Some unusual two-letter words that are acceptable to use in Scrabble.

aa	ba	er	ka	na	oy
ae	bo	es	la	ne	pe
ag	da	et	li	nu	pi
ai	de	ex	lo	od	re
al	ef	fa	mi	oe	sh
ar	eh	hm	mm	op	si
aw	em	ho	mo	or	ta
ay	en	jo	mu	os	ti

Florida's Disneyworld is larger than the entire city of Buffalo, New York.

LOVE POTION #9

People have been looking for aphrodisiacs since the beginning of recorded time. Most of the concoctions they've come up with are pretty weird and basically worthless. But some, it turns out, may actually work.

O RIGIN OF THE TERM
The word *aphrodisiac* comes from *Aphrodite*, the Greek goddess of love and beauty (also known as *Kallipygos*, or "Beautiful Buttocks" in Greek).

• Aphrodite was originally supposed to be the embodiment of pure beauty and heavenly love. But over the years she came to represent great prowess in sexuality and seduction as well.

• Eventually, according to the *Dictionary of Word and Phrase Origins*, her name was used "to describe any drug or other substances used to heighten one's amatory desires."

APHRODISIACS IN HISTORY

As sex therapist Dr. Ruth Westheimer says—and history proves— "an aphrodisiac is anything you think it is."

• In the Middle Ages people believed that "eating an apple soaked in your lover's armpit is a sure means of seduction." Others drank the urine of powerful animals to increase sexual powers.

• A 15th-century Middle Eastern book entitled *The Perfumed Garden for the Soul's Delectation* suggested that lovers eat a sparrow's tongue, and chase it down with a cocktail made of honey, 20 almonds, and parts of a pine tree.

• People once thought that eating any plant that looks phallic would increase male virility—carrots, asparagus, and mandrake root were especially popular. Bulbs and tubers—e.g., onions—which people thought resembled testicles, were also believed to increase sexual potency. And peaches, tomatoes, mangos, or other soft, moist fruits were considered aphrodisiacs for women.

• In *Consuming Passions*, Peter Farb and George Armelagos write that during the 1500s and 1600s, "Europe was suddenly flooded with exotic plants whose very strangeness suggested the existence of secret powers." For example:

A wolf's howl can be heard as far as seven miles away; a bullfrog's croak: one mile away.

Tomatoes brought back from South America were at first thought to be the forbidden fruit of Eden, and were known as "love apples." And when potatoes first arrived in Europe—the sweet potato probably brought back by Columbus and the white potato somewhat later—they were immediately celebrated as potent sexual stimulants....A work dated 1850 tells the English reader that the white potato will "incite to Venus."

• In the 20th century, everything from green M&M's to products like Cleopatra Oil and Indian Love Powder have been passed off as aphrodisiacs. Even in 1989, a British mail-order firm called Comet Scientific was offering an aerosol spray that it claimed made men "irresistible to women."

DANGEROUS APHRODISIACS

• Spanish fly, one of the most famous aphrodisiacs, is also one of the most dangerous. It has nothing to do with Spain or flies. It's really the dried, crushed remains of an insect known as the "blister beetle." Although it can constrict blood vessels, and thus may appear to be a sexual stimulant, it's actually a deadly poison. It can do irreparable damage to the kidneys.

• For thousands of years, people (especially in the Far East) have believed that by eating part of a powerful animal, a man can absorb its sexual vitality. This has led to the ingestion of such weird stuff as dried and powdered bear gallbladders, camel humps, and rhinoceros horns. (In fact, animal horns have been considered sexual stimulants for so long that the term "horny" became slang for "a need for sex.") It has also had a drastic effect on some endangered species. *U.S. News & World Report* noted in 1989 that "with a kilo of rhino horn fetching $42,800 in Taiwan, poachers have slaughtered rhinos so relentlessly that barely 11,000 survive." And in North America, poachers have killed thousands of black bears to get their golf ball-sized gallbladders.

THE REAL THING

Traditionally, scientists have dismissed aphrodisiacs as frauds. But new research into medicinal herbs and pheromones (chemical messengers) has produced some interesting results. Experts now believe that some aphrodisiacs may really work. Here are seven "maybe's."

1. Yohimbe: The bark of a West African tree thought for centuries to produce passion in African men. Research has found that the chemical yohimbine can in fact excite men by increasing blood flow. The drug was approved by the FDA 10 years ago as a prescription treatment for impotence.

2. Oysters: Traditionally considered an aphrodisiac because of their association with the sea and their resemblance to female sex organs. However, now we also know that they're very rich in zinc—a mineral necessary to male sexual health. A man deficient in zinc is at high risk for infertility and loss of libido.

3. Chocolate: Contains PEA, a neurotransmitter that is a natural form of the stimulant amphetamine. It has been shown that either love or lust increases the level of PEA in the bloodstream and that with heartbreak, the levels drop dramatically.

4. Caffeine: Research has shown that coffee drinkers are more sexually active than non-drinkers, but no one's sure if that's because of something in the caffeine, or just because it keeps people awake, and therefore interested, after bedtime.

5. DHEA: This hormone has been called the "natural aphrodisiac" by doctors. It's been shown in studies that blood levels of DHEA predict sexual thoughts and desire. DHEA became a food-supplement fad when it was hyped in the media as a way to increase energy and maybe even prevent cancer or heart disease (as well as boosting the libido).

6. Cinnamon: According to Dr. Alan Hirsch, director of the Smell and Taste Research Foundation, the aroma of cinnamon has the ability to arouse lust. As reported in *Psychology Today*, "Hirsch fitted male medical students with gauges that detected their excitement level, and then exposed them to dozens of fragrances. The only one that got a rise was the smell of hot cinnamon buns."

7. Androstenone: This is a pheromone. Scientists conducting research with animals found that androstenone produced by boars had a very positive effect on the sexual receptivity of sows. Androstenone is also found in human sweat.

FINAL THOUGHT

"Power is the great aphrodisiac." **—Henry Kissinger**

TOP-RATED TV SHOWS, 1973–1978

More of the annual Top 10 TV shows of the past 50 years.

1973-1974

(1) All in the Family
(2) The Waltons
(3) Sanford and Son
(4) M*A*S*H
(5) Hawaii Five-O
(6) Maude
(7) Kojak
(8) The Sonny and Cher
    Comedy Hour
(9) The Mary Tyler
    Moore Show
(10) Cannon

1974-1975

(1) All in the Family
(2) Sanford and Son
(3) Chico and the Man
(4) The Jeffersons
(5) M*A*S*H
(6) Rhoda
(7) The Waltons
(8) Good Times
(9) Maude
(10) Hawaii Five-O

1975-1976

(1) All in the Family
(2) Laverne and Shirley
(3) Rich Man, Poor Man
(4) Maude
(5) The Bionic Woman
(6) Phyllis
(7) The Six Million Dollar Man
(8) Sanford and Son
(9) Rhoda
(10) Happy Days

1976-1977

(1) Happy Days
(2) Laverne and Shirley
(3) The ABC Monday
    Night Movie
(4) M*A*S*H
(5) Charlie's Angels
(6) The Big Event
(7) The Six Million
    Dollar Man
(8) The ABC Sunday
    Night Movie
(9) Baretta
(10) One Day at a Time

1977-1978

(1) Laverne and Shirley
(2) Happy Days
(3) Three's Company
(4) Charlie's Angels
(5) All in the Family
(6) (tie) Little House on the Prairie
(6) (tie) 60 Minutes
(8) (tie) M*A*S*H
(8) (tie) One Day at a Time
(10) Alice

1978-1979

(1) Three's Company
(2) Laverne and Shirley
(3) Mork & Mindy
(4) Happy Days
(5) Angie
(6) (tie) 60 Minutes
(6) (tie) M*A*S*H
(8) The Ropers
(9) Charlie's Angels
(10) (tie) All in the Family

Average number of days each year when no major league sports are played: 5.

GIVE 'EM HELL, HARRY

A few words from Harry Truman, our 33nd president.

"It isn't polls or public opinion at the moment that counts. It is right and wrong and leadership—men with fortitude, honesty, and a belief in the right that makes epochs in the history of the world."

"We're going to lick 'em just as sure as you stand there!"

"Whenever the press quits abusing me, I know I'm in the wrong pew."

To his daughter: "Your dad will never be reckoned among the great. But you can be sure he did his level best and gave all he had to his country. There is an epitaph in Boot Hill Cemetery in Tombstone, Arizona, which reads, 'Here lies Jack Williams; he done his damnedest.' What more can a person do?"

"If they want to ask me some impudent questions, I'll try to give them some impudent answers."

"You won't get any double-talk from me. I'm either for something or against it."

"This is your fight. I am only waking you up to the fact that this is your fight. You better get out and help me win this fight, or you're going to be the loser, not I."

"I hope you will join me in my crusade to keep the country from going to the dogs."

"Some of the presidents were great, and some weren't. I can say that because I wasn't one of the great presidents, but I had a good time trying."

"I don't believe in anti-anything. A man has to have a program; you have to be *for* something, otherwise you will never get anywhere."

"My favorite animal is the mule. He has more sense than a horse. He knows when to stop eating—and when to stop working."

There were 16 contestants in the 1996 Arkansas Mosquito Cook-Off.

LET'S ROCK!

We'll bet you didn't know your favorite rock singers could talk, too. Here's some of the profound things they have to say, from The Great Rock 'n' Roll Quote Book, *by Merrit Malloy.*

"I'd rather have ten years of super-hypermost than live to be seventy by sitting in some goddamn chair watching TV."
—*Janis Joplin*

"When you're as rich as I am, you don't have to be political."
—*Sting*

"People used to throw rocks at me for my clothes. Now they wanna know where I buy them."
—*Cyndi Lauper*

"I'd rather be dead than singing 'Satisfaction' when I'm forty-five."
—*Mick Jagger*

"People have this obsession: They want you to be like you were in 1969. They want you to, because otherwise their youth goes with you, you know?"
—*Mick Jagger*

"Nobody loves me but my mother, and she could be jivin', too."
—*B. B. King*

"Rock journalism is people who can't write interviewing people who can't talk for people who can't read."
—*Frank Zappa*

"There are no more political statements. The only thing rock fans have in common is their music."
—*Bob Pittman, Vice President, MTV*

"Some American kid recognized who I was and he says, 'Your dad eats cow's heads.' My daughter says, 'You don't, Daddy. I've never seen you eat a cow's head.' I thought that was kind of sweet."
—*Ozzy Osbourne*

"I would think nothing of tipping over a table with a whole long spread on it just because there was turkey roll on the table and I had explicitly said, 'No turkey roll.'"
—*Steven Tyler, Aerosmith*

"Mainly, I helped wipe out the sixties."
—*Iggy Pop*

OH, FRANKIE!

You might be surprised at the role that trickery played in helping an up-and-coming singer get the "lucky break" he needed.

BACKGROUND
In 1942 a young singer named Frank Sinatra gave a performance at New York's Paramount Theater. Until then, his career had gotten little attention. But that night was different—Sinatra played to a packed house and gave such a powerful performance that about 30 bobby-soxers passed out and had to be taken away in an ambulance. The publicity that the incident generated helped catapult Sinatra to superstardom in less than a year.

BEHIND THE SCENES

The decisive moment in Sinatra's career actually came a few weeks *before* the Paramount show, when his press agent, George Evans, saw a teenage girl throw a rose on stage while Sinatra was singing. "I figured if I could pack the theater with a bunch of girls screaming, 'Oh, Frankie,' I'd really have something," he recounted later.

So Evans paid a dozen teenage girls $5 each to sit in the front rows during the performance and swoon. Rehearsing with them in the basement of the Paramount, he taught some of them to faint in the aisles during the slow songs, and taught others to scream 'Oh, Daddy,' when Sinatra sang "Embraceable You." He made sure the theater was full by giving away free passes to schoolkids on vacation. He even rented the ambulance that waited in front of the theater to take the girls away.

MASS HYSTERIA

Evans paid only 12 girls, but in a classic moment of mass psychosis, hundreds of others got caught up in the "excitement." About 20 girls who *hadn't* been paid to pass out fainted…and the whole crowd went crazy. The next time he played the Paramount, recalls a promoter, "they threw more than roses. They threw their panties and their brassieres. They went nuts, absolutely nuts." Sinatra-mania was born. Ol' Blue Eyes went on to become the most popular singer of his generation. But Evans wasn't around to enjoy it. Sinatra fired him a few years later in a dispute over money.

Experts say: If you don't remove an avocado's pit, it won't turn black, even when you peel it.

WHAT HAPPENED AT ROSWELL?

The "incident at Roswell" is probably the biggest UFO story in history. Was it a military balloon…or an alien spacecraft? You be the judge…

THE FIRST FLYING SAUCERS

In 1947, a U.S. Forest Service pilot named Kenneth Arnold was flying over the Cascade Mountains in Washington State in search of a missing plane when he spotted what he claimed were nine "disc-shaped craft." He calculated them to be moving at speeds of 1,200 miles per hour, far faster than any human-built aircraft of the 1940s could manage.

When he talked to reporters after the flight, Arnold said the crafts moved "like a *saucer* skipping over water," and a newspaper editor, hearing the description, called the objects "flying saucers." Thus, the expression "flying saucer" entered the English language, and a UFO craze much like the one that followed Orson Welles's 1938 broadcast of *War of the Worlds* swept the country. "Almost instantly," Dava Sobel writes in his article *The Truth About Roswell*, "believable witnesses from other states and several countries reported similar sightings, enlivening wire-service dispatches for days."

THE ROSWELL DISCOVERY

It was in this atmosphere that William "Mac" Brazel made an unusual discovery. On July 8, 1947, while riding across his ranch 26 miles outside of Roswell, New Mexico, he came across some mysterious wreckage—sticks, foil paper, tape, and other debris. Brazel had never seen anything like it, but UFOs were on his mind. He'd read about Arnold's sighting in the newspaper and had heard about a national contest offering $3,000 to anyone who recovered a flying saucer. He wondered if he'd stumbled across just the kind of evidence the contest organizers were looking for.

Brazel gathered a few pieces of the stuff and showed it to his neighbors, Floyd and Loretta Proctor. The Proctors didn't know what it was, either. And neither did George Wilcox, the county sheriff. So Brazel contacted officials at the nearby Roswell Army

Air Force base to see if they could help.

The next day, an Army Intelligence Officer named Jesse Marcel went out to Brazel's ranch to have a look. He was as baffled as everyone else. "I saw...small bits of metal," he recalled to reporters years later, "but mostly we found some material that's hard to describe." Some of it "looked very much like parchment" and some of it consisted of square sticks as much as four feet long. Much was metallic.

The stuff was also surprisingly light—Brazel later estimated that all the scraps together didn't weigh more than five pounds. Marcel and his assistant had no trouble loading all the debris into their cars and driving it back to the Roswell base. The next day, Marcel took it to another base, in Fort Worth, Texas, where it was examined further.

SUSPICIOUS FACTS

Was the Wreckage from Outer Space?

• Brazel and the Proctors examined some of the debris before surrendering it to the military. Although it seemed flimsy at first, it was extremely resilient. "We tried to burn it, but it wouldn't ignite," Loretta recalls. "We tried to cut it and scrape at it, but a knife wouldn't touch it....It looked like wood or plastic, but back then we didn't have plastic. Back then, we figured it doesn't look like a weather balloon. I don't think it was something from this Earth."

The Military's About-Face

• The morning after the military took possession of the wreckage, the media relations officer at Roswell hand-delivered a news release to the two radio stations and newspapers in town. The release stated that the object found in Brazel's field was a "flying disc," which in the 1940s was synonymous with "flying saucer." It was the first time in history that the U.S. military had ever made such a claim.

• A few hours later, though, the military changed its story: It issued a new press release claiming that the wreckage was that of a weather balloon carrying a radar target, not a "flying disc." But it was too late—the newspaper deadline had already passed. They ran the first news release on the front page, under the headline

AIR FORCE CAPTURES FLYING SAUCER
ON RANCH IN ROSWELL REGION

Kangaroos are lactose-intolerant.

Other newspapers picked up the story and ran it as well; within 24 hours, news of the military's "capture" spread around the globe.

• Interest in the story was so great that the next day, Brig. Gen. Roger Ramey, commander of the U.S. Eighth Air Force, had to hold a press conference in Fort Worth in which he again stated that the recovered object was only a weather balloon and a radar target that was suspended from it. He even displayed the wreckage for reporters and allowed them to photograph it.

Mr. Brazel's Unusual Behavior

• Mac Brazel refused to talk about the incident for the rest of his life, even with members of his immediate family, except to say that "whatever the wreckage was, it wasn't any type of balloon." Why the silence? His son Bill explains: "The Air Force asked him to take an oath that he wouldn't tell anybody in detail about it. My dad was such a guy that he went to his grave and he *never* told anyone."

• Kevin Randle and Donald Schmitt, authors of *UFO Crash at Roswell*, claim that shortly after Brazel made his famous discovery, "His neighbors noticed a change in his lifestyle....He suddenly seemed to have more money....When he returned, he drove a new pickup truck...he also had the money to buy a new house in Tularosa, New Mexico, and a meat locker in Las Cruces." Randle and Schmitt believe the military may have paid Brazel for his silence.

TRUST ME

Today, if the government announced it had captured a UFO— even if it was mistaken—and tried to change its story a few hours later by claiming it was really a weather balloon, nobody would buy it. But people were more trusting in the years just following World War II. Amazingly, the story died away. As Dava Sobel writes:

> The Army's announcement of the "weather balloon" explanation ended the flying saucer excitement. All mention of the craft dropped from the newspapers, from military records, from the national consciousness, and even from the talk of the town in Roswell.

Even the *Roswell Daily Record*—which broke the story in the first place—was satisfied with the military's explanation. A few days later, it ran a headline that was even bigger than the first one:

GENERAL RAMEY EMPTIES ROSWELL SAUCER

And that was the end of it...or was it? See page 401 for more.

In the 1800s, you could buy ketchup flavored with lobster, walnuts, oysters, or anchovies.

LEGENDARY TV FLOPS

There are plenty of bombs in TV history, but these three shows are legends.

MELBA.
A CBS sitcom starring singer Melba Moore as Melba Patterson, a single mother who ran "the Manhattan Visitors' Center." Premiered as a mid-season replacement on January 28, 1986—the day the *Challenger* space shuttle exploded. Drew the worst ratings of the 1985-86 season and was cancelled immediately. In August, CBS aired the other episodes it had commissioned. The night of its return was CBS's lowest-rated prime-time evening in the network's history.

TURN ON!
A half-hour of skits and jokes that was supposed to be "the second coming of 'Laugh-In'." It premiered on February 5, 1969, and turned out to be "just a bunch of stupid sex jokes." (The longest skit had two actors making faces at each other for several minutes while the word SEX flashed on screen.) Affiliates and sponsors hated it so much that it was cancelled the next day. In fact, the Denver ABC affiliate cancelled it *halfway through* the premiere, with the message: "The remainder of this show won't be seen." How bad was "Turn On!"? We can only speculate. The producers' settlement with the networks and sponsors stipulates that the "tapes would be locked up and never shown again."

YOU'RE IN THE PICTURE.
A game show hosted by Jackie Gleason. Four celebrity panelists sat in back of a 7'x10' picture frame and stuck their heads through porthole cutouts—making them part of a picture they couldn't see. With clues from Gleason, they tried to guess what the picture was. It debuted January 21, 1961. "Viewers who tuned into the show's third broadcast," writes Maxene Fabe in *Game Shows*, "saw only a bare stage containing an armchair in which Gleason sat. 'I apologize for insulting your intelligence,' he told his astonished viewers. 'From now on I promise to stick to comedy.'" The program was replaced the following week with "The Jackie Gleason Show."

MORE STRANGE LAWSUITS

More bizarre lawsuits from contemporary news reports.

THE PLAINTIFF: William H. Folwell, Episcopal bishop of Central Florida

THE DEFENDANT: U.S. government

THE LAWSUIT: The bishop hurt his knee while playing tennis at the Naval Training Center. He claimed the injury "prevented him from genuflecting," and sued for $200,000. The Feds countersued, saying the holy man had been sneaking onto the tennis courts and had no right to be there in the first place. They said he owed them $5,200 for use of the courts over the last five years.

THE VERDICT: Case dismissed. Neither side got any cash.

THE PLAINTIFF: Continental Airlines

THE DEFENDANT: Deborah Loeding, former wife of Continental pilot William Loeding

THE LAWSUIT: In 1994 William Loeding took a random drug test administered by the airline. Marijuana was detected, and Loeding was fired—although he swore he'd never gone near the stuff. He filed grievance after grievance with his union—and finally, during his third hearing, his ex-wife admitted she was responsible. To vent her anger at her ex-husband, she'd put pot in a loaf of rye bread she baked for him. Continental sued her for endangering passengers and causing her ex-hubby "significant distress in his personal and professional life."

THE VERDICT: Pending.

THE PLAINTIFF: Paul and Nancy Marshall, baseball fans

THE DEFENDANTS: San Diego Padres baseball team

THE LAWSUIT: In 1993, in a cost-cutting move, the Padres began trading high-salaried star players to other teams. When former batting champ Garry Sheffield was traded, the Marshalls filed suit charging the Padres with deceiving season ticket holders. (The

---

Alexander Graham Bell's father-in-law invented the burglar alarm.

team had sent out a letter saying players like Sheffield and Fred McGriff, an all-star first-baseman, "create the core of an excellent team for years to come.") The Marshalls asked for punitive damages and a promise that the Padres wouldn't trade McGriff.

THE VERDICT: Settled out of court. The Padres agreed to a more liberal ticket refund policy, and the Marshalls' suit was dropped. McGriff was traded to the Atlanta Braves five days later.

THE PLAINTIFF: James Houston
THE DEFENDANT: Northern Arizona University
THE LAWSUIT: According to news reports, Houston "is suing his alma mater because he believes that getting a doctorate was too easy." He is asking for $1 million.
THE VERDICT: Pending.

THE PLAINTIFF: Ethyln Boese, of Portland, Oregon
THE DEFENDANT: Restlawn Funeral Home
THE LAWSUIT: On July 25, 1996, a closed-casket funeral was held for Boese's husband, James. When it was over, Ethyln asked for a last look at the man she'd been married to for 50 years. When the casket was opened, she saw a stranger—in her husband's suit. At first, the funeral director wouldn't believe it was the wrong body. Finally he did, and found the right one. The family quickly got a different suit for the corpse, held a new funeral, and filed a lawsuit for $500,000 for "emotional distress."
THE VERDICT: Unknown

THE PLAINTIFF: Katie Rose Sawyer, age 11
THE DEFENDANT: Cody Finch, age 10
THE LAWSUIT: Fifth-graders Sawyer and Finch were "married" on the school playground in the fall of 1996. Then a few months later, they were "divorced" (another fifth-grader wrote up "Divores" papers). Katie said Cody kept bothering her, so she sued him under the New Mexico Family Violence Protection Act. "My mom told me, 'Don't get married again until you're an adult,'" Katie told reporters.
THE VERDICT: Unknown.

In a single day, a pair of termites can produce as many as 30,000 offspring.

AS SEEN ON TV!

We've all seen them—those cheesy TV ads for products no one needs, but millions of people buy. You've probably forgotten all about them. Well, heh-heh, we're here to remind you about...

GLH#9: Hair-in-a-can from the infamous Ron Popeil (GLH stands for "great looking hair.") A spray can of some sort of powdered pigment that sticks to your head. Just hold a few inches from your bald spot and spray! Comes in nine colors and according to the free brochure, you can use it on your dog!

THE CLAPPER: "Clap on, clap off!" From Joseph Industries, makers of the Chia Pet. "Clap twice and a lamp goes on, clap twice and it goes off. Only $19.95!"

INSIDE THE EGGSHELL SCRAMBLER: A piece of plastic with a curved needle attached. Impale the egg on the needle and it activates a motor. The needle spins inside the shell and *scrambles the egg*! "Outperforms a fork or whisk in every way! Scrambles the yolk and white of an egg right inside the shell in less than five seconds! You'll use it a lot and every time you do, you'll save washing a bowl and fork!"

THE GINSU KNIFE: From Dial Media. Ads showed a karate expert shattering bricks and kicking a watermelon, then fuming because he couldn't cut as well as the "amazing Ginsu knife!" Sounds vaguely Asian, but it's not—it was originally brought to the company by a salesperson who thought it was great because it never needed sharpening. But it was still just a knife...until the creative vice president of Dial came up with a Japanese-sounding name, a karate-theme ad, and the tag line: "But wait, there's more!"

THE VEG-O-MATIC: "This is Veg-O-Matic, the world-famous food appliance. Slice a whole potato into uniform slices with one motion....Simply turn the ring and change from thin to thick slices. Isn't that amazing? Like magic, you can change from slicing to dicing. No one likes dicing onions. The Veg-O-Matic makes mounds of

Difficult, Tennessee, gets its name because its residents couldn't agree on a name for the town.

them fast. The only tears you'll shed will be tears of joy. You can make hundreds of French fries in one minute. Isn't that sensational? Here's your chance to own one for only $9.99!" From Ronco.

THE SMOKELESS ASHTRAY: A plastic ashtray with a little fan that sucks smoke *in*. "Does cigarette and cigar smoke offend you? Does smoke irritate your eyes? If it does, you need the new Smokeless Ashtray....Helps clear the air you breathe. If you smoke, buy one and be considerate of those who don't smoke. If you don't smoke, buy one for those who do. Buy two or three. They really do make great Christmas gifts. And they're only $9.98!"

POCKET FISHERMAN: A fishing rod and reel that fold into a small carrying case. "Attaches to your belt...or fits in the glove compartment of your car!"

MIRACLE MOP: For $19.95, you get the original self-wringing mop "with a twistable shaft that lets you wring out the head without putting your hands into the dirty water!"

THE BUTTONEER: "The problem with buttons is they always fall off. *The problem with buttons is they always fall off.* And when they do, don't sew them on the old-fashioned way with needle and thread. Use The Buttoneer, the new automatic button fastener that attaches any kind of button!...Repair upholstery, pleat draperies, attach appliqués, ribbons, decorate toys, dolls...it's The Buttoneer!"

THE RONCO BOTTLE AND JAR CUTTER: "An exciting way to recycle throwaway bottles and jars into decorative glassware, centerpieces, thousands of things!...A hobby for Dad, craft for the kids, a great gift for Mom. The Ronco Bottle and Jar Cutter. Only $7.77!"

THE RONCO RHINESTONE AND STUD SETTER: A gizmo that attaches rhinestones and studs to jackets and jeans. "It changes everyday clothing into exciting fashions!...For young or old, the Ronco Rhinestone and Stud Setter is great fun!" Later marketed on TV as The Bedazzler.

DAMN YOU, STINK MAN!

*Until recently, all movies made in Hong Kong—including "chop sockey"
low-budget martial arts films—legally had to have English subtitles, because
it was a British colony. But chop sockey producers spend as little on transla-
tions as possible—typically it might take only two days and $128 to translate
a whole film. In Sex and Zen & a Bullet in the Head,* Stefan
Hammond *and* Michael Wilkins *list some of the most
ludicrous chop sockey subtitles. (These are real!)*

"You're a bad guy, where's your library card?"

"How can you use my intestines as a gift?"

"Quiet or I'll blow your throat up."

"Check if there's a hole in my underpants."

"No! I saw a vomiting crab."

"Damn you, stink man!"

"You're stain!"

"Bump him dead."

"Suck the coffin mushroom now."

"A big fool, with a gun, go to war. Surrendered and turned to a cake."

"You bastard, try this melon."

"Noodles? Forget it. Try my fist."

"Brother, my pants are coming out."

"Get out, you smurk!"

"Don't you feel the stink smell?"

"Take my advice or I'll spank you without pants."

"You cheat ghosts to eat tofu?"

"I'm not Jesus Christ, I'm Bunny."

"You're bad. You make my busts up and down."

"He's Big Head Man, he is lousing around."

"She's terrific. I can't stand her."

"You daring lousy guy."

"Well! Masturbate in hell!"

"The fart of God."
"What does it mean?"
"With a remarkable sound."

"Okay, I'll Bastare, show your guts."

"Suddenly my worm are all healed off."

"And you thought. I'm gabby bag."

Take your weight and divide by three. That's how much your legs weigh.

THE SECRET OF NANCY DREW

*The most famous girl sleuth in history had her own
secret for over 60 years: the identity of her creator.*

THE MYSTERY

As every fan knows, the author of the Nancy Drew series is Carolyn Keene. She began writing about the girl detective in 1930 (debut adventure: *The Secret of the Old Clock*), and today her work is as popular as ever. There are more than 20 million Nancy Drew books currently in print, in 18 languages.

The only problem: There *is* no person named Carolyn Keene—the name was invented by a man named Edward Stratemeyer. For over 60 years it was assumed that his daughter, Harriet Stratemeyer Adams, really wrote the books. Then in 1993, a real-life amateur sleuth uncovered the whole truth.

THE CLUES

1. *It was Edward Stratemeyer who first conceived the broad outlines of Nancy Drew, the 16-year-old amateur detective, in 1930.*

• Stratemeyer started out writing "dime novels" in the 1890s. During the Spanish-American War, he invented a fantastically popular series of juvenile stories starring the Rover Boys. Then he created teenage scientist Tom Swift and the Bobbsey Twins.

• In 1906, he realized he couldn't write stories fast enough to keep up with demand. So he began hiring newspaper reporters to write books from his plot outlines, paying them between $50 and $250 per novel. They never got credit—Stratemeyer made them sign a contract giving up all rights to their work, renouncing royalties, and promising never to reveal their identities.

• Thus the Stratemeyer Syndicate was born. By the 1920s, the syndicate was producing and selling millions of books a year. They starred Baseball Joe, Dave Dashaway, Bomba the Jungle Boy, the Motor Girls, and many more. In 1927, Stratemeyer invented one of his most popular series, the Hardy Boys (and its "author," F. W. Dixon).

• By the time of his death, Stratemeyer had developed more than 800 books for children and teenagers under 88 different pseudonyms. Just before he died in 1930, he came up with the idea that would be the Syndicate's biggest seller—Nancy Drew.

2. Stratemeyer's daughter, Harriet, took over the Syndicate. She later said she found the first three Nancy Drew manuscripts among her father's possessions.

• After graduating from Wellesley College in 1915, Adams went to work for her father—but not as a writer. Ironically, Stratemeyer didn't feel that women should work. "If they did," Adams recalled, "it was a disgrace and meant their fathers couldn't support them."

• Nevertheless, when Stratemeyer passed away in 1930, Adams and her sister took over the business. In the next 50 years, she outproduced her father, and is credited with writing 180 books and originating the plots for 1,200 others.

• Adams said that her father wrote the first three Nancy Drew books himself, and that in 1930, she found them, cleaned them up, and sent them off to be published. Then she took over the series and wrote the rest of them. Throughout her life, Adams was celebrated as the "real Carolyn Keene."

3. But there was a disparity between Nancy Drew and Adams's other characters.

• Nancy was independent, quick-thinking, in charge—a proto-feminist; Adams's other creations, like the Dana Girls, were flat and conventional.

• Critics and fans were puzzled by this. In a long analysis of the Nancy Drew series in *The Horn Book*, for example, Anne Scott MacLeod concluded that

> What Harriet Adams achieved in Nancy Drew was, apparently, as accidental as it was monumental. "If I made Nancy liberated, I was unconscious of the fact," Mrs. Adams said in 1980. It is ungenerous, but entirely believable. Adams's portraits of other women [in her other books]…seem ample evidence that she was [not] a feminist.

MYSTERY SOLVED
Adams wasn't a feminist—but Mildred Wirt Benson was.

In 1993 Geoffrey S. Lapin, a Nancy Drew fan, tracked Benson

down in Toledo, Ohio. The 87-year-old had been working there as a reporter for 50 years—and was still writing a weekly column for the *Toledo Blade* called "On the Go with Millie Benson."

But back in 1930, she was a reporter for the *Des Moines Register*. Edward Stratemeyer approached her about writing the first Nancy Drew story. He gave her a one-paragraph outline and paid her $125. She produced *The Secret of the Old Clock*.

At first, Stratemeyer wasn't happy with the character Benson had created. He felt Nancy was too independent and bossy at a time when girls were supposed to be delicate and dependent on men. But he had a deadline, and sent the manuscript to the publisher anyway.

By 1934—four years after the first Nancy Drew story was published—the series had outsold every other children's book in existence. Girls loved Nancy because she showed that they could have experiences on an equal level with boys. Benson told a reporter later:

> I sort of liked the character from the beginning. Now that kind of woman is common, but then it was a new concept, though not to me. I just naturally thought that girls could do the things boys did.

THE REAL NANCY DREW

"Mrs. Benson's life has tended to resemble her heroine's," commented a critic in the *New York Times*. "A doctor's daughter, she was the first woman to get a master's degree in journalism from the University of Iowa. She was [also] an accomplished pilot who "made nine solo trips to Central America to study pre-Columbian archaeology."

Benson wrote 26 of the first 30 Nancy Drew books, but never revealed her identity. She didn't want a lawsuit from the Stratemeyer Syndicate and besides, she "didn't want to get pestered."

After being discovered by Lapin, Benson was elected to the Ohio Women's Hall of Fame in 1993 and was honored by the University of Iowa at the first Nancy Drew Conference the same year.

Did she enjoy the attention? Well, yes, she admitted to the *New York Times*, but added: "I'm so sick of Nancy Drew I could vomit."

King Henry VIII owned tennis shoes.

THE NAKED TRUTH

Here's the latest BRI collection of "Nudes in the News."

THE NAKED USHERETTE

RIO DE JANEIRO, Brazil—"During a screening of *The Exorcist* at La Pampa Cinema in 1974, the audience was distracted by an usherette scampering backward and forward across the screen pursuing a rat with a mop. To cries of 'Get them off!' she started to disrobe. It was while dancing naked in front of the screen that she noticed the auditorium being cleared by armed police. Explaining her behavior, the usherette said later: 'I thought the audience was calling for me. I was as surprised as anyone.' "

—*Star Billing*, **by David Brown**

WHAT, NO DERBYS?

SEDGLEY, England—"Last May, police investigated claims that smartly dressed men were stripping off their suits and dancing naked in woodland near Penn Common, on the edge of the Black Country. 'We just do not know what these men are up to,' said Superintendent Malcolm Gough.

" 'It's been going on and off for about a year now, although it seems to stop after November,' said resident Judy Bardburn. She added: 'People who have seen them say that all they wear are black shoes and black socks.' "

—*Fortean Times* #90

COUNTRY COMFORT

NASHVILLE, Tennessee—"When singer-songwriter Kristi Lockwood said she was looking for a little exposure, she meant it.

"Wearing only cowboy boots and a cowboy hat Wednesday, Lockwood strolled down the city's famous Music Row, stunning other onlookers.

" 'Yeah, I saw Lady Godiva walking around,' said George McLain, who works at a recording company. 'She looked at us, and said "Hi guys." It was pretty amazing.' "

The singer admitted she was doing it all for the publicity.

The Chinese used to scatter firecrackers around the house. Reason: they make great fire alarms.

She said she'd been in Nashville for three years, "working real hard on my voice and getting good feedback on my songs, but nobody was paying much attention."

The police did. After getting a few calls, they found Lockwood, covered her, cited her for indecent exposure, and took her home.

—*Nashville Banner*, **February 15, 1996**

GEN. BUTT NAKED

MONROVIA, Liberia—"In the annals of Liberia's civil war, nothing tops the tale of Gen. Butt Naked. Nude except for lace-up leather shoes and a gun, the general would lead his Butt Naked Battalion—which was famed for its fearlessness and brutality—into battle. Why no clothes? The general says he believed 'it ensured protection from his enemies.'

"As the war wound down, so did Gen. Butt Naked's commitment to kill, until he gave it up and became an evangelical preacher. Today he wears a suit and tie as he roams the battered capital with a microphone preaching peace and reconciliation."

—**Wire service reports, August 3, 1997**

NAKED LUNCH

MELBOURNE, Australia—"Daring shoppers escaped the heat by taking off their clothes today in an Australian music store. About 50 patrons crowded Gaslight Music for its annual Nude Day promotion.

"The nude customers won free compact discs and were served a buffet lunch by a waiter and waitress and entertained by a pianist and an orator, all wearing only a smile...as the media looked on."

—*Reuters News Service*, **October 18, 1994**

NAKED LUNCH II

STOCKHOLM, Sweden—"A tourist in Stockholm could not catch the restaurant waiter's eyes, so he stepped outside, took all his clothes off and reentered, shouting: 'You Swedes only pay attention to nudes. Now will you serve me?' He was arrested for indecent behavior."

—*The World's Greatest Mistakes*, **by Steve Brummett**

PRIMETIME PROVERBS

TV comments about everyday life. From Primetime
Proverbs, *by Jack Mingo and John Javna.*

ON BRAINS

"If brains was lard, Jethro couldn't grease a pan."
—Jed Clampett,
The Beverly Hillbillies

Dr. Crane [about Sam]: "I was hoping for some insight."
Diane Chambers:"What insight could you possibly hope to gain from a man whose IQ wouldn't make a respectable earthquake?"
—*Cheers*

"When God was handing out brains, he mistook you for a cactus."
—Shirley Feeney,
Laverne and Shirley

"Yeah, she's beautiful, but you can't find her IQ with a flashlight."
—Bill Maxwell,
The Greatest American Hero

"If brains were money, you'd need to take out a loan to buy a cup of coffee."
—Diane Chambers,
Cheers

ON HEALTH

Dr.: "What you've got is a classic case of insomnia."
Balki Bartokomous: "Oh no…I knew it was something terrible! Okay, give it to me straight. How long have I got?"
Dr.: "Fifty or sixty years."
Balki: "Fifty or sixty years? Oh, my God, a slow death!"
—*Perfect Strangers*

"In the world of ulcers, Unger, you're what's known as a carrier."
—Dr. Gordon,
The Odd Couple

ON FEAR

Mr. Carlin: "I think I'm overcoming my agoraphobia.
Bob: "I didn't know you had a fear of open places."
Mr. Carlin: "I thought it was a fear of agricultural products. Anyway, wheat doesn't scare me anymore."
—*The Bob Newhart Show*

"Claustrophobia? That's a dreadful fear of Santa Claus."
—Vinnie Barbarino,
Welcome Back, Kotter

President Chester A. Arthur once sold a pair of Abe Lincoln's pants at auction.

FORGOTTEN POP HISTORY

Here are a few tidbits of obscure Americana, from the 1941 book Keep Up with the World, *by Freling Foster.*

DRAWERS ON SALE? DISGRACEFUL! A New York dry goods store shocked America in 1876 with the announcement that it would thereafter carry a full line of ladies' underwear. Until that time, all such garments were made in the home, being considered too intimate to be purchased in public. Besides, these unmentionables, when hung to dry on an outdoor clothesline, were always covered by a sheet to protect them from the vulgar gaze of passing males.

THE FIRST TALKING DOLL. A doll developed by Thomas A. Edison about 1888 is believed to be his least-known invention and the only toy of its time that ever actually talked. The doll had a small phonograph in its body that enabled it to recite nursery rhymes, a dozen of which were recorded for its mechanism. After making several hundred of these dolls, Edison was informed that, years before, his company had sold the right to manufacture phonograph toys to another firm. Edison stopped production and had the dolls destroyed. Of the few he saved and presented to friends, only two are believed to be in existence today.

OLD-FASHIONED FAMILY VALUES. In the early 1870s in Corinne, Territory of Utah, a law firm had so many divorce cases that it developed a slot machine and, through it, sold the necessary papers for $2.50 a set. At that time in the territory, no grounds for divorce were required, and these papers were so complete that they became legal when signed by the couple involved.

TAKE IT OFF! The strip tease is one of the only forms of theatrical entertainment that originated in the United States. It was introduced in N.Y. burlesque houses in the late 1920s to regain the patrons they'd lost to the new musical shows on Broadway that were featuring nudity.

The bullfrog is the only animal that never sleeps.

THE POLITICALLY CORRECT QUIZ

*"Political correctness" isn't as bad as it's made out to be—after all, there's
nothing wrong with trying to be sensitive to people's feelings. On the other
hand, people can get pretty outrageous with their ideas of what's
"appropriate." Here are some real-life examples of politically
correct (or "incorrect")behavior. How sensitive are you?
Can you spot the "correct"one? Answers on page 490.*

1. In 1994, an English charity offered low-income kids at a local
school free tickets to the ballet *Romeo and Juliet*. The school's head-
mistress, Jane Brown, turned them down. Why?

a) She thought the play was "too violent for children under 13."

b) She said the play was "blatantly heterosexist."

c) She said she was appalled by the "lack of ethnic diversity in
Shakespeare's plays."

2. In 1978 the city council of Woonsocket, Rhode Island, struck a
blow for political correctness by

a) Officially renaming the town's manholes "personholes."

b) Creating "ethnically diverse" streets, adding red and brown
stripes to the white and yellow center lines.

c) Installing urinals in all of City Hall's women's restrooms.

3. In 1997 the commissioners of Kelberg County, Texas, passed a
resolution eliminating the greeting "Hello" for official county business. They replaced it with

a) "Heaven-o"

b) "Peace on Earth"

c) "Howdy, y'all"

4. The Dutch founded the town of Fishkill, New York, in the
1600s (*kill* means "stream" in Dutch). In the 1990s, some residents
started a campaign to change the name, because

a) It sounds like their water is polluted.

One of the most popular soups in 1929: Peanut butter soup.

b) It discriminates against fish.

c) It celebrates "animal cruelty."

5. In the early 1980s, a white landlord in Tiburon, California, (near San Francisco) put cast-iron black "lawn jockeys" on many of his downtown properties. "It adds a little bit of charm to the place," he explained. But local activists protested that it also added a touch of racism. So the landlord painted the jockeys' skin "a pale Caucasian pink." Problem solved? Not exactly. In 1994

a) A local African American minister started a campaign to get the jockeys repainted black.

b) The International Jockeys' Union demanded that statues of women jockeys be included among the displays.

c) White supremacists picketed the statues to protest the "reverse racism."

6. In 1922, the high school basketball team from Dickinson, North Dakota, took on the nickname the "Dickinson Midgets." Seventy-four years later, in the summer of 1996, the town's school board decided the name was offensive and should be changed. The town responded by

a) Inviting a representative from Little People of America (an organization that protects dwarves' and midgets' rights) to discuss the issue.

b) Holding a recall election and replacing the school board.

c) Voting to change the name to the "Dickinson Little People."

7. Which of these incidents really happened?

a) A six-year-old in Lexington, North Carolina, kissed a classmate on the cheek and was suspended for "sexual harassment"—despite the fact he didn't even know what sex is.

b) A customer in a Quebec pet shop threatened to report the store to the government's French-language monitoring office because she was shown a parrot that only spoke English.

c) The 20,000 members of Britain's National Plumbers' Association were instructed by the government—at the risk of incurring a fine for sexist behavior—to stop talking about "ballcocks" and use the term "float-operated valves" instead.

MOVIE BLOOPERS

Here are a few mistakes to look for in popular movies. You can find more in a series of books called Film Flubs, *by Bill Gibbons.*

Movie: *Gone With the Wind* (1939)
Scene: Scarlett is running on the street in Atlanta.
Blooper: She passes an electric light as she is running, years before the invention of the incandescent bulb.

Movie: *Foul Play* (1978)
Scene: Goldie Hawn is sitting on a park bench, eating a sandwich.
Blooper: As she eats her lunch, "the sandwich is whole, then half-eaten, then uneaten again, then half-eaten, then it has just one bite out of it, then it disappears completely."

Movie: *Driving Miss Daisy* (1989)
Scene: Hoke and Daisy cross the state line from Georgia into Alabama. He comments that they're in Alabama...then two state troopers pull them over.
Blooper: They forgot to change uniforms. They're dressed as Georgia cops.

Movie: *Star Wars* (1976)
Scene: Luke returns safely after blowing up the Death Star.
Blooper: He accidentally calls out "Carrie!" to Princess Leia. (She's played by Carrie Fisher.) *Note:* It's in the re-released version, too.

Movie: *Maverick* (1994)
Scene: Mel Gibson is talking with a clerk at the railway station, in the Old West.
Blooper: You can see a white truck driving across the screen.

Movie: *Batman* (1989)
Scene: The Joker (Jack Nicholson) and his gang are defacing artwork in a museum.
Blooper: One of the gang splatters a portrait with pink paint. In the next shot, the work is back to its original state.

Often when actors are filmed in a car through the windshield, there's no rearview mirror.

Movie: *Indiana Jones and the Last Crusade* (1989)
Scene: Hitler signs an autograph for Jones.
Blooper: He spells his name wrong. He signs it *Adolph*, with a "ph"—the American spelling—instead of the German *Adolf*. And he signs it with his right hand; Hitler was a lefty.

Movie: *The Crusades* (1935)
Blooper: According to Gibbons, "The king actually flips back his cape and looks at his watch!"

Movie: *First Knight* (1996)
Scene: King Arthur's knights are charging into battle on horseback.
Blooper: There are tire tracks in the foreground.

Movie: *Psycho* (1960)
Scene: Janet Leigh is lying dead in the shower, after the famous "shower scene."
Blooper: The corpse swallows.

Movie: *48 Hours* (1982)
Scene: Eddie Murphy escapes from jail, with Nick Nolte's aid.
Blooper: Nolte puts Murphy in his car handcuffed. Then Murphy's hands are free—he stretches one arm over the back of the seat. Next scene: He's handcuffed again.

Movie: *Funny Farm* (1988)
Scene: Chevy Chase jumps into a lake with his clothes on. He gets out of the water and gets into his car.
Blooper: Next scene, his clothes have miraculously become dry.

Movie: *North to Alaska* (1960)
Scene: John Wayne gets into a fight in a bar.
Blooper: He loses his toupee. Then in the next scene, he's hairy again.

Movie: *Presumed Innocent* (1990)
Scene: Harrison Ford is besieged by journalists outside the courtroom. A reporter holds a cassette tape recorder up to Ford's face for a comment.
Blooper: It has no tape in it.

"THE TONIGHT SHOW" PART IV: JACK PAAR'S NEARLY FATAL BATHROOM JOKE

Did you know that bathroom humor nearly killed "The Tonight Show" in 1960? It was a big story that year—if you're old enough to have watched "The Tonight Show" back then, you probably remember it well. If not, here's the tale.

FEBRUARY 10, 1960
It began like any other night on "The Tonight Show." Jack Paar walked out onstage, greeted the audience, and began his monologue.

On this night, however, things would be different. Paar wanted to tell a joke he'd heard from a friend. The friend had learned it from his daughter, who learned it when her junior high school teacher told it to the class. After telling the joke, the teacher passed out typewritten copies of it for the kids to share with their parents. The girl's father liked the joke so much that he gave his copy to Paar.

The joke was slightly risqué by 1960 TV standards. But Paar figured that if it was appropriate for a junior high school class, it was appropriate for his television audience. "I could have read it in church," he joked years later. "Not on Sundays, but I could read it during choir practice on Wednesday."

Paar told the audience that he had debated reading the joke on the show, and hinted that it might not appeal to everyone. "There's a slight question of taste involved here," he said. "I do this only with full knowledge that we're an adult group gathered at this hour, and we're not here to do anyone any harm." And then he told the joke.

THE JOKE
"An English lady, while visiting Switzerland, was looking for a room, and she asked the schoolmaster if he could recommend any

---

In Yukon, Oklahoma, it's illegal for patients to pull their dentist's teeth.

to her. He took her to see several rooms, and when everything was settled, the lady returned to her home to make the final preparations to move.

"When she arrived home, the thought suddenly occurred to her that she had not seen a W.C. That's a water closet to the British. We would call it a bathroom or ladies' room, men's room. I guess a bathroom.

"So she immediately wrote a note to the schoolmaster asking him if there were a W.C. around. The schoolmaster was a very poor student of English, so he asked the parish priest if he could help in the matter. Together they tried to discover the meaning of the letters W.C. and the only solution they could find for the letters was a 'Wayside Chapel.' The schoolmaster then wrote to the English lady the following note:

"**DEAR MADAM:**

'I take great pleasure in informing you that the W.C. is situated nine miles from the house you occupy, in the center of a beautiful grove of pine trees surrounded by lovely grounds. It is capable of holding 229 people and it is open on Sunday and Thursday only. As there is a great number of people and they are expected during the summer months, I would suggest that you come early, although there is plenty of standing room as a rule.

'You will no doubt be glad to hear that a good number of people bring their lunch and make a day of it, while others who can afford to go by car and arrive just in time. I would especially recommend that your ladyship go on Thursday when there is musical accompaniment.

'It may interest you to know that my daughter was married in the W.C. and it was there that she met her husband. I can remember the rush there was for seats. There were ten people to a seat usually occupied by one. It was wonderful to see the expressions on their faces.

'The newest attraction is a bell donated by a wealthy resident of the district. It rings every time a person enters. A bazaar is to be held to provide plush seats for all the people, since they feel it is a long-felt need. My wife is rather delicate, so she can't attend regularly.

Pearls are made of calcium carbonate, the active ingredient in antacids.

'I shall be delighted to reserve the best seat for you if you wish, where you will be seen by all. For the children, there is a special time and place so that they will not disturb the elders. Hoping to have been some service to you, I remain

'Sincerely,

'The Schoolmaster' ''

THAT'S NO JOKE
The joke got a hearty laugh from the audience. Paar thanked them and said, "You're my kind of people."

But apparently they weren't NBC's kind of people. Then, as now, "The Tonight Show" was taped in the afternoon, and broadcast at 11:30 p.m. after NBC censors had a chance to look it over. They had never made any substantive changes in the show before…but that night they excised the entire water closet joke without telling Paar in advance. "Some idiot got concerned about the words 'water closet,' '' he later explained.

Paar was angry when he found out what had happened, but he thought the controversy would make for an interesting discussion on his show. He proposed airing the censored joke the following evening, to "let the viewers decide for themselves" whether it was appropriate. NBC refused. Paar was furious—he felt the censorship was damaging to his reputation, since it implied that he had told a smutty joke on TV.

THAT'S ALL, FOLKS
The following evening, Paar walked out onto the stage as usual… but rather than deliver his monologue, he vented his rage at NBC. Calling the censorship "a question of free speech," Paar announced that he was quitting "The Tonight Show." "There must be a better way to make a living than this," he said. "I love NBC, and they've been wonderful to me, but they let me down." Then he bade farewell to the audience, telling them, "You've always been peachy to me, always."

He walked off the stage and went home, leaving his shocked sidekick, Hugh Downs, to finish the show alone. "Is he gone?" Downs asked in amazement, telling the audience, "Jack frequently does things he regrets."

Food fact: "Exocannibals" eat their enemies. "Indocannibals" eat their friends.

HIDING OUT

The incident made headlines all over the country. But Paar was no-where to be found—he and his wife, Miriam, had escaped to Flori-da, where they hid out in a half-finished luxury hotel that a friend was building.

The Paars didn't have a phone at the hotel, but NBC somehow learned of their hiding place, and network president Robert Kint-ner flew down to talk things out. He eventually talked Paar into coming back...but only after he and Robert Sarnoff, the chairman of NBC, both publicly apologized for censoring the joke. Paar re-turned on March 7 after being absent nearly a month. "As I was saying before I was interrupted...," he joked with the audience. "There must be a better way of making a living than this. Well, I've looked. And there isn't!"

PAAR'S NO. 1 PROBLEM

Paar's protest increased his celebrity status and made him a hero of sorts with the public. Ironically, however, the bathroom joke that nearly ended his career was now making it almost impossible for him to use public restrooms, because wherever he went—even to the bathroom—admirers would approach him and congratulate him on his victory.

"Finally you reach the porcelain," he lamented, "and find that—with all eyes on your performance—you cannot! What to do? They are all watching! You panic because now they might think you are some kind of weirdo or voyeur looking around. You press the han-dle of the urinal, you whistle, and you wish you could get the bat-tery-jump starter from the trunk of your auto....I tell you, it's very hard being a star in a men's room."

Turn to page 327 for Part V of "The Tonight Show's" history.

*　　*　　*

Precise definition: "Egotist: A person more interested in himself than me."

—*Ambrose Bierce*

"EXPLOITATION 2000"

As the year 2000 gets closer, you can be sure someone will put together a film festival featuring all the cheesy flicks ever made with "2000" in the title. Here's a preview of what you can expect to see there.

CHERRY 2000 (1987)
Plot: In the year 2000, a man short-circuits his sex-toy robots and goes looking for replacement parts across dangerous terrain. On the way, he meets a real female—Melanie Griffith (before breast implants).

DEATH RACE 2000 (1975). The ads said: "In the year 2000, hit-and-run driving is no longer a felony, it's a national sport!"
Plot: Top driver "Frankenstein" (David Carradine) battles Machine Gun Joe Viterbo (Sly Stallone) to win the annual transcontinental race. The more people you run over, the better your score. Written by Charles Griffith (*Little Shop of Horrors*).

EQUALIZER 2000 (1987)
Plot: "Another Road Warrior-style post-Holocaust picture (set in Alaska, which is now a desert). A military/industrial compound protects the precious commodity of oil (sound familiar?). One of the guarding group's officers is betrayed, so his son takes off for the 'wasteland.' There he's captured by rebels, and eventually leads an assault on the compound." —*Film Encyclopedia of Science Fiction*

MADRID IN THE YEAR 2000 (1925) Early silent film.
Plot: Unknown. Featured special effects which were so unbelievable (even then) that audience members burst out laughing.

1 APRIL 2000 (1950) A propaganda film from the Austrian government, designed to convince Allied forces (then occupying Austria) to grant them self-determination. An historical curiosity.
Plot: Depicts the chaos that would result if Allied forces waited until April Fool's Day 2000 to give Austria its independence. Notable for introducing actor Curt Jurgens (who became a well-known movie star).

Sneakers get their name because they don't squeak like leather shoes do.

TEST-TUBE TEENS FROM THE YEAR 2000 (1993)
Original title: *The Virgin Hunters*

Plot: "When sex is banned in the year 2000, horny teenagers are left with no choice but to travel though time for some action."
—*VideoHound's Golden Movie Retriever*

"The fast-forwardable plot concerns the title characters' efforts to go back in time and stop Camella Swales (Morgan Fairchild) from banning conventional reproduction....This, folks, is what low-budget video is all about.
—*VideoHound's Complete Guide to Cult Flicks and Trash Pics*

BURGLARY IN THE YEAR 2000 (1909) The first movie ever released with the year 2000 in its title.

Plot: A professor invents a substance that enables objects like chairs and tables to get up and walk away. Two burglars steal the stuff and use it to commit a series of crimes. But they drink too much wine, fall asleep, and are nabbed by the police. According to a contemporary review in *Moving Picture World*, the effect offered "considerable magic" and audiences "laughed heartily."

ESCAPE 2000 (1982) Original title: *Turkey Shoot*.

Plot: In the year 1995, the world population has been subjugated; individuality is not permitted. People who refuse to conform are labeled "deviates" and are sent to behavioral modification centers—then they're hunted in jungles for sport. Critical comment: "Repulsive...If constant whippings, decapitations and burnings are your idea of a good time, this one's for you." —*Movies on TV and Video Cassette*

JONAH—WHO WILL BE 25 IN THE YEAR 2000 (1976)
This one is actually a good film.

Plot: Swiss director Alain Tanner's bittersweet story of eight disillusioned 1960s revolutionaries who are trying to adjust to life in the 1970s. The reference to 2000 comes up in the friends' spontaneous song about one character's unborn son, Jonah:

In the year 2000, Jonah will be 25 / At 25, the century will disgorge him. The whale of history will disgorge Jonah / Who will be 25 in the year 2000 That's the time left to us / To help get him out, out of the mess.

YOU CALL *THAT* ART?

It's interesting to study the paintings of the great masters...but sometimes it's even more fun to study the work of the great fakers. Like these folks.

HANS VAN MEEGEREN

Background: At the end of World War II, Dutch authorities began investigating the sale of Dutch national treasures to Nazi officials. They learned that Hans Van Meegeren, a struggling Dutch artist, had sold a priceless 17th-century Vermeer called *Christ and the Adulteress* to Nazi leader Hermann Goering for $256,000. Once the painting was repossessed and authenticated as a work painted during Vermeer's "middle period," Van Meegeren was arrested and charged with collaborating with the Nazis—a crime punishable by death.

The Truth: Van Meegeren defended himself by saying that there was no Vermeer "middle period," and that he had faked all six of the paintings attributed to those years of the artist's life. Van Meegeren also claimed to have painted two works by Dieter de Hoochs, and one by Terborch.

The judge didn't believe him. But to be sure, he sent the artist back to his studio (under guard) and told him to "paint another Vermeer." Van Meegeren quickly created something he called *The Young Christ Teaching at the Temple.* It was, by all appearances, painted in the style of Vermeer.

What Happened: The judge dropped the treason charges. But as each of the paintings Van Meegeren took credit for were tested and proven to be fakes, he was arrested again—this time for forgery and fraud. He was convicted and sentenced to a year in prison; he died from a heart attack one month after the trial.

DAVID STEIN

Background: In the mid-60s, a 31-year-old art collector named David Stein walked into the shop of one of New York's top art dealers with three watercolor paintings by Russian painter Marc Chagall. The dealer bought all three for $10,000.

The Truth: Stein had painted all three "Chagalls" that morning before lunch. He made the new canvases look old by soaking them in Lipton's tea, and forged letters of authentication at the frame shop while waiting for the paintings to be framed.

What Happened: As Stein put it, "I should have stuck to dead men." By pure coincidence, Marc Chagall happened to be in New York that very same day...and the art dealer who bought the paintings had an appointment to meet with him. The dealer brought the paintings to the meeting, and Chagall immediately denounced them as fakes. Stein was arrested and spent nearly four years in American and French prisons. But the bust was such a boost to his reputation that when he got out of prison, he was able to make a living from his own original paintings.

PAVEL JERDANOWICH

Background: In the spring of 1925, the Russian-born Jerdanowich submitted a painting called *Exaltation* to a New York art exhibit. The red and green colors were unusual for the period, and the face of the woman in the painting was distorted, but art critics from admired the work, and Jerdanowich was invited to exhibit at a New York show in 1926. He did—this time displaying a painting called *Aspiration* and explaining that he was the founder of the "Disumbrationist" school of painting. The following year, he showed two more paintings, *Adoration* and *Illumination*. Jerdanowich's groundbreaking work caused a storm, and he was hailed as a visionary.

The Truth: "Pavel Jerdanowich" was actually Paul Jordan Smith, a Latin scholar who hated abstract and modernist trends in art. When an art critic criticized his wife's realistic paintings as "definitely of the old school" in 1925, he set out to prove that critics would praise any painting they couldn't understand. "I asked my wife for paint and canvas," he recounted after admitting the hoax. "I'd never tried to paint anything in my life." The Disumbrationist School was born.

What Happened: Smith admitted the ruse to the *Los Angeles Times* in 1927, but the confession only fueled interest in his work. A Chicago gallery owner displayed the paintings in 1928, and later called the show "the most widely noticed exhibition I have ever heard of."

HAR-HAR! RAH-RAH!

Palindromes are phrases or sentences that are spelled the same way backward or forward. Some people spend their whole lives making new ones up. Here are some of Uncle John's favorites.

A dog! A panic in a pagoda!

I'm a boob, am I?

Dog doo! Good god!

"Do orbits all last?" I brood.

Ed, I saw Harpo Marx ram Oprah W. aside.

An admirer! I'm Dana!

Oh no! Don Ho!

Emil, a sleepy baby, peels a lime.

Party boobytrap.

He spots one last sale. No stops, eh?

Neil, an alien.

Go hang a salami! I'm a lasagna hog!

Tarzan raised Desi Arnaz' rat.

All erotic, I lose solicitor Ella.

Madame, not one man is selfless; I name not one, Madam.

Ron, I'm a minor.

Stressed was I ere I saw desserts.

So, Ed, I vow to do two videos.

Yo! Bozo boy!

Wonton? Not now.

Sis, ask Costner to not rent socks "as is."

Cigar? Toss it in a can, it is so tragic.

Too far, Edna, we wander afoot.

Diana saw I was an aid.

Mad? Am I, madam?

Angola balogna.

Tennis set won, now Tess in net.

Stella wondered: "No wallets?"

Star comedy: Democrats.

I Love Me, vol. I

Now, Ned, I am a maiden won!

Ma is a nun, as I am.

Did I do, O God, did I as I said I'd do? Good, I did!

Amoral aroma.

Alan Alda stops race car, spots ad: "Lana—L.A."

New York's Times Square was orginally known as "Acre Square."

TECHNO-SLANG

Here are some of the most descriptive new terms from pop culture and cyberspace, gathered by Gareth Branwyn in his book Jargon Watch.

Ant farms: Giant multiscreen movie complexes found in U.S. shopping malls.

Anus envy: A common condition among fans of Howard Stern or Rush Limbaugh who try to imitate their heroes.

Batmobiling: Putting up protective emotional shields just as a relationship enters an intimate, vulnerable stage. Refers to the retracting armor covering the Batmobile.

Begathon: A TV or radio fundraiser.

Blamestorming: Sitting around in a group, deciding why a project failed—and who's responsible.

Body Nazis: Hardcore fitness fanatics who look down on anyone who doesn't exercise obsessively.

Deboning: The act of removing subscription cards and perfume ads from a magazine before reading it.

Friday night pizza maker (from Japan)**:** Someone who gets drunk after work, then blows chow on the subway platform.

Geekosphere: The area surrounding your computer, where you display trinkets, toys, or monitor pets that have personal significance.

Height technology: Computer-geek for "ladder" as in, "Can I get some height technology in here?"

In the plastic closet: Said of those who refuse to admit they've had plastic surgery.

Meatspace: Computer-geek for the physical world (as opposed to cyberspace); also known as the carbon community or RW (Real World).

Panic merchants: Businesses, media outlets, and moralistic groups that make their living by exploiting common fears and anxieties.

Percussive maintenance: Whacking a device to get it working.

Prairie dogging: When someone raises a commotion in a *cube farm*, and everyone else's heads pop over the walls to get a look.

Slogo: A combination corporate logo and slogan—Nike's "Just Do It," for example.

Thong-a-thon: A sexploitation film that features lots of women in bikinis.

Tract mansions: Big expensive homes packed in tight rows.

Um friend: A sexual relation of dubious standing. "This is my...um...friend."

In 1790, it cost 1¢ per person to take the U.S. Census. In 1990, it was $10.45 per person.

CURSES!

We've all heard of one curse or another. Usually, we laugh about them. But perhaps sometimes there's a good reason for believing.

THE CURSE OF TOSCA

Curse: Nasty things happen to actors during performances of this opera.

Origin: Unknown, but productions have been plagued with problems at least as far back as the 1920s.

Among Its Victims:

• During a production at the Met in the 1920s, the knife with which Tosca "murdered" Scarpia at the end of Act II failed to retract. Singer Antonio Scotti was stabbed.

• In 1965 at Covent Gardens, Maria Callas's hair caught fire while she was singing the title role. It had to be put out by a quick-thinking Tito Gobbi, who was playing Scarpia.

• In a production in Rome in 1965, Gionni Raimondi's face was scorched during the firing squad scene.

• In 1993, Elisabeth Knighton Printy jumped off the wrong side of the stage in St. Paul, Minnesota, and plunged more than 30 feet to the ground, breaking both her legs.

Status: Ongoing. Last reported incident was in 1995, when Fabio Armiliatu, starring in a Roman production, was hit in the leg by debris from blanks fired in the execution scene. He was taken off in a stretcher. Two weeks later he returned to the stage; he fell and broke his other leg in two places while standing in the wings at the end of the first act.

THE SPORTS ILLUSTRATED JINX

Curse: If you appear on the cover of *Sports Illustrated* magazine, you're in for a slump or a defeat.

Origin: Unknown. For decades, sports stars have claimed that making *SI*'s cover was the fastest way to a slump.

Among its Victims:

• Studying the records of 58 baseball players going back to 1955 (because there are sufficient records to check in baseball), researchers found that "there was a distinct tendency for batting performance to decline...about 50 points from immediately before appearing on the cover until three weeks after the appearance."

Status: Scientists say that if there is anything to the *SI* jinx, it's because it spooks players and thus is self-fulfilling. Also: "This extra attention and effort might cause more injuries, fatigue, or other interruptions to the hitters natural flow, with the result that performance suffers."

THE OSCAR CURSE

Curse: Winning the gold statuette can ruin, rather than help, an actor's career.

Origin: Luise Rainer won back-to-back Oscars for *The Great Ziegfield* (1936) and *The Good Earth* (1937). Two years and five horrible movies later, she was considered a has-been. Hollywood columnist Louella Parsons wrote that it was "the Oscar curse." Parsons said her Ouija board had warned, "Beware, beware, the Oscar will get you if you don't watch out."

Among its Victims:

• Rita Moreno and George Chakiris (Best Supporting Actor and Actress, 1961, *West Side Story*). Disappeared from films after winning.

• Richard Dreyfuss (Best Actor, 1978, *The Goodbye Girl.*) His weight ballooned to 180 pounds, he stopped bathing, and he started binging on booze and drugs.

• Michael Cimino (Best Director, 1978, *The Deer Hunter*). Followed Oscar with three losers: *Heaven's Gate, Year of the Dragon,* and *The Sicilian.*

• Linda Hunt (Best Supporting Actress, 1983, *The Year of Living Dangerously*). "Last seen in the short-lived sci-fi TV series, *Space Rangers.*"

Status: Considered credible in Hollywood. High expectations that can't always be fulfilled accompany an Oscar. It's also attributed to salary demands, type-casting, greedy agents or studio bosses, and stars who believe their own press and become hard to work with.

WORD GEOGRAPHY

A few more words that were derived from the names of real places.

SUEDE
From: Sweden
Explanation: *Gants de Suede* is French for "gloves of Sweden." It was in Sweden that the first leather was buffed to a fine softness, and the French bought the *gants de Suede*. Suede now refers to the buffing processes—not to any particular kind of leather.

TURKEY
From: Turkey
Explanation: *Turk* means "strength" in Turkish. The turkey bird is a large European fowl named after the country of its origin. American colonists mistakenly thought a big bird they found in the New World was the same animal...so they called it a turkey.

CHEAP
From: Cheapside, a market in London
Explanation: The Old English word was *ceap* (pronounced "keep"), which meant "to sell or barter." Because *Cheapside* was a major market where people went to barter for low prices, the word gradually took on a new pronunciation...and meaning.

MAYONNAISE
From: Port Mahon, Spain (according to legend)
Explanation: The *-aise* suffix is French for "native to" or "originating in." *Mahonnaise* was supposedly created to celebrate a 1756 French battle victory over the British on the Spanish isle of Port Mahon.

COFFEE
From: Kaffa, Ethiopia
Explanation: According to legend, coffee beans were first discovered in the town of Kaffa. By the thirteenth century, the Kaffa beans had traveled, becoming *qahwah* in Arabia, *cafe* in Europe, and finally *coffee* in the New World.

Doctors, more than any other profession, are most likely to be late for a doctor's appointment.

COLOGNE
From: Cologne, Germany
Explanation: Scented water that was produced there beginning in 1709 was named for the city.

DENIM
From: Nimes, Frances
Explanation: The tough cloth used in jeans was also made in Nimes. It was called *Serge di Nimes*—later shortened to *di Nimes*, which became *denim*.

SLAVE
From: Slavonia, Yugoslavia
Explanation: After large parts of Slavonia were subjugated by Europeans in the Middle Ages, a *slav* become synonomous with someone who lived in servitude. Eventually *Slav* became *slave*.

LIMERICK
From: Limerick, Ireland
Explanation: The town was popularly associated with humorous verses that had five lines, the first two rhyming with the last, the middle two rhyming with each other. The poems became an English fad in the mid-19th century, and people naturally identified them with the town's name.

HAMBURGER
From: Hamburg, Germany
Explanation: People in the immigration-port city of Hamburg—called Hamburgers—liked to eat raw meat with salt, pepper, and onion-juice seasoning, a treat brought to them via Russia that we call *steak tartar* today. A broiled version using chopped meat eventually became popular in America.

TURQUOISE
From: Turkey/Europe
Explanation: Another Turkish origin. Turquoise comes from a number of places, but was probably first imported to Europe from Turkey. So it was called *turquoise*, which means "Turkish stone."

Americans spend an estimated $10 billion a year on gambling and games of chance.

LOONEY LAWS

Believe it or not, these laws are real!

It's illegal to ride an ugly horse down the street in Wilbur, Washington.

It's against the law to step out of an airplane while it's in the air over Maine.

If you don't like a statue in Star, Mississippi, hold your tongue—it's illegal to ridicule public architecture.

Ninth-grade boys can't grow moustaches in Binghamton, New York.

It's against the law to drink milk on a train passing through North Carolina.

Virginia law prohibits "corrupt practices or bribery by any person other than candidates."

You can't carry an ice cream cone in your pocket in Lexington, Kentucky.

It's illegal to spit against the wind in Sault Sainte Marie, Michigan.

Goats can't legally wear trousers in Massachusetts.

In Lawrence, Kansas, it's against the law to carry bees around in your hat on city streets.

In Washington, D.C., you're breaking the law if you paint lemons all over your car to let people know you were taken advantage of by a specific car dealer.

If you complain about the condition of the street in Baton Rouge, Louisiana, you can be forced to fix it yourself.

Oregon prohibits citizens from wiping their dishes. You must let them drip-dry.

It's illegal to swim on dry land in Santa Ana, California.

If you mispronounce "Arkansas" when you're in that state, you're breaking the law.

It's illegal in Hartford, Connecticut, to educate your dog.

You can't go barefoot in Austin, Texas, without a $5 permit.

It's illegal to play cards in the road in Somerset County, Md.

British anatomist Richard Owen invented the word "dinosaur" in 1841.

OH WHAT A TANGLED WEB

Some cultures consider the spider a sign of good luck: "If you wish to live and thrive, let a spider run alive." This old English rhyme may be a recognition of the important role spiders play in insect control. In fact, that's what webs—those amazingly beautiful tapestries strung between branches, leaves, doorways, etc.—are for. They're deadly traps. Here's some info on the spider webs to make them even more interesting.

W EB CONSTRUCTION
- Only about half of all spiders spin webs.
- All spider webs are made of silk.

• Although it's only about .00012" in diameter, a spider's silk is stronger than steel of equal diameter. It is more elastic than nylon, more difficult to break than rubber, and is bacteria and fungi resistant.

• These qualities explain why at one time web was used to pack wounds to help mend them and stop bleeding.

• Spiders have 1-6 kinds of spinning glands, each producing a different type of silk. For instance, the cylindrical gland produces silk used for egg sacs (males often lack this) and the aciniform gland produces silk used for wrapping prey. Some spiders have glands that produce very fine silk. They comb and tease the fine strands until it's like velcro—tiny loops and hooks which entrap insect feet.

• Silk is extruded through special pores called *spinneretes* which consist of different sized "spigots." Silk starts out as a liquid. As the the liquid silk contacts the air, it hardens. The spider may need different silk for different purposes. By changing how fast the liquid is extruded or by using a different silk gland, it can control the strength and quality of the silk.

• Why doesn't a spider get stuck on its own web? The spider weaves in non-sticky silk strands and only walks on those. Also, spiders have a special oil on their legs which keep them from sticking.

THE WELL-BRED SPIDER

• A spider can often be identified by the type of web it weaves. The ability to weave is inherited, so specific types of spiders build specific types of webs. In addition, individual spiders sometimes develop a personal style; sort of like a signature.

• The spider is a hunter and its web is a snare, designed to hold its prey. So the design of its web and the place where the spider builds it depend on the kind of insects it is trying to catch.

• The determining factor: There are more insects, especially crawling ones, closer to the ground. Strong flying insects are usually higher, so the web is stronger.

WEB-SPINNERS

There are five different types of webspinners.

Cobweb spiders: (example: Black Widows),

• Use "trip lines" to snare prey. From their web, several vertical lines are drawn down and secured tautly to a surface with globs of "glue."

• Some unfortunate insect becomes stuck to the glue and breaks the line. The tension of the elastic trip lines, once released, flings the victim up to the spider waiting in its web.

• Cobweb weavers usually build only one web and so, with time, the web becomes tattered and littered with bits of debris.

Sheet-builders:

• Construct a horizontal mat beneath a horizontal trip-line, much like a trampoline under an invisible wire.

• Flying or jumping insects that are stopped midair by the line are flung to the net below.

• As the prey struggles to regain its balance, the agile spider pounces and inflicts a deadly bite

Web-casting spiders: (example: Ogre-faced spiders),

• Use "web snares" much differently than others: Instead of attaching the web to a bush or wall, the spider carries it.

• The spider uses it much like a fishing net and casts it on passing prey. Each night it hunts. Afterward, it may either tuck the web away until the next day's hunt, or spin a new one.

Angle lines: (example: the Bola spider.)

• It first suspends itself from a trapeze line and hangs there upside down. Then it sends down a single line baited with a glob of glue.
• When an insect moves by, the Bola takes careful aim and casts the line toward the moving insect. If successful, it will reel in its prize.

Orb-weavers: (the most familiar webs.)

• Spin the largest and strongest webs. Some span more than 1 meter. Natives of New Guinea and the Solomon Islands used the webs of the orb- weaving spiders as fishing nets. They were reportedly strong enough to hold a fish weighing as much as a pound.

• These webs are especially tailored to capture flying insects—which is why they're vertically suspended.

• Many Orb-weavers meticulously take down their webs each day, and build a new one at night.

• Orb-weavers weave such intricate webs that they are often the focus of behavioral studies. For example: two Orb-weavers went along on Sky Lab II on July 28, 1973. Researchers were interested to know the effects of zero-gravity on weaving. After some adjustments, the spiders were able to weave fairly normal webs. One curious difference: the space webs were symmetrical while earth webs tend to be asymmetrical.

WEB FACTS

Experimenters have covered the eyes of web-spinning spiders and discovered that it did not keep them from finding their prey in the web. The secret: a web spinner uses its web as a giant feeler. Based on vibrations it feels in the web, a spider can determine the size and energy of prey, environmental conditions, and even the presence of another spider.

• Male spiders of some species use vibrations to communicate to the female. They strum the female's web—and must send just the right vibration to convince the female that they are mates...and not dinner.

F.Y.I.: In old English, the word "cob" meant spider.

OOPS—FALSE ALARM!

With people so nervous about bomb threats these days, it's inevitable that there are going to be some pretty bizarre false alarms. At the BRI, we've been keeping a file on them. Here's what we've collected so far.

A LIQUOR PROBLEM

Background: In 1978, security personnel at Pan American Airlines suspected that either maintenance crews or flight attendants were stealing miniature liquor bottles, which cost 35¢ apiece, from airplanes. So they attached a clock device to the liquor cabinet to record the times of the alleged thefts.

False Alarm: "While airborne," write Nash and Zullo in *The Misfortune 500*, "a flight attendant heard the ticking and thought it was a bomb. She alerted the captain, who rerouted the plane to the nearest airport, where passengers were quickly evacuated by emergency exits. The unscheduled landing cost Pan Am $15,000."

DIAL B FOR BOMB

Background: In November 1995, a Royal Jordanian Airlines plane en route to Chicago was forced to land in Iceland when it received a bomb threat.

False Alarm: It turned out that the culprit was a Chicago woman who was trying to keep her mother-in-law, a passenger on the plane, from visiting her.

HIT OR MISSILE

Background: On October 17, 1995, Joanna Ashworth heard a thud outside her Level Plains, Alabama, home. "She opened the door," reported the local Daleville *News Ledger*, "and saw a white object sticking out from the roof of the shed behind her home." It was an 18-inch missile. She called the police.

Level Plains officer Lt. Ralph Reed arrived shortly after 6 a.m. and climbed a ladder to look at the missile....He saw markings that could have been military, so he decided to leave it where it was. "My mother didn't raise no fool," Reed said. "I wasn't gonna touch it."

"Ska pash-wee," a Native American name for rosebushes, translates "mean old lady sticks you."

Reed contacted officials at nearby Fort Rucker, who decided to evacuate people from the area. They closed the roads nearby and called the bomb squad from Fort Benning in Georgia.

False Alarm: Fort Benning's Ordnance Explosive Detachment (OED) arrived four hours later. For about half an hour, they carefully worked on getting the object out of Ashworth's roof. Then they announced to the press that it was a cardboard model that could be purchased at any toy store.

Local police vowed to get to the bottom of things. "The investigation is not closed," Lt. Reed said, as the story made national news. A few days later a 14-year-old dropped by the police station to let them know it was his rocket. He'd shot it off at a nearby playground and had been wondering what happened to it.

BRITISH FARCE

Background: According to the *Fortean Times*: "A suspicious-looking cardboard box was found outside a Territorial Army centre in Bristol (England) in 1993."

False Alarm: "The TA called the police, who in turn called an Army bomb-disposal unit, who blew up the box—to find it full of leaflets on how to deal with suspicious-looking packages."

ANIMAL CRACKERS

Background: On May 28, 1996, an employee at the Wal-Mart Superstore in Enterprise, Alabama, found a suspicious-looking box in the parking lot. Police were called. Taking no chances, they roped off the area, then called the bomb squad at Fort Benning, Georgia.

False Alarm: A few hours later, their Ordnance Explosive Detachment (the same ones who showed up in Level Plains) arrived by helicopter. They X-rayed the package and determined that it contained suspicious-looking wires. The store and surrounding area were evacuated. Then the package was blown up. It turned out to contain a dead armadillo.

* * *

"My license plate says PMS. Nobody cuts me off."
—*Wendy Liebman*

RUMORS: BASED ON
A TRUE STORY

Some rumors are straight fiction, but some have a kernel of truth at the core —which makes them a little more believable. Have you heard any of these?

R umor: The baby face on Gerber baby food belongs to Humphrey Bogart, who modeled for the label as an infant.
Hidden fact: Bogart's mother *was* a commercial illustrator, and may have done some work for Gerber.
The truth: The Gerber company credits artist Dorothy Hope Smith with designing the Gerber baby. Besides: Bogart was already 29 when Gerber baby food hit store shelves in 1928.

Rumor: After World War II the Japanese renamed one of their cities Usa, so products manufactured there could be exported with labels that read, "made in USA." (We reported this in BR #5.)
Hidden fact: There really is a town in Japan called Usa, just as there are Usas in Russia, Tanzania, and Mozambique.
The truth: Usa predates the war. The town is very small, so it doesn't show up on every map of the country—which may contribute to the notion that it suddenly "popped up" out of nowhere. But even if a country wanted to pull such a stunt, U.S. Customs regulations wouldn't allow it: Imported goods must be stamped with the *country* of origin, not the city.

Rumor: If you write to the H.J. Heinz company in advance of your 57th birthday, they'll send you a free case of Heinz products. They do it to plug their "57 Varieties" slogan.
Hidden fact: The company actually did used to send free cases of food to people who wrote in to say they were turning 57.
The truth: They stopped in the 1950s. Now they won't send you anything, except maybe a form letter.

Rumor: "Mama" Cass Elliot of the Mamas and the Papas choked to death on a ham sandwich in 1974.
Hidden fact: When Cass died in 1974, it took a week for the

Some breeds of vultures can fly at altitudes as high as 36,900 feet.

autopsy reports to be released. In the meantime, her personal physician did speculate in newspaper interviews that she could have choked on a sandwich.

The truth: The autopsy showed that the cause of death was actually a heart attack caused by her obesity, not choking.

Rumor: Recently, a man somewhere in the South was chomping on a unusually hard plug of chewing tobacco. He took it out of his mouth... and discovered he'd been chewing on a human thumb.

Hidden fact: There was a real lawsuit filed in Mississippi in 1918 that resembles this rumor. Plaintiff Bryson Pillars bought some Brown Mule chewing tobacco, chewed the first plug without incident, then started chewing the second plug. According to court records, "when the appellant tackled the second plug it made him sick, but not suspecting the tobacco, he tried another chew, and still another...while he was getting 'sicker and sicker.' Finally, his teeth struck something hard. On examination, he discovered a human toe." The Supreme Court of Mississippi ruled against the R.J. Reynolds Tobacco Company, owner of the Brown Mule brand, arguing "We can imagine no reason why, with ordinary care, human toes could not be left out of tobacco. If toes are found in chewing tobacco, it seems to us that somebody has been very careless."

The truth: The rumor has been circulating for more than 50 years.

Rumor: In the 1960s the U.S. military forced the recall of U.S.S. *Nautilus* plastic submarine models. The models were so accurate that the government feared Soviet spies would buy them and learn our submarine secrets.

Hidden fact: In 1961 Vice Admiral Hyman Rickover *did* complain that a model kit of the Polaris nuclear submarine, made by the Revell Toy Company, revealed too much—including detailed floor plans of the engine and missile compartments. (Defense contractors that made the real submarine's missiles even used the models to demonstrate how their weapons systems worked.)

The truth: The military complained...but the model was never recalled. Super-accurate models annoy the military even today: In 1986 the Testor Model Company offered a surprisingly accurate model of the F-19 Stealth fighter—even before the U.S. Air Force acknowledged the plane existed.

WHAT'S A RUDNER?

You may not have heard of Rita Rudner before, but Uncle John thinks she's pretty funny. See what you think

"I want to have children while my parents are still young enough to take care of them."

"I'm going home next week. It's a kind of family emergency—my family is coming here."

"My mother used to tell me she had natural childbirth. I recently found out it was *her* version of natural childbirth—she took off her makeup."

"When I meet a man, I ask myself: 'Is this the man I want my children to spend their weekends with?'"

"My boyfriend and I broke up. He wanted to get married, and I didn't want him to."

"I got kicked out of ballet class because I pulled a groin muscle, even though it wasn't mine."

"In Hollywood, a marriage is successful if it outlasts milk."

"Before I met my husband, I'd never fallen in love… though I'd stepped in it a few times."

"My cousin married a man for money. She wasn't real subtle about it. Instead of calling him her fiancé, she kept calling him her financee."

"All I have to say about men and bathrooms: They're not real specific. It seems if they hit 'something' they're happy."

On marathons: "What would make 17,000 people want to run 26 miles? Maybe there was a Hare Krishena in back of them going, 'Excuse me? Could I talk to you for just a second?'"

"In high school, I was voted the girl most likely to become a nun. That may not be impressive to you, but it was quite an accomplishment at the Hebrew Academy."

A HISTORY OF THE YO-YO

What's it like being in the yo-yo business? They say it has its ups and downs.
Here's a brief history of one of the world's most enduring toys.

WHODUNNIT?

- The Yo-yo is believed to be the second-oldest toy in the world, after dolls. No one knows for sure when or where it was invented: some think China, others the Philippines.

- Most yo-yo experts agree that a version of the yo-yo was used as a weapon in the Philippines as far back as prehistoric times. Hunters wrapped 20-foot leather straps around heavy pieces of flint and hurled the rock at prey. If a hunter missed, he could pull the rock back and try again. (The name "yo-yo" comes from a Filipino expression that means "come come" or "come back.")

- Even when it fell into disuse as a weapon, the yo-yo retained an important role in Filipino culture: people used yo-yo contests to settle disputes. Yo-yoing became the national pastime of the islands. "To this day," says one game historian, "young, rural Filipinos spend weeks creating their own custom yo-yos out of rare wood or a piece of buffalo horn."

YO-YOS IN EUROPE

- The ancient Greeks played with yo-yos as far back as 500 B.C. They even portrayed yo-yoers in their art. In *World on a String*, Heliane Zeiger writes that terra-cotta yo-yos and "a piece of decorated pottery showing a youngster in a headband and tunic, playing with a yo-yo—both from the classical period in Greece—are currently on display in the Museum of Athens."

- "In 1790," Zeiger continues, "the yo-yo made its way from the Orient to Europe, where it became popular among the British and French aristocracies...and inherited some new names. In England the yo-yo was known as the *bandalore*, *quiz*, or *Prince of Wales's toy*. (A painting from the 1700s shows King George IV, then Prince of Wales, whirling a bandalore.)"

- In France, the yo-yo picked up the nicknames *incroyable*, *l'emigrette*, and *jou-jou*. "One contemporary account of the French

Revolution notes that several French noblemen were seen yo-yoing in the carts hauling them off to the guillotine." And Napoleon's soldiers amused themselves with yo-yos between battles.

Coming to America
Bandalores appeared in the United States in the 19th century. For about 100 years, they occasionally popped up as local fads in areas on the East Coast…then faded in popularity each time. They never disappeared completely but didn't attain greater success until the early 20th century.

ENTER DONALD DUNCAN

The turning point for the yo-yo came in 1928, when a businessman named Donald Duncan happened to see Pedro Flores, owner of the Flores Yo-Yo Corporation, demonstrating yo-yos in front of his store. Duncan was impressed with the huge crowds that had gathered to watch the tricks. He figured that a mass-produced yo-yo, if heavily promoted, would make a lot of money—so in 1929 he and Flores began manufacturing yo-yos on a larger scale. A year later Duncan bought Flores out for $25,000 and renamed the company after himself.

No Strings Attached
Yo-yo historians disagree on whether Flores or Duncan deserves credit for the innovation, but the yo-yos that Duncan manufactured in 1929 boasted an important new feature: the yo-yo string was looped loosely *around* the axle (the center post between the two halves of the yo-yo), rather than being firmly secured to it. This allowed a Duncan Yo-Yo to spin freely at the end of the string. It transformed the yo-yo from a device that could only go up and down to one that could perform an endless number of tricks.

Duncan started out with just one model—the O-Boy Yo-Yo Top—but by the early 1930s had a whole line of yo-yo products… and a trademark on the name "yo-yo." Legally, his company was the only one in the United States that could call its toy a yo-yo.

SALES HYPE

But it took more than a technical innovation to make the yo-yo a national fad. It took promotion—and Duncan was a promotional genius. He immediately created…

- **The "Yo-yo Champion."** Many Filipinos living in the United States had played with yo-yos since they were kids. Duncan hired 42 of them (including his former business partner, Pedro Flores), gave them each the title "Champion," and sent them on tour to demonstrate yo-yos all over the country. At its peak, the company had one demonstrator on the road for every 100,000 people in America.

- **The yo-yo contest.** To drum up local support, Duncan sponsored neighborhood yo-yo contests all over the country, awarding new yo-yos, "All American Yo-Yo Sweaters," baseballs, gloves, bicycles, and other prizes to winners.

HELP FROM HEARST

But Duncan's most productive effort came one afternoon in 1929, when he walked uninvited into the San Simeon mansion of newspaper press baron William Randolph Hearst, talked his way past the butler, and made a quick sales pitch to Hearst, telling him how he could use yo-yo contests to boost newspaper circulation.

Duncan's idea was simple: Hearst's newspapers would publicize his yo-yo competitions, and in exchange for the free publicity, Duncan would require all entrants to sell three Hearst newspaper subscriptions as the price of admission to the contests. Hearst knew a good idea—and a good product—when he saw one. He took Duncan up on the offer. The promotions worked; in 1931, for example, one month-long effort in Philadelphia helped sell three million yo-yos.

Picture Perfect

To make newspaper coverage of his product as exciting as possible, Duncan arranged to photograph as many actors, professional athletes, and other celebrities playing with yo-yos as he could. He got lucky: two of the first stars who agreed to the photos were Douglas Fairbanks and Mary Pickford—then Hollywood's biggest stars. Their superstar status guaranteed that other celebrities would enthusiastically follow suit.

Some celebrity endorsements went beyond mere photographs: he got Bob Hope to perform yo-yo tricks for U.S. troops during World War II, and talked a young singer named Bing Crosby into singing promotional songs for the company, including this one:

> What is the dearest thing on earth, that fills my soul with joy
> and mirth? My Yo-Yo.
> What keeps my sense in a whirl, and makes me break dates
> with my best girl? My Yo-Yo.

THAT'S A LOT OF YO-YOS

These promotional efforts paid off. By the early 1930s, annual sales had shot from thousands of yo-yos to millions. The yo-yo craze spread all over the world. Demand became so great that in 1946 Duncan had to build a huge plant in Luck, Wisconsin, to keep up. The factory could turn out 3,600 yo-yos an hour—but at times Duncan still couldn't fill all the orders...even running the plant 24 hours a day.

Still, long-term sales were unpredictable. In boom years, the demand for yo-yos was insatiable. Other years, the demand declined by as much as 90%.

UPS AND DOWNS

The biggest yo-yo craze in history took place in the 1960s. In 1962 alone, according to news reports, 45 million were sold—despite the fact that there were only 40 million kids in the country. This should have been the Duncan Yo-Yo Company's finest hour—but it was their undoing. Why?

1. To meet the demand, they expanded and got too far into debt.

2. They stuck with wood when they should have switched to plastic. Wood had to dry for as long as six months, so they couldn't increase production fast enough.x

3. They lost their "yo-yo" trademark. There was so much money to be made selling yo-yos that competitors challenged the trademark in court. As proof that the term had become generic, they pointed to a billboard Duncan itself had erected near its factory: *Welcome to Luck, Wisconsin, Yo-yo Capital of the World.* If there was a yo-yo *capital*, that must mean yo-yos were made elsewhere, too. In 1962 a Federal Court of Appeals ruled that the trademark was invalid because the word yo-yo was the name of the toy itself.

These problems, combined with increasing costs and competition from Frisbees, skateboards, and other toys, sent the company into a tailspin. In 1965 the Duncan Co. filed for bankruptcy.

Three years later, the Flambeau Plastics Corporation bought the rights to the Duncan name and began cranking out plastic yo-yos. The Duncan name survives to this day (its yo-yos still have an 80% to 85% market share), and yo-yo fads still come and go; Donald Duncan, Jr. is even still in the business, producing yo-yos for the educational market under the name Playmaxx. But for purists, the end of the era came in 1965.

YO-YO FACTS

• Donald Duncan applied his promotional genius to other products: he also invented the Eskimo Pie, originated the Good Humor ice cream truck, co-patented the first four-wheel hydraulic automobile brake, and was the first person to successfully market the parking meter to cities and towns. (At one point, his parking meter company manufactured 80% of all meters in the United States.)

• In the early 1900s Hubert Meyer of Toledo, Ohio, patented an edible yo-yo.

• The Lego company built yo-yos for sale in the 1930s, but like Duncan, it sometimes found itself with huge inventories and low demand. One year it had so many unsold yo-yos in its warehouses that it sawed them in half and used them for wheels on toy trucks and cars.

• In 1984 astronaut David Griggs brought a yo-yo on board the Space Shuttle as part of NASA's "Toys in Space" experiments. His finding: yo-yos don't "sleep" in space—they just reach the end of their string and bounce right back up.

• The world's record for yo-yoing was set by John Winslow of Gloucester, Virginia. He started on November 23, 1977 and didn't stop for five days—120 hours.

• The world's largest yo-yo, Big-Yo, is 50" tall and 31-1/2" wide, and weighs 256 pounds. The string is 3/4" braided Dacron rope. In 1980 the "You Asked for It" TV show launched it off Pier 39 in San Francisco. But the string accidentally got wet before the launch and Big-Yo kept spinning in a "sleeper" position until its axle overheated and the string burned through. The yo-yo plunged 30 feet into San Francisco Bay and frogmen had to keep it from drifting away until it could be retrieved and towed to shore.

Genetically speaking, a guinea pig is more closely related to a cow than it is to a rat.

CELEBRITY SUPERSTITIONS

They're only human, after all.

John Madden: As Oakland Raiders coach, he wouldn't let his team leave the locker room until running back Mark van Eeghen belched.

Confederate General Stonewall Jackson: Jackson always charged into battle with his left hand held over his head, for "psychic balance."

Alfred Hitchcock: The cameo appearance he made in each of film he directed was for good luck.

Michael Jordan: Always wears his North Carolina shorts under his Bulls uniform. "As long as I have these shorts on…I feel confident," he says.

The Barrymores: Lionel, Ethel, and John always gave each other an apple on the night of a show's premiere.

Jimmy Connors: Wouldn't compete in a tennis match without a little note from his grandma tucked into his sock.

Jack Lemmon: Whispers "magic time" as filming starts.

Thomas Edison: Carried a staurolite, a stone that forms naturally in the shape of a cross. Legend has it that when fairies heard of Christ's crucifixion, their tears fell as "fairy cross" stones. Also a lucky piece for Theodore Roosevelt and Woodrow Wilson.

Greta Garbo: Wore a lucky string of pearls.

Mario Andretti: Won't use a green pen to sign autographs.

Kichiro Toyoda: A fortune-teller told him it was good luck to change his product's name to *Toyota* and only use car names beginning with "C" (Celica, Camry, etc.).

John Wayne: Considered it lucky to be in a movie with actor Ward Bond.

John McEnroe: Thinks it's bad luck to play on a Thursday the 12th. Carefully avoids stepping on a white line on the tennis court.

Randy Johnson: Eats pancakes before pitching.

More than 50% of all the lakes in the world are in Canada.

FAMILIAR PHRASES

More unusual origins of everyday words.

PARTING SHOT

Meaning: A final cutting remark or severe look at the end of an argument.

Origin: Unlikely as it seems, this term apparently evolved from the term *Parthian shot* or *Parthian shaft*. In about 1 B.C. in Western Asia, Parthian warriors were known for firing arrows *backwards* as they were retreating from an enemy.

TO LICK SOMETHING (OR SOMEONE) INTO SHAPE

Meaning: Improve something/someone; make them presentable

Origin: Comes from the old belief that bear cubs were born featureless, as "shapeless masses of flesh and fur" and needed constant licking from their parents to achieve their final shape.

NO-MAN'S LAND

Meaning: Any desolate or dangerous place.

Origin: A thousand years ago in London, retribution for criminal acts was swift and severe. Most crimes were punishable by death. It was customary to transport condemned men just outside of the north wall of the city, where they would be hanged, impaled, or beheaded, and their bodies disposed of.. Long after the surrounding territory was settled, no one laid a claim to the land where the executions had been held. Since no one owned it, it was designated as *no-man's land.*

TAKE WITH A GRAIN OF SALT

Meaning: Be skeptical; examine something carefully before accepting a statement's accuracy.

Origin: In ancient times, salt was rare and people thought it had special powers. Among other uses, they sprinkled it on food suspected of containing poison. It became customary to eat a questionable dish only if it was accompanied with a dash of salt.

IT'S THE LAW!...OR IS IT?

Most of us think we know more about the law than we actually do. We challenge you to take the BRI's version of the Bar Exam. Can you tell the difference between legal myths and legal reality? Answers are on page 499.

P ROBLEM #1
Bill and his wife get divorced, and he's socked with a hefty alimony payment. His drinking buddy tells Bill to get out of it by declaring bankruptcy. Can he do it?

a) Yes—if he moves around a lot and doesn't hold a steady job.

b) Nope. In his case, love may be temporary...but alimony is forever.

c) Of course. Once the bankruptcy is final, all of his debts will be erased.

PROBLEM # 2

Susan and Tom are first cousins who've fallen in love. They want to get married and raise a family. Tom's brother tells them they're out of luck—it's not legal. So they do some research and find out:

a) Tom's brother is right. It's illegal in the United States for first cousins to marry.

b) They can get married, but first they'll have to undergo psychological and genetic testing to evaluate the chances of insanity or birth defects. If the results are okay, a court will grant permission.

c) They should start packing and head for Georgia.

PROBLEM #3

Speed-limit signs of 5 MPH are posted at the local mall. One of the mall's security officers calls the local police to have some teenagers arrested for speeding through the parking lot. The police dispatcher tells the security officer to forget it—he's not sending out an officer. Why not?

a) The security guard didn't have a radar gun, so the case would be thrown out of court for lack of evidence.

b) It's not the police's problem.

c) Speeding violations are a low priority for local police.

In Sarasota, Florida, it's illegal to wear a swimsuit while singing in a public place.

PROBLEM #4

You bounce a check at the corner grocery store. Legally, what can they do about it?

a) They're required to request payment as soon as the check is returned to them. If you make good on it immediately, they can only charge you for the amount of the check.

b) They can stick it to you and charge you for up to *ten times* the amount of the check.

c) If they wanted to, they could have you arrested for theft.

PROBLEM #5

Sally loses her bank card, but doesn't notice it's gone until a couple of days have gone by; then she calls the credit card company right away. What's her maximum liability?

a) $50.

b) None—the card is automatically insured.

c) $500.

PROBLEM #6

You have a great idea for a new product. Your friends advise you to get it patented right away. Is that the best idea?

a) Yes, it's always the best protection for your idea.

b) You can't get a patent for something until you're ready to produce it, so you'll have to get manufacturing deals set up first.

c) Not always. If you apply for a patent, you might be limiting your ability to make money from it.

PROBLEM #7

Your friend dies in a climbing accident in Yosemite National Park in California. Before he left, he told you, "If anything happens to me you can have my guitar." Do you have any legal claim to the instrument?

a) Sorry, no. Wills have to be in writing, signed by witnesses, and notarized.

b) Yes—as long as there were credible witnesses to the promise.

c) Sure, if he hasn't already promised the guitar to someone else.

Q&A:
ASK THE EXPERTS

More random questions, with answers from America's trivia experts.

A LOT OF BULL

Q: *Do animals see color?*
A: We often act as if they do, but the truth is, most don't. "Apes and some monkeys perceive the full spectrum of color, as may some fish and birds. But most mammals view color only as shades of gray." So, for example, "bulls don't charge because a cape is red. They charge because of the *movement* of the cape." (From *The Book of Answers*, by Barbara Berliner)

CARROT TRICK

Q: *What are the "baby carrots" sold in plastic bags at supermarkets?*
A: "Take a closer look. Right there on the bag, it says clearly: 'baby-cut.' These aren't now and never were baby carrots. In the early 1990s, a carrot packer in Bakersfield, California thought of a clever way to use his misshapen culls. Mechanically he cut them into short pieces, then ground and polished them until they looked like sweet, tender young carrots.

"Baby-cut packers today don't rely on culls....They use a hybrid carrot called 'Caropak' that grows long and slender; it doesn't taper much and has little or no core. In the processing shed, the carrots are cleaned, cut into pieces, sorted by size, peeled in abrasive drums, then polished. Bagged with a little water and kept cold, they stay crisp and bright orange." (From the S.F. *Chronicle*)

THREAD OF TRUTH

Q: *Is fiberglass really made of glass?*
A: "It is, literally, tiny strands of glass that are anywhere from .0004 inches to two-millionths of an inch in diameter. They can be from six inches to more than a mile long.

"It's made by either of two processes. The longer, thicker fibers are made by melting glass marbles, then drawing melted strands

---

Double-speak: The U.S. government called the invasion of Grenada a "predawn vertical insertion."

through holes in a platinum bushing. Shorter, thinner fibers are made by an *air-stream* or *flame blowing* process that pulls bits of melted glass into tiny fibers. As the glass fibers cool, they are sprayed with a polymer that protects their surface and keeps the fibers strong." (From *Everything You Pretend to Know and Are Afraid Someone Will Ask*, by Lynette Padwa)

THAT JUMPY FEELING

Q: *How far can a kangaroo jump?*

A: "One large kangaroo, at a single desperate bound, is reported to have cleared a pile of timber 10-1/2 feet high and 27 feet long." (From *Can Elephants Swim?*, compiled by Robert M. Jones)

STEEL AWAY

Q: *"What makes stainless steel stainless?"*

A: "Stainless steel is coated with a thin, transparent film of iron oxide and chromium. This prevents soap, food, water, and air from getting to the metal below and eating it away. Since its coating is smooth, stainless steel is [also] very sanitary. Bacteria, fungi, and dirt have nowhere to hide and are easily washed away....[Ironically, the metal] was developed in 1913 by British metallurgist Harry Brearly, who was searching for a better lining for cannons." (From *The Book of Totally Useless Information*, by Don Voorhees)

QUESTION WITH A-PEEL

Q: *Are most of a potato's nutrients in the peel?*

A: "In most cases, the vitamins are spread evenly throughout the potato. But eating the peel is still a good idea. Certain minerals that your body needs, such as calcium and zinc, are found in larger amounts in the peel....In baked potatoes, the peel *does* contain more than its share of vitamins. Baking causes vitamins and other nutrients to pile up in the peel....[However], potatoes are members of the nightshade family. The stems, seeds and skins of this family are poisonous—some more so than others....While the flesh of the potato (the white part) is okay, the leaves and skin contain [a small amount of] substances called glycoalkaloids....That's why you should never eat potato eyes—that's where the glycoalkaloids concentrate." (From *Know It All*, by Ed Zotti)

The Chilean Pudu, the smallest member of the deer family, is no larger than a rabbit.

THE GREAT REGURGITATOR

We found this in a book called David Wallechinsky's The Twentieth Century. *Sure, it's gross, but you can't say it's not fascinating.*

COMING OUT

Would you pay good money to watch someone throw up? Thousands once did, on both sides of the Atlantic.

Born in Egypt in 1892, Hadji Ali traveled to the United States in the early 1930s, where he appeared in fairs, carnivals, and vaudeville. Billed variously as "the Amazing Regurgitator" and "the Egyptian Enigma," Ali would swallow a variety of household objects—coins, buttons, stones, watermelon seeds, hickory nuts, costume jewelry, even live goldfish—washing them down with copious amounts of water.

As audience members called out specific items, he would spit them up, one at a time. Ali acquired a small but enthusiastic following, and his grand finale brought down the house every night: His assistant would set up a toy castle in a corner of the stage while Ali gulped down a gallon of water chased with a pint of kerosene. To the accompaniment of a dramatic drumroll, he would spit out the kerosene in a six-foot arc across the stage, setting the castle on fire. Then, as the flames shot high into the air, Ali would upchuck the water and extinguish the fire.

FLEETING FAME

Ali remained more a sideshow curiosity than legitimate vaudeville headliner; according to Joe Laurie Jr. in his book *Vaudeville: From the Honky Tonks to the Palace*, Ali "lasted four weeks" in one theater "before they got wise that he was killing their supper shows."

Even so, Ali's remarkable talent was recorded in at least three films: *Strange as It Seems*, a 1930 short subject, *Politiquerias*, a Spanish-language comedy made in 1931, and *Gizmo*, a documentary filmed in the 1930s that is occasionally shown on cable television today. He was also featured at Grauman's Chinese Theater in

Hollywood from 1930 to 1931. (Ali died during a theatrical tour of Great Britain in 1937.)

UP-AND-COMING STARS

To be sure, Ali's talent for selective regurgitation was not unique or unprecedented. A performer named MacNorton, headlined as "The Human Aquarium," made a living in Europe ingesting and disgorging live fish and frogs on stage. He tried to bring his art to the United States in the 1920s but was prevented from doing so by the American Society for the Prevention of Cruelty to Animals. Around the same time, German-born Hans Rohrl gained fame as "The Living Hydrant." He wowed audiences by propelling a mouthful of water 15 feet across a stage in a spray nearly 7 feet wide.

In fact, voluntary upchucking, through controlled expansion and contraction of the throat and stomach muscles, has been a popular form of entertainment since the 1600s. A French theatrical text published in 1812 noted that a highly distinguished member of the Faculty of Paris was capable of emptying the contents of his stomach at will, without nausea or excessive effort. Unlike Hadji Ali, however, there is no indication that anyone paid to see him perform.

*   *   *   *   *

ANDY WARHOL SAYS...

"Ghetto space is wrong for America. It's wrong for people who are the same type to go and live together. There shouldn't be any huddling together in the same groups with the same food. In America it's got to mix 'n' mingle. If I were president, I'd make people mix 'n' mingle more. But the thing is, America's a free country and I couldn't *make* them."

—*The Philosophy of Andy Warhol*, 1975

NEAR-DEATH EXPERIENCES

Death may be lurking closer than you think. Judging from these stories, it might be a good idea to have a box of Tuna Helper on hand, just in case. Here are a few classic "near misses."

TUNA SURPRISE

"During a robbery at a grocery store in Chicago, employee Vincente Arriaga was shot by the robber at a distance of 20 feet. According to a report in the *Chicago Sun-Times*, the bullet barely broke Arriaga's skin because it was slowed down as it passed through a box of Tuna Helper he was holding."

—*News of the Weird,*
January 10, 1996

A STIRRING STORY

"Someone fired a .45 caliber bullet into Ava Donner's kitchen. Luckily, she was holding a spoon. Donner was stirring a pot of macaroni and cheese when a bullet hit the stem of the stainless steel spoon, ricocheted off the refrigerator and landed on the kitchen counter....'If it had been an inch either way, it would have been in her chest,' said Donner's husband. Police suspect he shot was fired by youths target shooting in a nearby vacant lot."

—*San Francisco Chronicle,*
February 26, 1996

RADAR RANGE

"Two members of the British traffic police were in Berwickshire with a radar gun, checking for speeding motorists, when suddenly their equipment locked up with a reading of over 300 miles per hour. Seconds later a low flying Harrier jet flew over their heads and explained the mystery. When the policemen complained to the RAF, they were informed they were lucky to be alive. The jet's target-seeker had locked onto their radar gun as 'enemy' radar...which triggered an automatic retaliatory air-to-surface missile attack. Luckily for the traffic cops, the Harrier was unarmed."

—*Pilot* magazine

Top speed attained in the first American auto race in Chicago in 1895: 7.5 mph.

MODERN-DAY LATIN

Latin may be a dead language for most people...but not for the Vatican. In 1991 they published the Lexicon Recentis Latinitas, an 18,000-word dictionary updating Latin for modern usage. Here are some of the entries for you bathroom scholars.

AIDS: *syndrome comparati defectus immunitatis*

amnesia: *memoriae amissio*

baby doll: *tunicula dormitoria*

babysitter: *infantaria*

to be lazy at work: *neglegenter operor*

bestseller: *liber maxime divenditus*

bidet: *ovata pelvis*

bottlewasher: *machina lageonis expurgandis*

brainwashing: *coercitio mentis*

carburetor: *aeris benzinique mixtura*

car wash: *autocinetorum lavatrix*

cellulite: *cellulitis*

Christmas tree: *arbor natalicia*

cover girl: *exterioris paginae puella*

disc brakes: *sufflamen disci forma*

discotheque: *orbium phonographicorum theca*

flashbulb: *fulgor photographicus*

fax: *exemplum simillime espressum*

to flirt: *lusorie amare*

guerrilla warfare: *bellum tectum*

gulag: *campus captivis custodiendis*

hypertension: *hypertensio*

hypnotherapy: *hypnotherapia*

leased property: *locatio in emptionem convertibilis*

pinball machine: *sphaeriludium electricum nomismate actum*

photocopy: *exemplar luce expressum*

refrigerator: *cella frigorifera*

secret agent: *speculator tectus*

sycophant: *assentator turpissimus* or *adulator impundens*

television: *instrumentum televisificum*

traffic jam: *fluxus interclusio*

travel agency: *itinerum procuratio*

warmonger: *belli instigator*

washing machine: *machina linteorum lavatoria*

First U.S. president born outside the original 13 states: Abe Lincoln.

WHAT A TRIP!
THE CIA & LSD

Just say no to drugs? It may surprise you to know that the U.S. government was using them—and maybe even spreading them. This story is from It's a Conspiracy, *by the National Insecurity Council.*

D uring World War II, Nazi scientists tested hallucinogenic drugs (like mescaline) on inmates at the Dachau concentration camp. The Nazis were ostensibly trying to find a new "aviation medicine," but what they were really looking for was the secret to "mind control."

After dosing inmates for years, the Nazi scientists concluded that it was "impossible to impose one's will on another person...even when strong doses had been given." But they found they *could* extract "even the most intimate secrets" from subjects under a drug's influence.

After the war, U.S. military intelligence found out about the Nazi experiments and wondered if hallucinogenic drugs might be used for espionage. Could such drugs be sprayed over enemy armies to disable them? Could the drugs be used to confuse or discredit leaders in hostile countries? The possibilities seemed endless. So, in 1950, the CIA took over where the Nazis had left off.

THE CIA ON DOPE
• In 1953, the CIA initiated a full-scale "mind-control" program called Operation MK-ULTRA. Its experiments included hypnosis, electroshock, ESP, lobotomy—and drugs. The operation is said to have lasted 20 years and cost $25 million.

• According to the book *Acid Dreams: The CIA, LSD and the Sixties Rebellion*: "Nearly every drug that appeared on the black market during the 1960s—marijuana, cocaine, PCP, DMT, speed, and many others—had previously been scrutinized, tested, and in some cases refined by the CIA and army scientists. But...none received as much attention or was embraced with such enthusiasm as LSD-25 [lysergic acid diethylamide]. For a time CIA personnel were completely infatuated with the hallucinogen. Those who first

It takes about 30 minutes for aspirin to find a headache.

tested LSD in the early 1950s were convinced that it would revolutionize the cloak-and-dagger trade."

But how could the CIA find out if the drug was an effective secret weapon unless it was first tested on people?

THE SECRET DRUG TESTS

In 1973, the CIA destroyed most of its files on the MK-ULTRA project; but some files escaped destruction. From these files, Congress and the public learned, for the first time, that for years the CIA had been experimenting with drugs.

• To test LSD, the CIA had set up both clandestine operations and academic fronts. For instance, it established a "Society for the Investigation of Human Ecology" at the Cornell University medical school, which dispensed "grants" to institutions in the U.S. and Canada to conduct experiments with LSD.

• The LSD project was administered by the CIA's Technical Services Staff. A freewheeling atmosphere developed in which anyone was likely to be dosed without warning in the name of research. Before the program concluded, thousands of people had been involuntarily dosed.

• Not only the CIA, but also the U.S. Army was involved in LSD experiments. *Acid Dreams* reports that in the 1950s, "nearly fifteen hundred military personnel had served as human guinea pigs in LSD experiments conducted by the U.S. Army Chemical Corps." The Army even made a film of troops trying to drill while stoned on acid.

THE REST

The government had no choice but to admit it had given LSD to about 1,000 unsuspecting people from 1955 to 1958 and has paid millions of dollars to settle lawsuits that were filed when subjects given drugs became permanently incapacitated or committed suicide. A few examples:

• In a San Francisco operation code-named "Midnight Climax," prostitutes brought men to bordellos that were actually CIA safe houses. There, as reported in *Acid Dreams*, they would "spike the drinks of unlucky customers while CIA operatives observed, photographed, and recorded the action."

Quick fact: 20% of drivers get 80% of the traffic tickets.

- In one experiment, black inmates at the Lexington Narcotics Hospital were given LSD for 75 consecutive days in gradually increasing doses.

- In 1953, a civilian working for the Army was slipped LSD at a CIA party. He jumped to his death from a 10th-story window. It was ruled a suicide until 1975, when the government revealed the truth. The CIA apologized and Congress awarded his family $750,000.

- A CIA-funded psychiatrist in Canada dosed patients with LSD and used other mind-control techniques, trying to "reprogram" them. Nine of the patients sued the CIA for damages. The case was settled out of court in 1988.

- According to *Acid Dreams:* "A former CIA contract employee reported that CIA personnel actually helped underground chemists set up LSD laboratories in the San Francisco Bay area." Many counter-culture heroes believed this was true:

> "The LSD movement was started by the CIA. I wouldn't be here now without the foresight of the CIA scientists."
>
> —Timothy Leary

> "We must always remember to thank the CIA and the army for LSD. That's what people forget…They invented LSD to control people and what they did was give us freedom."
>
> —John Lennon

FOOTNOTE: THE OSWALD CONNECTION

- Was Lee Harvey Oswald given LSD by the CIA? In 1957, Oswald—then a 17-year-old marine—was assigned to the U.S. naval air base in Atsugi, Japan. According to *Rolling Stone*, this base "served as one of two overseas field stations where the CIA conducted extensive LSD testing."

- Two years later, Oswald was discharged and moved to the USSR, supposedly as a defector. "If Oswald was sent to Russia as a pseudo-defector, performing some covert task for the U.S., then it's quite possible he was given LSD as part of his training." (*Rolling Stone*)

Recommended Reading: *Acid Dreams: The CIA, LSD and the Sixties Rebellion,* by Martin Lee and Bruce Shlain

---

The longest-surviving Civil War veteran died in 1959.

NOTABLE BOOKS

*We can't identify the first book ever read in the bathroom,
but we have been able to find the stories behind
a few other publishing milestones.*

THE FANNIE FARMER COOKBOOK

Originally, cookbooks didn't give precise measurements for recipes—they just told readers to use a "pinch" of this, a "heaping spoonful" of that, and a "handful" of something else. Fannie Merrit Farmer, a domestic servant in the late 1850s, had no trouble following such recipes herself—but she found it almost impossible to give instructions to the young girl who helped her in the home where she worked. So she began rewriting the family's recipes using more precise measurements.

Forty years later, she had become the assistant principal of the prestigious Boston Cooking School. In 1896, she decided to publish her first book of "scientific" recipes, *The Fannie Farmer Cookbook*. Her publisher was so worried it wouldn't sell that he forced Farmer to pay for the printing costs herself. She did. It sold 4 million copies and permanently changed the way cookbooks are written.

DR. SPOCK'S BABY AND CHILD CARE

Dr. Benjamin Spock was a New York pediatrician with a background in psychology when Pocket Books approached him about writing a childcare book for new mothers. It wasn't the first time he'd gotten such an offer: in 1938 Doubleday had asked him to write a similar book, but he turned them down, saying he was inexperienced and wasn't sure he could write a good book. He almost rejected Pocket Books for the same reason—until the editor explained that it didn't *have* to be a very good book, "because at 25¢ cents a copy, we'll be able to sell a hundred thousand a year."

Feeling reassured, Spock accepted the offer and wrote *The Pocket Book of Baby and Child Care*. He began with the admonition "Trust yourself"—and wrote a book that was unlike any child-rearing book that had been written before. "The previous attitude in child-rearing books was, 'Look out, stupid, if you don't do as I say, you'll kill the baby,'" Spock recalls. "I leaned over backward not to be alarming and to be friendly with the parents."

His warm, supportive voice paid off; *The Pocket Book of Baby and Child Care* became the second-bestselling book in American history, second only to the Bible. It has sold an average of 1 million copies a year *every year* since it was published in 1946. Its impact on American culture has been profound. According to *The Paperback In America:* "For two generations of American parents, it has been the bible for coping with their newborns.... A comparison of new mothers to the number of books sold during the baby boom's peak years—from 1946 to 1964, when nearly 75 million babies were born in the United States—put the estimate of 'Spock babies' at one in five, and that failed to account for the number of women who shared or borrowed the book or used it to raise more than one child."

THE COMPLETE BOOK OF RUNNING

Jim Fixx was a part-time author and full-time editor at *Horizon* magazine...until 1976, when his boss "suggested" he find another job. Fixx didn't want another magazine job, but all he knew how to do was write, and he had four kids to support. He'd been running for about eight years, and knew there was no book that gave practical advice for beginning runners, so he came up with an idea to make a quick $10,000—a "breezy, superficial" book called *The Lazy Athlete's Look Younger Be Thinner Feel Better & Live Longer Running Book.*

As it happened, one of the last things he did for *Horizon* magazine was meet with Pulitzer Prize-winning author Jerzy Kozinski. "As Kozinski and I sat talking in his studio in midtown Manhattan," Fixx recalled, "the conversation turned to my book."

> "You have a big job ahead of you," Kozinski said "To write a book like that, you have to read everything that's been written on the subject." Until then I hadn't thought of doing anything of the sort. All I wanted to do was get the book written quickly and collect my check. But I realized that Kozinski was right. The conversation turned a modest and easily manageable plan into a two-year obsession.

The book came out in 1978. It immediately hit the bestseller list, and became the bible of one of the biggest sports in America. Years later, Fixx died of a heart attack while jogging.

REEL QUOTES

Here are some of our favorite lines from the Silver Screen.

ON INTELLIGENCE

Doc: "This kid is so dumb he doesn't know what time it is."
Golfer: "By the way, what time is it?"
Doc: "I don't know."
—W. C. Fields,
The Dentist

ON MARRIAGE

"If love is blind…marriage must be like having a stroke."
—Danny DeVito,
War of the Roses

"What's marriage anyhow? Just a tradition started by cavemen and encouraged by florists."
—Olivia de Haviland,
The Strawberry Blonde

"Marriage is forever—like cement."
—Peter Sellers,
What's New Pussycat?

ON SEX

"I like my sex the way I play basketball: one on one, and with as little dribbling as possible."
—Lt. Frank Dreblin,
The Naked Gun

ON RELIGION

Luna: "Do you believe in God?"
Miles: "Do I believe in God? I'm what you'd call a theological atheist. I believe that there is an intelligence to the universe, with the exception of certain parts of New Jersey. Do YOU believe in God?"
Luna: "Well, I believe that there's somebody out there who watches over us."
Miles: "Unfortunately, it's the government."
—Woody Allen's *Sleeper*

ON RELATIONSHIPS

"She dumped me cause she said I wasn't paying enough attention to her, or something. I don't know, I wasn't really listening."
—Harry,
Dumb & Dumber

"A guy'll listen to anything if he thinks it's foreplay."
—Susan Sarandon,
Bull Durham

"I'm not livin' with you. We occupy the same cage, that's all."
—Elizabeth Taylor,
Cat on a Hot Tin Roof

THE DISAPPEARANCE OF THE *MARY CELESTE*

One of the most famous unexplained disappearances ever recorded is the case of the Mary Celeste. In 1872 it was found drifting aimlessly in the Atlantic, in seaworthy condition and fully provisioned. But the entire crew had vanished without a trace. To this day, no one knows what happened.

BACKGROUND

On November 5, 1872, the *Mary Celeste* set off from New York carrying a cargo of 1,701 barrels of commercial alcohol. Her captain was Benjamin Spooner Briggs, a well-known seaman who allowed no drinking on his ship and regularly read the Bible to his men. The crew had been carefully chosen for their character and seamanship, especially because the captain had brought along his wife and two-year-old daughter. He was looking forward to a safe and pleasant voyage.

DISAPPEARANCE

One month later, on December 5, Captain Morehouse of the *Dei Gratia*—another cargo ship bound for Gibraltar—noticed a vessel on the horizon. It looked like it was in trouble, so he changed course to see if he could be of assistance. After calling out to the ship and getting no reply, Morehouse lowered a boat and sent two men to board. It was immediately evident that the ship, which turned out to be the *Mary Celeste*, was deserted. The men looked for underwater damage, but the vessel was not leaking, and was in no danger of sinking. There was evidence that the *Mary Celeste* had encountered bad weather, but on the whole she was in perfectly good condition and should have had no problem continuing her journey.

Stranger yet, there were six months' worth of provisions aboard and plenty of fresh water. All of the crew's personal possessions were intact—even the ship's strongbox. In fact, absolutely nothing was missing except some of the ship's papers and the ship's lifeboat. Captain Briggs, his family, and the crew had obviously abandoned the ship in a hurry...but why? What could have frightened them so much that they'd desert a seaworthy vessel for an overcrowded yawl and take their chances in the stormy Atlantic?

INVESTIGATION

Still puzzled by the disappearance of the crew, Captain Morehouse decided to claim the *Mary Celeste* as salvage. He put three men aboard her and proceeded with both ships to Gibraltar.

Officials in Gibraltar were suspicious of Morehouse when he showed up with a "salvage" ship in such good condition, still carrying valuable cargo. They investigated and discovered that:

• The *Mary Celeste*'s hull was perfectly sound, indicating she had not been in a collision. Nor was there any evidence of explosion or fire.

• The cargo of commercial alcohol seemed to be intact and complete.

• A phial of sewing machine oil was standing upright, spare panes of glass were found unbroken, and the furniture in the captain's cabin was in its proper place—all indications that the ship hadn't endured particularly rough weather.

• The fact that the crew had left behind all their possessions—even their tobacco—indicated that they had left the ship in a panic, afraid for their lives, but the investigators could see no reason for this.

• The most mysterious item aboard was a sword found under the captain's bed. It seemed to be smeared with blood, then wiped. Blood was also found on the railing, and both bows of the ship had strange cuts in them which could not be explained.

THE OFFICIAL WORD

Solly Flood, attorney general for Gibraltar, found the bloodstains suspicious and was convinced there had been violence aboard the *Mary Celeste*. However, the Vice Admiralty Court issued a verdict clearing Morehouse and his crew of any suspicion. After the ship's owners paid Morehouse a reward, the *Mary Celeste* was given a new crew, and went on to Italy, where her cargo was delivered. She continued to sail for 12 years but was known as a "hoodoo ship," so most seamen refused to set foot on her.

Fourth most popular plastic surgery performed on U.S. males: breast reduction.

WHAT HAPPENED?

The mysterious disappearance of the *Mary Celeste*'s crew had people all over the world imagining possible scenarios.

• Some believed a mutiny had occurred—the crew murdered the captain and his family, then took the ship. But if that were true, why did they abandon their prize?

• There was the possibility that pirates attacked the ship and killed everyone on it. But that made no sense because nothing was stolen.

• Perhaps an outbreak of disease panicked those left alive. But why would they subject themselves to the close quarters of the smaller boat, where the crowding would *guarantee* that everyone caught the disease?

• The most outrageous explanation offered was that the ship had been attacked by a giant squid several times, until everyone was killed. But a squid wouldn't have been interested in the ship's papers. And a squid wouldn't need the ship's lifeboat.

Because the story of the *Mary Celeste* got so much publicity, phony survivors started popping up and selling their stories to newspapers and magazines. But they all checked out false—no one who claimed to have been on board had their facts straight.

ONLY ONE EXPLANATION?

The mystery of the *Mary Celeste* has puzzled people for over a century. In all that time, say experts, only one feasible explanation has been proposed. This postulates that four things happened, in succession:

1. The captain died of natural causes while the ship was caught in bad weather

2. A crew member misread the depth of the water in the hold, and everyone panicked, thinking the ship was going down

3. They abandoned ship in such a hurry that they took no food or water

4. Everyone in the lifeboat either starved or drowned.

Is that what happened? No one will ever know.

HARD-BOILED: CLASSIC FILM NOIR QUOTES

Film noir—French for "black film"—generally refers to the tough-guy detective movies of the 1940s and 1950s. Peggy Thompson and Saeko Usukawa put together a collection of great noir lines called Hard Boiled. *Some samples:*

"I've met a lot of hard-boiled eggs in my time, but you—you're twenty minutes."
—Jan Sterling,
The Big Carnival (1951)

Charles McGraw: "You make me sick to my stomach!"
Marie Windsor: "Yeah? Well use your own sink."
—*The Narrow Margin* (1952)

"What do you want, Joe, my life history? Here it is in four words: big ideas, small results."
—Barbara Stanwyck,
Clash by Night (1952)

"I treated her like a pair of gloves. When I was cold, I called her up."
—Cornel Wilde,
The Big Combo (1955)

Psycho crook (Lee Marvin): "Hey, that's a nice perfume."
Moll (Gloria Grahame): "Something new. Attracts mosquitoes and repels men."
—*The Big Heat* (1953)

"She was giving me the kind of look I could feel in my hip pocket."
—Robert Mitchum
Farewell, My Lovely (1975)

Reporter (Audrey Trotter): "I don't like your manner."
Detective (Robert Montgomery): "I'm not selling it."
—*Lady in the Lake* (1947)

"I felt pretty good—like an amputated leg."
—Dick Powell,
Murder, My Sweet (1944)

"I don't pray. Kneeling bags my nylons."
—Jan Sterling,
Ace in the Hole (1951)

"What kind of a dish was she? The sixty-cent special—cheap, flashy, strictly poison under the gravy."
—Charles McGraw,
The Narrow Margin (1952)

"Personally, I'm convinced that alligators have the right idea. They eat their young."
—Eve Arden,
Mildred Pierce (1945)

Fight manager (William Conrad): "Everybody dies. Ben, Shorty, even you."
Boxer (John Garfield): "What's the point?"
Manager: "No point—that's life."
—*Body and Soul* (1947)

The speed of a roller coaster increases an average of 10 mph when it's raining.

QUEEN OF THE NILE

*She's one of the most famous queens in history...but
how much do you really know about her?*

For centuries, people have been enthralled by stories of Cleopatra. She was a tragic heroine in Shakespeare's *Antony and Cleopatra*; a scheming vamp in *Cleopatra*, Theda Bara's classic 1917 silent film; a buxom babe in Elizabeth Taylor's 1963 film flop. But most people know very little about the real Queen of the Nile. And much of what they *think* they know is false.

Belief: There was only one Cleopatra.

Truth: There were seven Queen Cleopatras in the Egyptian dynasty that began with King Ptolemy I in 323 B.C.; Cleopatra, who reigned from 15 B.C.–30 B.C. was the seventh and last. Her eldest sister was Queen Cleopatra VI, and her daughter (who never became queen) was also named Cleopatra.

Belief: She was Egyptian.

Truth: She was considered Greek. Cleopatra was one of King Ptolemy I's direct descendants; *he* had been a Greek staff officer of Alexander the Great before becoming king of Egypt following Alexander's death. Like the Egyptian pharaohs before them, the Ptolemaic dynasty adopted incestuous brother-sister marriage as a way to keep their bloodline "pure"; historians believe it's unlikely Cleopatra had any Egyptian blood at all. For that matter, she was the first Ptolemaic ruler who could even *speak* Egyptian.

Belief: She was one of the most beautiful women in the world.

Truth: At best, she had ordinary features; at worst, she was decidedly unattractive. "Her coins," Lucy Huges-Hallett writes in *Cleopatra: History, Dreams and Distortions*, "minted on her orders and therefore more likely to flatter than otherwise, show a strong, bony face with a hooked nose and a jutting chin, pretty neither by the standards of Cleopatra's day nor by those of ours." The ancient Roman historian Plutarch describes her as being not particularly good-looking, although her intellect, beautiful voice, and strong character made her desirable and enjoyable company.

JFK was a distant relative of Lisa Gheradini, the woman who posed for the Mona Lisa.

Belief: She was a great seductress.

Truth: This is based on her well-known affairs with Julius Caesar and Marc Antony. But in the days of ancient Rome, affairs between rulers were a common means of cementing alliances. Caesar is known to have had liaisons with several other queens and at least one king (one of his contemporaries described him as "every woman's man and every man's woman"); Mark Antony was also a notorious womanizer. Cleopatra, on the other hand, was completely celibate for more than half her adult life and is believed to have had only two lovers: Caesar and Marc Antony.

Belief: Caesar and Marc Antony were madly in love with her.

Truth: It *is* possible Caesar fell in love with Cleopatra (no one knows); but he really stayed in Egypt to get his hands on her fortune. And historians say he made her queen of Egypt because he didn't want to appoint a Roman who might become his rival.

Cleopatra's relationship with Marc Antony was also based on politics. At their first meeting, when they supposedly fell in love, they made a deal: Antony agreed to kill Cleopatra's sister so she'd have no challenge to her authority; Cleopatra became a loyal ally. Then he went back to Rome and his wife. When his wife died, he didn't marry Cleopatra—he hooked up with the sister of a political rival. Years later, he finally visited Cleopatra and the twins he'd fathered with her. Coincidentally, he also needed her treasure and her navy at the time.

Antony did commit suicide and die in Cleopatra's arms, but it wasn't for love; he was despondent because they'd been defeated in battle. Cleopatra committed suicide, too. For love? No. The Romans told her she was going to be paraded in disgrace through Rome in chains, and she couldn't take that.

Belief: She committed suicide by getting herself bitten by an asp.

Truth: Nobody knows for sure how she killed herself. "Plutarch had read the memoirs of her private physician, but even he was not sure," Huges-Hallett writes in *Cleopatra: History, Dreams and Distortions:* "It seems likely to have been the bite of a snake brought to her in a basket of figs, but it may be that she had some poison ready prepared and hidden in a hollow hair comb, or that she pricked herself with a poisoned hairpin. The only marks found on her body were two tiny scratches on her arm."

Expert advice: If you add honey to peanut butter, it won't stick to the roof of your mouth.

POLI-TALKS

Here are some comments about everyone's favorite—and everyone's least favorite—subject. From Ariel Books' compilation called "Politics."

"I am the future."
　　　　　—Dan Quayle

"The first law of politics: Never say anything in a national campaign that anyone might remember."
　　　　　—Eugene McCarthy

"There is something about a Republican that you can only stand for just so long. On the other hand, there is something about a Democrat that you can't stand for quite that long."
　　　　　—Will Rogers

"Democrats are the party that says government can make you richer, smarter, taller, and get the chickweed out of your lawn. Republicans are the party that says government doesn't work—and then gets they get elected to prove it."
　　　　　—P.J. O'Rourke

"It seems to be a law of nature that Republicans are more boring than Democrats."
　　　　　—Stewart Alsop

"I don't know a lot about politics, but I know a good party man when I see one."
　　　　　—Mae West

"I'm a fellow that likes small parties, and the Republican party is about the size I like."
　　　　　—Lyndon B. Johnson

"Republicans sleep in twin beds—some even in separate rooms. That is why there are more Democrats."
　　　　　—Will Stanton

"I'm a loyal Republican. I support the president [Ronald Reagan] when he's right—and I just keep quiet the other 95 percent of the time."
　　　　　—John LeBoutiller

"Democrats give away their old clothes; Republicans wear theirs. Republicans employ exterminators; Democrats step on the bugs. Democrats eat the fish they catch; Republicans eat 'em and hang 'em on the wall."
　　　　　—Sean Donlon

LET THERE BE LITE

At first glance, it seems incredible that the "lite" phenomenon—a 1980s diet food craze—started with beer. But after you read this two-part BRI report, it should make more sense. We can't help wondering if the whole notion of "diet food" isn't essentially a fraud. What do you think?

AN UNLIKELY BEGINNING

According to beer industry studies, 30% of American beer drinkers—mostly blue-collar males between the ages of 18 and 49—drink 80% of the beer produced in the country. That means that every major U.S. brewery is trying to attract the same customers.

Traditionally, it meant that "diet beer" was a recipe for losing money. Heavy beer drinkers weren't interested in dieting, and dieters weren't very interested in drinking beer. Why make a beer for people who won't drink it?

Those few breweries gutsy (or stupid) enough to brew a low-calorie beer were sorry they tried. In 1964, for example, the Piels Brewing Co. introduced Trommer's Red Letter, "the world's first diet beer." It lasted about a month and a half. Three years later, Rheingold Brewing Co. of New York introduced a low-cal brew called Gablinger's—described by critics as "piss with a head." One company exec lamented: "Everyone tried it—once." At about the same time, the Meister Brau Brewing Co. of Chicago came out with Meister Brau Lite. For some reason, they targeted it at calorie-conscious women. "It failed so badly," said one report, "that it practically took the entire Meister Brau Co. down with it."

LUCKY STRIKE

In the early 1970s, Miller Brewing Co. bought the rights to Meister Brau's brands. They got Lite Beer (which was still in limited distribution in the Midwest) as part of the deal, but no one at Miller paid much attention.

In fact, Lite Beer probably would have been quietly dumped right away if company executives hadn't stumbled on something surprising in Meister Brau's sales reports: Lite was actually *popular* in Anderson, Indiana, a steel town dominated by the same blue-collar workers who were supposed to hate "diet beer." Why did they like Lite? Nobody knew. Curious, the company sent representatives to find out. As Miller advertising executive Jeff Palmer recalls:

> The workers drank Lite, they said, because it didn't fill them up as much as regular beers. As a result, they felt they could drink more. And drinking more beer without having to pay more penalty in feeling filled up, is beer drinker heaven.

According to Palmer, the company did more research, and found that male beer drinkers were interested in a good tasting "light" beer but were "clear, if not vehement, that the concept of a *low-calorie* beer was definitely feminine and negative."

So if Miller could figure out how to make Lite taste better, and at the same time think of a way to get rid of the beer's "sissy" image, the company just might find a market for the brew.

LITE CHANGES

Miller president John Murphy decided it was worth a try. He ordered his brewmasters to come up with a beer that tasted like other Miller brands, but still cut the calories per can from around 150 to 96. It took them a little over a year.

Meanwhile, ad people went to work on positioning Lite as a "manly" brew that beer-lovers could drink without being ashamed. They decided to build an advertising campaign around "regular guy" celebrities, famous people with whom beer drinkers would be comfortable having a beer with in their neighborhood bars. The first guy they picked was Eddie Egan, the detective whose life was portrayed in *The French Connection*. "Unfortunately," one ad exec remembers, "he was under indictment at the time so we couldn't use him." Their next choice: journalist Jimmy Breslin. But he wasn't available either. The executives' third option: a few professional athletes...But Miller had a problem there, too—federal law prohibits using professional athletes in beer ads.

Miller was stuck. Who could they use?—who was left? While riding on a New York City bus, Bob Lenz, the ad executive in charge of Miller's account, came up with the answer. He noticed a poster of former New York Jet star Matt Snell, and it occurred to him that although advertising codes prohibited Miller from using *active* athletes to sell beer, there was no reason they couldn't employ *retired* ones. He called Snell.

"We taped him," Lenz recalls, "and once we saw the result, we knew we were onto something." Miller ultimately signed up dozens of *ex*-athletes for their ad campaign—from baseball players like Boog Powell and Mickey Mantle to bruisers like football's Deacon Jones and hockey's Boom-Boom Geoffrion.

SELLING THE BEER

As it turned out, using ex-jocks was a master stroke. Because they were a little older (and paunchier) than their contemporaries, they were easier for beer drinkers to relate to. Plus, they had nothing to prove—they were established heroes. If they said it was okay to drink "sissy" beer, no one was going to argue. "When Joe Frazier, Buck Buchanan, or Bubba Smith stroll into the bar and order Lite," wrote *Esquire* magazine in 1978, "you know you can too."

Every spot ended with the celebrities heatedly arguing about Lite's best quality—was it that it's "less filling" or that it "tastes great?"—followed by the tag line: "Everything you always wanted in a beer. And less."

When test marketing of Lite exceeded sales projections by an unprecedented 40%, it was attributed largely to the advertising campaign. Blue-collar workers not only felt comfortable drinking a "diet" beer, they also understood that "a third fewer calories" meant that drinking three Lites was only as filling as drinking two regular beers. So rather than cut calories, most Lite drinkers *drank more beer*, and the sales figures showed it.

LITE BONANZA

Lite was introduced nationally in 1975, and had an astounding effect on the Miller Brewing Co.

• In 1972, the company was the eighth-largest brewer, selling 5.4 million barrels of beer—compared to #1 Anheuser-Busch's 26.5 million barrels.

• By 1978—three years after the introduction of Lite—Miller was in second place and gaining, selling approximately 32 million barrels to Anheuser-Busch's 41 million. Schlitz, Pabst, Coors, and other brewers were left in the dust.

As *Business Week* put it, Lite became "the most successful new beer introduced in the United States in this century." Its ads became as well known as the most popular television shows. Some of its spokesmen became better known for their work with Lite than for their sports accomplishments.

THE LIGHT REVOLUTION

It was only a matter of time before other beer makers got into the act. In 1977, Anheuser-Busch brought its muscle "to light" when it introduced Natural Light beer.

Miller fought back, suing to keep any brewers from using the words *Lite* or *Light* in their brand names. But the company only won a partial victory. The court's verdict: Miller's competitors couldn't use the term *Lite*, but were free to use *Light*—since it's a standard English word and can't be trademarked.

Enthusiastic brewers started bottling their own light beers, and "light" became the hottest product in the beer business. By 1985, it made up 20% of the overall market. By 1994, it was a $16 billion business and comprised 35% of the market.

BACK TO THE FUTURE

Ironically, as the "light" category grew, Lite's revolutionary ad campaign began to look out of date. The market had changed, and a new light brews were aimed at young, health-conscious Americans—not blue-collar beer-guzzlers. "Light" had gone full circle; it was essentially being sold as a "diet" beer again.

The term "light" gradually took on a life of its own, too. It became a buzzword for *any* food that was lower in calories, or better for you, than the usual fare. This set the stage for an even bigger "lite" fad.

For Part II of Let There Be Lite, turn to page 410.

*   *   *

Sad but true: "If you're in jazz and more than ten people like you, you're labeled 'commercial.' "

—*Wally Stott*

"Chili" comes from an Aztec word that means "bowl of red."

YIDDISH-AMERICAN SLANG

A handful of Yiddish words have become common in the U.S.
If you've been wondering what they mean, here's the answer.

Chutzpa (hootz-pah): Clever audacity. Classic definition: "A child who kills both parents, then pleads for mercy because he's an orphan."

Drek: Junk. The bottom of the barrel.

Shtick: An act or a routine. (Usually associated with show business.)

Tchatchke (chotch-key): Toy, knick-knack, worthless gizmo.

Shiksa: A non-Jewish woman.

Schmuck: A fool; sometimes refers to an obnoxious person.

Schlemiel: Hapless individual. A person who always has bad luck; a fool.

Shlep: To haul around.

Shlock: Something that's poorly made, or made for low-class taste.

Kibitz: To offer unsolicited advice.

Klutz: Clumsy or inept person. From the German word for "wooden block."

Shmooze: To chat.

Meshugah (me-*shoo*-ga): Crazy.

Mensch: Compassionate, decent person. Someone both strong and kind.

Noodge: A pest. As a verb, "to pester or coax."

Putz: Dope, fool, schmuck.

Nosh: A snack. (As a verb, "to snack.")

Nudnik (nood-nik): A boring pest. A nudnik can even bore himself.

Bupkis: Nothing.

Shmo: A fool; a dumbo.

Shnook: A meek fool; sad sack.

Shpritz: To squirt. As a noun, a squirt of something.

Goniff: Sneaky thief; someone who takes advantage of others when able to.

Shloomp: Sloppy—e.g., clothes.

Farblunget: Totally confused; roaming aimlessly.

Greps: Belch; burp.

Shmeikel (shmeh-kel): Flatter insincerely; con or fast-talk.

Yenta: Nosy, gossipy person.

"THE TONIGHT SHOW" PART V: PAAR'S EXIT

By 1961, Jack Paar was one of the most celebrated stars in America. Who would have suspected that his job was making him sick?

END OF THE ROAD

One of the gifts of a skilled performer is the ability to make a difficult task seem effortless, to make it seem like anyone could do it.

So when Jack Paar announced in late 1961 that he was quitting "The Tonight Show" after only five years as host, viewers were surprised. Why would he give up such a great job? After all, he was such a natural at it.

But behind the scenes, it was a different story: people were amazed he'd lasted as long as he did.

BUTTERFLIES

Few people who watched Paar delivering his monologue and talking to guests understood how grueling an experience it was for him:

• Rather than just wing it through his monologues, Paar committed them to memory each night before going to bed by writing them out in longhand, over and over again, until he knew every word by heart. The process often took hours.

• He began to show serious signs of stress: he mumbled, washed his hands compulsively, and paced for hours worrying about the show.

• But the biggest secret was that, despite all his years as a performer, Paar had never gotten over his stage fright. "Jack used to duck under his desk in between commercials and throw up because he was so nervous," recalls Lew Hunter, the director of programming at NBC in the early 1960s. "It was amazing to watch him. That man went through hell to entertain people, and he'd already been on the air over two years when he was still doing that."

As Paar's tenure neared its end, he described his feelings about leaving. "I can't help but feel an overwhelming sense of relief that the ordeal is nearly over," he said. "The end is in sight at last, a release from days of living on my nerve ends and nights of sheer terror, going out before an audience of millions of viewers armed with nothing but a few notes....There never was a moment when I wasn't scared to death."

CHOOSING A REPLACEMENT

Two people were under serious consideration for Paar's job: Merv Griffin, host of the NBC game show "Play Your Hunch" and Johnny Carson, host of "Who Do You Trust" on ABC.

In the end, of course, NBC chose Carson. They figured that like Paar, Carson was a strong ad-libber and would be able to keep the show moving. They had no idea how good a choice they'd made.

For Part VI, "He-e-ere's Johnny," turn to page 359.

For Part VI, "He-e-ere's Johnny," turn to page 359.

*   *   *

RANDOM ORIGINS

The Jacuzzi

In 1943, Candido Jacuzzi's fifteen-month-old son suddenly contracted rheumatoid arthritis. The boy was in constant pain; the only thing that made him feel better was hydrotherapy treatments he got in the hospital. Candido decided to build a device that would enable him to have treatments at home. At the time his company, Jacuzzi Bros, Inc. was one of the world's largest manufacturers of submersible pumps. He adapted one so it would work in his bathtub. In 1955, they began manufacturing them as whirlpool baths. They were sold through drug stores at first—but when Hollywood discovered them, they became a symbol of luxury.

The Thimble

"The thimble was originally called a "thumb bell" by the English, because it was worn on the thumb; then it was referred to as a thumble, and finally its present name. It was a Dutch invention, and was first brought to England in 1695."

—from *Origins,* by J. Braude

LUCKY FINDS

*Here are three more stories of people who found
something valuable. It could happen to you...*

A HIDDEN VALUE

The Find: An 1830 painting

Where It Was Found: At an auction

The Story: In the mid-1990s, Wanda Bell paid $25 for an old
print depicting the signing of the Declaration of Independence.
One day, as she was cleaning the print, she noticed something underneath it. She removed it...and found an oil painting of a man.
Bell was curious to know more about it. In August 1997, she heard
that an "antiques roadshow" was offering free appraisals with experts from Sotheby's, so she took the painting there. Their assess-
ment: It's an early portrait painted by a famous New England artist
named Sheldon Peck. Estimated value: $250,000.

A ROLL OF FILM

The Find: The pilot show of "I Love Lucy"

Where It Was Found: Under a bed

The Story: In 1949, CBS offered Lucille Ball her own TV show, to
be based on her successful radio program, "My Favorite Husband."
She agreed...as long they'd let her real-life husband, Desi Arnaz,
co-star. CBS called the idea preposterous. "Who'd believe you were
married to a Cuban bandleader?" they said.

Lucy was determined. She and Desi decided to create a live show
and take it on the road to prove that audiences would accept them
together. "Desi moved quickly to assemble a first-rate vaudeville
act," write Steven Coyne Sanders and Tom Gilbert in their book,
Desilu.

> He called in an old friend, the renowned international Spanish
> clown Pepito, to devise some physical-comedy sketch material.
> Pepito rigorously coached the couple, as Desi recalled, "eight to ten
> hours a day" at the Coronado Hotel in San Diego.

The stage show was a huge success, so CBS agreed to film a sitcom
pilot. The synopsis: "Ricky goes to a TV audition. Pepito the

---

Clown, due to an accident, fails to appear and Lucy takes his place for the show." It was filmed on March 2, 1951.

"I Love Lucy," of course, became one of the most successful TV programs in history. But along the way, the pilot episode was lost. Fans and TV historians tried over the years to locate it, but it appeared to be gone for good. Then one day in 1989, Pepito's 84-year-old widow (he'd died in 1975) looked under a bed in her Orange County home and came across a can of film labeled "Lucy-Desi-Pepito" audition. It was the long-lost "Lucy" pilot. Desi, it turns out, had given it to Pepito as a thank-you for his help. The film, with an estimated value of over $1 million, was quickly turned into a TV special and home video.

A LUCKY MISTAKE

The Find: A unique coin

Where It Was Found: At a flea market

The Story: In 1970, Guy Giamo came across an interesting 1969 penny at a Northern California flea market. "What made it intriguing," reported the *San Francisco Chronicle*, "was that it seemed to be a 'double die' stamping, a Bureau of the Mint manufacturing error that gave the legends *Liberty* and *In God We Trust* a blurred, double-image look."

There are a lot of double-dies from 1955, worth more than $500 apiece. But double-die coins are easy to fake, and many are counterfeit. Giamo bought it anyway. Cost: about $100.

In 1978, he sent it to the U.S. Mint to find out if it was real. A few months later a Secret Service agent called and said simply: "The Treasury Department has determined your coin to be counterfeit, and it will be confiscated and destroyed." "That's it?" Giamo asked. "Affirmative," the agent replied, and hung up.

But that's not the end. A year later, Giamo was surprised by *another* call from the Treasury Department. "What the hell do you want now?" he asked bitterly. "We have a coin for you," he was told. Someone had re-examined his penny before it was melted down, and decided it was genuine. "We goofed," they told him.

Giamo's coin is the only double-die 1969-S penny in existence. Its estimated value: as much as $50,000.

TOP-RATED TV SHOWS, 1979–1984

More of the annual Top 10 TV shows of the past 50 years.

1979-1980

(1) 60 Minutes
(2) Three's Company
(3) M*A*S*H
(4) Alice
(5) Dallas
(6) Flo
(7) (tie) The Jeffersons
(7) (tie) The Dukes of Hazzard
(9) That's Incredible
(10) One Day at a Time

1980-1981

(1) Dallas
(2) 60 Minutes
(3) The Dukes of Hazzard
(4) The Love Boat
(5) Private Benjamin
(6) M*A*S*H
(7) House Calls
(8) The Jeffersons
(9) (tie) The Two of Us
(9) (tie) Little House on the
Prairie

1981-1982

(1) Dallas
(2) 60 Minutes
(3) The Jeffersons
(4) (tie) Joanie Loves Chachi
(4) (tie) Three's Company
(6) Alice
(7) (tie) The Dukes of Hazzard
(7) (tie) Too Close for Comfort
(9) ABC Monday Night Movie
(10) M*A*S*H

1982-1983

(1) 60 Minutes
(2) Dallas
(3) (tie) M*A*S*H
(3) (tie) Magnum, P.I.
(5) Dynasty
(6) Three's Company
(7) Simon & Simon
(8) Falcon Crest
(9) The Love Boat
(10) (tie) The A Team
(10) (tie) NFL Monday Night
Football

1983-1984

(1) Dallas
(2) 60 Minutes
(3) Dynasty
(4) The A Team
(5) Simon & Simon
(6) Magnum, P.I.
(7) Falcon Crest
(8) Kate & Allie
(9) Hotel
(10) Cagney & Lacey

1984-1985

(1) Dynasty
(2) Dallas
(3) The Cosby Show
(4) 60 Minutes
(5) Family Ties
(6) The A Team
(7) Simon & Simon
(8) Murder, She Wrote
(9) Knots Landing
(10) Falcon Crest; Crazy Like a Fox

What's your favorite fruit? The most-consumed fruit in the United States is the coffee bean.

ONE TOUGH LAMA

BRI member Sid Morrison found this in Atlantic *magazine, and sent it our way. We enjoyed it so much that we decided to reprint it.*

Here's how Atlantic *introduced this excerpt: "From an interview with Pema Jones, a 13-year-old Tibetan lama, in the Spring issue of* CyberSangha: The Buddhist Alternative Journal. *Jones, who is known as Rinpoche ("Precious One"), was born in India to a Tibetan mother and an American father; he lived in a Tibetan monastery until he was 7. He now lives in Wyoming, and is one of the youngest Buddhist teachers in the United States. The interview was conducted by Chris Helm."*

Chris Helm: It must be hard enough to be a 13-year-old boy in America, not to mention a Tibetan lama. How do your friends and family treat your connection with the Dharma?

Pema Jones: It's kind of weird. I have 2 older brothers, and they tease me about it. They call me "shrimpoche." The kids at school don't know I'm a lama. I would never tell them.

Helm: Why not?

Jones: I get dissed enough as it is just being Asian. They call me names like "nip" and "gook." It's not like when I was growing up in India. Everyone here in Wyoming is white. I consider it a good day when some goof in a pickup truck doesn't try to run me over.

Helm: How do you deal with people trying to hurt you?

Jones: It's pretty safe around here, but we Asians need to stick together. Some of my best friends in our gang are Chinese. It's strange to have Chinese friends when my family has been treated so badly by the Chinese, but this is America—I gotta live here with my own karma. Some skinhead doesn't care whether I'm Tibetan or Chinese. He just wants to stomp my head.

Helm: You're in a gang?

Jones: It's just for protection. It's like if a guy threatens one of us, there's nothing we can do on our own, but by getting a bunch of us together, we can defend ourselves. We don't have guns, and we don't do drugs or rob people. Can we talk about something else?

Helm: Sure. Do you like your students?

Babe Ruth wore a cabbage leaf under his baseball cap to keep cool during games.

Jones: Yeah, they're all right. They're kind of funny. It's like, they say they come for the teachings, but when they get into the interview room, they talk about other stuff.

Helm: What other stuff?

Jones: They mainly talk about the opposite sex. Men talk about problems with their wives, and women talk about their husbands and boyfriends. I don't get it. It's like, I have little enough time as it is with school and Little League and my chores, and they want me to be a shrink or something. And I'm only 13! I mean, I've got girlfriends and all, but what do I know about relationships?

Helm: So what do you tell them?

Jones: I talked to my dad about it, and he gave me a stack of business cards from one of his friends, a psychologist. I just hand my students one of the cards when they start talking about relationships. I put my name on the back of the card, and whenever my dad's friend gets a new client he takes me to Dairy Queen. It's cool.

Buddhism is no big deal; it's like being a doctor. There's suffering, you diagnose it, give someone a prescription, and hope they go to the drugstore. No one in America wants to go to the store, though. They all want to be pharmacists and sit around discussing different types of medicine. What's with that? Take some medicine and come back next week. I mean, don't get me wrong— Buddhism is choice.

Helm: So you're fully qualified to teach?

Jones: Sure. I mostly teach *Tonglen*, giving and receiving. It's what I think works best at times when people are trying to kill you or too many changes are happening at once, which seems to be the case in this country. You're basically a giant filter, like on an air conditioner. You suck in the bad air and breathe out the pure air. I see myself like an air-conditioning repair dude. I teach people how to filter and cool things down.

Helm: So if you can cool things down, why do you need to be in a gang?

Jones: It's a samsara and nirvana thing. If some guy disses me I can just tell myself that he really doesn't exist separate from me, you know? It's like he's dissing himself. That works fine. But what happens when he stops talking and starts beating on me? You need to be able to take care of yourself so you don't get killed. We live in samsara, and spacing out about nirvana doesn't help anyone.

Helm: Don't you see any contradiction in that? The Dalai Lama, for example, constantly teaches nonviolence, despite having been terribly oppressed all his life.

Jones: (*laughing*): Oh yeah,

right. The Dalai Lama is an awesome old dude and a killer teacher. But he's got, like, a dozen bodyguards around him when he's traveling. What do you think would happen if some butthead pulls a gun on His Holiness? Do you think those dozen bodyguards will practice nonviolence or bust some karate move on him? No way, man. A bodyguard sees this dweeb with a gun and he's gonna pop a cap in his ass.

* * * *

AND NOW...Another Anonymous Star: MARNI NIXON

Starring roles: The singing voice of Deborah Kerr in *The King and I* (1956) and *An Affair to Remember* (1957), Audrey Hepburn in *My Fair Lady* (1964) and Natalie Wood in *West Side Story* (1961).

Background: One of the world's most popular unknown singers, known as "The Ghostess with the Mostess." Sang in movie choruses. Her career began when someone heard she had a talent for mimicking other people's voices, and hired her to dub Margaret O'Brien's voice in the 1949 film *Secret Garden*.

Highlights: On her gift for mimicry: "It's a combination of intuition and imagining what they sound like. You take it from the quality of their existing voices and facial structure. Audrey Hepburn's speech pattern is much different from Natalie Wood's, for instance. I would try to stretch the membranes in my mouth to approach a particular shape. I imagined I could somehow change the tone and quality. Her hardest job: *My Fair Lady*.

• On dubbing: "Back then it was a dirty secret. I was threatened, you know. People told me if anybody knew, I wouldn't work in this town again,. And then it became an 'in' thing to know who was doing it. But now it's not a big deal, and I hope I've had something to do with changing people's attitudes about it."

President James Garfield kept fit by juggling Indian clubs.

IS YOUR NAME YOUR DESTINY?

*Ever met someone whose name matches their profession? Like a
Dr. Bones, or an attorney named Ms. Law...or a guy named
John who writes Bathroom Readers? It's an interesting phenomenon that's not—it turns out—all that uncommon. Here's
a Wall Street Journal article on the subject.*

WHAT'S IN A NAME?

What's in a name? Plenty, if it turns out to be your lot in life.

Once upon a time, the Butchers, the Bakers, and the Tailors took on names that advertised their professions. Today, business ought to be brisk for a hairdresser named Barbara Trimmer, for a chef named Susan Spicer—and for her younger brother, Tom Spicer, a specialty-herb broker. Life should be a song for Daniel Harp, who teaches music. "Consciously or unconsciously, they've got the essence of branding," says Alan Brew, a corporate-name consultant.

BRANDED

But no. Talk to some of the aptly named people like Judge Aaron Ment, Connecticut's chief court administrator, or Bob Crooks, a used-car salesman in Illinois—and you discover that being sad-dled with a vocationally appropriate or, in Mr. Crooks's case, a slyly judgmental name, isn't necessarily a blessing.

C. Martin Lawyer III, a legal-aid attorney in Tampa, Florida, tries to deflect the inevitable question before clients can even ask it: "My name is Martin Lawyer. Yes, I am an attorney. And, yes, Lawyer is my real name." Even with that as prologue, some cli-ents still don't get it. One called his office demanding to speak to her attorney. When the secretary asked the attorney's name, the annoyed woman responded: "I don't know. He won't tell me his real name. He makes me call him Mr. Lawyer."

OCCUPATIONAL HAZARDS

"Sometimes I wonder if people don't take me seriously enough," says Dr. Glass-Coffin, whose maiden name is Glass and whose husband's name is Coffin.

R. Bruce Money, a former banker and now a business professor at the University of South Carolina, says his first name is actually Richard, but he doesn't use it because people might start calling him "Rich Money."

Is it tempting to just legally change a troublesome name?

No way, sniffs John M. Hamburger, who says his family name predates the sandwich. But it is his fate to be president of a restaurant consulting and publishing firm in Roseville, Minnesota, and though he can trace his lineage back several generations to Germany, some people still break into nervous giggles when he makes business calls on restaurant companies.

FEIGNING INCREDULITY

Though he figures peoples' reactions to his name are their problem, not his, he still has had to endure being called "Hamburg-lar" and "Cheeseburger." But he has learned to turn the tables. When someone observes, "I bet you got a lot of jokes about your name as a kid," Mr. Hamburger shakes his head, deadpan: "No, why would I?"

Are people with unusual monikers drawn to professions that suit their names? Lewis P. Lipsitt, a child psychologist and Brown University professor whose hobby is collecting names that fit, says he believes something is at work subconsciously. Beginning in childhood, having an unusual last name "could easily become a repeated reminder of an interest area that, by golly, could eventually become yours," Dr. Lipsitt says.

TWO WAYS TO GO

Neal Goldsmith, a New York City psychologist, goes one step further. He speculates that people with job-related names may "either grow into or grow in opposition to" their names. "A man named Crook would be more likely than others to become either a cop or a criminal, and a person named Hamburger would be more likely to become a burger-joint owner or a vegetarian," Dr. Goldsmith says.

Why is a jackknife called a jackknife? Because it was invented by Jacques da Liege.

But over and over again, people say their careers are just a coincidence. Reeve Askew, a chiropractor, Larry Bone, an orthopedic surgeon, and Shawn Buckless, a university fund-raiser, all agree that their names didn't influence what they chose to do for a living.

Mr. Hamburger, the restaurant consultant, says that when he started out, he had a choice between working for a computer company and a restaurant company. "I chose the restaurant because it paid more," he says.

Mr. Roach, [a Terminix] inspector, says the name-job connection might seem fishy, but it's just a fluke. Still, both his mother and his brother also work for Terminix. "Destiny," he says, "works in strange ways."

* * * * *

APPROPRIATE AUTHORS

A list of honest-to-goodness real books and their
your-name-is-your-destiny authors, from Russell Ash
and Brian Lake's *Bizarre Books*.

A Treatise on Madness, by William Battie, M.D. (1768)
The Cypress Garden, by Jane Arbor (1969)
Motorcycling for Beginners, by Geoff Carless (1980)
Diseases of the Nervous System, by Walter Russell Brain (1933)
The Abel Coincidence, by J. N. Chance (1969)
Your Teeth, by John Chipping (1967)
The Boy's Own Aquarium, by Frank Finn (1922)
Illustrated History of Gymnastics, by John Goodbody (1983)
Running Duck, by Paula Gosling (1979)
Writing with Power, by Peter Elbow (1981)
How to Live a Hundred Years or More, by George Fasting (1927)
Causes of Crime, by A. Fink (1938)
Riches and Poverty, by L. G. Chiozza Money (1905)
Crocheting Novelty Potholders, by L. Macho (1982)
The Skipper's Secret, by Robert Smellie (1898)

It takes three minutes for a fresh mosquito bite to begin to itch.

ALPO AND GREEN SLIME

"The world of pizza is a world full of anger, anxiety and anchovies" says pop historian Tim Harrower. Literary scholar Gwen Foss invested years of research to create a glossary of pizza-maker's slang in an issue of Maledicta, the International Journal of Verbal Aggression. *Here's some of the more colorful lingo:*

Alpo: Italian sausage, also known as *dog food, Puppy Chow, Kibbles 'n' Bits*, and *Snausages*.

Beef darts: A game played during slow times, in which employees hurl bits of raw beef against the walls.

Birthday cake: A pizza with way too many items on it.

Blue quarters: Another kitchen game in which coins are heated in a 550°F oven until they turn blue.

Bondage pie: A pizza with S and M (sausage and mushrooms).

Carp: Anchovies, also known as *guppies* and *penguin food*.

Cheese off!: A friendly expletive meaning "Go away!"

Crispy critter: A burnt pizza.

Edgar Allen pie: A pizza with PO (pepperoni and onions)

Flyers and fungus: Pepperoni (because raw slices fly like Frisbees) and mushrooms.

Green slime: Green peppers, especially those that become slippery and slimy. Also known as *lizards* and *seaweed*.

Hemorrhage: Pizza with extra tomato sauce.

Master-baker: An oven tender.

Panty liner: The absorbent cardboard placed under a pizza when it's boxed.

Shroomers: Mushrooms.

Spoodle: A saucing tool that looks like a combination spoon/ladle.

Starver: A customer who orders a pizza then tells the driver that they didn't order one but offers to buy it at a discount.

Vulture pie: A pizza "with too many problems to send out to a customer," fit only as food for vultures—or employees.

Zap zits: Pop the bubbles in a pizza crust as it cooks.

Quitting smoking can reduce the amount of sleep you need each night by as much as an hour.

BASEBALL CURSES

Athletes are notoriously superstitious. But these "curses" are just fun…Right?

THE CURSE OF WRIGLEY FIELD

Curse: The Cubs will never make it to a World Series again

Origin: "As the story goes, the late Bill Sianis, founder of the Billy Goat's Tavern, tried to bring his pet goat into Wrigley Field [during the World Series] in 1945," wrote Mike Royko in the *Chicago Tribune*. "He was turned away because the goat smelled. That's when the curse was placed…and they haven't been in a World Series since."

The curse at work: Most years since 1945, the Cubs haven't even been in contention for a National League pennant. The club hasn't put together consecutive winning seasons since 1972.

• They finally won a division championship in 1984 and took the first two games in the best-of-five playoff series with the Padres. Then they lost three straight.

• They went back to the playoffs in 1989 and lost again.

• In 1997, the Cubs gave a beer company permission to use the curse as part of an ad campaign. They opened the season with a record-breaking 0-14 losing streak, their worst start in 121 years.

Status: Curse-lifting has been attempted on a number of occasions. The the current owner of the Billy Goat Tavern once went on "The Tonight Show" with a goat; it didn't work. In Royko's column, he blamed the "curse" on racism. The Cubs were slow to bring in black players in the late '40s, he said, which doomed them to poor teams in the '50s. Weird coincidence: Royko's column on the Cubs' curse was the last he ever wrote. He died shortly after.

THE CURSE OF THE BAMBINO

Curse: The Boston Red Sox will never win a World Series again.

Origin: On Jan. 5, 1920, Red Sox owner Harry Frazee announced he'd sold Babe "the Bambino" Ruth to the New York Yankees. Frazee got $100,000, plus a $300,000 loan for a mortgage at Fenway Park. The New York Yankees got the best player in baseball—a national treasure. The punishment for exchanging a gift of the gods for cold, crass cash? This curse.

Among other things, the ancient Egyptians worshipped cabbages.

The curse at work: Since then, the Yankees have won 34 pennants and 23 World Series. The Red Sox have won four pennants and lost all four World Series in heartbreaking fashion.

• 1946. After leading three games to two (in a best-of-seven series), Boston lost two in a row.

• 1967. They took the series to seven games against the Cardinals…and lost.

• 1975. In Game 6, Carlton Fisk's homer in the 12th inning gave Boston a 7-6 victory against Cincinnati in one of the most dramatic moments in baseball history. But the Reds still won Game 7, 4-3.

• 1986. Boston led the New York Mets three games to two. They were winning 5-4 in Game 6, with two outs and two strikes on the Met batter. It looked like the curse was about to be broken. Then disaster hit: The Mets tied the game on a wild pitch by the Red Sox pitcher, and the batter hit a grounder that went through Red Sox first-baseman Bill Buckner's legs; the Mets won the game, 6-5. Naturally, the Red Sox lost Game 7, too.

Status: People in Boston will stop believing in it when the Red Sox win a championship—and not a moment before.

THE CURSE OF COLAVITO

Curse: For trading slugger Rocky Colavito in 1960, the Cleveland Indians were doomed to bad baseball and bad luck.

Origin: April 17, 1960 was known as "the day Cleveland baseball died." That's the day the 26-year-old Colavito, hero of Indian fans, was dealt to the Detroit Tigers for a fading shortstop.

The curse at work: From 1960-93, the Indians finished no higher than third place—and that happened only once, in 1968.

• Bad luck ranged from player troubles—eg., in 1961, top young pitcher Sam McDowell, in his *first* major league start, broke two ribs throwing a fastball—to fan troubles: In June, 1974 they tried a 10¢ Beer Night; drunk fans poured onto the field, forcing a forfeit.

• July 1994. With Cleveland poised to reach the postseason for the first time since 1954, the players went on strike.

Status: Is it over? Hard to tell. The Indians made it to the World Series in 1995, but the best-hitting team in baseball batted .179 and lost in six games. Cleveland led the majors with 99 wins in '96, but choked against Baltimore in the divisional playoffs. As we write this, the Indians are in the World Series again. Maybe this time…

GROUCHO MARX, ATTORNEY AT LAW

Here's more dialogue from a recently rediscovered radio show featuring Groucho and Chico Marx—Five Star Theater, which aired in 1933.

(*Phone rings*)

MISS DIMPLE: Law offices of Beagle, Shyster, and Beagle ...Mr. Beagle? I expect him back from court any minute . . .

Door opens; footsteps heard.

MISS DIMPLE: Good morning, Mr. Beagle. How did you make out in court?

GROUCHO: Splendid, splendid, Miss Dimple. I got my client off.

MISS DIMPLE: You got him off?

GROUCHO: Yes, I got him off the streets for six months. They put him in the workhouse.

MISS DIMPLE: Oh...Well, there's a man out here who wants to talk to you about a job. (*Footsteps approach.*)

GROUCHO: Tell him I'll take it. But I won't work for less than a hundred dollars a week.

MISS DIMPLE: You misunderstand. He wants a job here.

GROUCHO: Oh, he wants a job. I think I can put him to work.

CHICO: I don't wanna work. I just wanna job.

GROUCHO: Hmm-m. How about references?

CHICO: Aw, that's awright. You don't need no references. I like your face.

GROUCHO: And I like your face—if it is a face. Have you had any experience?

CHICO: You bet. For 15 years I've been a musician.

GROUCHO: A musician? What do you get an hour?

CHICO: Well, for playing I get ten dollars an hour.

GROUCHO: What do you get for not playing?

CHICO: Twelve dollars an hour.

GROUCHO: That's more like it.

CHICO: Now for rehearsing I make a special rate—that's 15 dollars an hour.

GROUCHO: What do you get for not rehearsing?

CHICO: Oh, you couldn't afford that. You see, if I no re-

England is only two-thirds the size of New England.

hearse I no play. And if I no play, that runs into money.

GROUCHO: What would you want to run into an open manhole?

CHICO: Just the cover charge.

GROUCHO: Well, drop in some time.

CHICO: Sewer.

GROUCHO: I guess we've cleaned that up. Now go out and find some clients.

CHICO: Hey! We no speak about money.

GROUCHO: That suits me fine. If you promise not to say anything about it, I won't mention it either.

CHICO: Alright, but I gotta have more money.

GROUCHO: I'll tell you what I'll do. I'll give you 50 dollars a week and you can bring your own lunch.

CHICO: Well . . .

GROUCHO: Ok, I'll go even further. I'll give you 50 dollars a week and you can bring lunch for me too.

CHICO: I can't live on fifty dollars a week.

GROUCHO: That will make me very happy. You're hired.

CHICO: When do I start?

GROUCHO: Well, it's one o'clock now. If you start now you can be back here at three

with lunch. Bring me a cheese sandwich on white bread.

CHICO: I no gotta white bread, but I can give you rye.

GROUCHO: All right, then I'll take a quart of rye.

(*applause, commercial break*)

GROUCHO: Today is Monday. What have we have got on the books besides red ink? What's on the court calendar for this afternoon?

MISS DIMPLE: You know you have a suit on today.

GROUCHO: Certainly I have a suit on today. Do you expect me to come in my nightshirt? I only wear that for night court. Where's that assistant I hired last week?

MISS DIMPLE: Oh, Mr. Ravelli. He just phoned.

GROUCHO: Oh, he phoned, did he? Where did he get the quarter? He's been holding out on me. Say, I thought I told him to go out find some clients.

MISS DIMPLE: He said as soon as he finds a client he'll come see you.

GROUCHO: Oh, so he'll come in to see me. I suppose he doesn't think I'm good enough to go out and see him! Maybe he's ashamed to let me see where he lives. Where *does* he live?

MISS DIMPLE: He's been living here in the office ever since you hired him.

GROUCHO: No wonder he's ashamed.

MEANWHILE...

(*street noises*)

CHICO (yelling): Anybody want a lawyer? Nice fresh lawyer today? You want a lawyer, lady? Alright, it don't hurt to ask, you know. Hey, mister, how about you? You wouldn't want a lawyer, would you?

MAN: How do you know I wouldn't?

CHICO: Well, you wouldn't want this one.

MAN: As a matter of fact, I want a lawyer and I want one bad.

CHICO: I got just the man for you. He's terrible.

MAN: Well then, leave me alone. I got no use for your lawyer.

CHICO: Well, I got no use for him either, but I gotta get a client.

MAN: Say, what are you trying to do? Lay off me or I'll call a cop.

CHICO: You want to sue me? I got a good lawyer for you.

MAN: Oh, you...Officer, will you keep this nuisance away from me?

COP (Irish): Here you...move along, you're obstructing traffic.

CHICO: You want a lawyer?

COP: What would I be wantin' a lawyer for?

CHICO: I don't know. Take him home, wash him up, show him to the kids.

COP: Listen, what are you trying to do?

CHICO: My boss sent me down here to get clients.

COP: Well, you're not going to get any clients for a lawyer standing around here.

CHICO: At'sa fine. How am I gonna get clients?

COP: Hustle around....Use your imagination....But move along.

LATER...

(door opens; footsteps heard)

CHICO: Hey, Mr. Flywheel! I gotta client. This lady, she wants to see you.

We'll be back in a few pages with the conclusion
Check out page 407

Bees are born fully grown.

WRETCHED REVIEWS

Doesn't it bother you when a movie you love gets a thumbs-down from those two bozos on TV? Us, too. The Critics Were Wrong, *by Ardis Sillick and Michael McCormick, compiles hundreds of misguided movie reviews like these.*

THE WIZARD OF OZ

"Displays no trace of imagination, good taste or ingenuity... It's a stinkeroo."

—*The New Yorker*, 1939

LOVE ME TENDER
(Elvis's first film)

"[Presley is] a young man of hulk and probably flabby muscle, with a degenerate face, who sings emasculated innuendos in a southern drawl as he strums guitar. The weak mouth seems to sneer, even in repose, and the large, heavy-lidded eyes seem open only to be on the lookout for opportunities for self-indulgence....How a society as dynamic as our own throws up such a monstrosity is beyond the scope of this review."

—*Films in Review*, 1956

STAR WARS

"O dull new world! It is all as exciting as last year's weather reports....all trite characters and paltry verbiage."

—*New York*, 1977

JAWS

(*The ads showed a gaping shark's mouth.*) "If sharks can yawn, that's presumably what this one is doing. It's certainly what I was doing all through this picture."

—*The New Republic*, 1975

SNOW WHITE AND THE SEVEN DWARFS

"*Snow White* is a failure in every way. As a moving figure she is unreal, as a face and body she is absurd, and what she does is ludicrous....Another *Snow White* will sound the Disney death-knell."

—*Current History*, 1938

THE EMPIRE STRIKES BACK

"Malodorous offal.... Everything is stale, limp, desperately stretched out, and pretentious. Harrison Ford offers loutishness for charm, and becomes the epitome of the interstellar drugstore cowboy."

—*National Review*, 1980

Short people have been called "shrimps" longer than shrimps have.

STRANGE CELEBRITY LAWSUITS

*Here's a "strange lawsuits" for celebrity junkies—
people who read* People *magazine.*

THE PLAINTIFF: Elton John

THE DEFENDANT: The *Sunday Mirror*, an English newspaper

THE LAWSUIT: In 1992, the *Mirror* claimed that John had been spitting out chewed hors d'oeuvres at a Hollywood party, calling it a "new diet." The singer had recently gone public about his bulimia; he sued because "the story implied he was a sham"...and because he wasn't even at the party.

THE VERDICT: The singer was awarded $518,000 in damages. The *Mirror* issued a formal apology admitting the story was bogus.

THE PLAINTIFF: Catherine Deneuve, French movie star

THE DEFENDANT: Outspoken Enterprises, Inc., a San Francisco magazine publisher.

THE LAWSUIT: For five years, Outspoken Enterprises published *Deneuve* magazine. By 1996, it had 200,000 readers—making it one of the largest magazines for lesbians in the United States. The editor claimed the title was inspired by "the name of her first love," not the actress. But Catherine Deneuve didn't believe it. In January, 1996, she sued for trademark infringement.

THE VERDICT: The suit was apparently dropped when the magazine voluntarily changed its name to *Curve*.

THE PLAINTIFFS: French sexpot Brigitte Bardot and her neighbor, Jean-Pierre Manivet

THE DEFENDANTS: Jean-Pierre Manivet and Brigitte Bardot

THE LAWSUIT: Not surprisingly, it's about sex. In 1989, Bardot and Manivet lived next to each other on the French Riviera. Bardot owned a female donkey, Mimosa, and a mare, Duchesse; Manivet had a male donkey named Charly. Bardot, an animal activist, agreed to let Charly graze with her animals. But when Charly "be-

---

The ancient Romans died their hair with bird droppings.

gan to show male instincts toward the old mare," he lost his rights—Bardot had him castrated. Manivet was out of town at the time; when he returned, he sued Bardot for 4,500 francs (about $950) in damages, plus 10,000 for "moral prejudice." Bardot countersued, claiming Manivet's publicity about the case had harmed her image.

THE VERDICT: Everyone lost. The court ruled it was within Bardot's rights to "fix" the donkey, but not to protect her "image."

THE PLAINTIFF: Richard Belzer, of TV's *Homicide: Life on the Street*

THE DEFENDANTS: Hulk Hogan and Mr. T., professional wrestlers

THE LAWSUIT: In 1985, Belzer hosted a cable talk show called *"Hot Properties."* Hogan and Mr. T. appeared on one program as guests. According to news reports, the interview was "merely awkward" until Belzer asked them to show him some wrestling moves.

"I'm going to make him squeal," Hogan chuckled as he stood up." Mr. T. urged "the Hulkster" to show Belzer a "Pipsqueak Sandwich."

While the band played Chopin's funeral march in the background—and a Manhattan studio audience, including 50 children in wheelchairs, who had been invited to the show, watched in horror—Hogan demonstrated his "front chin lock." After a few seconds, the comedian collapsed. He recovered briefly—long enough to break for a commercial—and then he was taken by ambulance to Mount Sinai Hospital where nine stitches were taken in his scalp.

Belzer sued the two wrestlers for $5 million.

THE VERDICT: In 1988, the case was settled out of court.

THE PLAINTIFF: Michael B. Mukasey, stepfather of singer Mariah Carey

THE DEFENDANT: Mariah Carey

THE LAWSUIT: In 1993, Mukasey filed suit claiming that Carey had promised to let him market "singing dolls that looked like her." Underlying the lawsuit: His contention that he deserved a share of her earnings because "he helped her achieve stardom by… providing transportation to rehearsals and paying for dental work."

THE VERDICT: Case dismissed.

Funeral directors used to be known as "cold cooks."

THE HISTORY OF ROCK: QUIZ #2

*Now it's time to find out how much you know about
oldies from the 1960s. See page 492 for the answers.*

1. The Jefferson Airplane's "White Rabbit"—inspired by *Alice in
Wonderland*—was one of the rock classics of the 1960s. What
prompted singer Grace Slick to write it?

a) The rest of the group locked her in a room and told her not to
come out until she'd written some songs.

b) She read *Alice* to her niece and couldn't get over how "psyche-
delic" the story was.

c) She went to a Halloween party and saw Janis Joplin dressed as
Alice.

2. "Summer in the City" was the Lovin' Spoonful's biggest hit, a
#1 song in 1966. It was co-written by Spoonful leader John Sebas-
tian and...

a) Tommy Gershwin, nephew of composer George Gershwin. He
adapted it from an unpublished piece of music his uncle had left
him.

b) Mark Sebastian, John's brother. According to legend, Mark submitted the lyrics as a poem in his high school English class...and
got an "F" on them. John didn't think they were so bad and put
them to music.

c) Grace Slick. She'd just finished "White Rabbit" and was looking
for something new to work on.

3. Roy Orbison hit #1 in 1964 with "Pretty Woman." How did he
come up with the idea for the song?

a) His wife announced she was going to buy groceries.

b) His wife announced she was pregnant.

c) His wife announced she was leaving him.

4. In 1962, Frankie Valli and the Four Seasons were rudely interrupted while recording their soon-to-be #1 song, "Walk Like a Man." What happened?

a) The studio was robbed. The thieves took their money, jewelry...and all the instruments.

b) The building was on fire—fire fighters were smashing down the studio door as the group desperately tried to finish the recording.

c) A gang of fans broke down the door and chased the group all over the studio—finally cornering them in the men's room. Police had to rescue them.

5. In 1969, a group called Steam hit #1 with a pop tune called "Na Na Hey Hey Kiss Him Goodbye." How did they wind up with that title (which is also the chorus)?

a) One of the musicians was a Native American whose tribal name was "Nah nah hay-hay."

b) They couldn't think of any words, so they just stuck in some nonsense syllables.

c) One of the musician's kids, a three-year-old, came up with it.

6. In 1964, jazz trumpeter Louis Armstrong became the oldest artist ever to have a #1 song when his version of "Hello, Dolly" topped the charts. Why did he record the song?

a) "Dolly" was his first wife's name.

b) It was a publicity gimmick. He cut a deal with David Merrick, the show's producer: If Armstrong's record made the Top 10, Merrick said he'd pay the trumpeter an extra $100,000.

c) Someone gave it to Armstrong at the recording session. He'd never heard of the musical or the song, but thought it was decent enough to record.

7. Which of these classic 1960s rock songs was made up spontaneously—right in the middle of a live performance?

a) "When a Man Loves a Woman," by Percy Sledge

b) "All You Need Is Love," by the Beatles

c) "My Boyfriend's Back," by the Angels

One third of the entire population of Sweden emigrated to the United States in the 1800s.

THE EIFFEL TOWER, PART II

Room with a view: Among the amenities that Gustave Eiffel designed for the tower was a penthouse apartment at the top, complete with a grand piano and spotlights for shining on other Paris monuments. He built it for his own use.

EIGHTH WONDER OF THE WORLD
Most advances in architecture and engineering are incremental. If, for instance, you wanted to build the world's first 10-story building, you'd expect to study the construction techniques of 8- and 9-story buildings first.

But Gustave Eiffel didn't have that luxury. No one had ever built an iron tower like his of *any* size...let alone one that was twice as tall as the tallest building on earth.

AN ENGINEERING GENIUS

To accomplish his task, Eiffel devised some incredibly ingenious techniques:

• Unlike other massive engineering projects of the day, he had nearly all of the parts used in the tower prefabricated off-site in his workshops. This meant that when they arrived at the tower, the parts could be quickly riveted into place with a minimum of fuss.

• The rivet holes themselves were predrilled to a tolerance of one-tenth of one millimeter, making it possible for the twenty riveting teams to drive an average of 1,650 rivets a day.

• None of the girders used in the tower was permitted to weigh more than three tons. This made it possible to use smaller cranes to lift everything into place. As Joseph Harris writes in *The Tallest Tower:*

> Eiffel had learned that using small components was faster and safer, even if this method did require more riveting, for cranes could be smaller and more mobile. The chances of accidents were reduced, and if one did occur the consequences were less serious. Use of bigger girders would have slowed the entire operation and required more expensive and complicated construction methods.

Thanks to these and other safety measures, the Eiffel Tower—the world's tallest construction site—was also one of the safest. Of the hundreds of people who worked on the tower, only one, a riveter's assistant named Dussardin, fell to his death.

THE PIERS

In the early days of the project, there were actually four construction sites at the Eiffel Tower, one for each foot, or "pier." These piers did not join together until the 180-foot level…and once this point was reached, they had to be set *perfectly* level with one another to create a perfectly horizontal platform on which the remaining 800 feet of the tower could be built. If the piers were even slightly out of alignment, the tiniest discrepancy at the base of the tower would be magnified at the top: it would appear to lean.

Eiffel knew there was no way he could *guarantee* the piers would be vertical when finished—the margin for error was too great. So he installed temporary hydraulic pistons in the base of each of the feet. That way, as work on the tower progressed, he could "fine-tune" the entire tower into perfect alignment by slightly raising or lowering each foot. When the tower was properly aligned, workers could drive iron wedges into the piers to secure them permanently.

As it turned out, Eiffel had little to worry about. Even at the 180-foot level, the worst of the four massive piers was less than 2 1/2 inches out of alignment. All four were easily adjusted and secured in place. Even today, the tower is perfectly vertical.

FINIS

The Eiffel Tower was a marvel—not just for its ingenuity of design, but also because it was completed ahead of schedule and under budget. The Exposition was scheduled to open on May 6; work on the tower was finished on March 31.

Eiffel & Company earned back its money in record time. During the six months of the Exposition alone, the tower earned back more than $1.4 million of its $1.6 million construction cost; that, combined with the $300,000 subsidy provided by the French government, pushed the tower into the black even before the Exposition closed.

Average wage for the workmen who dug the Erie canal: $1 and one quart of whiskey per day.

The tower was such a magnificent structure that it won over many of its earlier critics. Among them was French prime minister Tirard. He had opposed the project at its inception, but awarded Eiffel the medal of the Legion of Honor after it was finished. The tower, a symbol of France's unrivaled technical expertise, became the symbol of France itself.

Not everyone who hated the tower experienced a change of heart. Guy de Maupassant, the novelist best known for *The Necklace*, was said to eat regularly at a restaurant on the tower's second floor. His reason: It was the only place in Paris where he was sure he wouldn't see the tower. (Even some of the characters in his novels hated the tower.)

TOWER FACTS

• Every seven years, the Eiffel Tower receives a fresh coat of more than 300 tons of reddish-green paint. Why reddish-green? Because, tower officials say, it is the color that clashes least with the blue sky over Paris, and the green landscape of the Champ de Mars below.

• The positions of the Eiffel Tower's four "feet" correspond to the "cardinal" points of a compass: they point exactly north, south, west, and east.

• In 1925 the City of Paris wanted to decorate the tower with electric lights as part of an arts exposition being held nearby, but the cost, estimated at $500,000, was too high. When automaker Andre Citroën learned of the project, he offered to pay for it himself...in exchange for the right to put his company name and corporate symbol in lights as well. The City agreed. "The Eiffel Tower," Blake Ehrlich writes in *Paris on the Seine*, "became the world's largest electric sign, its outlines traced in lights." The lights were so popular that the tower remained lit with various designs until 1937.

• Sad fact: The Eiffel Tower is the most popular landmark for suicides in France. In an average year, four people commit suicide by jumping off the tower or, occasionally, by hanging themselves from its wrought iron beams. The first person killed in a jump from the tower, in 1911, was not an intentional suicide—the man was a tailor named Teichelt who had sewn himself a "spring-loaded bat-wing cape" that he thought would enable him to fly. It didn't.

THE FIRST CENTERFOLD

*Whether you approve of the magazine or not, Playboy represents a
significant part of American culture. One of its trademarks
is the centerfold. Here's the tale of the first one.*

THE BARE FACTS

In the late 1940s, Marilyn Monroe was still an unknown actress, struggling to pay rent. One day in 1948 she borrowed a car to get to an audition, but had an accident on the way. As bystanders gathered, she announced she was late for an appointment and had no money for a cab. Tom Kelley, a photographer—gave her $5 and his business card.

A year later when Marilyn needed money, she went to Kelley's studio to ask if he had any work for her. He did—he was doing a photo shoot for a poster advertising Pabst Blue Ribbon Beer and his model had failed to show up. Marilyn happily stepped in and took the job.

A few weeks later Kelley called Monroe with more work. A Chicago calendar manufacturer named John Baumgarth had seen the Pabst poster and wanted a few "tasteful" nude pinup shots.
According to Anthony Spoto in *Marilyn*:

> [She] accepted at once. Two nights later she returned to Kelley's studio and signed a release form as "Mona Monroe."
>
> A red velvet drape was spread on the studio floor, and for two hours Marilyn posed nude, moving easily from one position to another as the photographer, perched ten feet above her on a ladder, clicked away.

Baumgarth paid Kelley $500 for all rights to the photos from the session, and Kelley gave Marilyn $50. They never met again.

PIN-UP GIRL

Baumgarth did nothing with the photos until 1950, when Marilyn began to get attention for her role in *The Asphalt Jungle*. He decided to use her picture on a pinup calendar. It was only meant to be a giveaway for service stations, tool dealers, contractors, etc. But in April 1952, *Life* magazine included a tiny reproduction of the calendar in a cover story they did on Marilyn. As a result, the picture became world-famous. And Marilyn became infamous.

"Marilyn blunted the potential effect on her career," says Spoto, "by giving interviews in which she explained that she had desperately needed money. The public bought it. But the saga of the pin-up calendar wasn't over."

PUBLIC EXPOSURE

Just as the furor surrounding Marilyn's pinup shot was dying down, Baumgarth got a visit from a fellow Chicagoan who wanted to use it. According to Russell Miller in *Bunny, the Real Story of Playboy*:

> Because of the risk of prosecution for obscenity, Baumgarth believed there was probably no other use to which the pictures could be put. He was surprised, therefore, when [a young man] showed up at his office, without an appointment, on the morning of June 13, 1953, and asked if he could buy the rights to publish the Monroe nude pictures in a magazine he was planning to launch.

The man was Hugh Hefner; the magazine was *Stag Party* (soon to be renamed *Playboy*). Baumgarth not only sold Hefner the magazine rights, but threw in the color separations as well—which saved the struggling Hefner—who'd barely scraped up enough money for the 48-page first issue—a bundle.

Hefner knew his magazine was finally on its way. Monroe—featured that year in *How to Marry a Millionaire*—was now a star. And Hefner could announce that she would be his first "centerfold." In December 1953, the premiere issue of *Playboy* hit the stands, with Marilyn beckoning from the front cover. Due in part to the famous pinup, *Playboy* was an instant success. Ironically, this exposure made the photos even more famous...and more valuable. Spoto concludes:

> More than any other portraits of a nude woman in the history of photography, those of Marilyn Monroe taken in 1949 became virtual icons, everywhere recognizable, ever in demand. Landmarks in the union of art with commerce, the photographs have appeared in calendars, playing cards, keychains, pens, clothing, accessories, linens and household items; for decades, entrepreneurs have become wealthy by claiming or purchasing rights to their dissemination.

THE ACME
ANTI-CASTRO SPY KIT

Like the Coyote and Road Runner, the CIA was obsessively trying to kill Fidel Castro in the 1960s. But like Coyote, they just couldn't seem do it. Was it because Castro was so wily... or because the CIA was so incompetent? Here are some examples of how the anti-Castro super-spies spent their time (and our money).

CONCOCTING WEIRD PLOTS
Seven plots against Castro that the CIA actually considered.

1. Use agents in Cuba to spread rumors that the second coming of Christ is imminent and that Castro is the anti-Christ.

2. Surprise him at the beach with an exploding conch shell.

3. Put thalium salts in his shoes or cigars during an appearance on "The David Susskind Show," to make his beard and hair fall out.

4. Put itching powder in his scuba suit and LSD on his mouthpiece so he would be driven crazy and drown.

5. Offer him exploding cigars designed to blow his head off.

6. Shoot him with a TV camera that has machine gun inside.

7. Spray his broadcasting studio with hallucinogens.

EMBARGOING BASEBALLS

In its war against Fidel Castro during the 1960s, the CIA literally tried to play hardball politics. "The CIA tried to cut off the supply of baseballs to Cuba. Agents persuaded suppliers in other countries not to ship them. (U.S. baseballs were already banned by the trade embargo the U.S. had declared.)" The bizarre embargo was effective. Some balls got through, "but the supply was so limited that the government had to ask fans to throw foul balls and home runs back onto the field for continued play."

—Jonathan Kwitny, *Endless Enemies*

Hey, men! What hair grows fastest? Your beard.

CONSULTING JAMES BOND

How out-of-control was the CIA in its anti-Castro frenzy? They even took Ian Fleming's jokes seriously. This anecdote from Deadly Secrets, *by Warren Hinkle and William Turner, says it all.*

"It was, even by Georgetown standards, one helluva dinner party. It was the spring of 1960. The hosts were Senator and Mrs. John F. Kennedy. The guest of honor was John Kennedy's favorite author, Ian Fleming.

"Kennedy asked Fleming what his man James Bond might do if M. assigned him to get rid of Castro. Fleming had been in British intelligence....He was quick to answer. According to his biographer, John Pearson, Fleming thought he would have himself some fun....

"[He] said there were three things which really mattered to the Cubans—money, religion, and sex. Therefore, he suggested a triple whammy. First the United States should send planes to scatter [counterfeit] Cuban money over Havana. Second, using the Guantanamo base, the United States should conjure up some religious manifestation, say, a cross of sorts in the sky which would induce the Cubans to look constantly skyward. And third, the United States should send planes over Cuba dropping pamphlets to the effect that owing to American atom bomb tests the atmosphere over the island had become radioactive; that radioactivity is held longest in beards, and that radioactivity makes men impotent. As a consequence the Cubans would shave off their beards, and without bearded Cubans there would be no revolution.

"Fleming was staying at the house of British newsman Henry Brandon. The next day CIA director Allen Dulles called Brandon to speak to Fleming. Brandon said his guest had already left Washington. Dulles expressed great regret. He had heard about Fleming's terrific ideas for doing in Castro and was sorry he wouldn't be able to discuss them with him in person.

"It is testimony to the resounding good sense exercised by the CIA during the Secret War that all three of Fleming's spoof ideas were in one form or another attempted—or at least seriously considered."

FAMOUS FOR 15 MINUTES

Here's another installment of our feature based on Andy Warhol's comment that "in the future, everyone will be famous for 15 minutes"

THE STAR: Shawn Christopher Ryan, 7-year-old resident of Castro Valley, California

THE HEADLINE: *Second-Grader Smells Smoke, Saves Sixteen*

WHAT HAPPENED: At 4 a.m. on February 9, 1984, Shawn awoke and smelled smoke. He ran into his mother's room, saw that her mattress had caught fire (she'd fallen asleep smoking), and woke her up. He helped her escape, then ran back into the apartment building and knocked on every door, waking up and saving all 16 neighbors. For a few weeks, he was a national hero. He was honored at the state capitol by the governor of California, received a commendation from President Reagan, and was lauded on the floor of the U.S. House of Representatives.

AFTERMATH: Ryan wasn't in the news again until 1995, eleven years later. Ironically, it was because he had pled guilty to the murder of two acquaintances (alleged drug dealers) while they were all high on methamphetamine. "I can't explain it," he said. "I'm not the kind of person to take a life, not for any reason." He was sentenced to 32 years in prison.

THE STAR: Diane King, a 33-year-old night-shift manager at a Portland, Oregon, Taco Bell

THE HEADLINE: *Good Samaritan Gets Heave-ho from Taco Bell*

WHAT HAPPENED: On August, 16, 1995, a fight broke out in a Taco Bell parking lot, leaving one teenager dead and one lying motionless in the street. King, a former nurse's aide, rushed to help. She left another employee in charge of the restaurant, even though she knew it was against company policy. Later, she explained, "I was worried he might die out there." When the police arrived, she went back to work. A few weeks later, she was fired. Newspapers reported the story as an example of both corporate insensitivity and a screwed-up society that discourages good samaritans.

Nutritional fact: There are more places to buy candy in the U.S. than there are places to buy bread.

AFTERMATH: Hundreds of people offered King jobs and money. *People* magazine ran a story on the incident. Oprah Winfrey flew King to Chicago for a show titled "Would You Help a Stranger in Distress?" Finally, Taco Bell—which had tried to reinstate King without admitting it had done anything wrong (she refused)—ran a full-page apology in the Portland *Oregonian*. "Sometimes big corporations make mistakes," it said. "In this case, we did, and we've learned from it." King ignored them and took a job at a convenience store. She also filed a $149,500 suit against Taco Bell for "shock, outrage, and emotional distress." No word on the outcome.

THE STAR: Nicholas Daniloff, Moscow bureau chief for *U.S. News and World Report*

THE HEADLINE: *U.S. Reporter Held Hostage by Soviets*

WHAT HAPPENED: In 1986 Gennadi Zakharov, a member of the Soviet Union's mission to the United Nations, was arrested in New York for spying. A few weeks later, the Soviets retaliated, arresting Daniloff in Moscow and charging *him* with espionage—with a possible death penalty. His arrest was front-page news. President Reagan and Secretary of State Schulz called it "an outrage," but swore they'd never trade a spy (Zakharov) for a hostage (Daniloff). The matter was so serious that it jeopardized the upcoming Summit meeting in Iceland between Reagan and Gorbachev. The United States even announced it was expelling 25 members of the Soviet delegation to the U.N. because they worked for the KGB.

Some fancy maneuvering followed. Daniloff was released. The United States waited awhile (so it didn't seem like there was any connection), then released Zakharov in exchange for a Russian dissident and allowed some of the expelled U.N. workers to stay. Daniloff was welcomed home...but a *day* after his release, he was already old news. The Reagan administration changed the subject. Their new focus—it was to avoid scrutiny of the deal they'd made political pundits suggested—was details of the Summit meeting.

AFTERMATH: Daniloff surfaced again in 1988 when he toured the country promoting his autobiography, *Two Lives, One Russia* (published on the second anniversary of his imprisonment). He became a professor at Northeastern University in Boston and a respected expert on Russia.

THE STAR: Lucy De Barbin, Dallas clothes designer who claimed to be Elvis's lover and mother of his child

THE HEADLINE: *Dallas Designer's Daughter Royal Descendent?*

WHAT HAPPENED: In 1987 De Barbin revealed her secret 24-year affair with Elvis in a book entitled *Are You Lonesome Tonight?: The Untold True Story of Elvis Presley's One True Love—and the Child He Never Knew.* She said they kept their involvement a secret so it wouldn't mess up his career. Later, she kept it quiet to protect Lisa Marie and the daughter she had with Elvis, Desir'ee. "I was so afraid of what was going to happen [if the secret got out]," she told a reporter. "I thought if one person found out, everybody would know." She didn't even tell Elvis they had a child, she said, although she hinted at it in a phone conversation just before the King's death: "I just said things like, 'I have a wonderful secret to tell you' and 'Her name is Desir'ee,' things like that. And he said, 'I hope what I'm thinking is true.'" De Barbin's publisher, Random House, believed her. And several experts confirmed that a poem the King had reportedly written for De Barbin was in his handwriting. But neither the public nor the Presley estate bought the story.

AFTERMATH: De Barbin never produced blood samples to prove that her daughter was Elvis's. Apparently, she offered no real evidence that they'd been lovers. The Presley estate claimed that because the book was not a success (it actually was), they didn't need to bother suing De Barbin.

THE STAR: Matthias Jung, a German tourist in Dubrovnik, Croatia

THE HEADLINE: *Brazen Tourist Has Dubrovnik All to Himself*

WHAT HAPPENED: Dubrovnik, Croatia, was one of the world's loveliest towns and a major tourist resort. But for seven months, from fall 1991 to spring 1992, the Serbs bombarded it with mortar shells. Tourism fell off, then disappeared. In August 1995, tourists warily started returning—only to be greeted with more shelling. They all fled...except one—Jung, a 32-year-old shopkeeper from Hanover. He wasn't a thrill-seeker; he just wanted peace and quiet for his vacation.

AFTERMATH: After a while, things got *so* quiet that Jung admitted he was bored and went north.

What a commuter! Moles are able to tunnel through 300 feet of earth in a day.

"TONIGHT SHOW" PART VI: HE-E-ERE'S JOHNNY!

After 30 years on the tube, Johnny Carson became synonymous with "The Tonight Show." Here's how he got the job.

RISING STAR

Johnny Carson had been working his way up the TV ladder for a decade. His first show was "Carson's Cellar," a comedy-variety program he created in 1951 for L.A.'s CBS affiliate. It only had a $25/week budget, so he couldn't pay guests for appearances. Much of the time, he had to fake it.

One afternoon he had a member of the studio crew run quickly past the camera. "That was Red Skelton," Carson joked. "Too bad he didn't have time to stay and say a few words!" Skelton heard about the joke and was flattered. He made several appearances on the show...then hired Carson as a writer for *his* TV program.

OPENING DOORS

Carson left "Carson's Cellar" in May 1954 to host a network game show called "Earn Your Vacation." But he continued to write jokes for Skelton on the side. Then on August 18, 1954, while rehearsing a stunt for his show, Skelton threw himself into a prop door that was supposed to open on impact. It didn't—Skelton was knocked cold with less than 90 minutes to go before airtime.

A few minutes later, Carson got a call from the show's producers, who were searching frantically for a replacement host. Carson agreed to fill in...and so impressed CBS with his performance that the network gave him his own primetime show: "The Johnny Carson Show."

It was Carson's first big break...and his first big flop. Years later, Carson lamented: "They told me, 'We've got to make the show *important*.'...How were they going to do that? With chorus girls. They were going to make me into Jackie Gleason! I'd come rushing on in a shower of balloons, with chorus girls yipping, 'Here comes the *star* of the show, *Johnny Carson!*'...That was my first big lesson. If you

---

don't keep control, you're going to bomb out, and there's nobody to blame but yourself."

BUILDING TRUST

Carson's next job was hosting a game show called "Do You Trust Your Wife?" The program was failing: the host, ventriloquist Edgar Bergen, had just been let go, and ABC was only renewing the contract month to month. Carson turned it around by dumping the husband-and-wife format and renaming it "Who Do You Trust?" so anyone could play.

Soon after, the show's announcer left. Word spread that Carson was looking for a replacement, and Chuck Reeves, producer of Dick Clark's "American Bandstand," decided to help. He'd been at a party emceed by Clark's next-door neighbor, a radio announcer named Ed McMahon. He liked McMahon's style...so he got McMahon an audition on "Who Do You Trust?"

SECOND BANANA

McMahon went to New York and talked on camera with Carson for a couple of minutes. Then he went home. Weeks went by, and he heard nothing. So, convinced he hadn't gotten the job, McMahon made plans to take a trip across the Atlantic.

As McMahon recalled in his biography, the day before he was scheduled to leave, he got a call from the show asking him to come back to New York. He cancelled the trip and went to meet with Carson's producer, Art Stark. They talked for a few hours, but he still didn't get a job offer. Finally, Stark asked McMahon if he was going to move to New York.

"I don't think so," McMahon replied.

"I thought maybe you'd want to."

"Why?"

"Well, I thought it might be tough for you, doing the show."

"What show?"

"Our show. You start Monday."

"*Next* Monday?"

"For Chrissake, didn't anybody tell you?"

And that's how Ed became the world's most famous second banana.

Check it out: On U.S. coins, all portraits (except Lincoln's) face left.

CANNED LAUGHTER

As on Groucho Marx's "You Bet Your Life," the jokes in "Who Do You Trust?" were scripted in advance. It was the best-kept secret of the show: only Carson's copy of the script contained the jokes. The television audience—and ABC's censors—were kept completely in the dark, which made for racier ad-libbing. With Carson at the helm, "Who Do You Trust?" became one of the surprise hits of daytime television. Meanwhile, Carson kept his talk-show skills fresh by guest hosting for Garry Moore, Dinah Shore...and Jack Paar.

HEEERE'S JOHNNY!

Carson guest-hosted "The Tonight Show" as early as 1958, but doubted whether he could ever fill Paar's shoes as permanent host. So when Paar announced in late 1961 that he was getting out, Carson wasn't sure he wanted to give up a safe, successful network quiz show to take a chance on "The Tonight Show." "How could I follow Jack Paar? I just wasn't sure I could cut it," he wrote years later.

In the end, of course, Carson decided to take the chance. He and McMahon signed on as the host and announcer of "The Tonight Show." On October 1, 1962, Carson made his debut. The deck was stacked wildly in his favor that first night—he was introduced by Groucho Marx and had Mel Brooks, Tony Bennett, Joan Crawford, and Rudy Vallee as his guests.

Overall, the reviews were positive. "Mr. Carson's style is his own," Jack Gould wrote in *The New York Times*. "He has the proverbial engaging smile and the quick mind essential to sustaining and seasoning a marathon of banter."

PAAR FOR THE COURSE

For some viewers, however, Carson was a big letdown. "America can now go back to bed," Robert Kennedy joked to Jack Paar a few days later.

Even the NBC pages were skeptical. "After that first night," says Kenneth Work, a history professor who was an NBC page in 1962, "the pages went down to the NBC coffee shop and all of them were convinced Johnny wouldn't make it. After working with Paar all those years, we were concerned he didn't have the excitement and outspokenness Paar had. I didn't think he'd last six months."

More to come! See Part VII on page 386 after these messages.

According to florists, America's favorite flower is the rose. Second place: the daisy.

UDDERLY SIMPLE

We all know these terms, but if someone were to ask you what they actually mean, would you be able to tell them? Here's the difference between the different kinds of milk sold in most supermarkets.

Whole Milk. Milk as it comes from the cow. The USDA requires it to contain at least 3.25% fat and 8.25% other solids. It's also about 88% water.

Low-Fat Milk. Milk with some fat (cream) removed. Depending on how it's labeled, it can contain 0.5% to 2.5% fat *by weight*. By percentage of calories, it's more. E.g., "1% milk" gets 24% of its calories from fat; "2% milk" gets 36% from fat. Vitamins A and D are found in the cream; when the cream is removed, the USDA requires dairies to "fortify" milk by putting the vitamins back in.

Skim Milk. All—or nearly all—of the fat is removed.

Evaporated Milk. Milk that has had 60% of its water removed. Sometimes it has a caramelized flavor, a result of the heating process used to remove the liquid.

Condensed Milk: Whole milk, mixed with as much as 40% to 45% sugar, then evaporated over heat.

Cream. When it's taken from skim or low-fat milk, cream is made into four different products: *regular cream* (18% milk fat by weight—not calories); *light whipping cream* (30%-36% milk fat); *heavy whipping cream* (36% or more milk fat); and *half-and-half:* (half milk, half cream—10%-12% milk fat).

Buttermilk. When cream is agitated, or "churned," the globules of fat separate out from the cream and clump together, forming butter. The globules are removed from the liquid, which is called "buttermilk."

Acidophilus Milk: When milk is pasteurized to kill bad bacteria, a lot of beneficial bacteria is killed along with it. In acidophilus milk, the lactobacillus acidophilus bacteria, which aids digestion by regulating bacteria in the digestive system, is put back in after pasteurization.

Soy Milk: Made from whole soybeans, which are pureed, boiled, filtered, and sometimes sweetened.

MYTH-SPOKEN

Everyone knows that Captain Kirk said, "Beam me up, Scotty" in every episode of "Star Trek" and that Bogart said, "Play it again, Sam" in Casablanca. But everyone's wrong. Here are a few common misquotes.

Line: "Beam me up, Scotty."
Supposedly Said By: Captain Kirk
Actually: That line was *never* spoken on "Star Trek." Not once. What Kirk usually said was, "Beam us up, Mr. Scott," or "Enterprise, beam us up." According to Trekkies, he came pretty close just once. In the fourth episode, he said, "Scotty, beam me up."

Line: "Don't fire till you see the whites of their eyes."
Supposedly Said By: Colonel William Prescott to American soldiers at the Battle of Bunker Hill, as they lay in wait for the British
Actually: Sounds like another American myth. There's no record of Prescott ever saying it, but there are records of both Prince Charles of Prussia (in 1745) and Frederick the Great (in 1757) using the command.

Line: "You dirty rat."
Supposedly Said By: James Cagney in one of his movies
Actually: Every Cagney impressionist says it, but Cagney never did. He made over 70 movies but never spoke this line in any of them.

Line: "Nice guys finish last."
Supposedly Said By: Leo Durocher in 1946, when he was manager of the Brooklyn Dodgers
Actually: While being interviewed, he waved toward the Giants' dugout and said, "The nice guys are all over there. In seventh place." When the article came out, reporters had changed his statement to "The nice guys are all over there in last place." As it was repeated, it was shortened to "Nice guys finish last." Durocher protested that he'd never made the remark but couldn't shake it. Finally he gave in, and eventually used it as the title of his autobiography.

Why is a newborn's skin wrinkled? It's too big for its body.

Line: "Gerry Ford is so dumb he can't walk and chew gum at the same time."

Supposedly Said By: President Lyndon Johnson

Actually: This remark was cleaned up for the public—what Johnson really said was, "Gerry Ford is so dumb he can't fart and chew gum at the same time."

Line: "How I wish I had not expressed my theory of evolution as I have done."

Supposedly Said By: Charles Darwin, on his deathbed

Actually: The Christian evangelist, Jimmy Swaggart, announced in a speech in 1985 that Darwin had spoken the words as he lay dying, and asked that the Bible be read to him. But it was an old lie started shortly after Darwin's death by a Christian fanatic who was speaking to seminary students. Darwin's daughter and son both deny that their father ever had any change of heart about his scientific theory. According to his son, his last words were, "I am not the least afraid to die."

Line: "I rob banks because that's where the money is."

Supposedly Said By: Infamous bank robber Willie Sutton

Actually: According to Sutton, it was a reporter who thought up this statement and printed it. "I can't even remember when I first read it," Sutton once remarked. "It just seemed to appear one day, and then it was everywhere."

Line: "Play it again, Sam."

Supposedly Said By: Humphrey Bogart, in the classic film *Casablanca*

Actually: This may be the most famous movie line ever, but it wasn't in the movie. Ingrid Bergman said, "Play it, Sam. Play 'As Time Goes By.' " And Bogart said "If she can stand it, I can. Play it!" But the only person who ever used "Play it again, Sam" was Woody Allen—who jokingly called his theatrical homage to Bogart *Play It Again, Sam* because he knew it was a misquote.

Line: "Elementary, my dear Watson."

Supposedly Said By: Sherlock Holmes, in Arthur Conan Doyle's books

Actually: Holmes never said it in any of the stories. It was a movie standard, however, beginning in 1929 with *The Return of Sherlock Holmes.*

Brain waves have been used to run an electric train.

BOND(S)...JAMES BONDS

*Every 007 fan has their own opinion of which actor—Sean Connery,
George Lazenby, Roger Moore, Timothy Dalton, or Pierce
Brosnan—made the best James Bond....but do you know
how each actor landed the role? Here are their stories.*

SEAN CONNERY

The role of James Bond turned Connery from a nobody into an international sex symbol in less than five years...but as Connery's fame grew with each Bond film, so did his frustration with the part. He worried about being typecast, he hated reporters, and he was annoyed by the crowds of fans that followed him wherever he went. And since his image was inextricably linked with the Bond character, he was angry that Cubby Broccoli and Harry Saltzman wouldn't make him a full partner in the 007 films and merchandising deals. He left the series in 1967 after making *You Only Live Twice*, his sixth Bond film.

GEORGE LAZENBY

In 1967 a friend asked George Lazenby, a part-time actor, to substitute for him on a blind date when his girlfriend suddenly came back to town.

The blind date "was supposed to be some up-and-coming agent, which was why he wanted to go out with her," Lazenby recounted years later, "but I didn't care. I was running a health studio in Belgium." Some months later, the agent remembered Lazenby and contacted him when the search for Connery's replacement in *On Her Majesty's Secret Service* got underway. "I got the part," Lazenby remembers, "and my friend's career fizzled."

So did Lazenby's: After fighting with the producers, the director, and co-star Diana Rigg during the making of *On Her Majesty's Secret Service*, he either quit or was fired, depending on who you ask.

When it premiered in 1969, *On Her Majesty's Secret Service* was panned by the critics and was a box-office disappointment; today it is considered one of the best of the Bond films.

Dry run: In his 7 Bond films, Roger Moore didn't smoke a cigarette or drink a single martini.

SEAN CONNERY (II)

Panicked by the drubbing *On Her Majesty's Secret Service* took at the box office, Broccoli and Saltzman paid a reluctant Sean Connery $1.25 million plus a huge share of the profits to return to the series in the 1971 film *Diamonds Are Forever*.

Connery needed the boost—most of his post-Bond films were box-office flops—but he quit the series again after just one film, turning down a reported $5 million for *Live and Let Die*. The role went instead to his old friend Roger Moore. (Burt Reynolds was also considered, but Broccoli insisted on an Englishman.)

Connery returned for a seventh and last time in the 1983 film *Never Say Never Again*.

ROGER MOORE

Moore was one of Ian Fleming's original choices for the Bond role, and he finally got his shot in *Live and Let Die*. Unlike Lazenby, Moore succeeded—largely by complementing, not imitating, Connery's interpretation of the role. As Raymond Benson writes in *The James Bond Bedside Companion*,

> From *Live and Let Die* on, the scriptwriters tailored the screenplays to fit Roger Moore's personality. As a result, James Bond lost much of the *machismo* image which was so prominent in the sixties. It seems Bond never gets hurt in any of the subsequent films—the Roger Moore Bond uses his wits rather than fists to escape dangerous situations.

Moore's departure from Connery's Bond was so dramatic that it inspired a Beatles-vs.-Rolling Stones-type rivalry among 007 fans over who was the best Bond. "People who saw their first Bond with Sean never took to Roger," says 007 marketing executive Charles Juroe, "and people who saw their first Bond with Roger never took to Sean. Roger's movies grossed more than Sean's." Moore made a total of seven Bond films between 1973 and 1985, tying Sean Connery. His last was *A View to a Kill*.

TIMOTHY DALTON

First choice for Moore's replacement was Irish actor Pierce Brosnan, star of the recently cancelled American TV series "Remington Steele." Brosnan was given the unofficial nod for the role, but when word of the deal leaked, it generated so much publicity for the failing "Remington Steele" that the show's ratings skyrocketed to fifth place in the Nielsens, their highest in history, prompting NBC to *un*-cancel the show and force Brosnan to serve out the remainder of his contract. With Brosnan out of the running, the job went to British actor Timothy Dalton, who appeared in *The Living Daylights* and *License to Kill*.

Dalton was considered by many 007 purists to be the best Bond since Connery; but he never dodged the stigma of being runner-up to Pierce Brosnan, and both films were box-office disappointments. In April 1994, amid rumors he was being fired, Dalton quit the series.

PIERCE BROSNAN

Two months after Dalton quit, Brosnan finally won the nod to play 007 in *Goldeneye*, the 18th film in the series. "Most of today's biggest male stars were eliminated from consideration for the role," the *New York Times* reported in 1994. "Hugh Grant was thought too wimpy, Liam Neeson too icy. Mel Gibson...was deemed not quite right. Even Sharon Stone was talked about for the part of Bond." Brosnan turned out to be a wise choice: *Goldeneye* was the highest-grossing Bond film in history, with more than $350 million in ticket sales around the world. He signed on for three more films.

DAVID NIVEN

There will always be debates over which Bond movie is the best, but there isn't much disagreement over which one was the worst: *Casino Royale*, starring David Niven as James Bond. By the time Cubby Broccoli and Harry Saltzman bought the film rights to Ian Fleming's other novels, the rights to his first book, *Casino Royale*, had already been sold to someone else.

Work on the film version of *Casino Royale* did not begin until 1967, when Sean Connery's Bond image was already well established. Rather than compete against Connery directly, the producers decided to make a Bond spoof starring Niven, Peter Sellers, and Woody Allen.

Budgeted at $8 million, *Casino Royale* was the most expensive Bond film to date, as well as one of the messiest. Seven different writers wrote the screenplay, five different directors worked on various parts of the film, and seven of the characters are named James Bond. "What might have begun as a great idea ends up a total mess," Raymond Benson writes in *The James Bond Bedside Companion*. "The film should not be considered part of the James Bond series."

POISON GAS

One of the ways the U.S. intelligence community protected itself against adverse publicity and budget cuts in the early 1960s was by sending agents to Hollywood to act as "technical advisors" in spy films, thereby making the spy business appear vital and heroic to the public. *Dr. No* and other early Bond films were no exception: they had real-life secret agents working on the set.

The agents turned out to be quite useful, as Bond scriptwriter Richard Maibum recalls:

> Before we got done, we had literally about ten technical agents, all telling us marvelous stories of what had happened to them all over the world which we incorporated into the plot. There were foreshadowings of things in the Bond films—the pipe that was a gun, and other gadgets. There were some things that we couldn't use, such as foul stuff smelling like an enormous fart that the OSS agents used to spray on people they wished to discredit.

❀　　❀　　❀

PRESENTING...THE FEJEE MERMAID

Background: In 1842 P.T. Barnum began displaying the body of what he claimed was an actual mermaid, which he said had been found by sailors near the faraway island of "Feejee." (That's how Barnum spelled Fiji.) He put the mermaid on display in August 1842, printing up more than 10,000 handbills, leading up to opening day.

What Happened: The "mermaid," one of the biggest hoaxes of Barnum's long career, was actually "an ingenious sewing together of a large fish's body and tail with the head, shoulders, arms, and rather pendulous breasts of a female orangutan and the head of a baboon." But it did the trick—at the peak of New York's "mermaid fever," ticket sales at Barnum's Museum hit nearly $1,000 a week. "In truth, by the close of 1843," says a biographer, "with the help of...a dried up old mermaid, Barnum had become the most famous showman in America."

HOW ABOUT A WILSON SANDWICH?

Every sport has its own language. Here's a bit of basketball lingo, inspired by the book How to Talk Basketball, *by Sam Goldaper and Arthur Pincus.*

Aircraft carrier: Big gun. Player you bring in to win the battle—a franchise center like Kareem Abdul-Jabbar.

Belly up: Play tight defense, right up against your opponent.

Brick: Lousy shot, tossed up with no idea where it's going. "Usually hits the backboard with a thunk."

Curtain time: Point at which there's no way one of the teams can win. "No miracle is big enough to make it happen."

East Cupcake: Hometown of a team's easiest possible opponent.

Fire the rock: Shoot well, as in "John Starks can fire the rock."

French pastry: Making an easy shot look tough and a tough shot look tougher.

Garbage man: Player who only seems to score when unguarded.

Garbage time: End of the game, when players just toss the ball up "without any pattern, grace, or apparent skill." (See *Curtain time.*).

Hatchet man: Heavy fouler, often the one who goes after the opponent's star player to take him out of the game.

Ice: "Coolest player on the court", one who is never fazed.

Kangaroo: Player who's such a good jumper you figure he or she must be related to one.

Leather breath: What players have when a shot has been blocked right back in their face.

Nose bleeders: Players who jump so high they "can suffer nose bleeds from the change in altitude."

Shake and bake: Taking it to the hoop using every move and fake imaginable.

Submarine: Getting under players after they've left their feet for a shot to knock them off-balance.

Suburban jump shot: Classic shot using perfect form. Used by players who grew up playing a less physical game in suburban gyms.

Three-sixty: Showy move involving dunking the ball while spinning in a full circle.

Wheel and deal: Making amazing offensive moves (wheel) and then passing the ball off (deal).

Wilson sandwich: What players eats when a shot's blocked back in their face. Other meals: a Spalding sandwich, a Rawlings sandwich, etc.

American milestone: The first laundromat opened in Fort Worth, Texas, on April 18, 1934.

THE CURSE OF THE HOPE DIAMOND

The Hope Diamond is probably the most famous jewel in the Western world...and it carries with it one of the most famous curses. How much of it is legend, and how much of it is fact? Even historians can't agree.

BACKGROUND

In 1668, a French diamond merchant named Jean-Baptiste Tavernier returned from India with a magnificent 112.5-carat blue diamond. No one knew exactly where he'd found it...but rumors spread that it was stolen from the eye of a sacred Indian idol—and people said it was cursed.

Nonetheless, King Louis XIV bought the Great Blue and added it to his crown jewels. Four years later, he had it re-cut into the shape of a heart (which reduced it to 67.5 carats).

In 1774, the diamond was inherited by Louis XVI. His wife, Marie Antoinette, apparently wore it; she was also said to have loaned it on one occasion to the Princesse de Lamballe.

> *"When the French Revolution broke out, the Princesse de Lamballe was murdered by a mob and her head paraded under the window where Louis the XVI and his family awaited execution. Marie Antoinette herself was executed in October 1793."*
> —*The Book of Curses*, by Gordon Stuart

THE HOPE DIAMOND

In 1792, in the midst of the French Revolution, the Great Blue diamond was stolen. It was never seen whole again.

> *"Thirty years later it emerged in Holland, owned now by an Amsterdam lapidary named Fals. His son stole the diamond and left Fals to die in poverty. After giving it to a Frenchman, named Beaulieu, Fals's son killed himself. Beaulieu brought it to London, where he died mysteriously."*
> —*The Book of Curses*

In 1830, an oval-shaped blue diamond weighing 44.5 carats turned up in a London auction house. Experts recognized it as a piece of the Great Blue, re-cut to conceal its identity.

A wealthy banker named Henry Philip Hope bought the jewel for about $90,000, and it became known as the Hope Diamond.

WAS IT CURSED?

Hope was warned about the gem's "sinister inflluence," but owning it didn't seem to have any effect on his life. He died peacefully.

However, in the early 1900s terrible things began happening again. Lord Francis Hope, a distant relative who'd inherited it, went bankrupt. Then his marriage fell apart. "His wife prophesied," says Colin Wilson in *Unsolved Mysteries*, "that it would bring bad luck to all who owned it, and she died in poverty."

She seemed to know what she was talking about. According to Colin Wilson, over the next few years:

•Lord Francis sold it to a French jewel dealer named Jacques Colot. He ultimately went insane and committed suicide.

•Colot sold it to a Russian prince. He lent it to his mistress, a dancer at the Folies Bergere. The first night she wore it, he shot her from his box in the theater. The prince was reportedly stabbed by Russian revolutionaries.

•A Greek jewel dealer named Simon Manthadides bought it. He later fell (or was pushed) over a precipice.

•A Turkish sultan named Abdul Hamid bought it in 1908. He was forced into exile the following year and went insane.

TEMPTING FATE?

One wonders why anyone would want the diamond at this point. But French jeweler Jacques Cartier took possession. He quickly re-sold it to Edward McClean (owner of the *Washington Post*) and his wife, Evalyn. A fascinated public watched to see if the "curse" would affect them. Did it?

• According to some accounts, McLean's mother and two servants in his household died soon after he purchased the jewel.

After her mother-in-law's death, Evalyn McLean had a priest bless the gem. In her autobiography she writes about the experience: "Just as he blessed it—without any wind or rain—this tree right across the street was struck by lightning. My maid

Maggie fainted dead away. The old fellow was scared to death and my knees were shaking. By the time we got home the sun was out, bright as anything."

— *Vanity Fair* magazine

Over the next 30 years, Evalyn McLean's family was decimated. Her father soon became an alcoholic and died. Her father-in-law went insane. The McLeans' beloved 10-year-old son, Vinson, was hit and killed by a car in front of their house. Their marriage broke up and Edward McLean went insane; he died in a mental institution. McLean's daughter Emily—who had worn the Hope Diamond at her wedding—committed suicide.

AFTERMATH

Through all the tragedy and even her own gradual financial ruin, Evalyn McLean scoffed at the "curse." She continued to wear the Hope Diamond until her death in 1947. Two years later, her children sold it to the famous diamond dealer Harry Winston, to pay estate taxes. He kept it (with no apparent ill effect) until 1958, then decided to give it away. He put it in a box with $2.44 in postage, paid $155 for $1 million insurance, and sent it to the Smithsonian Institution via U.S. mail. "Letters of protest poured in to the museum," writes Gary Cohen in *Vanity Fair.* "Some reasoned that the curse would be transferred to its new owners—the American people."

"Within a year, James Todd, the mailman who had delivered the gem, had one of his legs crushed by a truck, injured his head in a car crash, and lost his wife and dog. Then his house burned down. When asked if he blamed his ill fortune on the diamond, he said, 'I don't believe any of that stuff.'"

— *Vanity Fair* magazine

Today, the diamond is owned by the U.S. government. And we all know what kind of luck the United States has had since 1959.

* * * *

WHAT ABOUT LIZ? It's widely believed that Elizabeth Taylor once owned the Hope. Not true. She owns a larger diamond, often compared to the Hope, but now known as the Burton Diamond.

Watch out: there were over 15,000 vacuum cleaner-related accidents last year.

READ ALL ABOUT IT

*We've all heard the expression, "don't believe everything you hear."
Here are a few more reasons not to believe everything you read,
either. Take a look at these newspaper hoaxes, for example:*

B RITISH SCIENTIST FINDS LIFE ON THE MOON!
(*New York Sun*, 1835)
The Story: In 1835 the *Sun* reprinted a series of articles
from the *Edinburgh Journal of Science*, based on reports sent in by
Sir John Herschel, a respected astronomer. He was at the Cape of
Good Hope at the time, trying out a powerful new telescope.

In the first three installments, Herschel wrote that with his super-telescope, he could see amazing things on the moon: lakes,
fields of poppies, 38 species of forest trees, herds of buffalo with
heavy eyelids, bears with horns, two-footed beavers, etc.

In the fourth installment (August 28, 1835), he made the biggest
revelation of all: he had seen furry, bat-winged people on the lunar
surface. He wrote:

> They averaged four feet in height, were covered, except in the face,
> with short and glossy copper colored hair, and had wings composed of
> a thin membrane, without hair, lying snugly upon their backs from
> the top of their shoulders to the calves of the legs.

He said their faces looked like baboons' and officially named them
"Verspertilio-homo," or "bat-man."

Reaction: People were lined up at newsstands, waiting for the next
issue. Rival newspapers claimed to have access to the original
Edinburgh Journal articles and began reprinting the series. By the
fourth installment, the *Sun's publisher* announced his paper had
the largest circulation in the world—about 20,000. A book about
the moon discoveries sold more than 60,000 copies. A committee
of scientists from Yale University arrived at the offices of the Sun
to inspect the source writings by Herschel (they were given the
runaround until they gave up). One group of society ladies even began raising money to send Christian missionaries there.

The Truth: There was no *Edinburgh Journal of Science*...and the

---

According to the USDA: If you're an average American, you'll eat 1,425 lbs. of food this year.

Edinburgh Philosophical Journal (which is what they meant to quote) had gone out of business two years earlier. The whole thing was concocted by a young reporter named Richard Adams Locke, who said later that he'd written it as a "satire on absurd scientific speculations that had gotten out of hand." When the *Sun*'s editors realized how out of control their scheme had gotten, they admitted it was a fake…and scolded other newspapers for copying the story without giving them credit.

CIVIL WAR WOES: LINCOLN DRAFTS 400,000 MEN!

(*Brooklyn Eagle*, May 18, 1864)

The Story: On the morning of May 18th, two New York newspapers, the *World* and the *Journal of Commerce*, reprinted an Associated Press dispatch in which President Abraham Lincoln, lamenting recent Union setbacks in the Civil War, called for a national day of "fasting, humiliation, and prayer," and announced the drafting of 400,000 additional troops to fight in the war.

Reaction: Wall Street was rocked by the pessimistic proclamation: Stock prices plummeted, and gold prices soared as panicked investors looked for safe places to put their money. According to one Lincoln confidant, the story "angered Lincoln more than almost any other occurence of the war period."

The Truth: The story was planted by Joseph Howard, the city editor of the Brooklyn Eagle, who hoped to get rich by buying gold cheap before the story broke and selling it at inflated prices afterward. Howard wrote the fake AP report with an accomplice, then paid copy boys to deliver it to every newspaper in New York. Only two papers, the *World* and the *Journal of Commerce*, printed it without bothering to check if it was true. Howard and his accomplice were arrested were arrested two days after the story broke; they spent three months interned at an Army fort without trial before Lincoln personally ordered their release.

The Hidden Truth: As Carl Sifakis writes in *Hoaxes and Scams*,

> At the very time the phony proclamation was released, Lincoln had a real one on his desk, calling for the drafting of 300,000 men.
> When the president saw the impact of the false proclamation on the public and the financial markets, he delayed the real call up for 60 days until the situation cooled.

BROADWAY OBSESSION

What does it take to have a hit on Broadway? Well, judging from this story, it doesn't hurt to be at least a little crazy.

Obsession: Movie producer Ray Stark married the daughter of a former 1930s vaudeville star. As he learned more about his mother-in-law's life, he decided it had all the elements of a great film: determination (she'd become a star despite her homely appearance), romance (she fell in love with a handsome guy), tragedy (he was a gambler), and so on.

He made several unsuccessful attempts to get a film deal while the woman was still alive. No dice. When she died in 1951, he was so committed to the project that he bought the rights to her autobiography and convinced the publisher to burn all copies of the book except his...so no one else could make the film. Stark spent nine years working on the script, but still couldn't sell it. Finally in 1960, he gave up on Hollywood and took it to Broadway. If he couldn't make a movie, he'd make a musical.

What Happened: People were more receptive to the story in New York. Stark got some top talent working on it—producer David Merrick, director Jerome Robbins, lyricist Jule Styne, and others. Their first task was finding a leading lady. Front-runners were veterans like Mary Martin, Carol Burnett, and Eydie Gorme. But when Robbins and Styne went to a New York nightclub and saw a 21-year-old singer named Barbra Streisand, they wanted her for the part. Stark wanted a more glamorous star (ironically, since his mother-in-law, Fanny Brice, wasn't glamorous). But Robbins won out and Streisand got the part. Merrick ultimately dropped out of the project—but before he did, he convinced Stark to change the name of the play from *My Man* to *Funny Girl.*

Epilogue: Stark was proved right when his dream of a movie version finally came true in 1968. It was Streisand's film debut, and a huge hit; she won an Oscar for Best Actress.

Paul Anka wrote Johnny Carson's "Tonight Show" theme song.

THE RESURRECTION OF ELVIS, PART II

Here's what the Presley estate did to preserve Elvis's memory...and make a fortune from it in the process. Continued from Part I, page 177.

E**NTER PRISCILLA**
The effort to keep Elvis's estate out of bankruptcy was exhausting and probably contributed to his father Vernon Presley's death from heart disease in June 1979.

In his will, Vernon named three co-executors to take over his responsibilities: Elvis's accountant Joseph Hanks, the National Bank of Commerce, and Priscilla Presley—Elvis's ex-wife and the mother of his daughter, Lisa Marie. Priscilla had no business experience and had known nothing about the King's financial affairs during the marriage...but to everyone's surprise, she and her advisors took a leading role in rescuing the Presley estate for Lisa Marie.

FORCED INTO ACTION
With the bulk of Elvis's fortune gone forever, Priscilla was forced to make the best of what remained, namely: 1) Graceland, and 2) Elvis's name and likeness.

She immediately put both to work for the estate. First she opened Graceland to the public, charging $5 a head to the hundreds of thousands who visited each year. Then she took over the Elvis merchandising operations. Her strategy was simple but brilliant. "Since...the estate would have to rely on Elvis's memory to generate revenue," writes Sean O'Neal in *Elvis, Inc.*, "Elvis would be transformed into a symbol, a character that could be licensed to merchandisers. The estate would turn Elvis Presley into its own version of Mickey Mouse."

> The problem with this idea was that, during the last eight years of his life, Elvis's image was not very Disneyesque. His weight had ballooned and he had been addicted to prescription medication. By the time of his death, Elvis had become a grotesque caricature of the performer he once was. This Elvis would never do as the symbol of the new empire.

The average depth of the ocean is 2 1/4 miles.

Priscilla's solution to this problem was also simple and brilliant: she would act as though the 1977 Elvis never existed. Only the young Elvis, the King in his prime, would be acknowledged. It was this Elvis that would adorn the T-shirts, plates, shot glasses, billboards, and promotional literature of Priscilla's new empire. In her sanitized version of his life, he died after his *1968 Comeback Special*, an idol in his prime, like James Dean.

COPYCATS
The only problem with this approach was that it had no teeth. After the King's death, hundreds of companies had come out with Elvis posters, T-shirts, videos, calendars, velvet paintings, whiskey decanters, and just about anything else imaginable. The knockoffs were cheap and tacky; even worse, they competed against "official" Elvis memorabilia licensed by the Presley estate.

Obviously, without control of the Elvis image, Priscilla's strategy would never work…and Lisa Marie would inherit nothing. So the estate was forced to fight for control of Elvis in court.

The heirs to Bela Lugosi and Laurel and Hardy had put up strong fights, but those battles were nothing compared to the efforts of the Presley clan. They fought lawsuit after lawsuit, in state after state. They put up millions of dollars. But they still couldn't get the issue resolved.

The outcome in every state was different: In New York, for example, the estate won—Presley's name and likeness were considered their exclusive property; but in California and Tennessee, Presley's likeness was judged to be public domain. The upshot: Merchandisers who were chased out of one state could set up business in another. Then the Presley estate would have to start all over again and fight them there, too.

THE ELVIS LOBBY
As the legal battles continued, Priscilla and Co. adopted a new tactic. They began lobbying the Tennessee state legislature to create a "Personal Rights Protection Act." This act was finally passed in 1984, and though it only officially applied in the state of Tennessee, its passage was quickly felt all over the country. Reason: In the American legal system, the laws of the state in which a person dies

are the ones that apply in federal court. If someone in Missouri began selling an unlicensed Elvis poster, the Presley estate could now go into Missouri federal court and force the person to comply with Tennessee law. For the first time, the Presley estate had teeth all over the country.

Not long after the Tennessee law passed, California enacted a similar law, the Celebrity Rights Act, thanks in large part to a lawsuit filed by the heirs of comedian W. C. Fields (they had been trying to block a centerfold-style poster of Fields's head superimposed over another naked fat man's body).

Several other states, including Virginia, Florida, Utah, and Kentucky, passed their own versions of the law. And as more and more states followed, courts began recognizing that control of a celebrity's name and likeness were as "inheritable" as any other piece of property.

ELVIS PRESLEY ENTERPRISES

These laws changed the face of celebrity merchandising in America. Suddenly, officially licensed products featuring icons such as Marilyn Monroe and James Dean started popping up. And in Memphis, Elvis Presley Enterprises, the merchandising arm of the estate run jointly by Priscilla and Jack Soden, became the "Elvis police." They controlled every aspect of the Elvis image, from T-shirts to TV documentaries to random snapshots that had been taken by private photographers.

Priscilla's original strategy was implemented—and today there are no fat Elvis photos floating around, ruining the King's memory. Licensees only use "approved" pictures of the early Elvis; if they don't have one, they can pick from the estate's library of several thousand acceptable photos. And woe to anyone who tries to use Elvis's name or likeness—no matter how innocent the motivation—without the consent of Presley Enterprises. Charities, cities, artists, and even school teachers have received lawyers' letters.

The result of this effort has been impressive. In 1981, the Presley estate was on the verge of bankruptcy. By the 20th anniversary of Elvis's death, in 1997, it was worth nearly $200 million. And it just keeps growing.

The kitty-litter capital of the world is Quincy, Florida.

THEY WENT THATAWAY

*More morbidly fascinating details of the
death-styles of the rich and famous.*

CATHERINE THE GREAT

Claim to Fame: Empress of Russia, 1762-1796

How She Died: Like Elvis—from a stroke, suffered while going to the bathroom

Postmortem: There are probably more rumors about Catherine's death than that of any monarch in history (except "The King": Elvis). Most of them relate to her reputedly unusual sexual appetite. For some reason, many people believe a horse was being lowered onto her when the cable holding the beast aloft snapped, crushing her. That's 100% myth (perhaps invented by the French, Russia's enemies at the time).

The truth: Two weeks after suffering a mild stroke at the age of 67, Catherine appeared to be making a strong recovery. On Nov. 5 she began her day with her usual routine: she rose at 8:00 a.m., drank several cups of coffee, then went to spend 10 minutes in the bathroom. This morning, however, she didn't come out. When her footman Zotov finally looked in on her, he found her sprawled on the floor, bleeding and barely alive. She died the next day.

GEORGE EASTMAN

Claim to Fame: Founder of Eastman Kodak and father of modern photography

How He Died: Suicide

Postmortem: In 1932 the 78-year-old Eastman was tired and ill. On March 14 he updated his will; later in the day, he asked his doctor and his nurses to leave the room, telling them he wanted to write a note. It turned out to be a suicide note. "As methodically has he had lived his 71 years [sic]," the *New York Times* reported the following morning, "he penned a brief note, carefully put out his cigarette, placed the cap back on his fountain pen and removed his glasses before firing a shot through his heart."

Big surprise: About 60% of U.S. kids say they "don't want to be like their parents."

ISADORA DUNCAN

Claim to Fame: One of the world's most famous modern dancers

How She Died: From a broken neck

Postmortem: On September 14, 1927, Duncan climbed into the passenger seat of a Bugatti race car wearing a long red silk scarf. The scarf was a little *too* long: when the car started off, the tail end wrapped around the wheel and yanked Duncan out of the car, snapping her neck and dragging her for several yards before the driver realized what had happened. It was too late. Final irony: A day before she died, Duncan had told an *Associated Press* reporter, "Now I'm frightened that some quick accident may happen."

MARGARET MITCHELL

Claim to Fame: Author of *Gone with the Wind*

How She Died: Run down by an automobile

Postmortem: Mitchell was crossing busy Peachtree Street in downtown Atlanta with her husband. She was halfway across when she saw a speeding motorist bearing down on her. Mitchell had previously said she was certain she would die in a car crash. Perhaps that's why she panicked, darting back across the street and leaving her husband standing there in the middle of the road. She got hit; he didn't. She died in the hospital five days later. The driver who hit her turned out to be a 29-year-old taxi driver with 23 traffic violations on his record.

NELSON ROCKEFELLER

Claim to Fame: Former governor of New York; vice president under Gerald Ford; grandson of John D. Rockefeller, founder of Standard Oil

How He Died: According to official reports, he had a heart attack while sitting at his desk

Postmortem: It was a cover-up. He was actually alone in his townhouse with 25-year-old Megan Marshack, who was on Rockefeller's staff. She had reportedly been working with him on a book about his modern art collection, but as the New York *Daily News* reported, there were no work papers in the house—just food and wine. What really happened? Only two people know for sure...and one is dead.

It costs the Coca-Cola Company more to buy the can than it costs them to make the cola.

RADIO WAVES

Uncle John found this in a book called Reading the Numbers, *by Mary Blocksma. He's embarrassed to admit that when he was a kid, he thought FM stood for "foreign music," and AM stood for "American music." But after reading this piece, he finally understands what radio waves are.*

D id you ever wonder why the AM numbers on your radio dial are bigger than the FM numbers? Or what the difference is between regular (VHF) television channels and UHF channels? Or why you sometimes hear a CB radio in the middle of your favorite rerun? In fact, what do these things—plus electricity, microwaves, infrared waves, light waves, X-rays, and gamma rays, have in common? All are electromagnetic waves—all of which travel at the same speed—the speed of light—and each of which vibrates at a constant rate.

DOING THE WAVE

What makes one electromagnetic wave different from another is how fast it's vibrating, or the *frequency* (number) of the waves, called *cycles*, that go by per second. Frequency is measured in *hertz:* 1 hertz = 1 cycle per second. Very low frequency waves with long wavelengths, like electricity (AC power) vibrate at only a few cycles per second; 60 hertz is common in the United States. Radio waves begin at about 15,000 hertz. Compared to electricity, that sounds high, but it's nothing compared to X-rays, which vibrate at about 1,000,000,000,000,000,000 cycles per second (10 to the 18th power hertz), or gamma rays, at more than 10 to the 24th power hertz. Hertz are also referred to in larger, more easily used units:

1 cycle per second	= 1 hertz (Hz)	
1,000 hertz	= 1 kilohertz (kHz)	
1,000 kilohertz	= 1 megahertz (MHz)	= 1,000,000 hertz
1,000 megahertz	= 1 gigahertz (GHz)	= 1,000,000,000 hertz

George Washington's favorite tooth whitener: household chalk.

ON YOUR RADIO

How does this translate to your radio dial? The AM side, usually numbered from 550 to 1600 (some dials remove the last zero, leaving it 55 to 160), stand for *kilohertz*, although today's AM band extends from 525 to 1,700 kilohertz, or 525,000 to 1,700,000 cycles per second. The FM side of your dial is usually numbered from 88 to 108, which stands for *megahertz*. FM numbers are lower than AM numbers, but the frequencies are much higher—88,000,000 to 108,000,000 cycles per second. The FM stations are sandwiched between television stations, which are assigned frequencies according to channel: VHF channels 2 through 6 broadcast at 54 to 88 megahertz, below FM frequencies; while channels 7 to 13 broadcasting at 174 to 216 megahertz, and the UHF channels (14 to 83), broadcast at 470 to 890 megahertz, are above the FM channels. CB radio uses two bands, one of which is in 460 to 470 right under the UHF band, which accounts for its occasional television interference.

WHAT'S THE FREQUENCY?

Whatever it's broadcasting, each station is assigned its frequency by the FCC—the Federal Communications Commission—which has been regulating American broadcasting since 1934, to keep stations from interfering with one other. Each station operates strictly within its assigned channel, whose size depends on the type of broadcast. AM channels require only a 10-kilohertz band, while FM channels require closer to 200 kilohertz ,and television channels require 6,000 kilohertz each.

So how big is a radio wave? The length of a wave (cycle) is measured from crest to crest, or from the tip of one wave to the tip of the next. Very low frequency waves (lower than 30 hertz) can measure over 10,000 yards—more than six miles—from crest to crest. Medium frequency waves—AM broadcasting waves fall in here—are about 100 to 1,000 yards each. VHF waves—used for FM and television broadcasting—measure 1 yard to 10 yards. UHF waves are from about a yard to half an inch. Extremely high frequency waves, such as X-rays, are so small that they are measured in angstroms (one ten-billionth—0.0000000001—of a meter): light rays are approximately 3,900 to 7,700 angstroms wide, while an X ray might measure 1 angstrom, and gamma rays can be smaller than 0.000001 angstrom.

LIGHT VS. RADIO

It's the size of the electromagnetic wave, related to its frequency, which is really what makes a light wave (which you can see) different from and electrical wave, or a radio wave, or an X ray. The range is phenomenal -- frequencies run from 1 to more than 1,000,000,000,000,000,000,000,000,000 to 0.0000000000000001 meter.

*   *   *   *

SCIENTIFIC HOAXES

The Amazing Tomato-wheat-cow

Background: In September 1984, *Omni* magazine ran a story about "an amazing tomato-wheat-cow," a single plant-animal hybrid that had been created by two biologists at the University of Hamburg in West Germany. "With all the characteristics of a giant stalk of wheat," *Omni* wrote, "the skin can be tanned and used as leather, and several udder blossoms provide the grower with a steady supply of tomato juice." *Omni* attributed the genetic breakthrough to "Dr. Barry MacDonald and William Wimpey of the Department of Biology at the University of Hamburg."

The Truth: *Omni* got the story from the April issue of *New Scientist* magazine…which turned out to be the April Fool's issue. The "cow" was an obvious hoax—Wimpey's and McDonald's are the two largest hamburger chains in England—but *Omni* somehow missed the joke. According to one account, "fact-checking for the article was limited to leaving a message for Wimpey and MacDonald at the University of Hamburg. The message was not returned."

Bruno Bettelheim

Background: From the 1940s until he committed suicide in 1990, he was considered a pioneering psychologist in the study of the treatment and education of emotionally desturbed children.

What Happened: In 1997 biographer Richard Pollak (whose mentally ill brother had been treated by Bettelheim) discovered that Bettelheim "constantly falsified his credentials after arriving in the U.S. in 1939," had plagiarized the work of others throughout his career, and had never even earned a degree in psychology.

Las Vegas is growing so fast that the phone company issues new phone books every 6 months.

FOR CYNICS ONLY

*Are you the kind of person who always expects the worst—who's
never surprised by scandals or heroes who are exposed as phonies?
Then this page is for you. Read it and weep…or laugh…or whatever.*

DENNIS THE MENACE

Hank Ketcham, creator of the "Dennis the Menace" comic strip, considers his work a beacon for families. "The Mitchells represent what I hope America is," he said in 1990. But at last report, he was estranged from the real Dennis—his son—who inspired the strip in the first place. "We lead separate lives, there's very little communication," Ketcham told a reporter unapologetically. He added: "I don't want a closer relationship."

At age 46, Dennis was living in an Ohio trailer park with his second wife, working as a tire retreader. The cute kid with the cowlick told *People* magazine: "Dad can be like a stranger. Sometimes I think that if he died tomorrow, I wouldn't feel anything."

FAMILY VALUES

Nancy Reagan has publicly said she's against premarital sex. But it turns out the former first lady was pregnant when she and Ronald Reagan were married. Apparently, she claimed for years that her daughter Patti had been born prematurely. But in her 1989 autobiography, *My Turn*, she revealed the truth. As UPI reported when the book came out:

> For the first time she admitted that her daughter Patti "was born—go ahead and count—a bit precipitously but very joyfully October 22, 1952." The Reagans were married the previous March, two weeks after announcing their engagement. Mrs. Reagan told [reporters] she saw no conflict between her public disapproval of premarital sex and her daughter's conception. …"We're not talking about teenagers. And we knew we were going to get married."
>
> Critics have accused the Reagans of hypocrisy for preaching "family values" while having a tangled set of personal relationships.
>
> "It's true that we weren't always able to live up to the things we believed in," she said in the book, "but that doesn't mean we didn't believe in them."

Don't try this at home: the acid in your stomach is powerful enough to dissolve razor blades.

IT'S JUST MONEY

From 1989 to 1993, Catalina Vasquez Villalpando was treasurer of the United States—the person in charge of the U.S. Mint whose signature appeared on all paper money until 1993. But in 1994, she pled guilty to "evading federal income taxes, obstructing an independent counsel's investigation, and conspiring to conceal financial links to her former company" while she was serving in her government position. In addition to not reporting income, she concealed information about money she received from a telecommunications firm in which she was a senior vice president. (Coincidentally, the company was awarded several contracts from the federal government while she was in the Treasury Department.)

A WHALE OF A PROPERTY

When the first *Free Willy* film became a hit, kids started asking about the star. To their surprise, the real whale—named Keiko—wasn't doing too well. "The 3-1/2 ton whale spends his days endlessly circling a pool so shallow he has trouble remaining submerged," Ted Bardacke wrote in a 1994 *Washington Post* article. "Three times a day, he does a few tricks at Reino Aventura, the Mexico City amusement park that has owned him for more than a decade....He is sick with a herpes-type skin infection, he is dangerously underweight, and his teeth either never matured or are being worn down by constant contact with the pool's walls and bottom.

> Keiko is not the only one with a problem. With the killer whale still in captivity, Warner Bros., the studio behind *Free Willy*, has a public relations disaster swimming around in a Mexico City fish tank. Not only has the studio been unable to follow through on its promise to...let the whale go, but Keiko is slated to star—via outtakes from the first film and through robotics—in a sequel, *Free Willy II: The Return Home*....If Keiko is still languishing south of the border while in the sequel Willy is out in the wild...the new movie could draw more protests than viewers. "

Reino Aventura was willing to donate the whale, but not to pay his moving expenses. "Warner has made a lot of money on the film and only paid us $75,000," said a spokeswoman. "Now we have to deal with all this bad publicity. Warner should cough up the dough." Ultimately, the orca was moved to a more appropriate facility in Newport, Oregon and Warner was free—to churn out more *Free Willy* films, videos, and a TV series.

TONIGHT SHOW PART VII: THE CARSON YEARS

How long did Johnny Carson host "The Tonight Show"? Look at it this way: If Jay Leno wants to break the record, he'll have to stay on the job until 2022.

ROUGH RIDING

Carson's "Tonight Show" got off to a good start in 1962. His ratings were high all over the country—in Chicago, for example, he captured 58% of the viewing audience on the first night. By early 1963, his ratings were even beginning to surpass Paar's.

But Carson wasn't happy with the quality of the program. The interview format was inflexible—if a guest was scheduled for 10 minutes, they stayed on for 10 minutes, even if they ran out of things to say. Some nights were particularly awful. When an interview fell apart, Carson would become so frustrated, he'd yawn into the camera; his eyes would wander as his guests droned on and on.

MAKING CHANGES

In early 1963, the show's producer transferred to another program just as Art Stark, Carson's producer on "Who Do You Trust?" became available. Stark had helped Carson turn the game show into a surprise hit, and Carson hired him to do the same thing with "The Tonight Show."

Stark immediately went to work on the format. He and Carson agreed that from now on, if an interview ran out of gas they'd go to a commercial as quickly as possible, and the offending guest would slide down the couch and off-camera. When the commercials ended, a new guest or skit would begin the next segment. The flexible scheduling helped the show's pacing, and put a lot of pressure on guests to perform.

Robert Blake, a frequent guest during the Carson years, describes what it was like:

> You've got six minutes to do your thing. And you better be good, or they'll go to the commercial after two minutes....The producer, all the federales are sitting like six feet away from that couch. And

they're right on top of you, man, just watchin' ya. And when they go to a break, they get on the phone... They whisper in John's ear. John gets on the phone and he talks. And you're sitting there, watching, thinking...and then the camera comes back again and John will ask you something else or he'll say, "Our next guest is..."

Other Changes

• Whenever possible, Stark scheduled an attractive woman as the first guest, to appeal to what he felt was a largely male-chauvinist audience...and to break up what was otherwise an all-male show.

• He scheduled the biggest stars to run just *after* the midnight hour, so that viewers would have something to stay up for.

• The third guest would often be a singer or instrumentalist, and the fourth, an author. (When the show was cut from 90 minutes to an hour in 1980, authors disappeared almost completely.)

• And where Paar had abandoned comedy sketches entirely, Carson began putting them back in, borrowing liberally from the comedians of the day. Carnak the Magician was a recreation of Steve Allen's Question Man, Aunt Blabby borrowed heavily from Jonathan Winters, and Art Fern was inspired by Jackie Gleason.

CARSON ON STRIKE

By the mid-1960s, the show was on its way to becoming a national institution. Ten million people tuned in every night. Carson was a superstar: when he performed a stand-up comedy routine at the Las Vegas Sahara in 1964, he broke the all-time attendance record.

The program was also making huge money for NBC. It had a smaller audience than most prime-time shows, but because it was produced at a lower cost—and was on five nights a week—it earned more money.

Where's Johnny?

Despite his success, Carson was becoming increasingly unhappy with NBC—he didn't feel the network was giving him the star treatment he'd earned. On his second anniversary as host, NBC threw him a party. But instead of renting a swanky nightclub or restaurant for the occasion, they held it in a conference room on the fifth floor, and served cold hors d'oeuvres and drinks in plastic cups. "I've seen smoke come out of a guy's nose before," one person who was at the party recalled, "but I'm telling you this was steam. [Carson] was pissed off."

Another thing that drove Carson crazy was the show's 11:15 p.m. starting time. During the Paar years, most television stations had 15-minute newscasts at 11:00 p.m. But in 1965, many stations expanded to a half-hour, which meant they didn't switch over to "The Tonight Show" until 11:30—after Carson had finished his monologue.

One evening Carson decided he'd had enough. He refused to come onstage until 11:30, leaving Ed McMahon and band leader Skitch Henderson to fill in the first 15 minutes themselves. When he strode out at 11:30, Carson explained that the only people listening at 11:15 were "four Navajos in Gallup, New Mexico, and the Armed Forces Radio on Guam." NBC moved the starting time to 11:30. It was the beginning of a series of confrontations that would last as long as Carson was host.

Taking Control

The next big showdown came in April 1967, when the American Federation of Television and Radio Artists (AFTRA) struck all three networks. Carson, a union member, participated in the walk-out. The networks responded by playing reruns, with little protest from AFTRA members...but when NBC played a "Tonight Show" rerun, Carson accused NBC of violating—and thereby voiding—his contract. He refused to go back to work even after the strike ended. "I know of no business except the broadcasting industry in which a performer becomes a scab to himself and his union because of videotape," Carson said at the time. Like Paar before him, he went to Florida for the duration of the fight.

Who Do You Trust ?

Cynics suggested that Carson, who was making an estimated $700,000 a year, was really using the strike to get more money out of NBC. And while Carson admitted that money was an issue, what he really wanted was greater control over his show—and greater independence from NBC.

He got it. Americans were already hooked on "Tonight," and NBC was hooked on the estimated $25 million a year the show was bringing in. Besides, after years of ceding the late-night audience to NBC, ABC had launched "The Joey Bishop Show" opposite Carson. Bishop, a nightclub comic, had a style similar to Jack Paar's, and ABC hoped that he would enjoy similar success.

If NBC lost Carson now, his audience might leave, too. NBC couldn't afford to take the chance, so they agreed to Carson's demands for greater control and renegotiated his salary. Carson returned on April 24, 1967, one week after "The Joey Bishop Show" made its debut. Bishop, whose ratings were only half those of "The Tonight Show" even on his best nights, limped along until December, 1969.

LATE NIGHT FIGHTS

"The Joey Bishop Show" was one of the first attempts to steal Carson's crown as King of the Night, but it wasn't the last. Here are some other also-rans of the 1960s and 1970s:

• **"The Les Crane Show"** (1964-1965). Crane's show bore more similarity to a tabloid talk show than it did to "The Tonight Show": Crane and his guests tackled the controversial topics of the day, including homosexuality and adultery. He was fired four months into the show, rehired, then fired a final time on November 12, 1965.

• **"The Las Vegas Show"** (1967). In 1967 a consortium of independent TV stations calling itself the United Network made a stab at becoming America's fourth television network. The Las Vegas Show, featuring top casino acts, went on the air on May 1, 1967 …and went off the air on May 31, when the United Network ran out of money.

• **"Merv Griffin"** (1969-1972). Griffin—Carson's original rival for the "Tonight Show" gig—had his own syndicated evening show when CBS came to him about going up against Carson. Griffin didn't want the job—so he demanded double the salary that Carson was rumored to be getting, knowing that CBS would refuse. They didn't. According to Griffin, they agreed to pay him $80,000 a week. "Suddenly I felt sick," Griffin recalls, but he agreed to do the show. Griffin's ratings were consistently higher than Joey Bishop's, but remained far behind Carson's.

More roses are grown in Texas than in any country on earth.

• **"Dick Cavett" (1969-1974).** When Joey Bishop got the axe in 1969, Dick Cavett, a former writer for Jack Paar, signed on to replace him. Promoted as "the intellectual Carson," Cavett won strong critical praise, but low ratings

• **"Jack Paar Tonite" (1973).** Paar is said to have envied Carson's celebrity as it grew. So when ABC scaled Cavett's show back from four weeks a month to one in 1973, Paar agreed to take one of the weeks for himself. Paar, however, had lost touch with his audience. Ronald Smith writes in *The Fight for Tonight:*

> Parr looked like a refugee from another era with his bowties and wet-look toupee. Viewers didn't understand why he was being a cornball and showing his home movies. He embarrassed himself with his tirades against rock music and long hair....His sidekick was Peggy Cass, and together they looked like someone's parents videotaping an evening with dull friends.

Paar's ratings were terrible—worse than Cavett's—so in the Fall of 1973, he announced that he wasn't renewing his contract. "I guess the next event in my life will be my death," he lamented.

KING OF THE NIGHT
Once again, Carson was the unchallenged king of late-night television. His next serious challenger would not emerge for a decade.

*Still more to come? Maybe...
turn to page 418 to find out.*

*   *   *

LOST TRADEMARKS
These generic terms were once registered trademarks.

Cellophane: Invented by a Swiss chemist around 1900 and sold to DuPont in 1915. It was declared a generic term by a N.Y. court in 1941, because no other word could adequately describe it.

Dry ice: Once registered by the Dry Ice Corp. to describe "solidified carbon dioxide."

Escalator: Otis Elevator Co. had this trademark.

Linoleum: Originally a trademark of the Armstrong Cork Co.

LIFE'S AN ITCH

*Uncle John has been itching to write about this subject
for a long time. He bets you can't read to the end of
this chapter without scratching at least once...*

ITCH, ITCH, ITCH

"The itch," says Jeffrey Bernhard, of the Massachusetts Medical Center "is one of, if not the, most mysterious of all 'cutaneous intrusions.'" No one knows exactly why we itch, or how it works.

• Some scientists speculate that its function is to remove parasites and other foreign objects from the skin. Or it may serve as an "early warning system" for the body's borders. Sometimes itching is a warning of a serious disease.

• Itching has a lot in common with pain—they even travel through the same kind of nerve cells (neurons). In fact, scientists once thought itching was a *kind* of pain. Now they're pretty sure itching and pain are two entirely separate functions.

• Health experts divide itches into two different categories: *sensory itches* and *allergic itches*. They also say that scratching almost always makes itches worse.

SENSORY ITCHES

• These are caused when special nerve endings in your skin called *Merkel's discs* (but referred to by doctors as "itch nerves") detect pressure on your skin. They immediately send nerve signals to the spinal cord...which sends them on to the brain.

• Your brain checks out the signals: if they're caused by something your body's used to—like clothes you wear all the time—it files the signals away in your subconscious. You don't even notice they're there.

• But if the stimulus is new and unfamiliar—say you're wearing a new hat, or you have several days of new beard growth—your brain sends out a "foreign irritant" alert and makes you aware something's there. How? By making you itch—trying to get you to brush the irritant away.

• At the same time, your brain is sending signals to the muscles in

---

16th century French doctors prescribed chocolate as a treatment for venereal disease.

your hands and arms to start scratching. That's why you scratch even when you sleep.

• Fortunately, your brain adapts to new sensations fairly quickly. So if the irritant hangs around for a while, the brain will calm down and start rerouting signals to your subconscious. The irritant is still there, but the itch goes away.

ALLERGIC ITCHINGS

• *Allergic* itching is what happens when a foreign body—e.g., medication or an insect bite—irritates your immune system. The immune system responds by releasing *histamine,* the chemical that is the body's main response to allergies. Histamine is the stuff that gives you rashes.

• Histamine does several things to the nearby cells that makes it easier for them to fight off the allergen—it causes the blood vessels to dilate; it makes it easier for fluids to pass through the affected skin cells; and it stimulates nearby nerve endings.

• In most cases, your body will get rid of the histamine naturally in 18 to 24 hours; antihistamine medications can do the same job in a couple of hours, but serious allergies can take much longer.

WEIRD ITCHES

Of course, there are always itches that break the rules—inexplicable itches with no identifiable cause. Four, that Scott LaFee, in the *San Diego Union-Tribune,* has picked as the most interesting:

Mitempfindungen: "Otherwise known as a referred itch, occurs more or less in one spot when another spot is scratched."

Aquagenic pruritus: "Itching provoked by contact with water."

Atmknesis: Itching caused by, or apparently caused by, exposure to air while undressing."

Pruritus prohibitus: "An itch that can't be scratched because your hands are full, because you can't reach it, because it would be unseemly or embarrassing to do so. Most famous case involved Huckleberry Finn."

SCRATCH FEVER

• Why do itches get worse when you scratch them? Because when you scratch, you irritate a *second* set of nerve endings—the ones

Two most recognized men of the 1970s: Mohammad Ali and the Ayatollah Khomeni.

that transmit pain. So even if you get rid of the original irritant, you've created a whole new one—*you*.

• Scratching also temporarily thickens your skin. "It sets up what I call a hot spot," says Dr. Nia Terezakis, a New Orleans dermatologist. "Scratching thickens the skin, and when skin gets thicker, it itches more. You've got a nervous itch going. You stimulate the nerves to fire more and more."

• With allergic rashes, the problem is even worse. On top of irritating the nerve endings and thickening your skin, you also spread the histamine into unaffected cells—which makes the rash bigger.

SCRATCH FACTS

• Do you itch when you come in from the cold? That's because cold weather "numbs" your nerve endings…which makes them transmit signals more slowly. But when you get back into a warm environment, your nerve endings spring back into action and flood the brain with itch signals. Your brain makes you feel itchy until it adjusts to the warmth.

• Wool is itchier than most fabrics because it stimulates two types of nerve endings at once: the pressure of the wool against your skin activates the itch nerves, and the individual fibers tickle the nerve endings that are wrapped around your hair shafts.

• No one knows why people itch so strongly at the base of the shoulder blades, the very place that's impossible to reach and scratch. "It's an intense itching that drives people crazy," says Dr. David R. Harris, a Stanford University dermatologist. "And no one knows why this occurs. We think it might be a peculiar reaction to the nerve fibers, but we don't know for sure."

ITCHY INFO

• Chicken pox gets its name from the itch, not chickens. The ailment was originally called gican pox in Old English, which meant "itchy pox."

• It takes about three minutes from the time a mosquito bites you for the bite to begin itching.

• Everyone itches at least once a day. Even thinking about itching can make you itch.

SO YOU WANT TO BE A ROCK 'N' ROLL STAR?

*There have been some pretty amazing success stories in the history of rock.
But there's never been a better example of "overnight stars" than the
McCoys. One day they were in a local Dayton, Ohio, band called
Rick and the Raiders, and the next—literally—they were in New
York recording a #1 song. Here's the story of how it happened,
from* Behind the Hits, *by Bob Shannon and John Javna.*

THE STRANGELOVES

In 1965, a trio of New York writer/producers (Bob Feldman,
Jerry Goldstein, and Richard Gottehrer) decided to call
themselves The Strangeloves, record a few songs, and go on a U.S.
tour. In their first session, they recorded two songs called, "I Want
Candy" and "Hang on Sloopy." "I Want Candy" was released first.
It was an immediate hit.

The Strangeloves planned to make "Sloopy" (which they were
sure would be big) the follow-up, but they had to wait until "Candy" peaked on the charts before they could release another single.

ON THE ROAD

They decided to start performing "Sloopy" on their live tour anyway. During a gig in Tulsa, Oklahoma, another band heard and
realized that "Sloopy" was a sure hit. The leader of the band taped
the Strangeloves' performance and told the group he planned to
record it the same way when he got home.

This was trouble for the Strangeloves. There was no way their
version could be rushed out without undermining "I Want Candy"
as it headed up the charts…but now a rival band could steal the
song. They knew they had to do something quick; they just weren't
sure *what*.

FATE STEPS IN

Bob Feldman was afraid to fly. He insisted that the group drive
back to New York from Oklahoma. And since they were passing
through Ohio anyway, the group set up a quick concert in Dayton.

When the scheduled backup musicians didn't show, a local band was hired to fill in. It was Rick and the Raiders, led by 16-year-old guitarist Rick Zehringer.

The band impressed Feldman, Goldstein, and Gottehrer—who suddenly came up with a brilliant idea: Why not take this young group back to New York and have *them* sing "Sloopy" over the already-recorded music tracks! The trio talked to the boys' parents about the idea. Coincidentally, Zehringer's parents were starting their summer vacations the very next day. They agreed to chaperone the band, so the rest of the families agreed to let their kids go to the Big Apple. The two groups drove there the next morning.

Rick Zehringer: "They said, 'Do you want to come back tomorrow?' My parents' vacation started then. We said, 'Sure, it sounds like a great idea.' That's how easy it was. We were back in New York City the next day and went into the studio because everything had been prearranged and set up."

IT'S A HIT!

One problem they'd already solved: Their name was too close to a popular group called Paul Revere and the Raiders. But a Zehringer family album showed an early picture of the band with "The McCoys" written on the base drum. By the time they reached New York, the boys had become the McCoys again. In the studio, the McCoys sang "Sloopy" over the existing instrumental tracks, with Rick adding a guitar solo.

Rick Zehringer: "They gave us a small record player and a copy of the musical track and told us exactly what they wanted us to sing. We went out into the park for a few days, practiced singing it, and put the vocal on. They jumped up and down in the control room and yelled, 'Number One!' and a few weeks later, it was. That's how easy it was for us."

EPILOGUE

"Sloopy" hit #1 on October 2, 1965, sold over a million records and became a rock classic. The McCoys had several more hits. Rick Zehringer changed his name to Rick Derringer, and became a star on his own in the 1970s with the hit song "Rock and Roll Hoochie Koo."

Sonny Bono had only one big solo hit: "Laugh At Me."

YOU CALL THAT ART? II

Here are some more great art fakes.

D **S. WINDLE**
Background: In 1936 Windle entered a painting called *Abstract Painting of Woman* in the International Surrealist Exhibition taking place in London. The work was one of the most talked-about and admired paintings of the show.

The Truth: D. S. Windle ("De Swindle") was actually B. Howitt-Lodge, a portrait painter who hated surrealist art. He created his painting out of "a phantasmagoria of paint blobs, variegated beads, a cigarette stub, Christmas tinsel, pieces of hair, and a sponge." Howitt-Lodge chose the materials, he later admitted, because he wanted to create "the worst possible mess" and enter it in "one of the most warped and disgusting shows I've ever seen."

What Happened: Modernists were unmoved by his confession—they accepted Howitt-Lodge's work as genuine surrealist art, even if *he* didn't. "He may think it's a hoax," one fan told reporters, "but he's an artist and unconsciously he may be a surrealist. Aren't we all?"

ALCEO DOSSENA

Background: In 1922 the Boston Museum of Fine Arts paid $100,000 for the marble tomb of a wealthy Italian woman named Maria Caterina Savelli, who died in 1430. The tomb was supposedly carved by a famous Florentine sculptor named Mino da Fie-Savelli, and was so impressive that the museum set the exhibit up right at the building's entrance.

The Truth: As Kathryn Lindskoog writes in *Fakes, Frauds & Other Malarkey*, "No one seemed to notice that the Mino Tomb was dated one year after its sculptor was born, and that the brief Latin inscription on the tomb, which was naively copied from a book about the Savelli family, said, 'At last the above-mentioned Maria Caterina Savelli died.'"

What Happened: No one realized it was a fake until 1928, when an obscure Italian sculptor named Alceo Dossena sued art dealer

---

6 most-hated creatures in the U.S.: cockroaches, mosquitoes, rats, wasps, rattlesnakes and bats.

Alfredo Fasoli for $66,000, claiming that without his knowledge, Fasoli had been selling his copies of Renaissance art as the genuine article.

The Boston Museum of Fine Arts refused to accept that the Mino Tomb was fake...until Dossena produced photographs of the work in progress, as well as a toe that had broken off a figure carved in the tomb.

Museums all over the world scoured their collections looking for Dossena's fakes—hundreds were found. The Cleveland Museum of Art was particularly hard hit—after finding modern nails deep inside a "13th-century" Madonna and Child, it replaced the piece with a marble statue of Athena that cost $120,000. That statue also turned out to be a Dossena fake. For what it's worth, not everyone suffered from the scandal: Alceo Dossena flourished. People became so interested in his work that he was able to launch a career as a legitimate artist.

THOMAS KEATING

Background: In 1976 thirteen paintings by Samuel Palmer, a famous English artist, inexplicably came on the market at the same time.

The Truth: When the *London Times* challenged their authenticity, an English painter named Thomas Keating wrote in to confess that he had forged the paintings—as well as 2,500 other paintings during his illicit 20-year career, including works attributed to Rembrandt, Degas, Goya, Toulouse-Lautrec, Monet, Van Gogh, and others. Keating claimed he left a clue in every painting that proved it wasn't authentic—sometimes he used modern materials; other times he painted "this is a fake" on the canvas using lead-based paint, which would show up on X-rays. But he was never caught.

What Happened: Keating was in such poor health when he confessed that he was never put on trial. He became a cult hero in England for fooling art experts for so long, and his own paintings soared in value. One which he called *Monet and his Family in their Houseboat*, sold at an auction for $32,000. By the time of his death in 1983, his work was so popular that other forgers were cashing in by copying *his* work.

The tubeless auto tire was invented by a man named Frank Herzegh. He made one dollar for it.

TOP-RATED TV SHOWS, 1985–1990

More of the annual Top 10 TV shows of the past 50 years.

1985-1986
(1) The Cosby Show
(2) Family Ties
(3) Murder, She Wrote
(4) 60 Minutes
(5) Cheers
(6) Dallas
(7) (tie) Dynasty
(7) (tie) The Golden Girls
(9) Miami Vice
(10) Who's the Boss?

1986-1987
(1) The Cosby Show
(2) Family Ties
(3) Cheers
(4) Murder, She Wrote
(5) The Golden Girls
(6) 60 Minutes
(7) Night Court
(8) Growing Pains
(9) Moonlighting
(10) Who's the Boss?

1987-1988
(1) The Cosby Show
(2) A Different World
(3) Cheers
(4) The Golden Girls
(5) Growing Pains
(6) Who's the Boss?
(7) Night Court
(8) 60 Minutes
(9) Murder, She Wrote
(10) (tie) ALF
(10) (tie) The Wonder Years

1988-1989
(1) The Cosby Show
(2) Roseanne
(3) A Different World
(4) Cheers
(5) The Golden Girls
(6) Who's the Boss?
(7) 60 Minutes
(8) Murder, She Wrote
(9) Empty Nest
(10) Anything But Love

1989-1990
(1) Roseanne
(2) The Cosby Show
(3) Cheers
(4) A Different World
(5) America's Funniest Home
     Videos
(6) The Golden Girls
(7) 60 Minutes
(8) The Wonder Years
(9) Empty Nest
(10) NFL Monday Night Football

1990-1991
(1) Cheers
(2) 60 Minutes
(3) Roseanne
(4) A Different World
(5) The Cosby Show
(6) Murphy Brown
(7) (tie) Empty Nest
(7) (tie) America's Funniest Home
     Videos
(9) NFL Monday Night Football
(10) The Golden Girls

Knights in armor used to lift their visors when riding past the king—the original military salute.

THE SWORD OF DAMOCLES

Here's another tale from Myths and Legends of the Ages.

There was once a rich and powerful king in Greece named Dionysius. A clever, ruthless man, Dionysius had fought his way to the throne. In gaining the crown, he'd had made many powerful and bitter enemies. Yet there were many who envied Dionysius and wished they were in his place.

Among the king's courtiers was a man called Damocles. Damocles was constantly praising Dionysius and saying, "Oh great king, you are indeed blessed of the gods. Everything you could wish for is yours. How happy you must be!"

One day, when Damocles was speaking in his flattering way, Dionysius said, "Well now, Damocles, what are you saying? Would you like to be king in my place?"

Damocles was frightened. He didn't want the king to think he was plotting to seize the throne. Quickly he replied, "Oh no, great king. I was only thinking how wonderful it would be to enjoy your riches for even one day."

"It shall be as you desire," said King Dionysius. "For one day, you shall enjoy the position and power and luxury of a king. You shall know exactly what it feels like to be in my place."

The next day the astonished Damocles was led into the king's chamber. He was dressed in royal robes and told that he could do whatever he wished.

Suddenly, as he leaned back among his silken cushions, he gasped with horror. Just above his head was an enormous sword hanging by a slender thread! If the thread broke, the sword would instantly fall and kill him. He sat, pale and trembling. Pointing to the sword in terror, he whispered, "That sword! That sword! Why is that sword hanging above me? Hanging by so slender a thread?"

"I promised you," answered Dionysius, "that you should know exactly how it feels to live like a king, and now you know! Did you expect that you might enjoy all of a king's riches for nothing? Do you not know that I always live with a sword hanging over my head? I must be on my guard every moment lest I be slain."

Then Damocles answered, "O king, take back your wealth and your power! I would not have it for another moment. I would rather be a poor peasant living in a mountain hut than live in fear and trembling all the days of my life!"

Never again did Damocles envy the king.

*   *   *   *

READ ALL ABOUT IT!

Here's another newspaper hoax.
Nuclear War: It's Hell!
(The *San Francisco Chronicle*, 1960)

The Story: In 1960 the *San Francisco Chronicle* posed this question. If there were a nuclear war, "could an average city dweller exist in the wilderness tomorrow with little more than his bare hands?" The paper answered its own question by assigning outdoor columnist Harvey Boyd, his wife and their three children to spend the next six weeks living in a mountain wilderness area near San Francisco. The *Chronicle* called the series "The Last Man on Earth."

Reaction: In his articles, Boyd described the experience as "the most brutish, hellish, most miserable days of our lives." But after several days of struggle, his son learned to capture frogs and Boyd himself learned how to trap a deer. After ten days, Boyd reported, he was feeling "ahead of the game at last."

The Truth: Editors at the rival *San Francisco Examiner* decided to check up on The Last Man on Earth…and found a campsite filled with modern conveniences and store-bought foods, including "matches, canned spaghetti, fresh eggs, watermelon, and the current *Reader's Digest*." The only thing missing: the Boyds themselves: the Last Man on Earth and his family had already gone home.

Karate was not introduced to Japan until about 1917.

WHAT HAPPENED AT ROSWELL?

*"The Incident at Roswell" is probably the biggest U.F.O. story in history.
Was it a military balloon...or an alien spacecraft? You be the judge...*

DEJA VU
The Roswell story would probably stayed dead if Stanton T. Friedman, a nuclear physicist, hadn't lost his job during the 1970s. UFOs were Friedman's hobby...until he got laid off; then it became his career. "In the 1970s, when the bottom fell out of the nuclear physics business," he explains. "I went full time as a lecturer." His favorite topic: "Flying Saucers ARE Real," a talk that he gave at more than 600 different college campuses and other venues around the country.

In his years on the lecture circut, Friedman developed a nationwide reputation as a UFO expert, and people who'd seen UFOs began seeking him out. In 1978 he made contact with Jesse Marcel, the Army Intelligence Officer (now retired) who'd retrieved the wreckage from Mac Brazel's ranch 31 years earlier.

At Friedman's urging, Marcel gave an interview to the *National Enquirer*. "I'd never seen anything like it," Marcel told the supermarket tabloid, "I didn't know what we were picking up. I still believe it was nothing that came from Earth. It came *to* Earth, but not *from* Earth."

BACK IN THE HEADLINES

The *Enquirer* interview couldn't have come at a more opportune time: it was 1979, and Stephen Spielberg's film *Close Encounters of the Third Kind*, which had premiered several months earlier, had stoked the public's appetite for UFO stories. After lying dormant more than 30 years, the Roswell story blew wide open all over again.

From there the story just kept growing. Dozens of new "witnesses"to the Roswell UFO began seeking out Friedman at his public appearances to tell him their stories. Soon, the Roswell "cover-up" included humanoid alien beings." Over the years," Joe Nickell writes in the *Skeptical Enquirer*, "numerous rumors, urban legends, and outright hoaxes have claimed that saucer wreckage and the remains of its humanoid occupants were stored at a secret facility—the (nonexistent) 'Hangar 18' at Wright Patterson Air Force Base. People swear that the small corpses were autopsied at that or another site."

• For the record, neither Mac Brazel nor Jesse Marcel ever claimed to have seen aliens among the wreckage. No one came public with those claims until more than 30 years after the fact.

WHY BELIEVE IN ROSWELL?

• Why are UFO conspiracy theories so popular? Anthropologists who study the "Roswell Myth" point to two psychological factors that help it endure:

1) It appeals to a cynical public that lived through the Kennedy assassination, Watergate, Vietnam and other government crises, and who believe in the government's proclivity for covering things up. As *Time* magazine reported on the 50th anniversary of the Roswell incident,

> A state of mind develops which easily believes in cover-up. The fact that the military is known for 'covert' activities with foreign governments having to do with weapons which could wipe out humanity makes the idea of secret interactions with aliens seem possible. Once this state of mind is in place, anything which might prove the crash was terrestrial becomes a lie.

2) UFO theories project a sense of order onto the chaos of the universe...and they can even serve as an ego boost to true-believers, because they suggest that we are interesting enough that aliens with vastly superior intelligence actually bother to visit us. Believing in aliens, the argument goes, is much more satisfying than believing that aliens are out there but would never want to visit us.

WAS THERE A CONSPIRACY?

So is our government hiding evidence of an Alien crash-landing on earth?
In 1993 Congressman Steven Schiff of New Mexico asked the U.S. Government's General Accounting Office to look into whether the U.S. government had ever been involved in a space-alien coverup, either in Roswell, New Mexico or anyplace else. The GAO

spent 18 months searching government archives dating back to the 1940s, including even the highly classified minutes of the National Security Council. Their research prompted the U.S. Air Force to launch its own investigation. It released its findings in September 1994; the GAO's report followed in November 1995; then a second Air Force report was released in 1997.

PROJECT MOGUL

All three reports arrived at the same conclusion: what the conspiracy theorists believe were UFO crashes were actually top secret research programs run by the U.S. military during the cold war.

Take Roswell: according to the reports, the object that crashed on Mac Brazel's farm *was* a balloon, but no ordinary weather balloon: it was part of Project Mogul, a defense program as top secret as the Manhattan Project itself. Unlike the Manhattan project, however, Project Mogul wasn't geared toward *creating* nuclear weapons, it was geared toward *detecting* them if the Soviets exploded them.

In the late 1940s, the U.S. had neither spy satellites nor high-altitude spy planes that it could send over the Soviet Union to see if Stalin's crash program to build nuclear weapons was succeeding. Instead, government scientists figured, "trains" of weather balloons fitted with special sensing equipment, if launched high enough into the atmosphere, might be able to detect the shock waves given off by nuclear explosions thousands of miles away.

Up, Up, and Away

Project Mogul was just such a program, the reports explained, and the object that crashed on Mac Brazel's field in 1947 was "Flight R-4," a Mogul balloon train that had been launched from Alamogordo Army Air Field—near the Roswell Base—in June 1947. The train of 20 balloons was tracked to within 17 miles Mac Brazel's ranch; shortly afterwards, radar contact was lost and the balloons were never recovered…at least not by the folks at Alamogordo. The Roswell Intelligence officers who recovered the wreckage didn't have high enough security clearance to know about Project Mogul, and thus they didn't know to inform Alamogordo of the discovery.

On the whole, the program was successful—Project Mogul apparently did detect the first Soviet nuclear blasts. Even so, the project was discontinued when scientists discovered that such blasts could also be detected on the ground, making the balloon-borne sensors unnecessary. The project was discontinued in the early 1950s.

OTHER PROJECTS

The Air Force's 1997 report suggested that a number of other military projects that took place in the 1940s and 1950s became part of the Roswell Myth:

• In the 1950s the Air Forces launched balloons as high as 19 miles into the atmosphere and dropped human dummies to test parachutes for pilots of the X-15 rocket plane and the U-2 spy plane. The dummies, the Air Force says, were sometimes mistaken for aliens...and because it didn't want the real purpose of the tests to be revealed, it did not debunk the alien theories.

• Some balloons also dropped mock interplanetary probes, which looked like flying saucers.

• In one 1959 balloon crash, a serviceman crashed a test balloon 10 miles northwest of Roswell and suffered an injury that caused his head to swell considerably. The man, Captain Dan D. Fulgham, was transferred to Wright Patterson in Ohio for treatment. The incident, the Air Force says, helped inspired the notion that aliens have large heads and that aliens or alien corpses are being held at Wright Patterson for study.

NEVER SURRENDER

Do the GAO and Air Force reports satisfy people who previously believed the object was a UFO? Not a chance. "It's a bunch of pap," says Walter G. Haut, who worked at the Roswell base and after World War II, distributed the famous "flying saucer" news release in 1947, and is now president of the International UFO Museum and Research Center in Roswell. "All they've done is given us a different kind of balloon. Then it was weather, and now it's Mogul. Basically, I don't think anything has changed. Excuse my cynicism, but let's quit playing games."

"As the crow flies?" Crows don't fly in straight lines.

OLD WIVES' TALES

In modern society, an "old wives' tale" is a common misconception. But in ancient times, it was essential wisdom. Makes you wonder how the things we believe will look in centuries to come.

In primitive times, people believed disease and death were caused by the invasion of demons. To protect themselves, they devised complex magical rites and ceremonies. Every group had a healer who had been chosen to learn and pass on the tribe's medical "knowledge" and wisdom.

During the Middle Ages, these healers were "old wives" (*wife* simply meant "woman") or "quack-salvers" (from the words *quacken*, meaning "one who brags about their expertise," and *salve*, meaning a type of cure.) Obviously, this is where the term "quack" comes from. But originally it didn't imply fakery; "old wives" were respected members of society.

The following are some old wives' cures which have been used for centuries, some are strange and some, as it turns out, not so strange.

To reduce fever: Drink boiled onions or carry a key in the palm of your hand.

To treat gout: Walk barefoot in dewy grass.

For a headache: Rub an onion over your forehead. (Another suggestion, popular in the 17th century, was to drive a nail into the skull.)

To get rid of corns: Take brown paper, soak it in vinegar, and place it in a saucer under your bed. Dab the corn with saliva each day before breakfast.

For heart disease: Drink foxglove tea. (Foxglove contains digitalis which is used today to combat heart disease.)

To cure boils: Carry nutmeg in your pocket.

To treat cramps: Place a magnet at the foot of the bed to draw the pain from the body. Also wear a piece of "tarred yarn" around the upper leg.

Most popular target for shoplifters: food stores.

To get rid of warts: Procedures for getting rid of warts must be done in complete secrecy in order to be effective. Here are three different cures:

- Whirl a strip of bacon around your head until you get tired, then bury it. When it rots the warts will be gone.
- Rub each wart with a bean, a pickle, an onion, a slice of potato and the skin of a chicken gizzard—then bury them.
- Tie half of a grapefruit over the wart and wear it each night until the wart

To cure a cold: Fry some onions, mix them with turpentine, spread them on your chest. (Alternative: boil an old hog hoof and drink the water.)

The cure chicken pox: Lie on the floor of a chicken house and get somebody to chase a flock of hens over you.

To grow taller: Eat a banana. Each time you eat one, you will grow.

To have curly hair: Pour rum or the juice of wild grapes on your head, and eat bread crusts with carrots. But if you are a girl, be sure not to whistle or you will grow a beard.

To cure Asthma: Eat carrots.

To keep the brain clear: Sprinkle eyebrows with rosewater.

Relief from lumbago: Roll around in grass at the sound of the first cuckoo.

To gain strength: Drink rusty water from a rain barrel.

To cure rheumatism: Wear an eel skin around your waist.

To get rid of a headache: Stick a match in your hair. (Alternative: Tie the head of a buzzard around your neck.)

To get rid of freckles: Rub a live frog over your face.

To relieve a stomach ache: Take lily roots with wine.

To treat frostbite: Cow manure and milk, used as a poultice.

To cure Lameness, muscle aches and pains: Use skunk grease.

The diesel cruise liner Queen Elizabeth II gets 6 inches to the gallon.

GROUCHO MARX, ATTORNEY AT LAW

Here's the next installment of the radio adventures of Groucho and Chico Marx, from Five Star Theater *(which aired in 1933).*

MRS. BRITTENHOUSE: Is this a detective agency?

GROUCHO: A *detective* agency? Madam, if there's anything in it for me, this is Scotland Yard.

MRS. BRITTENHOUSE: This man told me he was taking me to a detective bureau.

CHICO: You're cuckoo, I did not. You stop me in the hall. You say you want a detective. I say, you go see Flywheel. You say alright. Well, here's Flywheel.

MRS. BRITTENHOUSE: Sir, are you or aren't you a detective? My time is money.

GROUCHO: Your time is money? I wonder if you could lend me ten minutes for lunch, or maybe a half an hour for the rent?

MRS. BRITTENHOUSE: For the last time, are you a detective?

GROUCHO: Madam, for the first time I *am* a detective.

MRS. BRITTENHOUSE: Well, you don't look much like a detective to me.

GROUCHO: That's the beauty of it. See? I had you fooled already.

MRS. BRITTENHOUSE: Is this man who brought me in a detective too?

CHICO: Sure, I'm a detective. I prove it. Lady, you lose anything today?

MRS. BRITTENHOUSE: Why, I don't think so. Heavens! My handbag has disappeared.

CHICO: Here it is.

MRS. BRITTENHOUSE: Where did you find it?

CHICO: Right here in my pocket.

GROUCHO: Isn't he marvelous, madam? He has the nose of a bloodhound, and his other features aren't so good either.

MRS. BRITTENHOUSE: Well, you're just the men I'm looking for.

CHICO: You're looking for us? Hey, are you a detective?

MRS. BRITTENHOUSE: No, no. You misunderstand me. You see, my daughter is getting married this afternoon.

GROUCHO: Oh, your daughter's getting married? I love those old-fashioned girls.

MRS. BRITTENHOUSE: We're having a big wedding reception, and I want you two men to come out this afternoon and keep an eye on the wedding presents. They're very valuable, and I want to be sure that nothing is stolen.

CHICO: How much you pay us? You know it's very hard work not to steal anything.

MRS. BRITTENHOUSE: I think fifty dollars would be adequate. But you understand, of course, that you're not to mingle with the guests.

GROUCHO: Well, if we don't have to mingle with the guests we'll do it for forty dollars.

MRS. BRITTENHOUSE: Dear, dear, I must hurry. My daughter can't get married unless I get her trousseau.

CHICO: Trousseau? You mean Robinson Trousseau?

GROUCHO: Your daughter's marrying Robinson Crusoe today? Monday? Wouldn't she be better off if she'd marry the man Friday?

MRS. BRITTENHOUSE: Well, I must hurry along now. Goodbye, gentlemen. I'll be looking for you this afternoon.

GROUCHO: Well, why look for us this afternoon when we're here right now?

(Later, at the Brittenhouse mansion)
MRS. BRITTENHOUSE: Hello, Mr. Flywheel. Hives, our butler, will take care of you. Oh, dear, I'm always so nervous at weddings. I'm really not myself today.

GROUCHO: You're not yourself, eh? Well, whoever you are, you're no bargain.

HIVES: Now, on these two tables here, gentlemen, are the presents. Please watch them very carefully. *(Receding.)* I'll have to leave you now.

(Tap at the window.)

GROUCHO: I think there's somebody at the window. You'd better let him in.

CHICO: Hey, boss. He's a great big guy and he looks very tough.

(Tap again.)

CHICO: Hey, who are you?

MAN: Never mind who I am. Who are you guys?

CHICO: We're a coupla detectives.

MAN: Oh, you're a coupla detectives. Ha, ha, ha! That's a hot one!

GROUCHO: Well, I've heard better ones than that, but it's fairly good.

MAN: Hey, what are you guys supposed to do here?

CHICO: I watch da presents. Flywheel, he watch me, but we got no one to watcha Flywheel.

MAN: Well, you can clear outta here. I'll do the whole ting for you.

GROUCHO: Ravelli, that fellow certainly is a prince. I'm getting out of here before he changes his mind.

(Opens and closes door. Footsteps)

MRS. BRITTENHOUSE: Why, Mr. Flywheel, I thought you were supposed to stay in that room with the presents!

GROUCHO: Madam, I couldn't stand being alone in that room. I just had to have another look at you. And now that I've had that look, I can hardly wait to get back to the presents.

MRS. BRITTENHOUSE: Why, Mr. Flywheel!

GROUCHO: Don't call me Mr. Flywheel, just call me Sugar.

MRS. BRITTENHOUSE: Oh, Mr. Flywheel, I simply love the things you say.

GROUCHO: Oh, Mrs. Brittenhouse—I know you'll think me a sentimental old softie, but would you give me a lock of your hair?

MRS. BRITTENHOUSE (coyly): Why, Mr. Flywheel!

GROUCHO: I'm letting you off easy—I was going to ask you for the whole wig.

MRS. BRITTENHOUSE: Well, we'll discuss that later. It's too bad you can't join us now for refreshments, but maybe some evening you'd like to have me for dinner.

GROUCHO: Have you for dinner? Well, if there's nothing better to eat, I wouldn't mind, but personally, I'd prefer a can of salmon.

HIVES: Mrs. Brittenhouse! Mrs. Brittenhouse!

GROUCHO: Is there no privacy here?

MRS. BRITTENHOUSE: Why Hives, what's the matter?

HIVES: The presents! The presents!

MRS. BRITTENHOUSE: What about the presents?

HIVES: They're gone. We've been robbed!

GROUCHO: Robbed? Where's Ravelli? Quick, find Ravelli!

CHICO: Here I am, boss. How you makin' out?

GROUCHO: Listen, Ravelli. I thought I told you to watch the presents.

CHICO: That's just what I was doing.

GROUCHO: There you are, Mrs. Brittenhouse. You have nothing to worry about.

HIVES: But, madam, the presents are gone.

CHICO: Boss, I watch them just like a bloodhound. You remember that big fellow? He came in da room . . . well, I watch him . . .

ALL: Yes. . .

CHICO: He walked over and picked up da presents and I watch him . . .

ALL: Yes. . .

CHICO: He took them out da window! He put them on a truck and I watch him . . .

ALL: Yes. . .

CHICO: But when da truck drives away . . . then I cannot watch no more.

GROUCHO: You're a genius. And now, Mrs. Brittenhouse, how about our fifty dollars?

Rule of thumb: if a plant is native to the Arctic circle, it doesn't have thorns.

LET THERE BE LITE, PART II

*First Lite Beer was a hit…then Light Beer…and then, Light Food.
Finally, it turned into the most comprehensive labelling law in
U.S. history. Here's the rest of this unlikely story.*

EATING LIGHT

By the late 1980s, the term "lite" had spread from beer to every kind of food imaginable. Consumers could buy "light" oil, cheese, salad dressing, ice cream, whiskey, pudding, crackers, hot dogs, even cat food (Tender Vittles Lite). In fact, by 1991 there were an estimated 10,000 "light" products on supermarket shelves.

"Next to foods that can be microwaved," reported a manager of the U.S.'s largest supermarket chain in 1989, "light foods are the fastest-growing segment in our stores. If two comparable products are on the shelf next to each other, the one that says "Light" will probably sell better."

What was behind the lite boom? Polls showed that although most Americans weren't inclined to radically alter diets or start exercising more, they still wanted to make some kind of "healthy" change. "Lite" food filled the bill perfectly. Everyone knew that "light" or "lite" on a package meant it was better for you. So by eating *lite*, people eat *right*—and still enjoy the same food they always had. It was a way to " have it all."

"Everyone wants to indulge," commented a food industry newsletter in 1990. "This way, you can indulge and not be so bad."

THE HEAVY TRUTH

But to a large extent, lite food was a hoax. It didn't have to be better for you, because legally, *lite* and *light* didn't mean anything at all. The terms could be applied to any product for almost any reason.

A "light" margarine might be lighter in color…or sold in a smaller package (which would make it lighter in *weight*). A "light" pudding might be lower in calories…or *higher* in calories, with a "lighter" texture. As the customer relations manager of Kroger

Supermarkerts tactfully put it: "It's kind of confusing for customers. When they pick up something that says 'Light,' it may not be at all what they expect." For example: According to published reports, on a shopping trip in 1990-91 you could buy...

• **Klondike Lite Frozen Dessert Bars.** Cutting down on fat? These babies had 7 grams of fat per serving—more than triple the FDA's recommendations for low-fat claims

• **Bertolli Mild & Light Olive Oil.** Light in color, but no change in calories.

• **Lipton's Lite Cup-a-Soup Chicken Soup.** Had exactly the same amount of calories at their regular chicken Cup-a-Soup.

• **Fleur-de-Lait "Ultra-Light" cheese spreads.** "Ultra-light" referred to the consistency of these whipped cheeses. Actually a high-fat item."

• **Sara Lee Light Classics cheesecake.** Had *more* fat and calories than its regular products. This product was so misleading that the attorneys general of nine states *sued* the company over it.

Not satisfied yet? You could always choose "Pillsbury Lovin' Lites cake mixes and frosting," Hostess Light Cupcakes," or "Spam Lite" (Fat was reduced from 16 grams per serving to 12). It seemed like ther was no end in sight to the fad.

But there was.

THE LITE AT THE END OF THE TUNNEL

In 1986 Jim Cooper, a bachelor congressman from Tennessee, arrived in Washington determined to stay in shape. He bought "light" food as part of his routine. When he got married a few years later, his wife suggested he read the fine print on the labels, to see what he'd *really* been eating. He was shocked, and began introducing legislation to regulate the use of terms like "lite" and "low-fat."

Gradually, the idea gained acceptance. The FDA, revitalized under President Bush, worked with Congress to develop a label law that would make it easy for consumers to see what they were getting. In 1993, after plenty of compromising, they came up with a set of rules that regulated nutrition claims, required nutritional labeling (at the time, 40% of all packaged foods provided no nutritional info at all), and gave specific definitions to words that *Consumer Reports* called "overused and underdefined"—such as "reduced," "low-cholesterol," "low-fat"…and of course, "lite" and "light."

As a result, we can now compare apples with apples…or low-fat salad dressing with low-fat salad dressing. And we know what it means when a label says Lite.

Here are some of the rules to remember the next time you go shopping:

Low-fat: Contains three grams of fat or less per serving

Low-cholesterol: One gram or less per serving. Plus, gets no more than 15% of its calories from saturated fat.

High fiber: Contains at least 20% of the required daily fiber—i.e., 5 grams.

Reduced or Less: Contains 25% less fat, sodium, cholesterol, or calories than the regular food.

More: Contains 10% more protein, minerals, fiber, etc. than the regular food.

Free: "Applies to foods that have none of the substance cited, or a nutritionally insignificant amount."

Light or Lite: Contains 1/3 fewer calories, and at least 40 fewer calories…or contains 50% of the fat in the regular product. If "light" describes a color or texture, it has to be specifically stated that way on the label—for example, "Light in Texture."

SKIRTING THE ISSUE

Labeling laws are important. But they don't keep food manufacturers from trying to pull a fast one. Case in point: When products calling themselves "light" failed to qualify for the term under the 1993 guidelines, the manufacturers tried to fake it. "They're turning to other words they hope sound almost as good," warned *Consumer Reports*. So Pringles "Light Chips" became Pringles "Right Chips;" Kraft "Deliciously Light" Dressing became "Deliciously Right" Dressing; and so on. "In the end," said one consumer advocate," the only protection you have is your own common sense."

THE TOMATO:
FACT & FICTION

You'd be surprised how tough it is to find good information on the subject of tomatoes. After months of searching, we found a book called
The Tomato in America, *by Andrew F. Smith, in which we discovered these interesting facts and fictions.*

F **ACT:** Tomatoes originated in South America.
Explanation: The first tomato plants grew wild in Peru. They weren't much like today's tomato—they were small and smooth. It took naturally occurring mutations to make them into the fruits we eat now. The mutated tomatoes were cultivated by native Central American farmers. Spanish explorers "discovered" them there and brought them to Europe.

FACT: Tomatoes were once considered an aphrodisiac.
Explanation: The first mention of them in Europe was in 1544, by Italian herbalist Pietro Matthioli. He called them *pomi'd'oro* ("golden apples") and classified them with mandrake (a member of the often-toxic nightshade family), which was widely regarded as an aphrodisiac. The result: Tomatoes were also regarded as a sexual stimulant. They acquired the nickname "love apples."

FICTION: Europeans thought tomatoes were poison and refused to eat them.
Explanation: Mostly a myth. The belief was limited to Britain (and later, British colonies). The reason: In 1597 an English physician and herbalist named John Gerard wrote that tomatoes were toxic—even though he was totally aware that they were eaten in Spain and Italy. Many English took his word for it, and carried the idea with them to the New World. Until about the 1700s, tomatoes were grown only for ornamental purposes in England. Then they gained a mild reputation for healing inflammations, ulcers, running sores, and gout. By 1728 the British were adding tomatoes to soups.

In what state can you find the Alabama swamps? New York. Wyoming Valley? Pennsylvania.

FICTION: Thomas Jefferson was the first to cultivate tomatoes in America.

Explanation: He was definitely an early advocate of the tomato in America—he was growing them in Monticello by 1809—but didn't introduce them; they were already here. The rumor probably started because Jefferson didn't hesitate to serve tomatoes to guests—many of whom tasted them for the first time at his home.

FICTION: In 1820, a man named Robert Gibbon Johnson announced he was going to eat a tomato on the courthouse steps in Salem, New Jersey. Until that time, people thought the tomato was poisonous, so, as Andrew Smith tells the story, "hundreds of onlookers gathered to see the spectacle of Johnson eating a tomato, expecting to see him fall frothing to the ground, then die a painful death….But much to everyone's surprise, Johnson survived and launched a new and mammoth tomato industry."

Explanation: In his book, Smith demonstrates that this is just a myth. True, the English didn't eat tomatoes—but the English weren't the only colonists in the New World. The Spanish had brought tomatoes to Georgia and the Carolinas; they were also brought by the French.

• By 1800, South Carolinians were exporting both seeds and recipes to other states, and many New Orleans gumbo recipes included tomatoes

• An 1806 *American Gardener's Calendar* trumpeted the tomato as "much cultivated for its fruit, in soups and sauces, to which it imparts an agreeable flavor."

FACT: Tomatoes became a permanent part of American culture when they were the focus of a health fad.

Explanation: In 1834 a book by Dr. John Bennet made big health claims for tomatoes. It caught the public's fancy—both quoting and debunking him made good newspaper copy. So many editors and commentators were touting the tomato's health virtues, that suddenly, they were hot. Within two years of Bennet's book, *The New York Times* was predicting quadruple sales for the coming year. The *Times* was right.

• In 1837, patent medicine "tomato pills" came out. Two rival manufacturers, Alexander Miles and Guy Phelps, engaged in heated tomato-pill wars, accusing each other in print of not really including tomatoes in their formulas (among numerous other charges). A massive ad campaign for tomato pills brought tomatoes to public attention like never before. The once-suspect *pomi'd'oro* was media-blitzed: cookbooks, newspapers, magazines, horticultural books, gardeners' calendars, agricultural periodicals, botanical texts—all now raved about the wonder fruit. Doctors actually started prescribing them. Miracle-cure tales sprang up: tomatoes had cured chronic coughs, liver trouble, dyspepsia, paralysis, consumption, even cholera. And they probably did help with some of these things because of the vitamins they contained.

MORE TOMATO HISTORY

• "Tomato-mania" died down over the next decade, but by then tomatoes were widely popular and a great cash crop in the United States. Growers' profits kept rising, and farms near big cities often abandoned other produce to grow only tomatoes.

• By the early 1850s, New England was growing millions of bushels a year, and tomatoes were considered one of the easiest and quickest vegetables to grow.

• Tomatoes began riding the transcontinental railroad in 1869, fresh from California, straight to New York. The next year, tomatoes ranked among the top three vegetables in America, along with peas and corn.

• Within a decade, 19 million cans of tomatoes a year found their way into U.S. pantries, and in another few years the number was four times that.

TOMATO BITS

• Settlers in Oregon ate their tomatoes pulverized into a thick paste they poured over hotcakes.

• In 1984 NASA sent 12 million tomato seeds into space for six years. Later, the seeds were given to schoolteachers across the country to grow in their classrooms. Public uproar over possible mutations led NASA director Gregory Marlins to recommend that students not actually eat the tomatoes.

• The world's biggest tomato, according to the *Guinness Book of World Records*, was grown in 1986 by Gordon Graham and weighed in at nearly 8 pounds.

The first tennis balls were stuffed with human hair.

TOP-RATED TV SHOWS, 1991–1997

More of the annual Top 10 TV shows of the past 50 years.

1991-1992
(1) 60 Minutes
(2) Roseanne
(3) Murphy Brown
(4) Cheers
(5) Home Improvement
(6) Designing Women
(7) Coach
(8) Full House
(9) Unsolved Mysteries
(10) Murder, She Wrote

1992-1993
(1) 60 Minutes
(2) Roseanne
(3) Home Improvement
(4) Murphy Brown
(5) Murder, She Wrote
(6) Coach
(7) NFL Monday Night Football
(8) Cheers
(9) Full House
(10) Northern Exposure

1993-1994
(1) Home Improvement
(2) 60 Minutes
(3) Seinfeld
(4) Roseanne
(5) These Friends of Mine
(6) Grace Under Fire
(7) Frasier
(8) Coach
(9) Murder, She Wrote
(10) NFL Monday Night

1994-1995
(1) Seinfeld
(2) ER
(3) Home Improvement
(4) Grace Under Fire
(5) NFL Monday Night Football
(6) 60 Minutes
(7) NYPD Blue
(8) Friends
(9) (tie) Roseanne
(9) (tie) Murder, She Wrote

1995-1996
(1) ER
(2) Seinfeld
(3) Friends
(4) Caroline in the City
(5) NFL Monday night Football
(6) The Single Guy
(7) Home Improvement
(8) Boston Common
(9) 60 Minutes
(10) NYPD Blue

1996-1997
(1) ER
(2) Seinfeld
(3) Suddenly Susan
(4) (tie) Friends
(4) (tie) Naked Truth
(6) Fired Up
(7) Monday Night Football
(8) Single Guy
(9) Home Entertainment
(10) Touched by an Angel

Long shot: Only one person in 2 billion will live to the age of 116.

WHAT'S A BLUE MOON?

You've heard the saying "once in a blue moon." And you've probably heard the song "Blue Moon." So what are these guys talking about? The diligent staff of the BRI has been searching the skies for the answer.

T**HE EXPRESSION**
According to the *Dictionary of Word and Phrase Origins*, the term "blue moon" first appeared in England in 1528. The source: A book (or booklet) entitled *Read Me and Be Not Wroth*, which said: "If they say the mone is blew / We must believe that it is true."

The term *once in a blue moon* was apparently derived from this sarcastic little rhyme about the upper class. It originally meant "never." But by the early 1800s it was used to describe "a very rare occurrence." This meaning is actually more correct, because two kinds of blue moons really do exist.

THE FACTS

• The moon does occasionally appear blue. In *The Moon Book*, Kim Long writes:

> This phenomenon [is] associated with unusual atmospheric conditions. A blue-colored moon, or one with a green color, is most likely to be seen just before sunrise or just after sunset if there is a large quantity of dust or smoke in the atmosphere. These particles can filter out colors with longer wavelengths, such as red and yellow, and leave green and blue wavelengths to temporarily discolor the moon.

• The term "blue moon" is also commonly used to describe a full moon that appears twice in one month. "This occurs approximately every 32 months," says Christine Ammer in *Seeing Red or Tickled Pink*. "A full moon comes every 29-1/2 days, when the earth's natural satellite is opposite the sun in the sky. Thus any month except February could see two full moons."

* * *

Musical Note: *Richard Rogers and Lorenz Hart wrote the song "Blue Moon" in 1934.*

The foreign city most visited by Americans is Tijuana.

TONIGHT SHOW PART VIII: SPECIAL GUEST HOST: PROFESSOR PEAR

Uncle John is sorry to announce that there's been a slight change in plans, and Johnny Carson will be on vacation until the next Bathroom Reader. Fortunately, we were able to recruit as a special guest the illustrious Professor Pear, who'll fill you in on all the wonderful things you can do with pears. And so, without further ado, heeeeere's... Professor Pear.

Thank you, Uncle John. It's great to be here.

"The pear must be approached with discretion and reverence; it withholds its secrets from the merely hungry." This observation, attributed to Paul Bunyard, is testimony that pears are one of the more mysterious of the fruits we commonly encounter. Unlike an apple, which is ready to eat from the day it is picked, a pear must go through a series of changes before it can deliver its full splendor. It would seem that the pear was not made for humans to easily enjoy; it must be manipulated in order to present us the flavor, texture, and juiciness that we consider attributes of high quality.

For one thing, pears do not ripen on the tree to our liking. If allowed to tree-ripen, pears typically ripen from the inside out, so that the center is mushy by the time the outside flesh is ready. In addition, the texture of tree-ripened pears is often more gritty than that of pears picked before they are ripe. So the frequently heard notion that pears are picked when they are still hard and green as a convenience for enduring the long truck ride to market misses the point. Pears are harvested when they are "mature," which in pear language means when they have reached the point where, after picking, they will ripen to good quality, sometimes with a little help, but definitely *off* the tree.

Now the next step after harvesting mature pears is to cool them down. Commercial storages cool them way down, to around 30° F (like drunks sleeping in the snow, they don't freeze at 32° because they have so much dissolved material in their juice—in the case of pears, it's sugar). The colder they are, the longer they'll stay in good condition. One unique quality of pears is that if they need to sit on the kitchen shelf, they will sit and sit and eventually decompose—without ever "ripening."

Ripening a pear must be a closely watched process, since there is a relatively narrow window between "too hard" and "too soft" where the glory of the perfect pear texture lies. The best quality is experienced when the pears are ripened by leaving them at 65°F-75°F. The amount of time varies from about five days for a typical Bartlett, to six or seven days for Bosc or Comice, to anywhere from seven to ten days for Anjou. As ripening begins, pears, like many fruits, begin to produce "the ripening hormone," ethylene gas, inside the fruit. This speeds the ripening along. In fact, the whole pear-ripening process can be kick-started by putting freshly bought or picked pears in a bag with a ripe banana or apple, both of which give off copious quantities of etyhylene gas. The bag keeps the apple or banana ethylene around the pears, which soak it up and quickly begin producing their own.

Determining when a pear is ripe depends somewhat on the eater's preference, but here is a time-honored method: hold the pear gently but firmly in the palm of your hand, as a baseball pitcher might hold the ball while studying the signs from the catcher. Apply the thumb of the same hand to the pear flesh just below the point where the stem joins the fruit. When the flesh beneath the spot yields evenly to gentle pressure from the thumb, it is ready to eat. If you have to push more than slightly, it's not ready yet. After years of study, scientists have found that a really juicy pear is best eaten while naked, in the bathtub, so that you needn't be concerned about the abundant juice streaming down your chin.

Thank you, Professor Pear.

Well, that's it for this edition.

**Johnny will be back in the next Bathroom Reader,
for the conclusion of "The Tonight Show" story.**

A snail breathes through its foot.

THE SECRET OF INVISIBILITY

Many years ago, during an extended visit to the bathroom, Uncle John entered a deep trance…and, suddenly, the secret of invisibility was revealed to him. And now we'd like to share it with you. Just follow these step-by-step instructions.

1.

2.

3.

4.

5.

6.

7.

8.

9.

10.

The Malaysian expression for "take a walk" translates as "eat the wind."

TWANG! A BRIEF HISTORY OF THE ELECTRIC GUITAR

"More than any other instrument," says Charlie McGovern of the Smithsonian Insititution, "the electric guitar has been the dominant shaping force in American music in the last half-century. It completely changed the direction of the blues. It pretty much rechanneled country music. You can't have rock-and-roll without it." It's also a relatively new instrument, whose history is still being written. Here's a quick summary of what we know so far.

THE PROBLEM WITH GUITARS

• In the 1920s, people thought of the guitar exclusively as a rhythm instrument. In bands, there were few single-note guitar solos—guitar players strummed as hard as they could in the background, trying to be heard over the other instruments. As one critic observed:

> In the Chicago and New Orleans jazz bands...the guitar had a rough time. No matter how hard the frustrated picker picked, he was usually drowned out by all sorts of horns and some bully on an eighty-eight key, five-hundred pound piano.

• Guitarists tried all sorts of tricks to be heard:

— They tried putting megaphones under the strings.

— They made bigger and bigger guitars.

— They used National Steel Guitars, which were made out of metal and came with built-in resonators.

— They put microphones up against the strings. This was a logical solution...except that microphones quickly produced feedback.

ELECTRIFYING FIRST

No one person can be considered the inventor of the electric guitar. But Lloyd Loar was the first to recognize their commercial potential.

• In the mid-1920s Loar, an employee of the Gibson Guitar Company, invented a microphone that fit in a guitar and picked up the sound better than most microphones. He proposed that Gibson, manufacture them, but they weren't interested.

The grey whale's heart beats nine times a minute.

• So Loar quit and formed his own company, Vivi-Tone, to manufacture "electric" guitars (acoustic guitars with a pick-up inserted). Unfortunately, he was ahead of his time, and quickly went out of business.

THE 1930s.

• Meanwhile, musicians all over the country were experimenting with their own ways to electrify guitars. In 1931, one inventor created the magnetic pickup—which "transformed string vibrations into electrical impulses that accurately reproduced sound."

• This breakthrough enabled the Rickenbacker Co., a tool-and-die maker, to manufacture a Hawaiian steel guitar with *built-in* pickups. They called it the "Frying Pan." In Seattle a year later, Paul Tutmar founded his Audiovox company, the first to manufacture electric guitars exclusively.

• But 1935 is generally considered the year the electric guitar was born. For the first time, major manufacturers—Gibson, Epiphone, and National—introduced electric models to the public.

THE FIRST GUITAR HEROES

Once the product was available on a wide basis, guitar players began showing the world what could be done with it.

• In the mid-1930s, for example, Aaron "T-Bone" Walker became the first bluesman to fully exploit the electric by strutting across the stage, doing splits, and playing the guitar behind his back. With this technique, he foreshadowed the stunts and styles of future rock 'n' roll greats like Chuck Berry and Jimi Hendrix. He also experimented with volume and feedback, demonstrating that it was the guitar and amplifier *together*—not the guitar alone—that made a new instrument.

• But the guitar player who made the biggest difference was Charlie Christian, who played with Benny Goodman's band from 1939 to 1941. He is credited with creating an identity for the electric guitar as a solo instrument. Christian would play staccato, horn-like, single-note phrases—a radical change from the accepted approach at the time. His style caused a revolution in technique and helped create the soon-to-be popular genre, bebop. In fact, his impact was so great the author of *The Art and Times of the Guitar*, wrote: "There is the guitar before Christian and the guitar after

Oregon has more ghost towns than any other state.

Christian, and they sound virtually like two different instruments."

THE SOLID-BODY GUITAR

Until the 1940s, electric guitars were still semi-acoustic. It took two electronic geniuses to bring about the solid-body electric.

Les Paul

• Paul began experimenting with electric sounds in the late twenties by jamming his mother's phonograph needle into the top of a guitar and plugging it in.

• In the 1940s he created an early prototype of the solid-body, which he called "The Log." It was little more than a 4'x4" board with strings anchored to a door hinge and a guitar body attached over the top for looks. He brought it to Gibson, and again, the guitar-maker missed an opportunity to revolutionize the guitar world.

• In 1952, when Gibson finally produced their first solid-body, they worked with Paul to create one of the most widely-used electric guitars ever made: the "Les Paul."

Leo Fender

• Fender is regarded as the father of the modern electric guitar—though, ironically, he wasn't even a musician. He just loved tinkering with electronics.

• In 1948, Fender came out with a Spanish-style solid body electric guitar he called the "Broadcaster." However, another music company owned that name; rather than go to court, he renamed it the "Telecaster." It was still regarded as a novelty by most guitarists

• It wasn't until 1954, when he created the most popular electric guitar of all time—the Stratocaster—that the electric guitar came into its own. The Strat was a new design, not based on that of acoustic or semi-acoustic guitars. For example: Most guitars in the early 1950s were heavy, and dug into guitarists' rib cages; Fender beveled the edges of the guitar so it would be more comfortable. The body was scalloped so every note on the neck was accessible; the volume and tone controls were in easy reach of the guitarist's hands; and so on. These and a host of other changes made the Stratocaster revolutionary in the 1950s...and opened the door to the electric guitar's popularity. Incredibly, the first Strats sold for only $75. Today they bring in as much as $20,000 as collectibles.

Venetian blinds aren't—they were invented in Japan.

THE FIGHT FOR SAFE MILK, PART II

On page 241 we told you about the battle to end the sale of adulterated milk. Part II is the story of the fight to pasteurize the U.S. milk supply. It's an instructive tale. In spite of proof that pasteurization could save lives, Americans resisted it because it was a new idea...and because it "cost too much."

SOLID PROGRESS

During the latter part of the 19th century, improvements were made in the quality of the milk sold in the United States.

Bottles: In 1884, for example, Dr. Henry G. Thatcher patented the first practical glass milk bottle with a sealable top. He got the idea while standing in line in the street for his own milk a year earlier. When the little girl ahead of him dropped her filthy rag doll into the milk dealer's open milk can, the dealer just shook the doll off, handed it back to the girl, then ladled Thatcher's milk as though nothing had happened.

Thatcher's bottle wasn't a solution to all of raw milk's problems, but at least it kept impurities out of milk after it left the dairy. Many dairies hated the bottles because they were expensive and broke relatively easily, but they caught on with the public and were soon in use all over the country.

The Lactometer: In the early 1890s, New York State began regulating the content of milk using a lactometer, a newly invented device that could measure the amount of milk solids in milk. For the first time, it was possible to compare pure milk with a test sample of a dairy's milk to see if it had been watered down or adulterated. If the milk tested didn't contain the same amount of milk solids as pure milk, the milk dealer could be fined or penalized.

BATTLING BACTERIA

But by far, the most important breakthroughs were scientific.

Five U.S. presidents have had the first name James, more than any other name.

The 1880s and 1890s were a period of great advancement in the understanding of bacteria and its role in causing disease.

In 1882, for example, a German scientist named Robert Koch discovered that bovine tuberculosis, a form of tuberculosis found in cattle, could be spread to humans through diseased milk. This form of tuberculosis attacked the glands, intestines, and bones, frequently killing the afflicted or leaving them deformed for life.

"Children seemed to be especially susceptible to bovine tuberculosis," James Cross Gilbin writes in *Milk: The Fight for Purity.* "[Victims] often spent years strapped into spinal frames…designed to prevent deformity while the body slowly overcame the infection."

Researchers discovered other diseases could be spread by milk as well. They found that if a cow's udders weren't cleaned before milking, bacteria from manure (or anything else on the udders) could fall into the milk. And if the person milking the cow was sick, *their* germs could infect the milk, too. There seemed to be no limit to the number of ways that milk could be infected with disease.

PASTEURIZATION

As it turns out, the solution to this problem had already been found. In the 1860s, French chemist Louis Pasteur invented the process of pasteurization, which uses heat to kill bacteria that cause liquids like milk and beer to spoil. But because his ideas were revolutionary, they spread slowly. The idea of pasteurizing milk didn't arrive in the United States until the 1880s—and even then, it took more than 30 years to find wide acceptance! That acceptance came largely through the work of one man.

MILK MAN

In the 1890s, Nathan Straus, co-owner of Macy's department store in New York, was already building a reputation as a philanthropist. In the winter of 1892, he distributed 1.5 million buckets of coal to impoverished New Yorkers so they could heat their homes. The following year, he organized a series of shelters that provided beds and breakfasts to the city's homeless population. In 1893 he tackled the problem of unsafe milk.

Straus had been reading up on Pasteur's work and the theoretical benefits of pasteurization. He knew that nearly 10% of all children

As far as anyone can tell, only humans get headaches.

born in New York City died by the age of five—and despite all the recent improvements in milk quality, he still suspected that milk was to blame for many of the deaths. His reasoning was simple: Milk spoiled quicker in the heat of summer, and the city's childhood mortality rate increased at the same time. He figured there had to be a connection between the two.

MILK BAR

In June 1893, Straus set up a milk-processing station in a neighborhood on East Third Street. The station pasteurized milk on the spot, then provided it at affordable prices to local families. The station also offered free medical exams for children and free hygiene advice for their mothers. Mothers who couldn't afford 2¢ for a pint or 4¢ for a quart of milk (less than the price of unpasteurized milk) could get coupons for free milk from local doctors and charities.

By the turn of the century, Straus had twelve milk stations in different parts of the city, distributing hundreds of thousands of bottles of pasteurized milk every year. He also had several milk stands where people could taste pasteurized milk for a penny a glass, to see for themselves that pasteurization didn't hurt the taste.

THE ORPHAN TEST

The final proof of the benefits of pasteurized milk came when Straus began providing milk to an orphanage that had seen death rates as high as 42% from tuberculosis and other milk-borne diseases. The orphanage was located on Randall's Island in the East River. All the milk it used was provided by a single herd of cows kept on the island, so it was easy to control the milk the orphans drank.

Straus started pasteurizing the orphanage's milk in 1898. Within a year, the mortality rate dropped to 28%, and continued downward in the years that followed.

AN UPHILL FIGHT

By the turn of the century, pasteurized milk stations like Straus's had been set up in Boston, Philadelphia, Chicago, and other major cities. The programs were voluntary and were run by charities. Although philanthropists were getting into the pasteurized milk business, the dairy industry was staying out of it. Citing the added cost of pasteurization, they refused to pasteurize their own milk, and blocked efforts to require it by law.

Another huge barrier was public resistance: most people were used to "pure" raw milk, and didn't understand science well enough to insist on pasteurization. The few dairies that *had* begun pasteurizing milk to increase shelf life and prevent spoiling did so mostly in secret, out of fear of losing sales to raw milk dairies.

Straus was instrumental in getting New York to create the post of inspector of dairy farms, making it one of the first cities in the nation to inspect the quality of milk at the source. In 1907, Straus tried to help pass a city ordinance requiring the pasteurization of all milk sold in New York. Many milk distributors, doctors, and even the city's Health Department opposed him, arguing that the health benefits of "clean raw milk" outweighed the risks. The ordinance failed.

PRESIDENTIAL SEAL OF APPROVAL

In 1907, the reform-minded president Teddy Roosevelt ordered his Public Health Service to look into the pros and cons of pasteurized milk. In 1908 the Service issued its report: Pasteurization, they found, did not affect the taste, quality, nutrition or digestibility of milk, but it did "prevent much sickness and save many lives."

Compulsory pasteurization was still many years away, though. A second attempt to require pasteurization of New York City's milk supply was defeated in 1909, and a similar ordinance that had passed in Chicago in 1908 was repealed in 1910 after the courts ruled the measure interfered with free trade.

Finally in 1911, the National Commission on Milk Standards issued a report arguing that "in the case of all milk not either certified or inspected, pasteurization should be compulsory." The American Medical Association followed with similar advice a few months later. These reports and others like them ignited a groundswell of public support for compulsory pasteurization. In 1912, Chicago passed a second pasteurization ordinance; this one stuck. New York passed a similar ordinance, but milk distributors succeeded in delaying and then watering down the law.

THE FINAL STRAW

In 1913, a typhoid fever epidemic struck New York claiming thousands of victims. By now there was proof that typhoid fever was carried by milk, and that it could be killed through pasteurization. New York City finally stopped dragging its feet. By the end of 1914, 95 percent of the city's milk supply was pasteurized. By 1917, nearly all of the 50 largest cities in the nation required pasteurization; the rest of the country would follow over the next several years.

The impact of pasteurized milk on public health was nothing short of astounding. In 1885 the infant mortality in New York City was 273 per 1,000 live births—more than 27%. By 1915 the infant mortality rate was 94 per 1,000, a drop of two-thirds.

PASTEURIZATION TODAY

Today the most popular method of pasteurization is called "flash pasteurization" or "high-temperature, short-time" pasteurization (HTST). Raw milk is heated to 161° fahrenheit and kept at that temperature for only 15 seconds, and then immediately cooled to 50° fahrenheit.

Products like half-and-half and whipping cream, which are expected to remain refrigerated for longer periods of time, are processed by "ultra-high temperature" pasteurization at 280° fahrenheit for two seconds.

*   *   *

THE
"EXTENDED SITTING" SECTION

A Special Section of Longer Pieces

Over the years, we've gotten
numerous requests from BRI members
to include a batch of long articles—
for those times when you know
you're going to be sitting for awhile.
Well, the BRI aims to please…
So here's another great way
to pass the…uh…time.

URBAN LEGENDS

Word to the wise: If a story sounds true, but also seems too good to be true, it's probably an "urban legend." Here's the inside poop.

G UESS WHAT I JUST HEARD?
At one time or another, just about everyone has heard about the poodle that exploded when its owner tried to dry it in a microwave…or the person who brought home a strange-looking chihuahua puppy from Mexico, only to learn it was really a rat.

Most of us now know these stories are urban legends—but only because they've been around a while. When individual stories become widely discounted as fables, new ones spring up to take their place.

WHAT MAKES A GOOD URBAN LEGEND?

People who study urban legends point to several characteristics that contribute to their believability and chances of survival.

✔ **They contain "details" that create the impression the story is true.** Take the story about the woman who tries on an imported coat at the mall, feels a sting on her wrist…and later dies from the bite of a poisonous baby snake that had hatched in the lining of the coat. The name of the mall (it's almost always nearby), the item of clothing, its price, and other seemingly corroborative details are usually included in the story.

✔ **They may contain a grain of truth, which implies that the *entire* story is true.** No word on what would happen if someone really did put a dog in a microwave oven, but if you've ever tried to hardboil an egg in one, you know it would probably be ugly.

✔ **The story reflects contemporary fears.** The poodle-in-the microwave story dates back to the days when few people owned microwaves, and fewer still understood how they worked. (If you aren't sure how yours works, see page 235). Other legends may be inspired by fear of attack, embarrassment, ghosts, or science.

IQ of the average police officer: 104

✔ **The person telling the story believes he knows the person who knows the person who witnessed or is involved in the story.** The listener thereby accepts it on faith, and when they tell the story, they can also claim a personal connection that makes the story more believable.

✔ **The story is reported in the media, either as fact or a rumor.** It doesn't really matter whether the news story gives it credibility or labels it a myth; either way, the legend is often given new life. In 1917, columnist H. L. Mencken published a fictional history of the bathtub in the New York *Evening Mail* that claimed President Millard Fillmore installed the first White House bathtub in 1851. The story isn't true—Andrew Jackson installed the first indoor plumbing, complete with bathtub, in 1833. Mencken later admitted the hoax. But it continues to appear in print to this day.

SIX URBAN LEGENDS

The Story: On October 10, 1995, the U.S. Chief of Naval Operations released the following transcript of what the story claims is "an actual radio conversation."

> NAVY: Please divert your course 15 degrees to the north to avoid a collision.
>
> CIVILIAN: Recommend you divert YOUR course 15 degrees to south to avoid a collision.
>
> NAVY: This is the captain of a U.S. Navy ship. I say again, divert YOUR course.
>
> CIVILIAN: No, I say again, you divert YOUR course.
>
> NAVY: THIS IS THE AIRCRAFT CARRIER ENTERPRISE. WE ARE A LARGE WARSHIP OF THE U.S. NAVY. DIVERT YOUR COURSE NOW!
>
> CIVILIAN: This is a lighthouse. Your call.

How It Spread: On the Internet.

The Truth: According to Patrick Crispen, who co-writes *The Internet Tourbus* (*http://www.tourbus.com*), "It turns out the Navy story is a very old urban legend," made fresh by new exposure on the Internet.

The first product Motorola developed was a record player for cars.

The Story: A traveler visiting New York City meets an attractive woman in a bar and takes her back to his hotel room. That's all he remembers—the next thing he knows, he's lying in a bathtub filled with ice; and surgical tubing is coming out of two freshly stitched wounds on his lower chest. There's a note by the tub that says, "Call 911. We've removed your left kidney." (Sometimes both are removed). The doctors in the emergency room tell him he's the victim of thieves who steal organs for use in transplants. (According to one version of the story, medical students perform the surgeries, then use the money to pay off student loans.)

Note: Uncle John actually heard this from a friend, Karen Pinsky, who sells real estate. She said it was a warning given by a real estate firm to agents headed to big cities for conventions.

How It Spread: French folklorist Veronique Campion-Vincent has traced the story to Honduras and Guatemala, where rumors began circulating in 1987 that babies were being kidnapped and murdered for their organs. The alleged culprits: wealthy Americans needing transplants. From there the story spread to South America, then all over the world. Wherever such stories surfaced—*including* the U.S— newspapers reported them as fact. The New York version surfaced in the winter of 1991, and in February 1992, the *New York Times* "verified" it. Scriptwriter Joe Morgenstern, thinking it was true, even made it the subject of an episode of the NBC- TV series "Law and Order. "

The Truth: National and international agencies have investigated the claims, but haven't been able to substantiate even a single case of organ theft anywhere in the world. The agencies say the stories aren't just groundless, but also implausible. "These incredible stories ignored the complexity of organ transplant operations," Jan Brunvald writes in *The Baby Train and Other Lusty Urban Legends*, "which would preclude any such quick removal and long-distance shipment of body parts."

*　　*　　*　　*

The Story: One of the most potent forms of marijuana in the world is "Manhattan White " (also known as "New York Albino"). The strain evolved in the dark sewers of New York City as a direct result of thousands of drug dealers flushing their drugs down the

Angel Falls, the highest in the world, was named after a U.S. pilot named Jimmy Angel.

toilet during drug busts. The absence of light in the sewers turns the marijuana plants white; raw sewage, acting as a fertilizer, makes it extremely potent.

The Truth: Most likely an updated version of the classic urban myth that alligators live in the New York sewers.

* * * *

The Story: A young woman finishes shopping at the mall and walks out to her car to go home. But there's an old lady sitting in the car. "I'm sorry ma'am, but this isn't your car," the woman says.

"I know," the old lady replies, "but I had to sit down." Then she asks the young woman for a ride home.

The young woman agrees, but then remembers she locked the car when she arrived at the mall. She pretends to go back into the mall to get her sister, and returns with a security guard. The guard and the old lady get into a fight, and in the struggle the old lady's wig falls off, revealing that she's actually a man. The police take the man away, and under the car seat, they find an axe. (The story is kept alive by claims that the mall has bribed reporters and police to keep the story quiet.)

The Truth: The modern form of the tale comes from the early 1980s and places the action at numerous malls...New York, Las Vegas, Milwaukee, Chicago, and even Fresno, California, depending on who's telling the story. Folklorists speculate the tale may date all the way back to an 1834 English newspaper account of "a gentleman in his carriage, who on opening the supposed female's reticule [handbag] finds to his horror a pair of loaded pistols inside."

* * * *

The Story: Two young men are driving home from a party one rainy night and notice a beautiful young woman standing by the side of the road. She doesn't have a raincoat or umbrella, so they stop and offer her a ride. She accepts, and while they drive her to her house, one of the young men gives her his jacket to wear.

About a block from the young woman's house, they turn around to say something to her...but she is gone. They drive to her house anyway, knock on the door, and the woman who answers tells them, "that was my daughter. She was killed two years ago on the same spot you picked her up. She does this all the time."

The next day the young men look up the girl's obituary in the library. There it is—complete with a picture of the girl they picked up. Then they go to the cemetery...and find the jacket she borrowed resting on her tombstone.

The Truth: Another oldie-but-goodie. According to folklorist Richard Dorson, it predates the automobile. The story "is traced back to the 19th century," he writes, "in America, Italy, Ireland, Turkey, and China; with a horse and wagon picking up the benighted traveler." In the Hawaiian version, the girl hitches a ride on a rickshaw.

* * * *

The Story: A woman catches a cockroach and throws it in the toilet. Rather than drown it, she decides to kill it quickly with bug spray. Her husband comes home a few minutes later, sits down on the toilet, and drops his lit cigarette into the bowl. *Kaboom!*

Burned on his behind and on his private parts, the man calls 911. As the paramedics are carrying him to the ambulance, he tells them what happened...and they laugh so hard they drop the stretcher, breaking his arm.

How It Spread: It apparently began in Israel: The *Jerusalem Post* reported the story in August 1988... then retracted it a few weeks later because it could not be substantiated.

The Truth: Urban legends featuring broken arms brought on by paramedics laughing at the embarrassing way in which a patient has injured himself, are so numerous they're practically a category unto themselves. The storyteller's fear of being embarrassed in a similar way is what keeps them alive.

* * * *

"A lie can travel halfway around the world before the facts have even put their boots on."

—*Mark Twain*

THE NEWSPAPER HOAX THAT SHOOK THE WORLD

The media's power to "create" news has become a hot topic in recent years. But it's nothing new. This true story, from a book called The Fabulous Rogues, *by Alexander Klein, is an example of what's been going on for at least a century. It was sent to us by BRI member Jim Morton.*

Most journalistic hoaxes, no matter how ingenious, create only temporary excitement. But in 1899 four reporters in Denver, Colorado, concocted a fake story that, within a relatively short time, made news history—violent history at that. Here's how it happened.

THE DENVER FOUR

One Saturday night the four reporters—from Denver's four newspapers, the *Times, Post, Republican,* and *Rocky Mountain News*—met by chance in the railroad station where they had each come hoping to spot an arriving celebrity around whom they could write a feature. Disgustedly, they confessed to one another that they hadn't picked up a newsworthy item all evening.

"I hate to go back to the city desk without something," one of the reporters, Jack Toumay, said.

"Me, too," agreed Al Stevens. "I don't know what you guys are going to do, but I'm going to fake. It won't hurt anybody, so what the devil."

The other three fell in with the idea and they all walked up Seventeenth Street to the Oxford Hotel, where, over beers, they began to cast about for four possible fabrications. John Lewis, who was known as "King" because of his tall, dignified bearing, interrupted one of the preliminary gambits for a point of strategy. Why dream up four lukewarm fakes, he asked. Why not concoct a sizzler which they would all use, and make it stick better by their solidarity.

The strategy was adopted by unanimous vote, and a reporter named Hal Wilshire came up with the first suggestion: Maybe they could invent some stiff competition for the Colorado Fuel and Iron

---

An alligator has a brain the size of your thumb.

Company by reporting the arrival of several steel men, backed by an independent Wall Street combine, come to buy a large site on which they planned to erect a new steel mill. The steel mill died a quick death; it could be checked too easily and it would be difficult to dispose of later.

Stevens suggested something more dramatic: Several detectives just in from New York on the trail of two desperados who had kidnapped a rich heiress. But this story was too hot; the editors might check the wire services or even the New York police directly.

Thereupon Toumay and Lewis both came up with the obvious answer. What they needed was a story with a foreign angle that would be difficult to verify. Russia? No, none of them knew enough about Russia to make up an acceptable story. Germany was a possibility or perhaps, a bull-ring story from Madrid? Toumay didn't think bull-fighting was of sufficient interest to Denverites. How about Holland, one of the reporters offered, something with dikes or windmills in it, maybe a romance of some sort.

THE PLOT THICKENS

By this time the reporters had had several beers. The romance angle seemed attractive. But one of the men thought Japan would be a more intriguing locale for it. Another preferred China; why the country was so antiquated and unprogressive, hiding behind its Great Wall, they'd be doing the Chinese a favor by bringing some news about their country to the outside world.

At this point, Lewis broke in excitedly. "That's it," he cried, "the Great Wall of China! Must be fifty years since that old pile's been in the news. Let's build our story around it. Let's do the Chinese a real favor, let's tear the old pile down!"

Tear down the Great Wall of China! The notion fascinated the four reporters. It would certainly make the front page. One of them objected that there might be repercussions, but the others voted him down. They did, however, decide to temper the story somewhat.

A group of American engineers had stopped over in Denver en route to China, where they were being sent at the request of the ruling powers of China, to make plans for demolishing the Great Wall at minimum cost. The Chinese had decided to raze the ancient boundary as a gesture of international good will. From now on China would welcome foreign trade.

By the time they had agreed on the details it was after eleven. They rushed over to the best hotel in town, and talked the night clerk into cooperating. Then they signed four fictitious names to the hotel register. The clerk agreed to tell anyone who checked that the hotel had played host to four New Yorkers, that they had been interviewed by the reporters, and then had left early the next morning for California. Before heading for their respective city desks, the four reporters had a last beer over which they all swore to stick to their story and not to reveal the true facts so long as any of the others were alive. (Only years later did the last survivor, Hal Wilshire, let out the secret.)

The reporters told their stories with straight faces to their various city editors. Next day all four Denver newspapers featured the story on the front page. Typical of the headlines is this one from the Times:

GREAT CHINESE WALL DOOMED!

PEKING SEEKS WORLD TRADE!

THE SNOWBALL EFFECT

Within a few days Denver had forgotten all about the Great Wall. So far, so good. But other places soon began to hear about it. Two weeks later Lewis was startled to find the coming destruction of the Great Wall spread across the Sunday supplement of a large Eastern newspaper, complete with illustrations, an analysis of the Chinese government's historic decision—and quotes from a Chinese mandarin visiting in New York, who confirmed the report.

The story was carried by many other papers, both in America and in Europe. By the time it reached China it had gone through many transformations. The version published there—and the only one that probably made sense in view of the absence of any information on the subject from the Chinese government—was that the Americans were planning to send an expedition to tear down the Chinese national monument, the Great Wall.

Such a report would have infuriated any nation. It led to particularly violent repercussions in China at that time. The Chinese were already stirred up about the issue of foreign intervention—European powers were parceling out and occupying the whole country. Russia had recently gotten permission to run the Siberian railway through Manchuria. A year previously German marines had seized the port town of Kiachow, and set up a military and naval base there. France followed by taking Kwangchowan. England had sent a fleet to the Gulf of Chihli and bullied China into leasing Weihaiwei, midway between the recent acquisitions of Russia and Germany.

Faced with this danger of occidental exploitation, possibly even partition, the Chinese government under Emperor Kwang-Hsu began to institute radical reforms, to remodel the army along more modern lines, and to send students to foreign universities to obtain vital technical training.

An important segment of Chinese society bitterly resented not only foreign intervention, but all foreign cultural influences, as well as the new governmental reforms. In 1898 Empress Tsu Hsi made herself regent and officially encouraged all possible opposition to Western ideas. A secret society known as the Boxers, but whose full name was "The Order of Literary Patriotic Harmonious Fists," took the lead in verbal attacks on missionaries and Western businessmen in China by openly displaying banners that read "Exterminate the foreigners and save the dynasty."

THE SPARK THAT LIT THE FIRE

Into this charged atmosphere came the news of America's plan to force the demolition of the Great Wall. It proved the spark that is credited with setting off the Boxer Rebellion. A missionary later reported: "The story was published with shouting headlines and violent editorial comment. Denials did no good. The Boxers, already incensed, believed the yarn and now there was no stopping them."

By June 1900, the whole country was overrun with bands of Boxers. Christian villages were destroyed and hundreds of native converts massacred near Peking. The city itself was in turmoil, with murder and pillage daily occurrences and the foreign embassies under siege.

Finally, in August, an international army of 12,000 French, British, American, Russian, German, and Japanese troops invaded China and fought its way to Peking. There, the troops not only brought relief to their imperiled countrymen, but also looted the

Emperor's Palace and slaughtered innumerable Chinese without inquiring too closely whether they belonged to the "Harmonious Fists" or just happened to be passing by. The invading nations also forced China to pay an indemnity of $320 million and to grant further economic concessions. All this actually spurred the reform movement, which culminated with the Sun Yat-Sen revolution in 1911.

Thus did a journalistic hoax make history. Of course, the Boxers might have been sparked into violence in some other fashion, or built up to it of their own accord. But can we be sure? The fake story may well have been the final necessary ingredient. A case could even be made that the subsequent history of China, right up to the present, might have been entirely different if those four reporters had been less inventive that Saturday night in the Hotel Oxford bar.

*   *   *

And Now It's Time For A Little...WEIRD MUSIC
Here are some real (no kidding) albums you can get:

• "Music to Make Automobiles By"
Volkswagen made this recording "to inspire their workers." It features the sounds of an auto assembly line backed with an orchestra.

Not to be confused with:
   • "Music to Light Your Pilot By," from the Heil-Quaker
     Corporation (a heater and air-conditioner manufacturer),
   •"Music to Relax By in Your Barcalounger"
   •"Music to Be Murdered By" (from Alfred Hitchcock)

• "The American Gun: A Celebration In Song"
A late-night TV special, not available in stores. Rage International offered this country music classic with a *free* oiled plastic rifle case. Songs include: "Thank You, Smith & Wesson," "America Was Born with a Gun in Her Hand," "Never Mind the Dog, Beware the Owner," and the ever-popular "Gun Totin' Woman."

KING KONG

King Kong was one of the most influential movies of all time. As both enter-
tainment and a vehicle for special effects, it was unsurpassed. Even its pro-
motion foreshadowed modern advertising techniques. We all know the char-
acter, but few of us know anything about how the film was made.

PART I: ADVENTURE FILMS

The early 1900s were years of discovery in which transcontinental railroads, steamships, and airplanes were opening up
the last unexplored corners of the world.

• In 1909 U.S. explorer Robert Peary became the first person to
reach the North Pole.

• In 1911 Roald Amundsen was the first to step foot on the South
Pole.

• In 1927 Charles Lindbergh made the first nonstop flight across
the Atlantic Ocean from New York to Paris.

Thanks to the new medium of motion-picture film, it was now
possible for explorers to take cameras with them and bring back
footage of an exotic world that audiences at home would otherwise
never see.

The Partners

Merian C. Cooper and Ernest Schoedsack were part of the new
breed of filmmaker/explorer. Cooper, a former fighter pilot, and
Schoedsack, a combat photographer, had met during World War I.
In 1925 they reunited and traveled to Persia (now Iran) to film a
feature-length documentary about the migration of 50,000 Bhaktia-
ri tribesmen over a 12,000-foot mountain range and across the Karun river in search of grazing land for their herds.

Even today, the film—called *Grass*—is considered a classic.
"The crossing of the torrential Karun river," Eric Barnow writes
in *Documentary*, "with loss of life among men, women, children,
goats, sheep, donkeys, and horses, provided one of the most spec-
tacular sequences ever put on film."

Cooper and Schoedsack followed up with *Chang*, a film about
tribal life in the remote jungles of Siam (now Thailand). Like

---

If a female ferret goes into heat and can't find a mate, she'll die.

Grass, it was a critical success that also made money at the box office. One critic called it "the most remarkable film of wild beast life that has reached the screen....Man-eating tigers, furious elephants in thundering stampedes, leopards, bears, monkeys, snakes, and other animals are shown in...one tense thrill after another."

Chang was popular with theater *audiences*, but theater *owners* complained that the movie would have played to larger audiences if it had contained a love story. Cooper took their message to heart.

PART II: GORILLA MY DREAMS

In 1929 Cooper and Schoedsack split up: Cooper stayed in New York to tend to his investments in the fledgling aviation industry; Schoedsack and his wife shot another film in the Dutch East Indies.

While he was stuck behind his desk in New York, Cooper began reading up on the newly discovered Komodo dragons. The world's largest species of lizards, they are found in only one place on earth: the island of Komodo in the South Pacific.

The Island That Time Forgot

The dragons gave Cooper the idea for another film, set on an imaginary island "way west of Sumatra." It would be about modern man's discovery of the island, and an encounter with huge "prehistoric" animals there. As the plot developed in Cooper's imagination, he explained,

> I got to thinking about the possibility of there having been one beast, more powerful than all the others and more intelligent. Then the thought struck me—what would happen to this highest representative of prehistoric animal life in our materialistic, mechanistic civilization? Why not place him at the pinnacle of the tallest building, symbol in steel, stone and glass of modern man's achievement and aspiration, and pit him against modern man?

Evolutionary Thinking

That central character, Cooper decided, should be a gigantic ape. An ape would be better at approximating human emotions than an elephant or dinosaur.

He wrote up a proposal for the film in 1931 and pitched it to

Paramount and Metro-Goldwyn-Mayer. He suggested filming the jungle scenes on location in Africa and on Komodo Island, and casting a real ape in the lead—a character he named "Kong." The studios liked the concept, but the Great Depression was underway, and they refused to risk so much money on a film that relied on animal actors and expensive on-location filming. Cooper put the idea aside.

PART III: THE SPECIAL EFFECTS MAN

In 1932 David Selznik, head of production at RKO studios, hired Cooper as his executive assistant. Like many Hollywood studios in the 1930s, RKO was on the verge of bankruptcy. Cooper's job was to help Selznik review studio projects to see which ones were likely to make money, and which ones should be scrapped.

One project that Cooper looked over was test footage from *Creation*, a movie about shipwrecked sailors who land on an island of prehistoric animals. The dinosaur footage was created by Willis O'Brien, a former cowboy, prize-fighter, and newspaper cartoonist who was now a pioneer in trick photography.

Stop-Motion Animation

As a feature film, *Creation* didn't work because the footage was boring—Cooper called it "just a lot of animals walking around"—and there wasn't much of a plot. But Cooper was still amazed by what he saw: the dinosaurs were lifelike and huge, and the backdrops were incredibly realistic.

It turned out that the creatures were less than eight inches tall. O'Brien had made the footage with miniature models on a tabletop in his garage, using a procedure called "animation in depth" (now known as stop-motion animation). O'Brien filmed the animation frame by frame: he took pictures of his models, then moved them slightly and photographed them again. He repeated this painstaking process again and again, 24 times for each second of animation. When played back at ordinary speed, the models appeared to move by themselves.

O'Brien also knew how to combine the footage with human action sequences, making it appear as if dinosaurs and humans were in the same scenes.

Greek temples were originally painted in bright colors; time has just bleached them white.

Cooper had stumbled onto someone who could actually make his *Kong* movie work. With animation in depth, he wouldn't need a real ape, and he wouldn't need to film on location—he could film all of the ape sequences right on O'Brien's workbench for a fraction of the original cost.

PART IV: GOING APE

RKO agreed to pay for a test reel of animation footage showing Kong in action, and O'Brien's assistant, Marcel Delgado, was assigned the task of designing the ape model that would make or break the film. Cooper told him to make it look somewhat human, so audiences would feel sorry for it at the end of the movie.

The first model was apelike, but still too human; so was the second model. So Cooper changed his instructions. "I want Kong to be the fiercest, most brutal, monstrous damned thing that has ever been seen." O'Brien argued that if the ape was too apelike, no one would sympathize with it, but Cooper disagreed. "I'll have women crying over him before I'm through, and the more brutal he is, the more they'll cry at the end."

What a Doll!

The test Kong was 18 inches high and covered with sponge rubber muscles and trimmed rabbit fur. "I never was satisfied with the fur," Delgado later recalled, "because I knew it would show the fingerprints of the animators." (He was right—even in the finished film, Kong's fur "bristles" as if it is being blown by the wind; an unintentional effect caused by the animators' fingers disturbing the fur as they move the model between shots.)

RKO executives watched the footage...and immediately commissioned the film. Cooper called Shoedsack in, and the two became partners again.

PART V: WRITE ON

Finding someone to write a satisfactory script proved as hard as building a good ape: The first writer died of pneumonia before he could start work, and the second couldn't figure out how to make some of the key parts of the plot seem believable, such as how

---

Q: Whose song is sweeter, the male or female canary? A: Male. Female canaries can't sing.

Kong gets to New York.

Finally Schoedsack turned to a real adventurer to write the story: his wife Ruth Rose. She had never written a screenplay in her life, but her travel experiences as an explorer made her perfect for the job. "Put *us* in it," Cooper and Schoedsack told her. "Give it the spirit of a real Cooper-Schoedsack expedition."

The Story
The finished version of the story did just that: it featured a crazed documentary filmmaker named Carl Denham (Robert Armstrong) who learns of Skull Island from a Norwegian skipper and plans an expedition to the island to make the ultimate travel-adventure film. With him on the voyage is Ann Darrow (Fay Wray), a beautiful but desperate young woman he rescues from the mean streets of New York City only hours before the ship sets sail. Hired to add "love interest" to the documentary, Darrow delivers more than expected when she capture's Kong's heart.

PART VI: SPECIAL EFFECTS
Like the *Star Wars* films that would follow four decades later, *King Kong* was a milestone in special effects filmmaking. Willis O'Brian and his crew performed camera miracles the like of which no one had ever seen.

Making the Monkey
All of the ape sequences were made using models. There isn't a single man-in-an-ape-suit scene in the entire film (although at least two actors would later claim to have been the "man inside Kong").

O'Brien and Delgado made the ape footage in total secrecy, with only Cooper, Schoedsack, and top RKO executives allowed to monitor their progress. The secret was kept for several years after the film was released, and few people had any idea at all how the ape scenes had been created. One rumor had it that RKO had built a full-sized, walking robot ape that was controlled by several men who rode inside. The reality was much different.

Kong was billed as a 50-foot-tall ape. Actually, he was portrayed as much smaller than that in the film.

• The ape model used in the jungle scenes was only 18 inches tall; the one used in the Empire State Building scenes was 24 inches tall.

• Since the modelers were working on a scale of 1 inch as equaling 1 foot, that means Kong was 18 feet tall in the jungle and 24 feet tall in the city.

Why the difference in sizes? Cooper wanted Kong large enough to be terrifying, yet small enough to take a believable love interest in tiny Fay Wray. Eighteen feet was initially set as the standard... but when work began on the Empire State Building scenes, he and Schoedsack saw that Kong looked too small against the skyscrapers. "We realized we'd never get much drama out of a fly crawling up the tallest building in the world," Schoedsack said later.

You Big Ape

There were no full-scale models of the complete ape, although the studio did make full-size models of the body parts that had contact with human actors. A huge hand suspended from a crane was made to lift Fay Wray aloft; and a huge foot and lower leg were made for the scenes in which Kong stomps natives to death.

The most complicated piece of all was the full-sized head-and-shoulders model, which was made of a wood and metal skeleton covered with rubber and carefully trimmed bearskins. The plaster and balsa wood eyeballs were as large as bowling balls, and the mouth, complete with a full set of huge balsa wood teeth, opened wide enough for Kong to chew on the natives.

The head-and-shoulders unit was large enough to hold the three men who controlled Kong's facial expressions using levers and compressed-air hoses connected to the movable mouth, lips, nostrils, eyes, eyelids, and eyebrows.

PART VII: THE VOICE

Sound effects were also a challenge: in some scenes Kong roared for as long 30 seconds, and though RKO had a sound effects library with more than 500,000 different animal sounds, even the longest elephant roars only lasted 8 seconds.

Americans throw away an estimated 27% of their food every year.

RKO sound man Murray Spivack went to the zoo at feeding time to get his own sounds. He got Kong's sounds from the lion and tiger cages, as he later recounted:

> The handlers would make gestures like they were going to take the food away from them and we got some pretty wild sounds. Then I took some of these roars back to the studio and put them together and played them backward. I slowed them down, sort of like playing a 78-rpm record at 33, until the tone was lowered one octave, then I re-recorded it. From this we took the peaks and pieced them together. We had to put several of these together in turn to sustain the sound until Kong shut his mouth, because Kong's roars were many times longer than those of any living animal.

For the affectionate sounds Kong makes when he's with Ann Darrow, Spivack grunted into a megaphone, then slowed the recording down until he thought it sounded like a big ape.

PART VIII: THE SCENERY

Their revolutionary approach to special effects included innovation with scenery. The "location" sequences were filmed on miniature sets that used a combination of special effects:

• The background details were painted on glass.

• Objects in the foreground, such as trees, rocks, and logs, were modeled in miniature using clay, wire, and even toilet paper.

• Sometimes the human footage (a person crouching in a cave, for example) was shot in advance. Then, in a process known as "miniature projection," a tiny screen would be set up in the tabletop jungle set where the ape animation was filmed. The human footage was then projected onto the screen frame by frame, making it seem as if the cave was part of the jungle. In the finished film, Kong appears to be towering over someone hiding in a cave.

PART IX: KONG ON THE RAMPAGE!

Cooper and Schoedsack wanted a powerful, one-word title for their film, so they named it *Kong*. But David Selznick was afraid that *Kong* would be mistaken for just another travel film (like *Grass* or *Chang*). So just before the film was released, he changed the name to *King Kong*.

America's favorite vegetable: broccoli. America's least favorite veggie: Brussels sprouts.

When work on the film began, everyone in Hollywood thought it would fail. But when RKO showed the finished film to theater owners, the response was so enthusiastic that the studio launched the biggest promotional campaign in its history. "THE PICTURE DESTINED TO STARTLE THE WORLD!," advertisements blared in national magazines.

The promotions paid off—in New York City, *King Kong* was booked at both the Radio City Music Hall and the New Roxy, the city's two largest theaters, with a total of more than 10,000 seats.

Even that wasn't enough. It made no difference that the Depression was on—as Goldner and Turner write in *The Making of King Kong*, "in the first four days of its run, *King Kong* set a new all-time world attendance record for any indoor attraction, bringing in $89,931....To accommodate the crowds it was necessary to run ten shows daily."

The movie made so much money that it lifted RKO out of debt for the first time in its history.

PART X: CENSORING KONG

By the time *King Kong* was re-released in 1938, the Hays Office and its infamous Production Code controlled Hollywood, and the film had to be re-edited before it could be shown in theaters. Censors removed all of the scenes of Kong stomping the natives to death, chewing them in his teeth, and dropping a woman (played by 19-year-old Sandra Shaw, Gary Cooper's future wife) off the side of a hotel building after he mistakes her for Fay Wray.

The censors also removed a scene of Kong "accidentally" removing Fay Wray's clothing. All of the remaining violent scenes were darkened, so that it would be harder to see what Kong was doing. (Some of the cut scenes were rediscovered decades later and reinserted into the film.)

PART XI: KONG FACTS

• Many of the sets used in *King Kong* were hand-me-downs from earlier films, and were in turn used in later films when *Kong* was finished. The Great Wall on Skull Island was made with remnants from the 1927 Cecil B. DeMille epic *The King of Kings* (after *King Kong* it was used in a film called *She*, and *The Return of Chandu*, a

Bela Lugosi serial. It was ultimately set on fire during the burning-of-Atlanta scene in *Gone With the Wind)*.

• Fay Wray provided all of her own screams in *King Kong*, spending an entire day at the sound studio screaming herself hoarse.

• The finished film was 13 reels long. A superstitious man, Cooper refused to let it go out at that length. He wanted it longer. So O'Brien went back to work...and created one of the most elaborate sequences in the entire film, one in which Kong attacks an elevated train just before he climbs the Empire State Building. (The film was later edited down to 11 reels, keeping the train scene but losing many jungle scenes using prehistoric creatures that had been recycled from *Creation*, O'Brien's unfinished dinosaur film.)

PART XII : KONG-SPLOITATION

Like every other classic Hollywood movie monster, King Kong was the inspiration for dozens of sequels and imitations—most of them terrible—over the next 60 years. Here are some of the real stinkers:

Son of Kong (1933)

Carl Denham returns to Skull Island and finds Kong's albino son trapped in quicksand. He rescues the young ape, and it becomes his protector for the rest of the film. The film did modestly well in the United States, but was much more successful overseas...particularly in Malaysia, the area where King King and son were supposedly captured.

The Ape Man (1943)

When horror films went out of vogue in 1935, Bela Lugosi found himself out of work. When they came back in 1939, Lugosi was so desperate that he took any job that came along...including this one. In the film, he plays a mad scientist-turned-ape as a result of "attempting to harness the physical power of apes for man." One critic called it "a prime example of the kind of film that destroyed Lugosi's career."

White Pongo (1945)

A.k.a. *Blonde Gorilla* (but not to be confused with *White Gorilla*, which was filmed two years later using the same costume). An undercover cop joins explorers in the search for a white gorilla that just may be the missing link. The *Video Movie Guide* says: "Reverently referred to by fans of genre films as the worst of all crazed-gorilla-missing-link jungle movies."

Nabonga (1944)

Julie London plays a grown woman who's lived in the jungle since surviving a plane crash as a young girl. The kind ape Nabonga protects her from the other jungle beasts. Later, Nabonga teams up with Buster Crabbe to protect London from evil treasure seekers.

Konga (1961)

Originally titled *I Was a Teenage King Kong*. A mad professor invents a growth serum that turns Venus flytraps into people-eating monster plants...and injects some of the stuff into his pet chimp, Konga, turning him into a giant killer ape.

King Kong vs. Godzilla (1963)

Two of the world's all-time great monsters meet for what was billed as "the cosmic clash of all time." It began as *King Kong vs. Frankenstein*, a film proposed by Willis O'Brien. He couldn't get financing in the U.S., so he took it to Japan...where they turned it into a Godzilla flick. The plot: Godzilla chows down on a nuclear submarine and heads for Japan. Meanwhile, on a nearby island, an ape eats some weird berries and grows into King Kong. The two monsters fight on Mt. Fuji, and the ape wins.

King Kong Escapes (1968)

Another Japanese Kong film. This time King Kong battles Gorosaurus, "a relative of Godzilla," and Mechanikong, a robot replica of himself.

A•P•E (1976)

A low-budget Korean *Kong* rip-off, complete with rubber snakes, a big naugahyde gorilla paw for the blonde to sit in, "a stuntman in a moth-eaten monkey suit," and ads that read, "Not to be confused with *King Kong*." Film critic John Stanley calls it "not very O•R•I•G•I•N•A•L," but there is one redeeming moment: when "A•P•E" is being chased by soldiers, he gives them the finger.

LOOKING FORWARD, LOOKING BACK

*This article is actually a speech given by Apple Computer guru Guy Kawa-
saki to a graduating high school class in Palo Alto, California. It was reprinted in a local magazine in Ashland...and Mrs.Uncle John liked it so much
that she cut it out and put it on the refrigerator. For a month, everyone who
saw it commented on how much they enjoyed it...And finally, Uncle John
realized that if even grown-ups liked it that much, it must be worth
reprinting.Guy kindly gave us his permission—and here it is.*

Speaking to you today marks a milestone in my life. I am 40
years old. Twenty-two years ago, when I was in your seat, I
never, ever thought I would be 40 years old.

The implications of being your speaker frightens me. For one
thing, when a 40-year-old geezer spoke at my baccalaureate ceremony, he was about the last person I'd believe. I have no intention
of giving you the boring speech that you are dreading. This speech
will be short, sweet, and not boring.

I am going to talk about hindsights today. Hindsights that I've
accumulated in the 20 years from where you are to where I am.
Don't blindly believe me. Don't take what I say as "truth." Just listen. Perhaps my experience can help you out a tiny bit. I will
present them ala David Letterman. Yes, 40-year-old people can still
stay up past eleven.

RULE #10: Live off your parents as long as possible.
When I spoke at this ceremony two years ago, this was the most
popular hindsight—except from the point of view of the parents.
Thus, I knew I was on the right track.

I was a diligent Oriental in high school and college. I took college-level classes and earned college-level credits. I rushed through
college in three and a half years. I never traveled or took time off
because I thought it wouldn't prepare me for work and it would delay my graduation.

Frankly, I blew it.

You are going to work the rest of your lives, so don't be in a rush

---

to start. Stretch out your college education. Now is the time to suck life into your lungs—before you have a mortgage, kids, and car payments.

Take whole semesters off to travel overseas. Take jobs and internships that pay less money or no money. Investigate your passions on your parent's nickel. Or dime. Or quarter. Or dollar. Your goal should be to extend college to at least six years.

Delay, as long as possible, the inevitable entry into the workplace and a lifetime of servitude to bozos who know less than you do, but who make more money. Also, you shouldn't deprive your parents of the pleasure of supporting you.

RULE #9: Pursue joy, not happiness.

This is probably the hardest lesson of all to learn. It probably seems to you that the goal in life is to be "happy." Oh, you maybe have to sacrifice and study and work hard, but, by and large, happiness should be predictable.

Nice house. Nice car. Nice material things.

Take my word for it, happiness, is temporary and fleeting. Joy, by contrast, is unpredictable. It comes from pursuing interests and passions that do not obviously result in happiness.

Pursuing joy, not happiness will translate into one thing over the next few years for you: Study what you love. This may also not be popular with parents. When I went to college, I was "marketing driven." It's also an Oriental thing.

I looked at what fields had the greatest job opportunities and prepared myself for them. This was brain-dead. There are so many ways to make a living in the world, it doesn't matter that you've taken all the "right" courses. I don't think one person on the original Macintosh team had a classic computer science degree.

You parents have a responsibility in this area. Don't force your kids to follow in your footsteps or to live your dreams. My father was a senator in Hawaii. His dream was to be a lawyer, but he only had a high school education. He wanted me to be a lawyer.

For him, I went to law school. For me, I quit after two weeks. I view this as a terrific validation of my inherent intelligence.

RULE #8: Challenge the known and embrace the unknown.
One of the biggest mistakes you can make in life is to accept the known and resist the unknown. You should, in fact, do exactly the opposite: challenge the known and embrace the unknown.

Let me tell you a short story about ice. In the late 1800s, there was a thriving ice industry in the Northeast. Companies would cut blocks of ice from frozen lakes and ponds and sell them around the world. The largest single shipment was 200 tons that was shipped to India. One hundred tons got there unmelted, but this was enough to make a profit.

These ice harvesters, however, were put out of business by companies that invented mechanical ice makers. It was no longer necessary to cut and ship ice because companies could make it in any city during any season.

These ice makers, however, were put out of business by refrigerator companies. If it was convenient to make ice at a manufacturing plant, imagine how much better it was to make ice and create cold storage in everyone's home.

You would think that the ice harvesters would see the advantages of ice making and adopt this technology. However, all they could think about was the known: better saws, better storage, better transportation.

Then you would think that the ice makers would see the advantages of refrigerators and adopt this technology. The truth is that the ice harvesters couldn't embrace the unknown and jump their curve to the next curve.

Challenge the known and embrace the unknown, or you'll be like the ice harvesters and ice makers.

RULE #7: Learn to speak a foreign language, play a musical instrument, and play non-contact sports.
Learn a foreign language. I studied Latin in high school because I thought it would help me increase my vocabulary. It did, but trust me when I tell you it's very difficult to have a conversation in Latin today other than at the Vatican. And despite all my efforts, the Pope has yet to call for my advice.

Learn to play a musical instrument. My only connection to music today is that I was named after Guy Lombardo. Trust me: It's better than being named after Guy's brother, Carmen. Playing a musical instrument could be with me now and stay with me forever. Instead, I have to buy CDs at Tower.

I played football. I loved football. Football is macho. I was a middle linebacker—arguably, one of the most macho position in a macho game. But you should also learn to play a non-contact sport like basketball or tennis. That is, a sport you can play when you're over the hill.

It will be as difficult when you're 40 to get twenty-two guys together in a stadium to play football as it is to have a conversation in Latin, but all the people who wore cute, white tennis outfits can still play tennis. And all the macho football players are sitting around watching television and drinking beer.

RULE #6: Continue to learn.

Learning is a process, not an event. I thought learning would be over when I got my degree. It's not true. You should never stop learning. Indeed, it gets easier to learn once you're out of school because it's easier to see the relevance of why you need to learn.

You're learning in a structured, dedicated environment right now. On your parents' nickel. But don't confuse school and learning. You can go to school and not learn a thing. You can also learn a tremendous amount without school.

RULES #5: Learn to like yourself or change yourself until you can like yourself.

I know a 40-year-old woman who was a drug addict. She is a mother of three. She traced the start of her drug addiction to smoking dope in high school.

I'm not going to lecture you about not taking drugs. Hey, I smoked dope in high school. Unlike Bill Clinton, I inhaled. Also unlike Bill Clinton, I exhaled.

This woman told me that she started taking drugs because she hated herself when she was sober. She did not like drugs so much as much as she hated herself. Drugs were not the cause, though she thought they were the solution.

She turned her life around only after she realized that she was in

---

The average female mannequin is 8 feet tall. The average woman is 5 feet, 4 inches tall.

a downward spiral. Fix your problem. Fix your life. Then you won't need to take drugs. Drugs are neither the solution nor the problem.

Frankly, smoking, drugs, alcohol—and using an IBM PC—are signs of stupidity. End of discussion.

RULE #4: Don't get married too soon.

I got married when I was 32. That's about the right age. Until you're about that age, you may not know who you are. You also may not know who you're marrying.

I don't know one person who got married too late. I know many people who got married too young. If you do decide to get married, just keep in mind that you need to accept the person for what he or she is right now.

RULE #3: Play to win and win to play.

Playing to win is one of the finest things you can do. It enables you to fulfill your potential. It enables you to improve the world and, conveniently, develop high expectations for everyone else too.

And what if you lose? Just make sure you lose while trying something grand. Avinash Dixit, an economics professor at Princeton, and Barry Nalebuff, an economics and management professor at the Yale School of Organization and Management, say it this way: "If you are going to fail, you might as well fail at a difficult task. Failure causes others to downgrade their expectations of you in the future. The seriousness of this problem depends on what you attempt."

In its purest form, winning becomes a means, not an end, to improve yourself and your competition.

Winning is also a means to play again. The unexamined life may not be worth living, but the unlived life is not worth examining. The rewards of winning—money, power, satisfaction, and self-confidence—should not be squandered.

Thus, in addition to playing to win, you have a second, more important obligation: To compete again to the depth and breadth and height that your soul can reach. Ultimately, your greatest competition is yourself.

RULE #2: Obey the absolutes.

Playing to win, however, does not mean playing dirty. As you grow older and older, you will find that things change from absolute to relative. When you were very young, it was absolutely wrong to lie, cheat, or steal. As you get older, and particularly when you enter the workforce, you will be tempted by the "system" to think in relative terms. "I made more money." "I have a nicer car." "I went on a better vacation."

Worse, "I didn't cheat as much on my taxes as my partner." "I just have a few drinks. I don't take cocaine." "I don't pad my expense reports as much as others."

This is completely wrong. Preserve and obey the absolutes as much as you can. If you never lie, cheat, or steal, you will never have to remember who you lied to, how you cheated, and what you stole.

There absolutely are absolute rights and wrongs.

RULE #1: Enjoy your family and friends before they are gone.

This is the most important hindsight. It doesn't need much explanation. I'll just repeat it: Enjoy your family and friends before they are gone. Nothing—not money, power, or fame—can replace your family and friends or bring them back once they are gone. Our greatest joy has been our baby, and I predict that children will bring you the greatest joy in your lives—especially if they graduate from college in four years.

And now, I'm going to give you one extra hindsight because I've probably cost your parents thousands of dollars today. It's something that I hate to admit, too.

By and large, the older you get, the more you're going to realize that your parents were right. More and more—until finally, you become your parents. I know you're all saying, "Yeah, right." Mark my words.

Remember these ten things: If just one of them helps just one of you, this speech will have been a success.

THE ANATOMY
OF LAUGHTER

*And you thought reading the funny stuff we put in the Bathroom Reader
was just a way to kill time. Well, it's not—while you're giggling at
Uncle John's prose, you're actually getting some exercise and
improving your health. Don't believe it? Here's proof.*

HARDEE HAR HAR

Even after centuries of scientific research, no one knows for sure why human beings (plus a few other primates, including chimpanzees, apes, and orangutans) laugh.

People have ideas, though.

> *"A 2-pound turkey and a 50-pound cranberry—
> that's Thanksgiving dinner at Three Mile Island."*
> **—Johnny Carson**

• Charles Darwin speculated that laughter, which begins in infants as young as three months old, served as an evolutionary "reward" to parental care-giving. Laughter in infants sounded and felt so different from crying, he believed, that even prehistoric parents must have interpreted it as a sign of well-being, kind of like the purring of a kitten. The parents enjoyed the laughter, which encouraged them to continue caring for the child.

• Sigmund Freud believed (of course) that laughter was closely intertwined with lust.

> *"[On old age:] First you forget names, then you
> forget faces, then you forget to pull your zipper up,
> then you forget to pull your zipper down."*
> **—Leo Rosenberg**

• Contemporary theorists believe that laughter evolved as a means for primates to diffuse tension and reduce the likelihood of confrontation when meeting and interacting with others.

FUNNY BUSINESS

Even if scientists still don't know why we laugh, they've learned a lot about it. For example:

• You use 15 different muscles in your face to laugh.

• The *sound* of laughter is created when you inhale deeply and then release the air while your diaphragm moves in a series of short, spasmodic contractions.

• The typical laugh is made up of pulses of sound that are about 1/15th of a second long and 1/5th of a second apart. When tape recorded and played backward, laughing sounds virtually the same as it does when it's played forward.

• Hearty laughter produces physical effects similar to those resulting from moderate exercise: The pulse of the person laughing can double from 60 to 120, and the systolic blood pressure can increase from 120 to 200—about the same thing that happens when you exercise on a stationary bicycle. Stanford University researcher Dr. William Fry even refers to laughter as "a kind of stationary jogging."

> *"I saw a TV commercial that said, 'Kiss your hemorrhoids goodbye.' Not even if I could."*
> —John Mendoza

• When people stop laughing, just as when they stop exercising, the muscles in the body are more relaxed than they were before the laughing started. Heartbeat and blood pressure are also lower. This leads scientists to believe that laughing is a means of releasing stress and pent-up energy.

THE BEST MEDICINE

One of the most interesting things researchers have learned is the powerful healing effect of laughter.

Well, actually they're *re*-learning it after centuries of neglect: In the Middle Ages, doctors "treated" their patients by telling them jokes, but modern medicine discounted the curative properties of laughing.

That began to change in 1979, when editor Norman Cousins wrote *Anatomy of an Illness,* in which he credited watching humorous videos with helping him reduce pain and recover from ankylosing spondylitis, a life-threatening degenerative spinal disease. The

---

book inspired researchers to look into whether laughter really did aid in healing and recovery from illness.

THE LAUGH TEST

In 1995, two researchers at the Loma Linda University School of Medicine had 10 medical students watch a 60-minute videotape of Gallagher, a stand-up comedian famous for smashing watermelons and other objects with a sledgehammer.

The researchers found that after watching the video, there was a measurable decrease in stress hormones, including epinephrine and dopamine, in the students' blood, plus an increase in endorphins, the body's natural painkillers. But the most changes were found in the students' immune systems. These included:

√ Increased levels of gamma interferon, a hormone that "switches on" the immune system, and helps fight viruses and regulates cell growth

√ Increased numbers of "helper T-cells," which help the body coordinate the immune system's response to illness

√ More "Compliment 3," a substance that helps antibodies destroy infected and damaged cells

√ An increase in the number and activity of "natural killer (NK) cells," which the body uses to attack foreign cells, cancer cells, and cells infected by virus

Some of the levels even began to change *before* the students watched the video—just from the expectation that they were about to laugh. "Say you're going to your favorite restaurant," Dr. Berk explains. "You can visualize the food; you can almost taste it. You're already experiencing the physiology of enjoying it. Your immune system [also] remembers....By using humor to combat stress, you can condition yourself to strengthen your immune system."

> *"Everything is drive-through. In California they*
> *even have a burial service called Jump-in-the-Box."*
> —**Wil Shriner**

GETTING THE JOKE

In 1995 Peter Derks, a psychologist at the College of William and Mary, tested how the brain stimulates laughter. He hooked re-

---

In 1915, the average income for an American family was $687 a year.

search subjects up to an EEG (electroencephalogram) topographical brain mapper, then told the subjects jokes. His findings:

- At the start of the joke, the brain processes the information in the left lobe, the analytical side that processes language.

- As the joke progresses, the primary activity shifts to the frontal lobe, where emotions are processed.

- Just before the punch line is delivered, the right side of the brain, which controls the perception of spatial relationships, begins coordinating its activity with the left side of the brain. This is the point where the brain is trying to "get" the joke.

- "What humor is doing," Derks says, "is getting the brain into unison so it can be more efficient in trying to find explanations for—in this case—the punch line. Laughter may also have long-term therapeutic effects." Derks suspects that joke-telling may even help stroke victims and the elderly recover lost brain function.

"I date this girl for two years—and then the nagging starts: 'I wanna know your name.'"
—**Mike Binder**

THE LAUGHTER GENDER GAP

Robert Provine, a psychology professor at the University of Maryland, has studied the laughter that takes place in conversations between men and women. (How? He and his assistants eavesdropped on more than 1,200 conversations that took place on the street and in offices, shopping malls, cocktail parties, and other public places around Baltimore.)

" My father's a strange guy. He's allergic to cotton. He has pills he can take, but he can't get them out of the bottle."
—**Brian Kiley**

His findings:

- "We found that far and away the most laughter takes place when males were talking and females were listening, and the least took place when females were talking and males were listening. Male-male and female-female conversations fell somewhere in between." Provine believes that this is because

---

Q: What is the most common disease in the world?   A: Tooth decay.

females are better listeners and are more encouraging in conversation.

• Men are more likely to make jokes than women are, and women are more likely to laugh at them than men are. These differences, Provine says, are already apparent when children begin telling their first jokes, usually around the age of six.

"I feel good. I lost 20 pounds on that deal a meal plan. Not that Richard Simmons plan. This is where you play cards, lose, and don't have enough cash to eat."
—John McDowell

ANIMAL LAUGHTER

Chimpanzees, apes, orangutans and a few other primates laugh, but no other animals do. Chimps laugh at the relief of tension, when tickling each other, and when playing chasing games. Their laugh sounds like rapid panting, but unlike humans, they are unable to regulate or control the air as they breathe out, which means they can't change the way it sounds. This lack of ability to control airflow is same thing that deprives them of speech.

Just because primates can't talk, it doesn't mean they can't share jokes. Chimps and gorillas that have learned sign language have been known to sign one another for laughs. Sometimes they give incorrect signs in "conversation," and then laugh audibly with each other; other times they urinate on humans and then sign "funny."

SILKWOOD

Karen Silkwood has been the subject of numerous articles, books, and a major movie, but few people know what really happened to her. Here, from the book "It's a Conspiracy," are the details of her controversial life and mysterious death.

On November 13, 1974, Karen Silkwood left a group of co-workers at the Hub Cafe in Crescent, Oklahoma, headed to a crucial meeting with a *New York Times* reporter. On her way out, she told them that she had proof that the plutonium plant where they all worked—Kerr-McGee's Cimarron River plant—had repeatedly covered up safety violations and falsified records. But she never made it to her meeting.

A little more than 7 miles outside of Crescent, Silkwood's car went flying off the straight highway and crashed into a concrete culvert, silencing Silkwood forever. Official statements claim that Silkwood fell asleep at the wheel, but evidence suggests otherwise.

KAREN SILKWOOD VS. KERR-McGEE

• Soon after she started working for Kerr-McGee in 1972, Karen Silkwood joined the local branch of the Oil, Chemical, and Atomic Workers Union (OCAW). In the spring of 1974, she was elected to the governing committee and began to voice her concerns about the company's safety record. She believed Kerr-McGee was sloppy in its handling of radioactive materials and indifferent to the health of its workers.

• She became even more concerned when several coworkers were directly exposed to plutonium—perhaps the most toxic substance on earth. And a production speedup that required employees to work 12-hour shifts increased the danger.

• On August 1, 1974, Silkwood herself was contaminated when airborne plutonium entered the room in which she was working. She began worrying about her own health as well as the effects of company safety lapses on her coworkers. She began carrying a notebook with her constantly to record the infractions she observed.

• On September 26, she and two other local union officials flew to Washington D.C., to meet with national OCAW leaders. They

---

alleged serious health and safety violations and charged that plant documents had been falsified to conceal defective fuel rods. National union leaders were so alarmed that they immediately took Silkwood to testify before the Atomic Energy Commission.

• This charge had "very deep and very grave [consequences]," according to OCAW official Steve Wodka—"not only for the people in the plant, but for the entire atomic industry and the welfare of the country. If badly made pins were placed into the reactor without deficiencies being caught, there could be an incident exposing thousands of people to radiation."

• After presenting her charges in Washington, Silkwood returned to Kerr-McGee and continued to document the safety violations she observed on the job.

CONTAMINATION

• On Tuesday, November 5, Silkwood was in the metallography lab, where she was handling plutonium in a safety case called a "glovebox." When she finished her work, monitoring devices revealed that she had been contaminated again—this time from her hands all the way up to her scalp.

• The contamination on her coveralls was up to forty times the company limit. Any exposure above the company limit required emergency decontamination—scrubbing repeatedly with a mixture of Tide and Clorox, which left Silkwood's skin raw and stinging. Within a few days, she noted, "It hurt to cry because the salt in my tears burned my skin."

• Health officials required Silkwood to supply urine and fecal samples so they could monitor the radioactivity level in her system. Samples taken over the next few days showed new, extremely high levels of radiation. Baffled by the source of the contamination, officials eventually checked her apartment. They found that it was so contaminated that most of its contents had to be removed and buried. While officials gutted her apartment, Kerr-McGee lawyers interrogated Silkwood, insinuating that she had smuggled plutonium out of the plant.

• Her health began to deteriorate. She began to lose weight and had trouble sleeping. A series of doctors prescribed sedatives to re -

lieve her anxiety. Now, terrified by the trauma of decontamination scrubbings, the burial of her belongings, and the high levels of contamination in her body, Karen Silkwood believed she was dying.

• She spent November 10 to 12 in Los Alamos, New Mexico, undergoing tests to assess how much radiation she had absorbed. Doctors determined that she was in no imminent danger—the amount of plutonium that her body had absorbed was below the maximum absorption that "cannot be exceeded without risk." But no one could assure her that the radioactivity would not lead to cancer or other health problems in the future.

• Then, on November 13, six days after the contamination was discovered in her house, Silkwood drove to meet a reporter from *The New York Times*, with documents she believed would prove Kerr-McGee's criminal neglect. En route, her car veered across the road and down the left-hand shoulder, and slammed head on into a concrete culvert, killing her.

WAS IT A CONSPIRACY? #1

Was her car wreck an accident—or murder?

• The official explanation of Karen Silkwood's death is that she brought it on herself: she took too many tranquilizers and dozed off while driving. "An autopsy revealed that her blood, stomach, and liver contained methaqualone, a sleep-inducing drug, and it was surmised that she fell asleep at the wheel," according to the *Encyclopedia of American Scandal*. "Justice Department and FBI investigations found no wrongdoing."

• This was possible. To cope with insomnia, changes in her work shift, and growing tension at the plant, Silkwood had gotten a prescription for sleeping pills. Her boyfriend, Drew Stephens, says that she had taken them for tranquilization, not for sleep—especially during the last week of her life. (Ms.)

• But colleagues who had been with Silkwood shortly before the accident said she appeared alert, spoke clearly, and acted normally. "It would never have crossed my mind that she might not be capable of driving a car safely," one coworker said. What's more, the road her car went off was perfectly straight, and Karen was an excellent driver—she'd won several road rallies in previous years.

• When Silkwood left her colleagues to meet with the reporter from *The New York Times*, she was carrying a brown manila folder and a large notebook. One coworker who had been at the Hub Cafe recounted some of Silkwood's last words: "She then said there was one thing she was glad about, that she had all the proof concerning the health and safety conditions in the plant, and concerning falsification. As she said this, she clenched her hand more firmly on the folder and the notebook she was holding." (*Ms.*)

Suspicious Facts

• Silkwood's manila folder and notebook disappeared after the accident. "A trooper at the scene reported stuffing the papers back into the car," said one reporter, "but they were gone when it was checked a day later."

• The road was straight. If, as the police suggested, she fell asleep, her car would probably have drifted to the right because of the road's centerline, or crown, and the pull of gravity. But instead it crossed the road and went off the left shoulder.

• Experts disagreed about the meaning of the tire marks at the accident. Police said her car left two sets of rolling tracks with no evidence of having attempted to brake or control the car. An investigator hired by the OCAW, however, thought the car had been out of control, as if it had been hit or pushed by another car.

• Experts also disagreed about a scratch along the side of the car. Police said it was made when the car was towed away from the culvert. But the OCAW analyst said microscopic exams showed metal and rubber fragments in the scratch, as if another car had bumped Silkwood's.

• Several years after the accident, family members filed a lawsuit against Kerr-McGee, claiming that the company intentionally contaminated Silkwood. In 1979, an Oklahoma jury ordered Kerr-McGee to pay Silkwood's estate more than $10.5 million in damages. The decision against Kerr-McGee was later overturned on appeal because the "award was ruled to have infringed on the U.S. government's exclusivity in regulating safety in the nuclear power industry" (*Encyclopedia of American Scandal*). Four years later, however, the U.S. Supreme Court ruled that "courts could impose punitive damages on the nuclear-power industry for violations of safety." Kerr-McGee eventually settled the suit for $1.3 million. Under the out-of-court agreement, the company admitted no guilt for the automobile accident.

WAS IT A CONSPIRACY? #2

If Silkwood was murdered, could agents of the U.S. government be responsible?

Suspicious Facts

• At least forty pounds of plutonium—the active ingredient in nuclear warheads—were missing from the Kerr-McGee plant. Silkwood was among the first to suggest this, and company officials later confirmed it.

• According to *The Progressive*, the Justice Department, "ignoring evidence that suggested the possibility of foul play at the accident site...shut down its investigation of Karen Silkwood's death early in 1974 with a four-and-a-half-page summary report dismissing the possibility of murder or any relationship of missing plutonium to the case."

• According to *Rebel* magazine, "Every attempt to get the government to release related intelligence files has been replied to by the Justice Department with claims of 'national security' and 'state secrets.' The FBI even tried to get a permanent gag order against Silkwood attorneys forbidding public disclosure of what they were finding."

• Attorneys working on the lawsuit brought by Silkwood's estate alleged that there was a relationship—and perhaps a conspiracy—between Kerr-McGee and the FBI. These attorneys said that Silkwood was being spied on and that transcripts of her private conversations were later passed from a Kerr-McGee official to both an FBI agent and an author (alleged to have CIA and Navy-intelligence links) who later wrote a disparaging book about Silkwood's activities.

• Attempting to clarify the relationship between Kerr-McGee, the FBI, and the author, Silkwood attorney Danny Sheehan repeatedly pressed the author in court to tell who had commissioned her book. The FBI objected 30 times, citing "national security." Finally, after conferring with FBI officials, the judge told Sheehan, "The information you seek is sinister and secret, and should never see the light of day." (*The Progressive*)

• The Oklahoma City Police Department (OCPD) also appears to have been involved in Kerr-McGee spying operations. "Silkwood estate investigators insist they found [OCPD] Intelligence Unit officers on Kerr-McGee's security payroll during the time Silkwood was being spied on," according to *Rebel* magazine. Moreover, "an FBI source claims OCPD's Intelligence Unit had been infiltrated by either CIA or [National Security Agency] undercover agents, and OCPD-gleaned FBI surveillance reports on Silkwood were transmitted via a NSA code classified top-secret."

• Sheehan, still trying to uncover possible CIA links to the case, pressed on until finally, he says, he was warned by a former Carter White House source to call his investigator off: "You're in way over your head. You don't have any idea how sensitive this issue is. You'd better contact your man…and tell him to stand down.… They'll kill him. And I promise you, no one will do anything about it." (*Rebel*)

• As for the missing plutonium, the English weekly *The New Statesman* suggests that "there is evidence that the material was sold on the black market to South Africa, Israel or Iran under the Shah. In our opinion, [Silkwood] had that kind of evidence—that's why she was killed."

RECOMMENDED READING
• "The Real Enemies of Karen Silkwood," by Anthony Kimmery (*Rebel* magazine, Feb. 20, 1984)
• "Karen Silkwood: The Deepening Mystery," by Jeffrey Stein (*The Progressive* magazine, Jan. 1981)
• "The Case of Karen Silkwood," by B. J. Phillips (Ms. magazine)Washington, D.C., to meet with national OCAW leaders.

*　　*　　*

TALES OF THE CIA
As the Cold War ended, the CIA decided it needed to project "a greater openness and sense of public responsibility." So it commissioned a task force. On December 20, 1991, the committee submitted a 15-page "Report on Greater Openness." It is stamped SECRET, and agency officials refuse to disclose any of it's contents.

SEX IN *ALADDIN*: ANATOMY OF A RUMOR

This article by Lisa Bannon, which appeared in the Wall Street Journal *on October 24, 1995, tells the story of how a significant rumor was born. It's one of the best investigative pieces we've ever seen on the spread of an urban legend.*

A STARTLING DISCOVERY

Anna Runge, a mother of eight, was so enamored with Walt Disney Co. that she owned stacks of its animated home videos, a *Beauty and the Beast* blanket, and a Disney diaper bag. "Disney was almost a member of the family," she says.

Until, that is, an acquaintance tipped her off to a startling rumor: The Magic Kingdom was sending obscene subliminal messages through some of its animated family films, including *Aladdin*, in which the handsome young title character supposedly murmurs, sotto voice, "All good teenagers take off your clothes."

"I felt as if I had entrusted my kids to pedophiles," says the Carthage, New York, homemaker, who promptly threw the videos into the garbage. "It's like a toddler introduction to porn."

A PERSISTENT RUMOR

By now, just about everyone had heard the rumors that so shocked Runge. Indeed, Disney catapulted into the headlines on reports that there are subliminal sexual messages in three popular Disney videos: *The Lion King* and *The Little Mermaid*, as well as *Aladdin*. The charges were reported around the world: TV news shows broadcast the offending snippets in slow motion, among them a scene from *The Lion King* in which dust supposedly spells out the word "sex."

Disney denies inserting any subliminal messages. And the three allegedly obscene sequences are hardly crystal clear; even using the pause button on a VCR, viewers may debate whether they exist. Yet they have quickly become the stuff of suburban myth, like the "Paul is dead" rumor from the heyday of the Beatles, or the persis-

---

Vital Stat: The world's biggest chicken-eaters, per capita are the Saudi Arabians.

tent allegations that Procter & Gamble Co.'s moon-and-stars logo symbolizes devil worship.

As the rumors spread, though, so did a common refrain: Where does this stuff come from?

In the case of *Aladdin*, the allegation crisscrossed the country, traveling mostly through conservative Christian circles and helped by, among others, Runge; a high-school biology class in Owensboro, Kentucky; an Iowa college student; and a traveling troupe of evangelical actors. It was passed on by some people who didn't believe it, by others who thought it was a joke, and by a Christian magazine that later—and apparently to no effect—retracted its story. At least two waves of the rumor swept the country, from very different starting points.

AN AVUNCULAR BISHOP

Most people probably first heard about the allegations in early September 1995, after the Associated Press ran a story saying a Christian group had identified the three subliminally smutty incidents. The articles described the *Aladdin* and *The Lion King* scenes as well as one in *The Little Mermaid* in which it said an avuncular bishop becomes noticeably aroused while presiding over a wedding ceremony. Disney quickly fired back. "If somebody is seeing something, that's their perception. There's nothing there," says Rick Rhoades, a Disney spokesman. Aladdin's line is "Scat, good tiger, take off and go," Disney says. The company maintains that Simba's dust is just that, dust. And Tom Sito, the animator who drew the Little Mermaid's purportedly aroused minister, says, "If I wanted to put Satanic messages in a movie, you would see it. This is silly."

AN INADVERTENT FIND

The Associated Press, as it turns out, didn't ferret out the story itself. It picked up the item from the *Daily Press* in Newport News, Virginia. The reporter on that story, Jim Stratton, himself stumbled on the allegations inadvertently. On a slow day at the end of August, Stratton, who at the time covered health and medicine for the paper, was casually flipping through a copy of *Communique*, a biweekly newsletter published by the American Life League, an anti-abortion group based in Stafford, Virginia. He was struck by an article warning parents about a scene from *The Lion King* in which Simba, the cuddly lion star, stirs up a cloud of dust. "Watch closely as the cloud floats off the screen," the newsletter instructed, "and you can see the letters S-E-X."

Bemused, Stratton called the league, where a spokeswoman told him about the illicit messages in *Aladdin* and *The Little Mermaid*. He decided to see for himself and gathered a dozen or so reporters around a newsroom TV to view *The Lion King* scene. They weren't convinced. "We didn't make a final decision either way on what exactly people were seeing," he says. Still, he decided to write a breezy tongue-in-cheek article about all three incidents for his paper. "We handled it lightly," he says.

Stratton's source for the story, the American Life League, meanwhile, hadn't actually found the alleged subliminal scenes itself, either. Its article was prompted by phone calls and letters from Christian groups. One of the callers had first read about the *Aladdin* allegation in the March issue of *Movie Guide* magazine, a Christian entertainment review based in Atlanta.

ALADDIN EXPOSED

In a story titled "Aladdin Exposed," *Movie Guide* alleged that, in a scene on the balcony with love interest Princess Jasmine and her pet tiger, Aladdin murmurs the "take off your clothes" line. The article likened the line to allegedly demonic messages in 1970s rock songs that can only be heard when the albums are played backward. "Thousands were seduced into following the suggestions of these same messages," the magazine wrote. It urged "moral Americans" to write to Disney's chairman, Michael Eisner, asking him to remove the "manipulative subliminal messages."

Overlooked by the *Movie Guide* reader who repeated the allegations to the American Life League, though, was one important fact: *Movie Guide* later ran a retraction. After its piece ran, *Movie Guide* received a letter from Disney saying that the line was actually "Scat, good tiger, take off and go." *Movie Guide*'s publisher, Ted Baehr, decided to clear up the matter once and for all, and took the video to a digital recording studio to decipher the questionable passage syllable by syllable. Although the line is hard to understand, *Movie Guide* concluded, it "falls short of the charge of subliminal-viewer manipulation," as the newsletter put in its July issue. Adds Baehr, "We messed up by not listening before."

THE PLOT THICKENS

Movie Guide, in any case, hadn't ferreted out the alleged subliminal message on its own, either. Baehr says the publication received a "flood of letters and calls complaining about *Aladdin*" in December, January, and February.

One of the letter writers was Gloria Ekins, Christian education director of First Christian Church in Newton, Iowa. "I heard it from my daughter" last winter, Ekins says. Her daughter Jenny, 17, heard it from her friend Jane Ford, a classmate at Newton Senior High School. Jane, in turn, first learned of the *Aladdin* message from her older brother, Matthew Ford, a college senior at the University of Northern Iowa in Cedar Falls, Iowa.

Ford would prove to be one of the central figures in the *Aladdin* saga: He heard the line on his own. The college student, who works part time at a local video store and a movie theater, is an electronic media major who hopes to go into the movie business. A self-confessed movie buff, he happened to be watching *Aladdin* one day last January when he stumbled across the alleged line. He had no moral or religious purpose in spreading the word about it. He simply thought it was funny....

"We were all sitting around the dorm back in January watching *Aladdin* and I couldn't figure out something he was saying," Ford recalls. "I said, 'Rewind that,' and then we heard it." He adds, "My friends think it's funny because it's a Disney movie." Months later, when the *Aladdin* line showed up on the national news, Ford never imagined he helped start it all. "When I saw the news," he says, "I just thought I wasn't the only one who noticed it."

A SECOND WAVE

In fact, almost a year earlier, in the spring of 1994, another teenager did notice the supposedly salacious line—and he started a separate wave of the rumor that also ended up tearing through Christian circles. Jon Wood, now a 16-year-old sophomore at Green Mountain Senior High School in Lakewood, Colorado, says he was watching his younger sister's new copy of the video when he "heard a whisper." He adds, "It was weird, I just felt like something was wrong. I heard something in the background and rewound it, and I just heard it."

Jon, who says he was "shocked" by the line, immediately called his 16-year-old brother, Jake, into the room to show him, too. A few weeks later, the boys showed it to their aunt, Chris Leach, of nearby Fort Collins, Colorado, who had just bought the video for her own five children.

Leach, whose husband is a pastor, passed the word on to a friend from religious circles, Glen Lee, who at the time was the youth pastor at Calvary Temple Assembly of God, a Pentecostal church in Owensboro, Kentucky. Lee in turn told a neighbor, Becky Tomes.

Tomes, the mother of two toddlers, listened to the tape in June 1994 with her husband, but "we didn't really hear it," she says. That didn't stop her, though, from spreading the rumor to another friend, Sheryl Arnold, who listened for herself and decided that, no doubt about it, it was indeed an obscene subliminal message. "We have surround-sound TV," she explains. "And when I listened to it, it was very clear."

Arnold told a friend of hers from church, Eva Sturgeon, a Pentecostal singer at Calvary Temple. After church one day, Sturgeon passed the word to her brother's girlfriend, Casey Ranson, now a junior at Apollo High School, a public school in Owensboro. Intrigued, Casey brought the *Aladdin* cassette into school and played it for her English and biology classes. "Nobody believed me when I told them, so I brought it to school and when I played it, they heard it," Casey says.

SOME SKEPTICISM

Casey herself told, among others, a classmate named Whitney Underhill, who says with some skepticism, "The more I listen to it, it doesn't sound like 'take off your clothes.' It drops off and is hard to understand." But Whitney nevertheless repeated the tale to a friend of hers, Johnny Henderson, who at the time was a senior at Owensboro High School. He told a schoolmate, Courtney Lindow, who in turn told another classmate, Lauren Hayden.

Lauren proved to be a providential choice. Her father, P. J. Hayden, is principal of a Catholic elementary school in Owensboro, St. Angela Merici Elementary. Lauren told him the tale, and Mr. Hayden promptly spread the word among his school's parents, showing the *Aladdin* scene at parent–teacher meetings. "I know a lot of our parents are concerned about subliminal messages," Mr. Hayden says. "I tell them, monitor [Disney movies] like you would anything else. The Disney name is not as…clean as we thought it was."

Among the parents he alerted was Lisa Bivens, who has three daughters. On a February afternoon, she took her children to a local church to see a performance by Radix, a traveling evangelical troupe of performers based in Lincoln, Nebraska, that uses song and dance to bring home biblical stories and tell morality tales. After the show, Bivens mentioned the *Aladdin* episode to the troupe's leader, 30-year-old Doug Barry. In May, Barry and Radix traveled to tiny Carthage, New York, 45 minutes from the Canadian border, for another performance. Among the audience members was Runge, the mother of eight. They spoke together later at a brunch, and as talk turned to the dangers of sex and violence in the media, he repeated the *Aladdin* tale, throwing in another allegation he had heard from a teenager who wrote to him, about the supposed "S-E-X" in *The Lion King*.

IT SMELLS "PERVERT"

Runge was furious—and determined to do something about it. Over the summer, she began calling Christian organizations and conservative groups, from Pat Robertson to Phyllis Schafly. She hit pay dirt when she reached the American Life League, which politely thanked her for passing on the *Aladdin* allegation—it had already heard that one from *Movie Guide*'s readers—but which promptly published the article about *The Lion King* that led to the Associated Press story that started the avalanche of unwanted publicity for Disney.

No matter that Runge wasn't even sure initially that all the allegations were true. "I really couldn't see *The Lion King* one myself," she admits, "until my teenagers traced it for me on the screen." No matter that her source, Barry of Radix, now says he isn't convinced himself about all the allegations "I'm not sure about *The Little Mermaid*," he says. Nor does it concern Mrs. Runge that *Movie Guide*, after spreading the *Aladdin* rumor, has since retracted its story.

"It may be Disney," Runge explains. "But it still smells 'pervert' to me."

ENCYCLOPEDIA BATHROOMICA

A BRI member recently sent us this "encyclopedia," which first appeared as "Encyclopedia Tropicana" in the Miami Herald *in 1986. We think it makes entertaining bathroom reading and it's the biggest piece we've ever included in a Bathroom Reader. It was written by Joel Achenbach, author of* Why Things Are.

INTRODUCTION

The TV is on the blink...You play with the dials, look behind the set, trace the wires and cables from the box to the wall, lips moving as you think. But you're only pretending to discern the pattern. In your heart you know the truth: You live on the brink of the third millennium yet couldn't teach a thing to a caveman.

No one expects you to be able to fix the TV set. That's for repairmen. Experts. But the shameful fact is, you don't really even know what a TV is. The basic principles elude you. You haven't a clue as to what this thing is that you stare at every day. You are glad the circuitry is hidden. You are happy to be out of touch. You are a Modern Person.

We've been thinking about your problem. A recent survey by Northern Illinois University showed 85% of the public to be "technologically illiterate." Only one person out of five knew how a telephone works. Four out of 10 thought rocket launchings caused major changes in the weather.

Almost without exception the great discoveries of human history have been acts of tremendous courage, rebellions against conventional wisdom, statements of heresy. The established powers killed Socrates, rebuked Copernicus, exiled Galileo, hounded Darwin. People died for knowledge that enriches us all. We repay the debt by abdicating all responsibility for the comprehension of ordinary things. If this stupefaction weren't so general it would be an outrage.

That's just how we feel.

So we had to ask ourselves: If we don't explain to [BRI] readers the facts of modern life...who will? Do we want them to just hear about it on the street? In alleys or something? Do we want to be responsible when our once-reputable readers wind up in the seedy back rooms of taverns, flipping through black-and-white diagrams of the insides of a Thermos? No, it would be too ugly. Read this, read it in public, with pride. Walk tall. Get with it. Do it for Socrates.

AIR

Air is made up of tiny particles, called molecules, which are of different makes and models, with the most common, the Ford Escort of molecules, being "nitrogen." There also is a fair amount of "oxygen," plus some "carbon dioxide," and tiny traces of other gases, like "argon," "xenon" and, "neon." Scientists have recently become worried about the ingredients of the air. The burning of coal and oil causes an increase in carbon dioxide in the atmosphere, a problem made worse by clear-cutting in the huge Amazon jungle, where vegetation cranks out a lot of oxygen. If the carbon dioxide gets too high, the atmosphere will begin to capture more of the sun's heat, and warm up, and melt the polar ice caps, and ruin crops, and plummet the planet into a period of turmoil and decay. But probably not in your lifetime.

AIRPLANE

Ever notice how a fast runner seems to glide over the ground, barely touching it, while a big plodding jogger seems to make the ground shake? Air acts the same way. The faster it is moving, the less pressure it exerts. Remember that. It will be important later.

Now we've got a plane knifing through the air. Air molecules are just standing there, minding their own business, chatting with their neighbors, when suddenly they are sliced apart by this wing. Air molecules react in a strange way when this happens. They race desperately along the top and bottom of the wing, looking for each other.

The top of the wing is curved; the bottom is straight. So the air at the top has a longer distance to travel than the air on the bottom. But, driven by some primal atmospheric instinct (actually, by a nearly incomprehensible law of fluid dynamics) they arrive at the same time. How did they do this? The air on the top of the wing moved faster than the air at the bottom!

Faster air above the wing, slower air below the wing. That means there is more pressure under the wing than above it, and the wing rises, carrying the plane with it.

B

BATTERY
The battery works for the same reason that fillings hurt when you bite into aluminum foil. (See *Fillings, why they hurt.*)

BLUE, WHY SKY IS
You must first understand what "blue" is. Blue is a color, one which, like pornography, defies easy definition, though we sure know it when we see it. Scientists can measure blue. It is what "light" looks like when it is coming at us in a particular wavelength (OK, you nerds, it's 480 nanometers).

Wavelength, we rush to say, is not a word to be feared. It is not even in the same league as, for example, Stakhanovism (*see Names to Impress Your Date*). A wavelength is just what it sounds like. A wave. Of a certain length. Blue has shorter wavelengths, red longer. The sunlight, a mixture of lights of all sorts of wavelengths, comes bounding into the clear sky from deep space. It hits the air molecules and starts ricocheting all over the place. With every skip, every bounce, many of the longer light waves—red—get soaked up by the molecules. But the blue keeps bouncing around. (This is a function of the shape and shimmy of air molecules.) By the time the light zigzags into our eyes, it's mostly blue.

This is when dust comes into the picture. Dust has a different shape from air molecules, a different shimmy. It soaks up the blue light. The less dust in the sky, the bluer it is. At dawn and dusk the sunlight comes in at a low angle, and must wade through gobs and gobs of dust hovering close to the Earth. So the sky turns orange, and then red.

BOMB, HYDROGEN, *how to build*
We are going to tell you the secret of the hydrogen bomb. The secret is a substance as familiar as your morning cup of coffee.

Now keep all this stuff to yourself. Inside a hydrogen bomb is an old-fashioned atom bomb that looks just like a soccer ball. It's the trigger. That's how mean hydrogen bombs are. They use atom bombs just to get them started. Below the atom bomb is a carrot-shaped container of nuclear fuel—various types of hydrogen atoms. The theory is this: Blow up the soccer ball, and the pressure will cause the carrot to compress, fusing the hydrogen atoms together. This simulates the events in the center of the sun. As two hydrogen atoms become one helium atom, they lose some of their weight. The lost weight, or mass, is converted to pure energy. KA-BLAMM!

The big problem is convincing the atomic bomb blast to squeeze the hydrogen evenly, the way you would crush a beer can, rather than just knock the whole contraption to kingdom come. The answer is to build the bomb *like a* Thermos (*see Thermos*) with "radiation reflectors" on the inside. A Thermos uses shiny glass, a hydrogen bomb uses super-thin sheets of Uranium-238, a metal. When the soccer ball explodes, there is a period of one-millionth of a second before the fireball can even begin to move, when invisible gamma rays and X-rays surge outward at the speed of light, bounce off the reflective casing, and pile-drive back into the carrot of hydrogen. The atoms fuse. And you get more bang for your buck.

Scientists needed something that would hold the carrot in place during the rocky ride from silo to target. But it had to be a special something: strong, yet totally unable to slow down or reflect the pressure from the atom bomb explosion. They looked and looked for the right material. Finally they got it: styrofoam.

A one-megaton bomb, big enough to thoroughly flatten Miami, would be the size of a suitcase. It would fit under your bed.

C

CAMERA, POLAROID
Light peeks through the shutter, hits the film. The film is like plywood. It has layers, each coated with silver bromide. The film is designed so that the top layer reacts to blue light. The next reacts to yellow. The next, red. As the sheet of film is ejected, the camera douses it with dyes. Red dye sticks to the part of the film that reacted to the red light. Same with the blue and yellow.

When the dyes soak through

to the bottom layer—the layer that you will put in your photo album—blue, red and yellow dye is represented in approximately the same intensity and the same place within the picture frame as the light from the original image. We stress "approximately."

CHIP, SILICON

The breakthrough that made small, efficient computers possible. Computers are basically machines that utilize the great speed of electricity to make millions of decisions in a matter of seconds. Computers see no grays: every problem is reduced to a series of yes-no decisions indicated by the turning on, or off, of a current. (Question: Is the number seven a prime number? Computer's methodology: Is it evenly divisible by two? No. By three? No. By four? No. By five? No. By six? No. Answer: Yes, it is a prime number.)

This process, though fast, requires astoundingly elaborate circuitry, resembling a bafflingly complex street map, miles and miles of printed circuits forking off in all sorts of directions, wherever the options and alternatives take it. Original computers did this with wires and solder, and all of the

circuitry required them to be the size of a 7-Eleven.

The silicon chip is a fingernail-sized slab which can be mass-produced and upon which tens of thousands of tiny, discrete circuits can be etched.

CLOCKS, DASHBOARD
How they work: They don't.

CORK, HOW IT GETS INTO CHAMPAGNE BOTTLES

The mushroom-shaped cork is steam-heated until it is very spongy, and then it is crammed into the bottle with a cramming tool. OK, so if it is so warm and mushy and slides in so easily, why doesn't it pop right back out from the pressure of the gas? Because at the time it is corked, champagne is flatter than Alfalfa singing "Lady of Spain." It earns its bubbles later, through fermentation in the bottle. By that time, the cork is dry and fat and holding fast.

D

DATE, NAMES TO IMPRESS YOUR

Bruno, Giordano. In the 17th century he conceived of the universe as being infinite in time and space, filled with suns surrounded by planets. For this revelation he was accused of heresy and burned at the stake.

Condamine, Charles Marie de la. Went to South America in 1735 to measure curvature of the Earth. Instead he discovered rubber.

Ham–First American chimpanzee in space. Emerged from capsule snarling, tried to bite photographers.

Semmelweis, Ignaz. A Hungarian physician in 1847, discovered concept of germs. Suggested doctors wash their hands once in a while. Infant mortality plummeted.

Stakhanov, Aleksei. Miserable Russian coal miner who worked so hard and so efficiently he yanked out seven times as much coal as the average miserable coal miner. In 1935 the Soviet government announced the start of "Stakhanovism," a system in which workers are encouraged to increase production, which no doubt sent a big thrill through the shafts.

Tull, Jethro. English agriculturist, brought horseshoes to England from France in early 18th century.

F

FACTS, UNTRUE, THAT REFUSE TO DIE

The Missing Link. Supposedly an extinct creature halfway between apes and humans on the evolutionary chart. It's not missing. Or if it is, no one's looking for it. Darwin didn't say humans evolved from apes. Both evolved from a common ancestor—an extinct ape-like creature.

Double-jointed people. No such thing. In some people, the ligaments that attach muscle to bone are more elastic.

Positive to negative flow of electricity. Wiring diagrams always show current flowing from positive to negative. But it's the other way around. The mistake was made by Benjamin Franklin after his famous experiment with the kite. Once the error was discovered there were too many books in print to change.

Columbus sailing off the edge of the world . No one was actually worried about this. Pythagoras proposed a spherical world as early as the sixth century B.C. Then, in the second century A.D., the Roman astronomer Ptolemy proved the Earth was spherical, pointing out the round shadow of the Earth during a lunar eclipse, and the obvious fact that the masts of sailboats come into view on the horizon before the hull.

The Fifth Dimension. A 1960s pop group. As far as spatial and temporal dimensions are concerned, we know of only four: length, breadth, height, and time. It was the last that finished off the singing group.

What steam looks like. It looks like nothing. You can't see steam, just as you can't see any gas. What you think is steam is actually condensed water vapor. Look at the spout of a steaming kettle. There is a brief space, just outside the spout, where you cannot see anything. That's steam.

FILLINGS, *why they hurt when you bite into aluminum foil*
What you are feeling is the basic fact of nature that makes batteries possible. There are two kinds of substances that can conduct electricity. One kind is just dying to send its electrons off on imperialistic forays, the other is so willing to take in foreign electrons that it will accept even those with obviously faked passports.

But despite all the intentions, the electrons can't go anywhere without a middle-man to negotiate the passage. In your mouth, saliva serves this purpose admirably, creating a slick path from the aluminum foil to the metal alloy in your filling. There is a mass migration of electrons (an electric current), which, when it occurs in the area of your back molar, comes as something of a shock. In the typical car battery, the electron donor and recipient are carbon and zinc, and the conducting liquid is sulfuric acid.

G

GUILLOTINE, *consciousness after use of*
Named after French physician J. I . Guillotine (1738-1814), who improved upon previous designs by angling the blade, making it more of a slicer than a chopper. Because of oxygen stored in brain at any given moment, says Dade County Chief Medical Examiner Joe Davis, an executed person is probably conscious for up to 10 seconds after the beheading, and can probably see and hear. We checked it out with a few neurologists. They were sharply divided on the subject.

Sophie, did you know that a pig has 44 teeth?

H

HEISENBERG'S UNCERTAINTY PRINCIPLE

You're at a cocktail party. Clive, whom you hate, is acting superior. You make an innocuous comment to the effect that it must be 100 degrees outside Clive says, "Of course, Heisenberg's Uncertainty Principle tells us that it is impossible to make a completely accurate measurement." Here's what you should say: "Fool! Dolt! Boob! Heisenberg said it is impossible to determine simultaneously and with unlimited accuracy the position and the momentum of a particle, but because Planck's Constant is so small, the Uncertainty Principle is meaningless except when discussing the motion of atomic particles, like electrons. Idiot." Hopefully this outburst will help quell future references to Heisenberg's Uncertainty Principle.

HELIUM, *source of*

It sends balloons, and your voice, high. It's a naturally occurring element, but where does it occur? In the ground.

Helium is mined from gas wells in Texas, Oklahoma, and Kansas. The United States is the world's leading helium producer, and relations with Germany were sorely strained before World War II when we refused to sell the stuff to Hitler. He wanted it for his zeppelins, but he had to make do with the highly volatile hydrogen instead. Which explains why the Hindenburg blew up over New Jersey in 1937.

HUMOR, *sense of*

A "sense of humor" is a measurement of the extent to which you notice that you're trapped in a world almost totally devoid of reason. Laughter is how you release the anxiety you feel about this.

L

LIGHTBULB

You flip a switch, and, godlike, you create light. But don't bask in the glow too long. Better to give credit where it's due—the electron, a basic component of matter so filled with energy it can't sit still for an instant.

Electrons usually can be found zipping around the nuclei of

their atoms at unfathomable speeds, trapped by an attractive force. But given a little shove, the electrons of certain elements—notably metals—are only too happy to promiscuously bounce from nucleus to nucleus.

The shove comes from a flood of free electrons produced by a generator or a battery. The flood turns into a torrent, cascading through the metal pathway—the wire—at close to the speed of light. This little drill actually produces light because not all materials carry electrons as freely as, say, copper wire.

The tungsten element in the center of a 60-watt lightbulb is not nearly so casual about its electrical relations. This unwelcome intrusion of three billion billion electrons a second plowing through its personal space causes a fit of apoplexy. It gets hot. White hot, in fact. It would burn itself to ash in no time, which was the slight flaw in early light bulb designs, except that the interior of the modern glass bulb is an airless vacuum. The lack of surrounding oxygen allows the filament to burn and glow in impotent rage for weeks before it loses its cool completely.

M

MATCH

Most tools seem complex but are actually fairly simple. Matches are the opposite. The humility of their design belies a deeper engineering genius. Consider: The common match was invented in 1805, nearly 200 years after the first telescope.

For much of the 19th century, workers in match factories succumbed to a horrible disease called "phossy jaw." We won't describe it.

There are actually two types of matches, the "Safety Match" and the "Strike-Anywhere Match." For simplicity's sake we will refer to the latter as the "Dangerous Match." The Dangerous Match can be lit with your fingernail, or, if you're as tough as Clint Eastwood in those old spaghetti westerns, your beard. The tip is coated in a chemical called phosphorus. White phosphorus is so flammable it bursts into flame upon contact with the air. There is more than a pound of the stuff in a human body, in blood, muscles, bones and teeth. Why don't teeth burst into flame when you talk? That's for another volume of the Encyclopedia Bathroomica. Know now simply that the modern Dangerous Match uses red phosphorus, calmer than its white cousin. Rub the match on sandpaper or any rough surface and the friction heats the match to the ignition point. The flame then fires down into the match's "tinder," easy-to-burn chemicals like sulfur, potassium chlorate, and charcoal, melded together with glue and wax.

But there's also dirt bits and powdered glass down there, to keep things under control. To make things yet more comfy for all concerned, the entire stick of wood has been soaked in a chemical that prevents smoldering.

The Safety Match is a radical departure. The thinking behind the Safety Match is that although the phosphorus and the "tinder" are wild and unpredictable when stuck together, they are harmless and mediocre when solo, like Lennon and McCartney. So the phosphorus is not even on the match, it's on the box, or the "pack," what have you. You know, on that black scratchy strip. To light the Safety Match one simply has to press it against the strip, "close cover before striking," and yank, unless the match in question is the last in the pack, in which case it will not light no matter how many billion times you try.

OVEN, MICROWAVE

No doubt it will not enlighten you to hear that microwaves are a type of high-frequency electromagnetic wave that penetrates food and causes atoms to violently agitate creating "heat."

Figure it like this. Right there in your kitchen is a radio station, KMWV. This station plays only one rock group, over and over, called Magnetron. Magnetron's music is so stupid only food can hear it. The little food molecules react by doing a dance. First the molecules line up in rigid formation. Then they suddenly flip around, facing the opposite direction. Back and forth, back and forth, kind of like the Twist or maybe even the Time Warp. They do this a couple billion times every second. It's what you call a fast dance.

An exterminator once told us that a microwave could not kill a roach. So we called an entomologist at the University of Florida to see if this was true. He did an experiment.

"There was never any reason to suspect that a microwave would not kill a cockroach. There is even less reason now," he said "It blew up like a potato."

P

PERPETUAL MOTION DEVICES
Don't work.

R

REFRIGERATOR

You put a package of bologna into your refrigerator, and it gets cold. The question is: Where does the cold come from? The answer is: The cold doesn't come from anywhere. The heat leaves. It goes into the air around the refrigerator. Here's how it gets there.

There are pipes in your refrigerator—you can sometimes see them in the freezer compartment. Flowing through these pipes is a liquid called a "refrigerant." This is a special

kind of liquid that evaporates—turns into gas—at a fairly low temperature, such as the temperature of your bologna. But to evaporate, a liquid must draw heat from somewhere. That's why when you moisten your finger and wave it in the air, it feels cooler; the water is evaporating and drawing heat from your skin.

So the refrigerant draws heat from the pipe it's in, which in turn draws heat from the air around it, which in turn draws it from your bologna.

The refrigerant now goes into a "compressor." This is the thing you hear when your refrigerator's running, and it sort of squeezes the refrigerant gas, which turns it back into a liquid. (Strange but true: If you compress a gas enough, it turns into a liquid.) The liquid, still under pressure, flows through pipes that are outside your refrigerator's cold compartment—these are the pipes you can usually see behind the refrigerator. The liquid gives off heat—the heat it goes from inside your refrigerator—to these pipes, and they give it off into the room air. Your bologna is warming your house, just a little bit.

The refrigerant, now that it has given up its heat, is ready to go back and get some more. It goes through a valve—sort of a trapdoor—back into the cold part of the refrigerator. As soon as it's through the valve, it's no longer being squeezed, so it quickly evaporates again, thus sucking up more heat, and the whole cycle repeats: get squeezed from gas back into liquid, give off heat, leave pressurized area, turn back into gas, suck up heat.

The cycle continues. It would be a very boring occupation, refrigerant.

ROCKET LAUNCHERS,
effects on weather
Don't be stupid.

T

TELEPHONE
The incredible thing about telephones is not that people can instantly talk to each other across the continents, but that you can recognize the other person's voice. Incredible that, somewhere along the suboceanic cables, or in the empty space between microwave transmission towers, your voice doesn't become that of a robot, or a total stranger, someone from Boston, for example.

The secret is inside the phone. It's a metal plate called a diaphragm. This thing is a direct steal from nature's design of the human eardrum. You hold the phone to your mouth and say something like, for example, "Honest, the check's in the mail." The sound of your voice ripples through the air in distinctive waves, molecules knocking each other along, a chain reaction of croquet balls. Your ripple pattern is different from everyone else's; that's what makes voiceprint I.D. an accurate tool.

The sound hits the diaphragm inside a phone, raining down like sheets of rain. The metal plate just vibrates.

But then comes the next trick: The metal plate is attached to a pack of carbon granules, like in certain cigarette filters. These granules have an electric current running through them. When the metal plate shakes, the granules jitter about, causing surges in the juice. The better the engineering of the phone, the more accurately your voice is translated into an electrical language. Like Morse code, this electrical message races along the phone lines at close to the speed of light, directed by switches and circuits that we here at the Encyclopedia Bathroomica do not understand and do not wish to learn about. The final miracle comes on the other end, where the whole process is reversed. The phone lines lead to a magnet inside your friend's phone. As the electrical current hems and haws in the pattern of your voice, the magnet tugs at the metal diaphragm. The metal plate vibrates. Sound comes out of the phone. "Honest, the check's in the mail." Sounds like… you.

TELEVISION

When you watch TV, you are not watching a moving picture. You are watching a moving dot. But this is one mighty fast dot. It races back and forth in a blur, moving line by line from the top of the screen to the bottom, a total of 525 lines. It does this at roughly 21,600 miles an hour.

The dot is actually a stream of electrons projected from the back of the TV to the inner surface of the picture tube, which is coated with phosphorus.

Phosphorus glows when hit by a stream of electrons; the more torrential the stream, the brighter the spot. By varying the brightness of every dot on every line on your screen, the electron beam paints a picture with strategically clustered dots, the same way those computer portraits are done at the mall. Your picture tube paints a different picture on your screen 30 times every second.

So why do you see it as "Seinfeld," and not a series of stills? Think of those decks of cards you got as a kid, the ones that you could riffle with your thumb to make a moving picture. Same principle. The mind fills in the gaps.

THERMOS

The question is: How come soda keeps cold and coffee keeps hot? How does the Thermos know?

The first thing to remember is that you must always capitalize the word Thermos, because it is a trademarked name for a "vacuum bottle."

Second, know that it is a container within a container. The inside container is a glass bottle. Between the bottle and the outer container is a No Man's Land, with close to zero air molecules. A vacuum, almost. Vacuums

---

don't transfer heat very well. (If you don't care why, skip to the last paragraph.)

Heat is transferred in one of three ways: conduction, convection, and radiation. Conduction means, basically, molecules smacking into each other like dominoes, sending energy down the line. Since a vacuum means an absence of molecules, there are no molecules against which to smack, conduction doesn't happen in a Thermos. Convection is when molecules cruise through traffic on their own, weaving and darting, trying to get across town; e.g., steam bubbles rising from the bottom of a boiling pot. But the inside of a Thermos is a solid: it keeps its molecules close to the vest.

Radiation defies easy analogy. It's kind of like…beauty. There's a little bit of it in everything. The hotter the source, the greater the radiation. It comes at you in waves, piercing everything in its way, stone or flesh. Like light from the sun, it can leap across a vacuum. Like beauty, it can melt the coldest of hearts. There is no protection from the withering power of beauty, but with a Thermos you can put silver on the inside of the bottle, reflecting back some of the radiant energy from your coffee or soup or what have you, postponing the inevitable.

]So what happens is, the vacuum and silvered side combine to prevent heat from escaping from the inner container if it's filled with something hot, and prevent heat from entering the inner container if it's filled with something cold.

TIME, LOST

The year before 1901 A.D. was, of course, 1900 A.D. The year before 101 A.D. was, of course, 100 A.D.

So what was the year before 1 A.D.? Zero A.D.? Was there ever a May 15, Zero A.D.?

No. Historians decided they just couldn't cope with a Zero year. The historical record leaps from December 31, 1 B.C. to January 1, 1 A.D.

TOILET

The humble toilet is too often the butt of indelicate jokes. We are going to do our best to refrain from infantile humor here, except to note, as we must, that the toilet was invented by a man named Thomas Crapper.

With the possible exception of the clock, Crapper's porcelain pew is the most efficient household device that doesn't require

Niagara Falls was created by a glacier.

electricity.

Here's an experiment to perform in the privacy of your own bathroom. Remove the top from your toilet tank. Now fish the curlers and tissues and hair spray and toothpaste and Comet from the bowl, where they have fallen. You should have removed them before lifting the cover. Now, look inside the tank. You'll see three main things: a rubber stopper at the bottom of the water, a big hollow float at the top of the water, and a tall post connected to the float by a long arm. When you press the handle to flush, the stopper pops up out of a hole in the bottom of the tank, and water, pulled by gravity, rushes down into the bowl. When a bowlful of water (about five gallons) has gone through, the stopper is now hanging in air, and gravity pulls it back into the hole.

Meanwhile, the air-filled float has sunk along with the water level, thereby opening a special valve (called a "ballcock") at the top of the tall post. This opening causes water to pour back into the tank from the house's water pipes, until the float rises again to the top of the tank and shuts off the water.

A very smooth system, until some object—for the sake of argument we will say a Cabbage Patch Doll—stops up the drain at the bottom of the bowl.

Meanwhile, no one has informed the tank, which is continuing to flush water into the bowl, causing the water level to rise toward a disastrous spillover.

Now that you know how a toilet works, you don't have to stand in helpless horror. Lunge for the float at the bottom of the tank and lift it to the closed position. Then radio for assistance.

TUNNELS, CONSTRUCTION OF

How do they dig underwater tunnels? Do they work in scuba gear? And how do they pump the water out afterwards? And how do they protect against leaks that would flood and drown people?

Easy. They dig real deep, under the riverbed.

V

VELCRO

Hooks and eyes. It's that sim-

Until 1867, Alaska was known as Russian America.

ple. One strip is covered with tiny nylon hooks, the other with tiny nylon eyes. Invented by Swiss engineer Georges de Mestral in 1948 after he returned from a hunting trip and noticed thistle blossoms clinging to his pants. He looked under a microscope. The blossoms were covered with tiny hooks. Velcro comes from velours, velvet, and crochet hook.

WORDS, PRETENTIOUS

Some capsule definitions of pompous, commonly misused terms:

Existentialism. No God, no fixed human nature. Man on his own, responsible for self. This freedom to define his own life is the source of man's dread.

Metaphysics. The big questions. What is ultimate nature of being? Are people basically good or evil? Why am I always late?

Entropy. Degradation of energy from order to disorder. The natural tendency of everything to degenerate. An ice cube, nice and symmetric, melts into a mess. So does the universe. All neatly put together with planets and stars and meteors all spinning around like clockwork, it is slowly getting messier and messier. Ultimately the galaxies will look like the floor under your refrigerator: nothing but fuzz. Things will be bleak indeed. Suffice it to say that this state is known as The Heat Death of the Universe. The good news is that you'll never have to clean under your refrigerator again.

Debenture -- An IOU from a corporation to a person.

WORLD, HISTORY OF

One-celled life appeared on Earth about three billion years ago and fitfully evolved into different plants and animals. Human beings proved most adaptive, learning to control their environment as other creatures could not.

After relying solely on hunting and gathering, Man started farming about 10,000 years ago. With their surplus food, they learned to sell. And shop. With their surplus time, they learned to write. So began civilizations. But civilizations were transitory, destroyed by external challenges, internecine tensions, political folly, and presumptions of divinity.

The Greeks developed a remarkably modern society, replete with science, philosophy, dramatic performances, and democracy. The Greeks were routed by the Romans. The Roman empire spanned the West at the birth of Jesus, whose teachings inspired first a cult and then a revolutionary religion. Rome was sacked by barbarians, beginning a thousand years of disorder, poverty, and intellectual stagnation sometimes known as the Dark Ages.

Meanwhile, in the Cast, a cerebral society was developing that revered age and wisdom but was slowed in its progress by a slavish devotion to custom and tradition. It was very mysterious to Westerners.

A bubonic plague called the Black Death killed a third of Europe. Papal domination subsided, and monarchs consolidated their support through ambitious foreign wars and ostentatious patronage of the arts. The invention of the printing press contributed to the intellectual flowering known as the Renaissance. Mastery of ocean navigation expanded European influence to much of the world. Later, the Industrial Revolution increased wealth and dehumanized the workplace. European empires gradually declined as their colonies revolted. Shifts in the balance of power erupted in world war. Communist revolution swept through Czarist Russia. Fascist Germans,

driven by master race hysteria, initiated another world war. The United States and the Soviet Union emerged as superpowers and have since fought proxy wars in poor nations. Meanwhile, in the East, China and Japan modernized, becoming less mysterious and more threatening to Western supremacy.

The accelerated development of technology in this century has led to greater leisure time, a rise in service industries, a decline in reading in favor of television viewing, a fundamental alteration and general contamination of the environment, and the construction of vast arsenals of bombs powered by the force that holds atomic nuclei together. The long-term significance of these changes has been largely ignored.

POLITICALLY CORRECT QUIZ ANSWERS (page 267)

1. b) She objected to the play's "blatant heterosexuality." At a news conference, Brown announced that "until books, film, and the theater reflect all forms of sexuality," she would not be "involving her students in heterosexual culture." Other school officials talked about sacking her, calling the decision "ideological idiocy."

2. a) They renamed the town's manholes "personholes."

3. a) They changed it to "Heaven-o." The man behind the resolution, a local flea market owner named Leonso Canales, Jr., explained: "When you go to school and church, they tell you 'hell' is negative and 'heaven' is positive. I think it's time to set a new precedent, to tell our kids that we are positive adults."

Employees at the county courthouse immediately began answering their phones with the new phrase. County officials called the greeting a "symbol of peace, friendship, and welcome in an age of anxiety." But linguists called it bizarre. "Linguistically and historically, 'hello' has nothing to do with 'hell,' " said one. "It stems from an old German greeting for hailing a boat."

4. c) Animal rights activists initiated a campaign to change the name of the town of Fishkill to something less "cruel." Mayor George Carter scoffed at the idea. "I think if they'd look the word up, they'd find out what it means," he told the press.

5. a) Rev. Jerry Buckner of the Tiburon Christian Fellowship demanded that the jockeys be returned to their original color. Why? It turns out that from 1875 to 1900 black jockeys were American sports heroes. According to a story by Mike Dougan, in the *San Francisco Examiner:*

> Buckner says black lawn jockeys were intended to honor—not demean—the real black jockeys who dominated American horse racing in the latter part of the 19th century.
>
> "All of the original jockeys were black, and most people aren't even aware of that fact," he said. He noted that the first 13 winners of the Kentucky Derby—beginning with Oliver Lewis in 1875— were blacks who often owned the horses they rode.
>
> Those who protest the display of black lawn jockeys are "histori-

cally illiterate," Buckner asserted.

But that didn't matter to people like Kerry Pierson, a black activist from nearby Mill Valley. According to Dougan,

> Pierson said that regardless of their origin, lawn jockeys have become for blacks a form of "degradation art."
>
> "You usually find them at country clubs and private clubs. What they represent to black people is that when you pass through a portal where those little jockeys are, you are passing into the pre-Civil War era, and you can expect to be treated as such."

The landlord, caught in the middle, was at a loss. "I don't know what to do," he said. (We don't know what he finally decided.)

6. b) Apparently they weren't happy about giving up their school mascot—a sketch of a frowning, belligerent midget, so they replaced three members of the school board. One of the boardmembers who was dumped, Diane Melbye, said simply: "I understand that people are desperately clinging to what they have known in the past, but the mascot is not appropriate." But the dentist who'd spearheaded the recall vote responded that he was angry that "70-plus years of tradition [had been] taken away from us in 15 minutes." He was one of the three elected to the school board.

7. All of them.

a) In September 1996, first-grader Jonathan Prevette was suspended for a day for "sexual harassment." When his outraged parents took it to court, the case received worldwide publicity...and the school was widely ridiculed. Finally, after about six months, the U.S. Education Department exonerated Prevette and called on school officials to use "good judgment and common sense" in fighting harassment. The school changed the charge to "unwelcome touching." Prevette's comment: "See, I told them I was just trying to be friends!"

b) The incredulous shop owner called newspapers himself.

c) The rule applies not only to ballcocks, but to stopcocks, too. (They have to be called "stop-valves.") "This is political correctness gone mad," said the head of the National Plumbers' Association. One plumber responded with an announcement that he would now charge $22 to fit a *stopcock*, but $45 to fit a *stop-valve*.

In about 250 B.C., Archimedes invented the screw

ANSWERS TO ROCK QUIZ (from page 39)

1. b. "Hound Dog" was written in 1952 by Jerry Lieber and Mike Stoller specifically for Willie Mae "Big Mama" Thornton. Her record went to #1 on the R&B charts in 1953. Then a lounge act named Freddie Bell and the Bellboys made a joke out of it in 1955. That's the version that Elvis copied.

How did he first hear it? In 1956, after "Heartbreak Hotel" had hit #1, Elvis was signed to do his first gig in Las Vegas. Later he'd be king of the town. But the first time around, he was fired—a two-week engagement at the Frontier Hotel was shortened to one week when audiences failed to respond to the hip wiggler. But Elvis still lucked out: he wandered into the lounge and watched Freddie Bell's group perform their humorous takeoff of "Hound Dog." He thought it was hilarious...and decided to do it himself. **Note:** The Bellboys had already recorded the song, and Elvis may have picked up a copy of their record to refresh his memory before he recorded his own version.

2. c. Blackwell had just taken a job writing for a publisher called Shalimar Music when Moe Gayle, the head of the company, called him into his office with an unusual offer: Elvis Presley was interested in recording "Don't Be Cruel," but the deal was contingent on Blackwell giving up half his writer's credit (and thus half the royalties) to Presley. "Elvis Presley?" Blackwell answered. "Who the hell is Elvis Presley?"

Blackwell recalls: "I just felt that I was getting the shaft, man. It took them about two weeks to convince me. They pointed out that if Elvis did become big, I would make a good deal more money this way than not doing it at all. And if he didn't become big, I really wasn't losing anything...so I said okay."

It may have been an unjust arrangement, but it wound up an extremely lucrative one for Blackwell. "Don't Be Cruel" was released in July 1956 as the flip side of "Hound Dog." The double-sided hit reached #1 in August and stayed there for over two months; it was on the charts for six months, becoming the year's #1 record and Elvis's favorite early record. Blackwell was instantly established as a major songwriter. He went on to write "All Shook Up," "Great Balls of Fire," "Return to Sender," and many more hits.

The filaments for the first electric lamp were made of bamboo.

3. a. Fats Domino wrote the song from real life: "I was walkin' down the street and I saw a little lady spankin' a baby. And I heard somebody say 'Ain't That a Shame.'" But Pat didn't relate to it— he objected to it because the grammar was bad.

"[When the record company asked me to record] 'Ain't That a Shame,' I balked," Boone says. "I said, 'Look, I just transferred to Columbia University, I'm an English major. I don't want to record a song called "Ain't That a Shame.'" I mean, 'ain't' wasn't an accepted word. It is now in the dictionary, but I was majoring in English and I felt that this was going to be a terrible thing if it was a hit. I tried to record it 'Isn't That a Shame,' but it didn't work.'"

He finally gave in and used the original lyrics. It hit #1 on the charts. Domino's version was a hit, too—but with Boone taking the lion's share of sales away, it only reached #10.

4. a. In the mid-1950s, "respectable" people—including Mrs. Kern— thought doo-wop rock was a travesty. Apparently, she… According to one account, was so appalled and outraged by the Platters' treatment of the song that she explored ways of stopping it legally. Of course, when the Platters' record became a hit—and sold more copies of "Smoke Gets in Your Eyes" than anyone had before—her opinion changed. And she never turned down a royalty check.

5. c. Hard to believe, but although he may have been the most influential rock musician ever, Berry only had one #1 song—a novelty tune full of sophomoric sexual innuendo called "My Ding-a-Ling." He'd been using it to close his concerts and did it as "My Tambourine" on a live album in the mid-1960s. Then in 1972 he recorded it live again, in London. For some reason his record company released it as a single. As Bob Shannon and John Javna wrote in *Behind the Hits*: "It's kind of depressing for music fans that the biggest single Chuck Berry ever had was this…this…*thing*! But what the hell, at least Chuck got a hit out of it."

6. a. Radio stations found all kinds of reasons not to play it: it was too suggestive, he cursed on it (the part where he goes "We-ell-a" sounded like he was saying "Weh-hell-a"), he sounded black (most stations didn't play songs by black artists). But when the record was banned by BMI (Broadcast Music Inc., which licenses music for airplay) because it was "obscene," the record died.

Sun Records knew it could be a hit—and Jerry Lee Lewis could be another Elvis—if it was handled right. So they took Lewis to New York to try to get him on "The Ed Sullivan Show." They flew to New York, but Sullivan wouldn't listen—Lewis didn't have a hit, and Sullivan didn't like that kind of music, anyway. So they called NBC and got the talent coordinator there to set up a meeting with the producer of "The Steve Allen Show" (a variety program that ran head to head with Sullivan's). Allen's biggest coup had been to introduce Elvis Presley as a guest after Sullivan had turned him down the first time. Now the Sun people hoped they could get Allen to do it again. They took Lewis with them to the meeting. When the TV execs asked to hear a record, Lewis stepped out and played in person. The NBC execs were blown away and scheduled him for *that* Sunday night.

What people at NBC never found out was that the song Jerry Lee was going to play—"Whole Lotta Shakin'"—had been banned. Why? Because after NBC agreed to have Lewis on, the head of promotion for Sun Records called BMI and convinced them that if NBC didn't mind about the lyrics, why should they? He neglected to add that no one at NBC had actually heard the lyrics. But BMI gave in, and the way was clear for Jerry Lee's appearance.

On July 28, 1956, America was introduced to Jerry Lee Lewis and "Whole Lotta Shakin' Goin' On" on "The Steve Allen Show." Jerry went crazy, playing piano with his feet and inadvertently involving Allen himself. At one point he jumped off his piano stool to play standing up and sent the stool careening across the stage: Allen, who was stomping and clapping with the rest of the audience, tossed it back toward Jerry. Then Allen grabbed another piece of furniture and tossed it. Reportedly, he was about to throw a potted plant when Jerry finished playing. The exposure sent the record zooming up the charts. By the end of August it was a million-seller and Jerry Lee was the hottest new rocker in America.

7. b. Little Richard was so incensed by Boone's cover version of "Tutti Frutti" (which outdid Richard's on the charts), he purposely made the follow-up, "Long Tall Sally," too fast for Boone to sing. Nonetheless, Boone figured out how to adapt "Long Tall Sally" and gave Richard a run for his money. Little Richard's version did beat out Boone's—barely. Richard hit #7 in *Billboard*, Boone hit #8.

ANSWERS TO ROCK QUIZ #2 (From Page 347)

1. a. The story told in Grace Slick's biography is that members of the Great Society (Slick's first band) kept trying to get her to write music. Finally they practically locked her in a room and told her she couldn't come out until she'd written some songs. She emerged with several, including "White Rabbit," which was loosely based on a classical piece by Ravel called "Bolero." However, Slick has said repeatedly that "White Rabbit" isn't about drugs. Her explanation: "We were talking about opening up, looking around, checking out what's happening. We were also talking about the fifties mentality, which was really bottled up." She added: "Feeding your head is not necessarily pumping chemicals into it."

Most of the imagery she used came directly from Lewis Carroll's two books, *Alice's Adventures in Wonderland*, and *Through the Looking Class* (see page 79). Three examples from the book *Behind the Hits*:

1. **"One pill makes you larger."** Alice was about three inches tall and wandering around Wonderland when she spotted a caterpillar. It was about the same height as her, except that it was sitting on top of a mushroom, smoking a hookah. She asked it how she could get big again; as the caterpillar was walking away, it turned back and said, "One side makes you larger, the other side makes you smaller." Alice asked, "One side of what?" The caterpillar replied, "The mushroom." There weren't any pills in the story, but maybe they were magic mushrooms.

2. **"When the men on the chessboard get up and tell you where to go."** The premise of *Through the Looking glass*: Alice is trying to get her cat to play chess with her; she falls asleep and dreams that she's a pawn on the chessboard and has to get to the other side to become a queen. Each chapter of *Through the Looking Glass* takes place on a different square of the chessboard, and the characters in it are characters in a game of chess. Occasionally they do tell her where to go (of course, she's lost). At one point, the White Knight guides her across a brook that turns out to be the space between the squares on the board.

3. **"When logic and proportion have fallen softly dead."** Everything is out of whack in Wonderland (although Carroll wrote a book about symbolic logic). What could be more illogical than the dialogue at the Mad Hatter's tea party? About proportion—Alice goes from three inches to 15 feet high. Hard to keep a sense of proportion with that

---

Explosive fact: The 3,000 calories you might eat are equal in energy to about 6 pounds of TNT.

pening. She mentions that it's rather uncomfortable to be so many different heights in one day.

By the way: The dormouse, who's sitting in a teacup at the Mad Tea Party, says, "Twinkle twinkle little bat. How I wonder where you're at." He doesn't say, "Feed your head."

2. b. In 1966 there was an amusing story coming from Lawrenceville Academy, a New Jersey prep school: People said that a student named Mark Sebastian—John's 15-year-old brother—had submitted the poem that became "Summer in the City" to his English teacher ...and had gotten an "F." It might well have been true—John Sebastian didn't particularly like the poem when he first saw it, either. But he did like the chorus—the part that went, "But at night there's a different world." Mark gave it to John and asked if he could do anything with it. John said he'd see. He put Mark's poem aside for a few months and in the interim came up with a little piano figure that he liked but didn't have a song for. Then one night as John was going to sleep, Mark's chorus, his own piano riff, and a set of new lyrics popped into his head.

"[Bassist] Steve Boone contributed a middle section," Sebastian says, and the song was done. His first impression of the song: certain notes sounded like car horns. "I said, 'Gee, this sounds sort of like Gershwin—sort of like "An American in Paris." Maybe we could put traffic on it.' "

The band went into New York's Columbia Studios for two nights. On the first, they did the entire instrumental track. The second night was for vocals...and sound effects. Sebastian says, "I remember this hilarious old sound man who'd never had a job with a rock 'n' roll band before looking at us quite puzzled as we auditioned pneumatic hammers to find the one that had the right intestinal tone to it." For car sounds, the old man brought in tapes of traffic jams and horns that he'd used when he worked in radio. The band listened to them for hours, then chose their favorites. John wanted the automobiles to start off softly, so the sound-effects man threw in a Volkswagen horn at the beginning.

The song was released in the summer, of course, and within a few weeks was #1 in America. It was the Spoonful's only #1 hit in their phenomenal string of seven consecutive Top 10 records between September 1965 and December 1966.

3. a. It started with a shopping trip. Roy and Billy Dees, a songwriter Orbison had been collaborating with, were sitting in the Orbisons' house when Orbison's wife, Claudette, announced she was going into town to buy some groceries. "Do you need any money?" Roy asked. Dees said, "A pretty woman never needs any money." Then he turned to Roy and said, "Hey, how about that for a song title?" Orbison liked the idea of doing a song about a "pretty woman," but not the part about the money. After Claudette left, they began turning the phrase into a song. And when she returned, carrying bags of food, she was greeted by the debut performance of her husband's second #1 tune.

4. b. The Four Seasons and a bunch of side musicians were in a recording studio in the Abbey Victoria Hotel on Seventh Avenue in New York City, recording "Walk Like a Man." After a few takes, it was obvious to everyone in the studio that something was wrong. But Bob Crewe, the producer, refused to pay attention. "Another take," he kept saying. Here's the story of the unusual session, as told by a participant, guitarist Vinnie Bell:

> As we were recording, there was a sudden pounding on the door. And there was the smell of smoke. And plaster was starting to fall from the ceiling. And water was leaking in...while we're recording! And there's this pounding on the door of the studio, and Bob Crewe wouldn't unlock it—he kept saying, "We'll open it in a second, there's one more take." And the water's pouring onto us, and we've got electric guitars in our hands—we were afraid we were gonna be electrocuted. Finally, the [firemen] axed their way right through the door—and Crewe's trying to push them out! And then we could see the smoke pouring through. It seems that the floor above us in that hotel was on fire! It was barely audible from inside the studio, but you could hear fire engines and all that—the whole bit. And this guy was so intent on making the record—on getting another take—that he kept trying to push these guys out...until they knocked him on the floor.

And that was it for the recording session.

5. b. The story behind this record—which was certified gold in 1969 and still refuses to die—is almost unbelievable. Paul Leka was a producer at Mercury Records in 1969. He persuaded the label to sign a friend named Gary De Carlo, and they did a recording ses-

---

sion together. They thought everything they recorded was good enough to be a hit, so they decided to record one really cheesy song for the B side of De Carlo's first single release. That way they'd save the good stuff for later.

The day of the B-side session, Leka ran into a friend he once wrote songs with. They remembered a tune called "Kiss Him Good-by" they'd written years earlier and decided to make that the stinker. The only problem: It was just two minutes long. They wanted to make it twice as long to make sure it never got on the air—no disc jockey would dare play a four-minute record—so they added a chorus…except they couldn't think of any words for it. So Leka just started singing "Na-na-na…" and someone else started singing "Hey-hey." And that was it. They didn't bother with lyrics because it was just a B-side.

To Leka's astonishment and embarrassment, when Mercury heard it, they decided to release it as an A-side. The musicians all agreed it should come out under an alias—and came up with Steam because at the end of the recording session, they'd seen a humongous cloud of steam coming out of a New York manhole cover.

6. c. Satchmo was making an album of show tunes, and David Merrick was trying to promote his new musical, so he encouraged performers to sing it. Armtrong had never heard of "Hello Dolly." And though he liked the tune, he was appalled that after all the innovative work he'd done in his career, his biggest hit was this silly, simple song.

7. a. Percy Sledge worked as an orderly at Colbert County Hospital in Alabama during the day and sang with a band called the Esquires Combo at night. One evening, the Esquires Combo was playing at a club in Sheffield, Alabama, and Sledge just couldn't keep his mind on the songs he was supposed to be singing. He was upset about a woman. Overcome by emotion, he turned to bass player Cameron Lewis and organ player Andrew Wright and begged them to play something he could sing to. Anything—it didn't matter what. The musicians looked at each other, shrugged, and just started playing. And Percy made up "When a Man Loves a Woman," one of the prettiest soul ballads ever written, on the spot.

Force exerted by the human jaw: 175 pounds. By the jaw of an African lion: 937 pounds.

Here are the answers to "It's the Law... Or is it?" (page301), according to the book *Legal Briefs*.

1. b. Nice try, Bill, but no dice. A number of debts can't be discharged by bankruptcy, including alimony, child support, certain tax fines and claims, most student loans, court fines and penalties, and court-ordered restitution.

Another note: If Bill goes on a spending spree right before he declares bankruptcy (within 40 days), he's stuck with those debts, too, if
- The purchase totals more than $500
- It was payable to a single creditor
- The money was spent on luxury goods or services

2. c. At last count, 31 states say "No" to marriages between first cousins. But Tom and Sue can still get married in Alabama, California, Colorado, Connecticut, Delaware, Florida, Georgia, and a bunch more.

Note: Cancel your tuxedo rental and send the caterers home if the proposed marriage is between a brother and sister, a parent and child, an aunt and nephew, or an uncle and niece. No state allows these marriages.

3. b. Traffic signs and theft/damage disclaimer signs aren't always enforceable on private property. Police can't give you a court-enforceable ticket for exceeding a private speed limit or making a privately prohibited turn onto a public highway. Courts have ruled that a person violating this type of sign is only "negligent."

F.Y.I: Police can't issue citations for accidents or other traffic violations on private property, either.

Another bit of interesting info: Signs on private property (like shopping centers) that claim to waive responsibility for theft and damage to your vehicle or possessions while you're doing business there may *not* be valid. A court has to base its decision on what they see as the property owner's "duty" to provide a reasonably safe environment for people and their possessions.

Food for thought: What country has the lowest birthrate in the world? The Vatican.

4. c. Depending on your history, they *could* have you arrested. Writing a bad check is considered a theft ranging from a misdemeanor to a second-degree felony. The penalty depends on the amount of the check and the legal history of the person who bounced it. In any event, most state laws limit the amount a store can charge you for a bounced check. Usually the fee has to be reasonable, and it has to be agreed to in writing.

5. a. If a bank card is lost or stolen, the owner's liability depends on how quickly the loss is reported to the company that issued the card. If it's within 2 working days, liability is only for the first $50. If it's within sixty days, liability is up to $500. If the loss isn't reported within 60 days of the owner's last financial statement, the owner is responsible for all charges—even if they total more than $500.

6. a. or c. Although a patent provides exclusive rights for 17 years, it may take time…and while you're waiting, companies can infringe on it.

Plus, sometimes it's smarter to keep it secret. A good secret can last forever. Had Coca-Cola's formula been patented, for example, it would have expired years ago and everyone could be using it now. By keeping the recipe a secret, Coca-Cola has been able to enjoy its exclusivity for many more years. Bear in mind, however, that keeping a secret can be pretty difficult.

7. b. Only a handful of states honor oral wills. These include California, Illinois, Kentucky, New York, and Ohio. They have strict procedures that must be followed, including having witnesses who are not beneficiaries and putting the words in writing within a certain period of time after the verbal bequest is made.

How'd you do? We'll test you again in the next edition.

Want more satisfaction? Here's

THE ULTIMATE IN BATHROOM READING!

Over 300 All-New Pages !

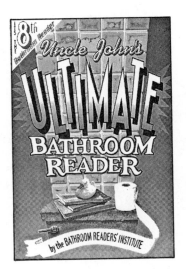

Uncle John's Ultimate Bathroom Reader

$12.95

And No Bathroom Is Complete Without...

The Best of Uncle John's Bathroom Reader!

- *All your favorites— the funniest, oddest, most intriguing articles, quotes, and trivia from volumes 1-7*

- *522 Pages—it's the Biggest and Best!*

- *Available for $16.95*

A Truly Satisfying Experience for the
Connoisseur of Bathroom Reading

AVAILABLE AT YOUR LOCAL BOOKSTORE!

WATCH FOR THE BRI'S OWN WEB SITE!

Starting January 1998...

www.unclejohn.com
www.bathroomreader.com

More favorites from Uncle John. • Trade great stories
Help write future editions • Order hard-to-get BRI books.

Go With the Flow!

THE LAST PAGE

FELLOW BATHROOM READERS:
The fight for good bathroom reading should never be taken loosely—we must sit firmly for what we believe in, even while the rest of the world is taking pot shots at us.

Once we prove we're not simply a flush-in-the-pan, writers and publishers will find their resistance unrolling.

So we invite you to take the plunge: Sit Down and Be Counted! by joining The Bathroom Readers' Institute. Send a self-addressed, stamped envelope to: BRI, PO Box 1117, Ashland, Oregon 97520. or contact us through our Web site at: *www*.bathroomreader.com. You'll receive your attractive free membership card, and a copy of the BRI newsletter (if we ever get around to publishing one), and earn a permanent spot on the BRI honor roll!

                                 ☞   ☞   ☞

UNCLE JOHN'S NEXT BATHROOM READER IS IN THE WORKS!

Don't fret—there's more good reading on its way. In fact, there are a few ways *you* can contribute to the next volume:

1. Is there a subject you'd like to see us cover? Write to us or contact us through our Web site (*www*.bathroomreader.com) and let us know. We aim to please.

2. Got a neat idea for a couple of pages in the new *Reader*? If you're the first to suggest it, and we use it, we'll send you a free book.

3. Have you seen or read an article you'd recommend as quintessential bathroom reading? Or is there a passage in a book that you want to share with other BRI members? Tell us where to find it, or send a copy. If you're the first to suggest it and we publish it in the next volume, there's a free book in it for you.

Well, we're out of space, and when you've gotta go, you've gotta go. Hope to hear from you soon. Meanwhile, remember:

Go with the flow.